Remembering Roy Campbell
The Memoirs of his Daughters Anna and Tess

Poetic Justice: *A Memoir of My Father, Roy Campbell* **by Anna Campbell Lyle**

In the Shadow of a Poet: Memoirs **by Teresa Campbell**

**Edited by
Judith Lütge Coullie**

WINGED LION PRESS

REMEMBERING ROY CAMPBELL
Preface © 2011 Joseph Pearce
Introduction, Notes and Appendix © 2011 Judith Lütge Coullie
Poetic Justice © 2011 Francesca de Carondelet Bento
In the Shadow of a Poet © 2011 Francisco Campbell

cover photograph:
(R-L) Anna, Tess, Mrs S.G.Campbell (Roy's mother), Roy and Mary Campbell in St. Mark's Square, Venice.
(Used by permission the Campbell Collection, UKZN.)

Published by Winged Lion Press
Hamden, CT

All rights reserved. Except in the case of quotations embodied in critical articles or reviews, no part of this book may be reproduced or transmitted in any form or by any means, electronic or mechanical, including photocopying, recording, or by any information storage or retrieval system, without written permission of the publisher.

10-9-8-7-6-5-4-3-2-1

ISBN: 978-1936294-04-6

Dedication

In the spirit of Tess and Anna's sisterly bond, I dedicate this book to my own sisters, Beverley, Elizabeth and Debbie.

Roy, London, 1949 (Tess)

Table of Contents

Preface by Joseph Pearce i

Editor's Introduction v

Acknowledgments xxv

Poetic Justice: by Anna Campbell Lyle 1

Additional Illustrations 141

In the Shadow of a Poet: by Teresa Campbell 163

Appendix 1—Roy Campbell Timeline 305

Index 319

Roy: Portugal, circa 1955 (Tess)

Preface
by Joseph Pearce

Roy Campbell exploded onto the British literary scene in May 1924 with the publication of THE FLAMING TERRAPIN, a vibrantly original tour de force that challenged the prevailing nihilism of the period with an unbridled zest for life. The sheer verve, vigour and irrepressible energy of the poem won over the critics, one of whom wrote with breathless excitement about the "exuberant relish of the sheer sonority and clangour of words, words enjoyed for their own gust, and flung down to fit each other with an easy rapture of phrase".[1] Almost overnight, the twenty-two year old had been rocketed into the ranks of the illustrissimi of English letters. And yet, almost ninety years later, posterity seems to have relegated him to a place among the lowly footnotes of twentieth century literature, in which he is remembered more for his friendships and enmities with more illustrious contemporaries than as a poet in his own right. The impression that his legacy has left on twentieth century literature is that of a muse that burst into glorious flame in a dazzling display of prosodic pyrotechnics and then fizzled out, or rather sputtered and sparked without ever really catching fire again. Such an impression is justified, up to a point, to the extent that Campbell seldom, if ever, reached the heights to which he ascended in THE FLAMING TERRAPIN. Whereas T.S. Eliot eclipsed the youthful brilliance of THE WASTE LAND with the maturity of FOUR QUARTETS, his magnum opus, Campbell's youthful brilliance seems to eclipse all that followed it. It might almost be said that he never grew up, artistically speaking.

As with all sweeping statements the preceding one requires an element of qualification. If it is true that Campbell never improved upon the dash and dare of his earliest work, it is emphatically not true to dismiss his other work as being of little worth or even worthless. On the contrary, Campbell remains one of the major poets of the twentieth century and much of the rest of his corpus warrants a place in the cannon, its ignominious exclusion from which constitutes nothing less than a literary scandal.

Broadly speaking, Campbell's corpus can be divided into several periods. There are the African poems, the Provençal poems, the Spanish poems, the British poems, and the Portuguese poems.

It is in the African poems that Campbell comes closest to capturing the breathless brilliance of THE FLAMING TERRAPIN. In "Zulu Song", "Zulu Girl" and "The Serf" he displays a degree of formal discipline and lyrical flourish that is seldom achieved in much of his later verse, and in "The Sisters" he gallops erotically alongside his sexually charged subjects, handling his mount with tactfully suggestive dexterity. In "The Theology of Bongwi the Baboon" the poet indulges in theological subversion similar to that indulged in by Yeats in "An Indian Upon God" but does so with a playfulness that is utterly devoid of cynicism. On the contrary its joviality and *joie de vivre* have more in common with the satirical verse of G.K. Chesterton, which becomes apparent if Campbell's poem is read alongside "Race Memory (by a dazed Darwinian)", Chesterton's satire on a similar theme. There is no poetry written in the twentieth century that can match the best of these African poems for invigorating freshness and primitive intensity.

Campbell's muse rekindled something of this freshness after his escape from the puritanical prurience of the Bloomsburys in England and his discovery of the residual Catholicism of Provence. Settling near Martigues, Campbell fell in love with the briny earthiness of the peasants and fishermen with whom he assimilated with consummate ease. The Provençal poems reverberate with enthusiasm for his adoptive culture, embracing the primal matter of soil and sea as a means of seeing the soul of man. The purifying impact of Provence is seen in poems such as "Autumn", in which all is stripped away so that the "clear anatomy" is revealed in its quintessential simplicity, and it also surfaces in the religious imagery that begins to proliferate at this time. The presence of Catholic imagery in the absence of Catholic faith is exemplified most poignantly in the tranquil agnosticism of "Mass at Dawn", whereas the embryonic desire for faith is evident in the imagery of "Saint Peter of the Three Canals" in which the apparently faithless frivolity of the early verses makes way for the tacit acceptance or desire for faith implicit in its invocatory finale.

It was not, however, until the poet's arrival in Spain in 1933 that the Faith finally claimed the poet, or, at least, that the poet finally acclaimed the Faith,

> *under the stretched, terrific wings,*
> *the outspread arms (our soaring King's)—*
> *the man they made an Albatross!*[2]

Campbell's conversion to Catholicism unfolds majestically in his sonnet sequence, "Mithraic Emblems", the earliest of which were written in Provence and the last of which were written in Spain. Taken as a whole they display a soul in transit. Whereas the early sonnets show the poet groping with an uncomprehended and incomprehensible paganism, the later sonnets show an emergent Christianity that does not so much vanquish Mithraism as make sense of it. In the final sonnets, the sun is no longer a god to be worshipped, but only a symbol of the Son, the true God, who gives the sun its meaning and purpose. The Mithraic emblem is transformed by Christian typology and becomes Christ transfigured:

> *Oh let your shining orb grow dim,*
> *Of Christ the mirror and the shield,*
> *That I may gaze through you to Him,*
> *See half the miracle revealed.*³

Campbell's reception into the Catholic Church on 24 June 1935 confirmed him in his love for Spain, which he later described as "a country to which I owe everything as having saved my soul".⁴ It also accentuated still further his alienation from the secularist ascendancy in British literature, an alienation that had been expressed with shrill abandon in his verse satire, THE GEORGIAD two years earlier. Campbell's conversion would also serve to alienate him from the new generation of socialist poets, such as Stephen Spender, W.H. Auden, Louis MacNeice and Cecil Day-Lewis, an alienation that would become bitterly combative when Campbell's vociferous support for Franco's Nationalist forces in the Spanish Civil War brought him into conflict with the equally vociferous support of the new generation of poets for the communist and anarchist Republican forces.

Campbell's position as an outsider was confirmed by his choice of the "wrong" side during the Spanish Civil War and he was never really accepted thereafter among England's literati, even after he returned to live in London at the end of the Second World War. There were exceptions, such as his friendship with J.R.R. Tolkien, C.S. Lewis, Edith Sitwell and Dylan Thomas, but for the most part Campbell had become something of a pariah. This is perhaps the real reason that he is seldom read and studied these days. It is not so much for any real or alleged deficiency in his poetry that he is neglected, as for a supercilious refusal to accept the dissident voice in an age of "political correctness". And it is for this reason that the publication of these memoirs by Campbell's daughters is to be heartily welcomed.

Anna's and Tess's memoirs, and the interviews that they granted me so graciously when I visited them in Portugal, the country in which Campbell spent his final years, were crucial to my research for my biography of their father.

I am, therefore, deeply in their debt. I felt then, as I feel now, that the memoirs deserved to be published in their own right and I'm delighted that Judith Coullie, a leading Campbell scholar in the poet's native South Africa, has finally brought this worthy project to final fruition.

Roy Campbell was a great poet but he was also a great man, in the sense that he was larger than life. Finding oneself in his company is to find oneself intoxicated with the pure pleasure of his presence. One would like to meet him in the flesh, perhaps in that tavern at the world's end that Chesterton mentions, in which we will meet "Dickens and all his characters". In the absence of such a celestial rendezvous, this journey through Campbell's life in the terrestrial presence of his daughters is pleasure enough.

Joseph Pearce, associate professor of literature and writer in residence at Ave Maria University in Florida, is the author of BLOOMSBURY AND BEYOND: THE FRIENDS AND ENEMIES OF ROY CAMPBELL *(HarperCollins 2001), which was published in the United States under the title* UNAFRAID OF VIRGINIA WOOLF: THE FRIENDS AND ENEMIES OF ROY CAMPBELL *(ISI Books 2004). He is also the editor of* ROY CAMPBELL: SELECTED POEMS *(Saint Austin Press 2002) and is editor of the* SAINT AUSTIN REVIEW *(www.staustinreview.com).*

---

[1] DIAL, November 1924
[2] Roy Campbell, "Mithraic Emblems: Mithras Speaks 2"
[3] Roy Campbell, "To the Sun"
[4] Quoted in Matthew Hoehn, OSB, ed., CATHOLIC AUTHORS: CONTEMPORARY BIOGRAPHICAL SKETCHES 1930-1947 (Newark, NJ: Saint Mary's Abbey Press, 1947), 104.

Tess and Anna, Étang de Berre, 1930 (Francesca)

Editor's Introduction[1]
Tess and Anna

Teresa Mary Campbell was born in Wales, in a dilapidated cottage cum stable, on 26 November 1922. She was the first-born child of the handsome young South African poet, Roy Campbell, and his strikingly beautiful English wife, Mary Garman. Tess's arrival in the world has a ring of the fairytale about it: born into what can justifiably be called poverty-stricken circumstances, she was blessed with exceptional parents whose future looked bright with the promise of aesthetic riches and worldly greatness. The very walls of their primitive abode must have trembled with the youthful passions of her parents: undaunted by parental disapproval on both sides, they married in February 1922, within months of having met, when both were still in their early twenties. They were deeply in love. They eschewed material comforts and embraced the sacrifices necessitated by the artist's life. Mary, herself an artist, relished her role as muse for Roy's forceful poetry, and Roy threw himself headlong into feverish creative outpouring.

Fame came quickly to Tess's father. His long poem, THE FLAMING TERRAPIN, was published to great critical acclaim in 1924, when he was just 22. Fame aside, the Campbells were nevertheless in financial difficulty and Roy decided to return to his native South Africa. After about seven months, Tess and Mary joined him.

It was at the cottage at Sezela on the coast of the Indian Ocean, loaned to them by an admirer of Roy's, that Anna Margaret Campbell was born on 1 February 1926. The family's time in South Africa was not as idyllic as had been hoped. Having failed to reconcile with his father and having antagonised most of his white compatriots with what he referred to as his "negrophilist" sentiments, Roy, Mary and their infant children decided to return to England. They left South Africa in December 1926, before Anna's first birthday.

Over the next three decades, the family's fortunes were mixed. They moved between England, France, Spain and Portugal living in what—for many readers—will seem to be romantically exotic places: on the outskirts of Martigues in the Provençal countryside; in the ancient city of Toledo; in the mist-soaked

---

[1] Parts of this introduction appear in "Telling the life story, anxiously: The memoirs of Teresa and Anna Campbell", BIOGRAPHY 33 (2) 2010: 309-332.

hills of Sintra. Roy continued to write and publish poetry and prose, and translated important works from French, Spanish and Portuguese, while Mary continued to draw and paint. There were many shared pleasures and much joy, but most of the time money was limited. This was not only because neither parent had regular jobs. The economic difficulties of a world in tumult were merely intensified for the bohemian Campbells. They lived through the most turbulent times: post World War I England, the Depression, the Spanish Civil War and World War II and its aftermath. How all of this impacted on Roy and Mary Campbell and their growing daughters is recounted in vivid and intimate detail by Tess and Anna in their memoirs.

Memoir and Biography

Tess and Anna both subtitle their autobiographical narratives "memoirs". Theorists of life writing differentiate between autobiography and memoir:

As a general rule, traditional autobiography makes the individual life central, while memoirs tend to focus on the times in which the life is lived and the significant others of the memoirist's world. [...M]emoir writers are more concerned with making their lives meaningful in terms of the lives of others and in terms of their communities rather than in terms of individual accomplishments. [...] Like the autobiographer, they want to make their lives count in the public record; unlike autobiographers they tend to be less sure that their lives will count.[2]

In practice, however, writers tend to use the terms autobiography and memoir rather more loosely than specialists do and the distinction between the two can be difficult to maintain. There is more to muddy the waters. As Helen M. Buss points out, whereas in our age we tend to subsume memoir into the broader category of autobiography, this was not always so: "the 18th and early 19th centuries subsume[d] it into the genre called 'biography'" (596). Tess and Anna's memoirs, although autobiographically intimate in many respects, are clearly closer, generically, to biography in that both aim to create narrative portraits of their parents, to tell of the lives that they, as daughters, shared with them. Neither of the Campbell daughters make their own lives central to their narratives. Tess and Anna tell the story of their parents' lives, before and after the daughters were born; each ends with their parents' deaths.[3] There is

---

[2] Buss, Helen M. "Memoirs." ENCYCLOPEDIA OF LIFE WRITING: AUTOBIOGRAPHICAL AND BIOGRAPHICAL FORMS. Ed. Margaretta Jolly. London & Chicago: Fitzroy Dearborn, 2001: 595-597.

[3] Anna's memoir does give some account of her and Tess's lives after Mary's death—almost 22 years after Roy's—but it is a perfunctory addendum to the primary narrative.

much about each of these memoirists' own lives that is not told: they say little about romantic liaisons, about their husbands or marriages, their children's lives or their experiences as parents, or about their own commitment to Catholicism.[4] In some respects, their memoirs are not dissimilar to the autobiographies of their father, Roy; BROKEN RECORD (1934) and LIGHT ON A DARK HORSE (1951), too, are remarkably reticent when it comes to his private life as husband and father. In LIGHT ON A DARK HORSE, for instance, the chapter on marriage barely discusses marriage or parenting (Tess and Anna were adults by the time this was written) and we learn little about his wife except that she is very beautiful. Instead, the narrator boasts about which rivals he was able to overcome. While the reserve that characterises Tess and Anna's memoirs may in part be motivated by a similar sense that the wider world has no need to know of private affairs, their restraint is rather more obviously motivated, and justified, by their desire to focus on their father. Tess and Anna's titles indicate the trans-generic nature of their texts: Tess's is entitled IN THE SHADOW OF A POET: MEMOIRS; Anna's is entitled POETIC JUSTICE: A MEMOIR OF MY FATHER, ROY CAMPBELL.[5] The titles show that their father, the poet Roy Campbell, is to have the lion's share of the attention.

These memoirs blur the distinctions between autobiographical and biographical; they are autobiographical biographies, if you will. Obviously, this is because Tess and Anna are intimately acquainted with their biographical subject. Although some readers may prefer their biographers to be more impartial, this is not a universally endorsed view. Virginia Woolf, for instance, maintained that the best biographical insights often occur when qualities shared by biographer and subject intersect, activating the biographer's curiosity about herself in reflective examination of the subject.[6] In the case of Mary and Roy Campbell's daughters, an examination of the lives of their parents necessarily involves an inquiry into their own lives and identities. For many biographers and readers alike, the desirability of a personal connection between portraitist and subject goes further than Woolf's endorsement of shared characteristics. They consider acquaintance of biographer and subject to be an empowering

---

[4] I learnt a little more about these aspects of their lives in meetings with Tess and Francesca, her niece, and in correspondence with them.

[5] Anna's memoirs were first published in 1986 in a limited print run of 150 copies by Typographeum Press (Francestown, N.H.). Terry Risk of Typographeum told me that he edited the manuscript. Tess's memoirs were unpublished.

[6] Virginia Woolf. "The Art of Biography." COLLECTED ESSAYS, 4. London: The Hogarth Press, 1967 (1925): 226.

qualification, if not an essential one, for writing a life.⁷

Readers of Poetic Justice and In the Shadow of a Poet will, I have no doubt, find that the writers' intimacy with—and love for—the principal biographical subject is "an empowering qualification." We do not simply learn that these two daughters loved their father, and why they did—troubled and troublesome as he sometimes was—but see their tenderness enacted in the narratives. The narratives were written because of that love. And that love informs all that is written. So while more scholarly, impartial biographical accounts will have the advantage of adhering to a truth-criterion which "does not consist in the authenticity of an inside view but in the consistency of the narrative and the explanatory power of the arguments,"⁸ Campbell's daughters' recollections are enriched by conveying, along with intimate details, a depth, an emotional charge that cannot but be missing in more impersonal, more balanced accounts.

There are important textual/aesthetic and ethical consequences when the biographical project is rooted in the narrators' experiences of their lives with—and experiences of—the biographical subjects, as is the case for Tess and Anna. The tension between biography and autobiography, when biography is effected *through* autobiography, is perhaps in part due to the unevenness of status between the writer (someone who is not famous, but finds a mandate to write only because of her relationship to the biographical subject) and the biographical subject (a well-known person). This uneven relationship is, of course, exacerbated when the biographer is a child of the biographical subject.

In such instances, the rhetoric of witnessing and confessing—which informs autobiography—infuses the rhetoric of interpretation and argument, which is more characteristic of biography. If biography predominates over autobiography, then it will be interpretation and argument which colour the self-representational project. As biographers, both Tess and Anna engage in interpretation and argument, returning again and again to polemical defences of Roy's politics and his qualities as father, husband and friend, not relying wholly on personal impression and quoting other documentary sources so as to legitimise their claims.

With regard to his politics, Tess devotes a significant proportion of the narrative to the argument that Roy's detestation of Communism (for which he sided with Franco and was, Tess says, labelled "by most of the intellectuals of

---

⁷ Catherine Parke. Biography: Writing Lives. New York and London: Routledge, 2002: 3-4.

⁸ Schlaeger, Jürgen. "Biography: Cult as Culture." In The Art of Literary Biography. Ed. John Batchelor. Oxford: Clarendon Press, 1995: 59.

the world a fascist bully'") was based on Communism's rejection of religion and its totalitarian "violation of the human spirit"; nevertheless, she says, his life was far more communist than the lives of many Communist card holders: "He lived his Communism in his Christianity". Tess points more than once to her father's prediction that communism would ultimately fail. She also addresses the other criticisms levelled against him and insists that in spite of some evidence to the contrary in his writings, Campbell was in reality against racism his whole life. In his early twenties, Campbell wrote of how the white colonialists, who seemed to him to be smug in their exploitation of the natives, grew in wealth and comfort:

> *In fair Banana Land [...]*
> *Our sturdy pioneers as farmers dwell,*
> *And, 'twixt the hours of strenuous sleep, relax*
> *To shear the fleeces or to fleece the blacks:*
> *Where every year a fruitful increase bears*
> *Of pumpkins, cattle, sheep, and millionaires—*
> *A clime so prosperous both to men and kine*
> *That which were which a sage could scarce define;*
> *Where fat whiter sheep upon the mountains bleat*
> *And fatter politicians in the street* (THE WAYZGOOSE, LL. 2-14)[9]

And at the other end of his career, in 1952, Campbell, Alan Paton, Laurens van der Post, Enslin du Plessis and Uys Krige signed an open letter to the South African government protesting against plans to remove "Coloured" voters from the voters' roll. In LIGHT ON A DARK HORSE: AN AUTOBIOGRAPHY,[10] Campbell says that he has "no colour prejudice". But what he says next shows why it is necessary for his daughters to protest that anti-racism was a feature of his politics and personal philosophy. He goes on to make the offensive statement that, "Hybrids between Negro and white [...] are neither hardy, strong, nor intelligent as a general rule" (185).

There have also been charges against Campbell of anti-Semitism, homophobia, sexism, bigotry, élitism and a range of prejudices. In his defence, Anna argues that her father had many Jewish, English and homosexual friends. Yet in his autobiographies (and elsewhere), he makes outrageous statements. The

---

[9] In COLLECTED WORKS I, eds. Peter Alexander, Michael Chapman and Marcia Leveson. Craighall: AD. Donker, 1985: 67.

[10] Page references refer to the Penguin edition (Hammondsworth: Penguin, 1971). The autobiography is reproduced in COLLECTED WORKS III, eds. Peter Alexander, Michael Chapman and Marcia Leveson. Craighall: AD Donker, 1985.

English (and Germans), he says disparagingly, "seem to prefer animals [...] to their own species and exult in the killing of men" (310) and both English and German tend to political naiveté "'putting two and two together' when they should be kept in separate compartments" (324). Fame eludes those who refuse to kowtow "to the homosexual and yiddish freemasonries" (248). His scorn for "the smug little Sunday School world of Bloomsbury 'queerness'" (263) arises from the failure of these men to conform to his masculine ideal. That these "males [are] under the domination of females" (263) cannot be blamed upon the females for, one can infer, females are underlings and cannot be expected to know better unless they are taught by real men.

> This state of affairs... is absolutely the fault of the husbands. No woman will ever forgive a husband who does not give her a thoroughly good hiding when she knows she has deserved one. On the contrary, she will hate and despise him, and make a fool of him at every turn and corner, if he does not behave like a man. (263-4)

The thing is, though, as Campbell's biographers and his daughters demonstrate, Campbell's diatribe is not based on practice: Mary was the dominant partner and Campbell did not reject male or female homosexuality *per se* but rather was responding to the way it was lived by his enemies, the Bloomsburies. For he also says that homosexuality should be "gay, as at sea, not tearful and tragic"; it should not be (in a not too veiled reference to Vita Sackville-West and her husband) "a sort of obligation for board of lodgings" (262).[11]

Much more difficult for his daughters to rebut is the charge of fascism. Anna does this by deviating from the dominant narrative mode into expostulation. Here is an excerpt from one such impassioned discussion:

> Of course Roy was labeled a "fascist". He was one of the few Western writers who was a militant anti-marxist. That is, he wrote *clearly* against all the satanical zombies, inhabited by seven devils, who have made rivers of blood and tears wherever they have appeared. Yes, Roy was one of the few who never compromised. He condemned Lenin and Stalin when it was literary lunacy to do so.[12]

---

[11] I have discussed LIGHT ON A DARK HORSE in more detail in "The Race to be Hero: Race and Gender in Roy Campbell's LIGHT ON A DARK HORSE", SCRUTINY2, 6 (2), 2001.

[12] Elsewhere she says that the description of his controversial pro-Franco poem, FLOWERING RIFLE, as "fascist propaganda" is "baffling": "If Roy was a fascist, then so was Christ!". Neither daughter mentions that their father never actually signed up as a member of the Fascist political party (Alexander, 177). Many of RC's contemporaries, as well as his biographer Peter Alexander, felt that he was extremely naïve politically and thus did not grasp the

Anna also defends her father's philosophy of poetry, quoting a lengthy passage from his speech when he was awarded an Honorary Doctorate from the University of Natal in 1954. His death in 1957 occurred "just as he was becoming well-known by a larger public [...]. His political enemies were frightened of his pen while he was alive, but once he was silenced they went to work with a will". Furthermore, she seeks to restore her father's reputation against what she argues are the errors of one of his biographers,[13] the malice of the Bloomsburies,[14] and the denunciations of the poets MacNeice, Auden, Day-Lewis and Spender.

Not only do they have to defend their father against his enemies, Anna and Tess also have to rescue him from his own bombastic characterisations of himself. For instance, Roy claimed that he had fought with the Spanish Army, when in fact his efforts to join were unsuccessful. For Anna, this was not an outright lie,

> It was Poetic Justice.[15] He did his best to get in and that was equivalent, for him, with having done so. The courage needed was the same. He really longed to fight the communists physically, but since he was unable to do so *fought for Christianity and against Communism with his pen.* (italics in original)

Later, she says "he always made light of his gifts as poet, but exaggerated his prowess in the fields of action". Tess says that her father represented a conundrum to "most people [...] owing chiefly to his own reports about himself—the ones about him being a cattle-man, horse-dealer, bull-fighter, soldier at the front in the Spanish Civil War, and so on"; although he did do these things, she says (but not quite as successfully or as intensely as he claimed), "he was essentially a poet, scholar, a thinker and a prophet".

But Roy and Mary's daughters also have to address other, less comfortable,

---

implications of his support for the party that defended the Catholic Church.

[13] Peter Alexander, ROY CAMPBELL, A CRITICAL BIOGRAPHY. Oxford: Oxford University Press, 1982: Anna criticises the biographer on five occasions. It should be pointed out, however, that Alexander's biography is not questioned by Tess and that it was written "with the full support" of Mary Campbell (n.p. dustcover).

[14] Anna describes them as boycotting her father's work and, in a "conspiracy of silence" refusing to run reviews of his new publications in any of the many journals they controlled.

[15] This is the title of her memoirs. The term usually means a conclusion in which virtue is rewarded and evil punished, often in an especially appropriate or ironic manner. Here, Anna seems to imply that it is true—in some sort of poetic or metaphoric sense—that he fought against the communists because he did so in ways that were available to him (that is, through literary means) and that his inaccurate statement that he fought physically is of little significance.

facets of their parents' reputations: for one thing, there are the allegations of sexual promiscuity (both heterosexual and homosexual);[16] for another, there is Roy's drinking. Having been raised by teetotallers, the excessive drinking started as soon as he was away from the family in Oxford, when he was not yet out of his teens. It was to continue, with varying intensity, throughout his life.[17] Roy's inebriety was often extreme; for instance, when he first met Laurie Lee in Toledo, he told him he was drinking four and half litres of wine a day[18] and there were many occasions—some of which are alluded to in the memoirs—when he drank himself into a stupor. The alcoholism was to cause severe damage to the young Anna's fragile disposition.

Tess and Anna occasionally differ with regard to which were the worst binges[19] and Tess downplays the severity of Roy's alcohol abuse, saying, euphemistically, about one such occurrence that he had an adventure when "He had had one too many". Nevertheless, one of her first memories of their new home in Provence is of an intense argument between her parents, in the course of which Tess realised that Roy's hidden liquor had been discovered by Mary:

> My awakening to the fact that my father drank was very gradual because at Martigues it was not evident. [...A]nd even later, when he had a crisis, I learnt to take it for granted. If he drank, it seemed natural. If he had been a teetotaller, that would have surprised me. His drinking never surprised or disturbed me.

Tess does tell of other crises, but almost every time her father's drinking is mentioned, it is either excused or minimised. For instance, although he felt very

---

[16] The most talked about affair—the one that serves as the pivot of *Dark Outsider*, Antony Akerman's biographical play about Roy and Mary Campbell—is that between Mary and Vita Sackville-West (Johannesburg: Witwatersrand University Press, 2000). According to Anna, the affair persisted over many years. Tess denies that this was a physical relationship.

There have also been claims that Roy indulged in homosexual sexual relationships while at Oxford. Tess along with Roy's most recent biographer, Joseph Pearce, deny this. It would appear, however, that Anna hints at homosexual or bisexual affairs at Oxford when she alludes to T. W. Earp's influence on Roy. Alexander also notes that Harold Nicolson's reference to RC as "another Rimbaud" indicates that RC had told him about homosexual adventures (78).

[17] This was, according to Anna, one of the reasons why Mary's father was opposed to the marriage.

[18] Alexander, 157.

[19] Tess says it was after he discovered the Vita affair. Anna reports several occasions when Roy's drinking was completely out of control for prolonged periods.

guilty because of his drinking (and this, she adds, was for him a spur to prayer),

> he had a great sense of self-preservation and seldom went all out. He never drank spirits[...].[20] His usual drink was wine mixed with water. [...] Although my mother used to try and prevent my father abusing drink, all through their life together she always kept him company in this. She [...] was a very natural drinker, she never wanted more than the measure.

It seems to me that however "natural" her father's drinking may have appeared to Tess, the fact that both she and Anna remember not only the rows and drunkenness (and doubtless we are not privy to every incident), but also those instances when Roy drank little or nothing, underscores the seriousness of the impact that his drinking had on the family. One is not likely to recall vividly those brief periods of relief if the predicament which was temporarily suspended was not significant.

It is in regard to this aspect of their lives with her biographical subject, that Anna's account (more markedly than Tess's), while still outwardly employing the (biographical) rhetoric of argument and interpretation, slips into the (autobiographical) confessional mode. She remembers (rather self-consciously[21]) an occasion in Toledo when she was called to fetch her insensible father from the tavern when his drinking was "suicidal". She worried constantly about him, and felt (in an inversion of the parent-child roles) that it was her responsibility to take care of him. She recalls that she tried to overcome this all-consuming, impossible compulsion at the tender age of eleven. Her father was preparing to go to Spain to join up. Anna recalls: "I could not stop him from doing this[...]. I was beginning to realise that he got on just as well whether I was worried about him or not. So I decided to put him out of my mind as much as possible." The attempt was not wholly successful, and this desire to protect her father from himself was not the only problem that she faced: in her childhood, her mother "was rather remote" and "never seemed to notice what we were eating: sometimes we would be given bread and milk, or sour milk, every night for our suppers, for weeks on end." This was exacerbated greatly when Mary converted to Catholicism, as she would be in church for most of the day. Anna recalls that "I became desperately lonely," and, "The fear that something would happen to [Mary] was quite irrational and obsessive." Tess was another cause of extreme anxiety for Anna. At an expensive

---

[20] As noted elsewhere, there were times in his life when he drank gin.
[21] She says, "I know that this is beginning to sound like Little Nell and her grandfather."

convent boarding school in Madrid, Anna says that in addition to suffering persistent hunger because they were not given enough food, she worried about Tess who, instead of objecting to their inadequate rations, was dieting obsessively and being teased about it:

> ...Tess and I, knowing what sacrifices our parents were making in sending us to the Assumption, could not possibly worry them by telling them that we were slowly starving to death.[... A] sarcastic, but well-intentioned, nun [...] used to call attention to Tess's strangeness, which was a terrible mortification to me [...].
>
> Gradually, what with being half starved and seeing my dearly loved sister made ever more a subject for mockery, I began to be frightened of other people. It was a slow process and only became really bothersome when I was eighteen.

The "really bothersome" nature of this fear resulted in more than one nervous breakdown, often accompanied by suicidal tendencies. Anna's psychological crises—which seem to have been prolonged—are not explained or described in detail.[22]

"Children," Anna remarks, "are very resilient ([nevertheless...] they pay later for their early sufferings)". Neither Tess nor Anna blame Roy and Mary for their subsequent problems, and both defend them as loving parents and applaud their unique gifts as individuals.

Tess describes her mother as "calm and stable", "original [...] in all aspects of her life", "very perfect physically" with an "exotic beauty". "She was very cultured [... and] a great enthusiast of poetry and highly artistic." Furthermore, she had an inexhaustible "vitality and a very controversial mind, so that wherever she was, things were never dull". Anna's praises for Mary are similarly warm:

> Mary—darling Mother! [...] How much she did for Roy and Tess and me! [...] Until I was about twenty-five years old, Mary could do no wrong in my eyes, so that I often followed her when my own instincts told me to do the contrary.[23]

---

[22] Anna mentions in passing that in 1950, after a six month convalescence in Italy, she met Roy and Tess (who was "skeletal") in Paris. She gives no details of the nature of the illness from which she was recovering.

[23] Anna's obvious love and admiration for her mother notwithstanding, what is omitted from this passage is a criticism of Mary's need to intervene and shape the lives of her husband and children. Anna says that although Mary did so much for her family "often her plans went wrong. [...] Every time we were just becoming completely independent,

Their father earns warm praise too. Tess describes him as tall and slim, with "a delicate face" and "large mystical eyes". He had " a magnetic effect on women". She recalls her mother's compliments about his skills as a baby-minder, and his "immense pride in his two little daughters" and his kindness when she suffered a nervous breakdown which resulted in a suicide attempt. For Anna, Roy was "gentle to a fault [...]. I used to feel that he was on such a different plain from other people that he often suffered from loneliness, as though he was not really in this world, but came down to it from time to time". Of his soul-destroying work to support his troubled family in the last fifteen years of his life, she says "he often came near to saintliness". He was emotionally and practically supportive of both her and Tess when they were experiencing psychological illnesses.

Such love and admiration notwithstanding, both daughters suffered greatly. In Tess's case, she developed what is now known as anorexia nervosa when in her teens. This was to persist for many years, and culminated in extremely severe depression, hospitalisation in an institution for the mentally ill[24] and a suicide attempt.

The memoirs thus reveal some of the writers' deeply personal and painful experiences, while allowing us glimpses into Campbell's life and his impact on his daughters. They will interest both Campbell scholars as well as those readers who know little or nothing about Campbell, a man who, argues Michael Hanke, lived "what may well have been the most exciting life of any poet of the twentieth century".[25]

Roy Campbell's Place in Literary History

History, no less than any other story, requires countless decisions regarding what to include, what to omit. This does not only hold for details; events and characters may also be excised from the storyline so as to establish themes and maintain a clear focus. The pleasures of narrative coherence and integrity thus

---

she would interfere and muddle us all up again.
And yet to put all the blame on her is very unjust. It was also my complete dedication to her as a person that was wrong."

[24] Anna describes this more harshly as "a lunatic asylum"; doctors had recommended that Tess be certified and confined there for the rest of her life. The costs of Tess's treatment necessitated Roy's (after he had been invalided out of the army) taking a job as a clerk with the War Damage Commission. Once, when Anna and Roy had been to visit Tess there, Anna describes another occasion on which she was to experience concern for her parent: "my heart bled for Roy who was pale and silent".

[25] Michael Hanke (ed.), CAMPBELL AND THE ROMANCE COUNTRIES, Wissenschaftlicher Verlag Trier, 2006.

gained for the most part outweigh possible losses and concerns for discarded narrative material. We keep our eyes on the peaks and the paths leading there.

The process of selection, itself subject to historical trends and ideological shifts, pertains not only to mainstream history but also to narrower, more specialised branches. In histories of literature, for instance, key movements and periodised approaches tend to result in accounts which focus on unifying themes and most notable practitioners. Scholars have thus identified essential characteristics of Modernism, and the many Big Names of Modernism feature in most studies of the movement and can therefore be readily reeled off: Woolf, Eliot, Faulkner, Joyce, Pound…. While accounts of Modernism seldom fail to emphasise the contradictions and paradoxes which characterise this movement, those who fell outside of its parameters or who conformed only partially tend to be ignored. In an age of free verse, remarks Alan Paton, Campbell "submitted himself to the discipline of rhyme and form." Reminding critics and literary historians of poetic forms, to say nothing of some of the sentiments expressed therein, that were fast losing ground, Campbell's poetry is, for most, easily dismissed. Except that, as Paton goes on to say, "No one in our century did it more brilliantly than he."[26] Paton's view is not often nowadays reiterated. While Malvern van Wyk Smith, in 1990, argues that with Campbell South African poetry "came of age"[27] and that Campbell's imagery and thinking about the Africa-Europe nexus "became pervasive" in South African poetry after WWII,[28] Campbell's works are not now, in post-apartheid South Africa, often taught and his legacy is seldom honoured. Few South Africans who have not made a special study of South African literature know of him.[29] However, of late a handful of literary critics have sought to rescue from obscurity some of the causalities of literary historical narrative conciseness,

---

[26] "Roy Campbell: Poet and Man" (1957), reproduced in CAMPBELL IN CONTEXT, ed. Coullie and Wade. Durban: Killie Campbell Africana Library Series, 2004: 564.

[27] Van Wyk Smith is concerned with Campbell's impact on South African literature and thus focuses on a narrow body of early works; within these confines, he argues that "The two key South African works in Campbell's *oeuvre* are […] THE FLAMING TERRAPIN (1924), and the prophetic valedictory lyric, "Rounding the Cape"[…]. Both transformed the debate about domicile and appropriation at the core of South African English poetry and provided a fertile mythology for its furtherance" (GROUNDS OF CONTEST: A SURVEY OF SOUTH AFRICAN ENGLISH LITERATURE. Kenwyn: Jutalit, 1990: 47).

[28] ibid.: 81.

[29] See Jean McBean's essay on Campbell's place in the hierarchy of famous Durban High School Old Boys (of which Campbell was one). He is honoured by having a school house named after him, and a bust of him is prominently displayed in the school grounds, but few contemporary schoolboys know why he was famous.

like the mavericks Wyndham Lewis (founder of Vorticism) and Roy Campbell.

From the start of his literary career, Campbell was hailed by contemporaries as re-energising English poetry by a yoking of European and African imagery and forms in what Michael Chapman refers to as "the anti-Georgian modernist manner".[30] "When Bloomsbury shilly-shallied," Chapman argues, "Campbell, the rough-neck, shouted, harangued and celebrated the physicality of existence. In his poetry the images are concrete, the verbs active, and even as he strikes the pose of the visionary, he relishes the colloquial word, and especially the insult".[31]

There is no doubt that the insults which peppered some of the longer satirical poems were prompted by intense anger. Nor is there any doubt that the vehemence of his animosity corroded Campbell's poetic craft in these satires. Nevertheless, there remained times when Campbell was able to rise above such furies to write fine poetry or craft translations which shone, and there can be little doubt that when the mastery returned, his enemies ensured that his work remained beyond the pale of English literary recognition. Tess and Anna's memoirs seek to redress this. While the memoirs are unmistakably charged with deep filial loyalty (which, one might argue, leads to the writers' refusal to acknowledge certain of their father's ideological and artistic weaknesses), they do demand that we re-examine Campbell's poetic achievements and also his motivations.

Roy Campbell — Man of Contradiction

The Roy Campbell that Tess and Anna recall is the husband and father who loved his wife and daughters deeply, whose generosity to his fellow human beings—of all persuasions, from all walks of life—was undeterred by hardship in his own life. They defend his political positions—his anti-racism, his rejection of socialism and communism and his consequent support for Franco—by explaining that these were but the product of a deeply felt concern for justice and spiritual values. But their primary goal is not to campaign for revision on this basis; they want their father to be given his due place amongst the Great Names of his time.

"Don't look for consistency in Campbell, just look for life, look in Campbell himself for disciplined indiscipline, and in his poetry for tumultuous orderliness", advises Paton.[32] And this is what Peter Alexander, the biographer to

---

[30] Michael Chapman, SOUTHERN AFRICAN LITERATURES. London and New York: Longman, 1996: 178.
[31] ibid.: 181.
[32] "Roy Campbell: Poet and Man" (1957), CAMPBELL IN CONTEXT, ed. Coullie

whom Paton gave all the papers he, and—before him—W.H. Gardner, had gathered for a biography of Campbell, does. Alexander argues that the conflict of loyalties the schoolboy was to feel between his father and his schoolmaster, A.S. Langley, "gave rise to a deep-rooted contradiction in his character; hatred of one father-figure and love of another made [Campbell] both hate authority and long to be subjected to it." This, Alexander adds, helps explain RC's "natural anarchy and his attraction [...] to the orderliness of the European dictatorships. It explains both his early anti-clericalism, and his later adherence to the authoritative teachings of Roman Catholicism. And it explains both his hatred of 'regimented' modern life, and his happiness in the British Army."[33] Alexander refers also to RC's bisexuality as "yet another facet of his divided nature" (21) (both Anna and Tess deny this about their father) and to his need to make enemies so that he could be both victim and hero (6).[34]

Often his own worst enemy, Campbell's outrageous statements did not always reflect his true feelings but were intended to shock or to avenge him for some insult or injury he had suffered. He hated hypocrisy, yet filled his autobiographies—and the stories he told about his experiences—with false boasts and inaccurate claims.[35]

There is no pigeon hole into which he will fit, no historical narrative in which he can be assigned a role and part that he will play dutifully, consistently.

Perhaps the greatest casualty of historical clarity and explanatory effectiveness are those messy non-conformists who cannot be dismissed with a sentence or two. Someone like Campbell, whose work and life can be selectively deployed to substantiate quite contrary interpretations, is rather too troublesome for critical analyses of twentieth century literary and political developments. Excluding a handful of scholars who take his work seriously, in the main Campbell comes to be remembered, if at all, as someone whose early promise was not fulfilled, who "ended up raving about communists" and whose *oeuvre* represents "the sad case of the dislocated colonial."[36]

Against this view, Tess and Anna emphasise their father's courageous stand (in his poetry and in life) against racism and colonial parochialism, against nepotistic literary cliques and against the brutalities of Communist regimes. They recall many instances of Campbell's easy and warm friendships with people of the working and peasant classes, his principled refusals to kowtow

---

and Wade. Durban: Killie Campbell Africana Library Series, 2004: 564.
[33] ROY CAMPBELL: A CRITICAL BIOGRAPHY. Oxford: Oxford University Press, 1982: 9.
[34] Alexander is quoting William Plomer.
[35] See Alexander 132.
[36] Chapman, 182.

to prevailing literary, political and religious (or, in this case, anti-religious) trends. Their obvious love for their parents does not cause Tess and Anna to hide the dark troubles[37] which clouded their parents' lives and stained their own formative years—and readers familiar with some of the more famous or infamous incidents and quarrels will be riveted by the daughters' intimate revelations and their interpretations of such matters; Tess and Anna ask us to see their parents' failings as ordinary human weaknesses which manifested themselves in extraordinarily beautiful and talented and good people.

Readers will be moved by the love that shines through in these memoirs. Nevertheless, we must not allow ourselves a facile judgment reliant on the excision of the contradictions, forgetting neither Campbell's anti-racism nor his spirited jibes against mixed race couples; his profound concern for his fellow humans nor his pro-Franco sympathies; his liberal generosity and kindness to all sorts of people nor his tirades against prominent homosexuals. In an essay entitled "Roy Campbell—Man and Poet"[38], Alan Paton praises Campbell's intelligence yet says that the mystery of Campbell lies in "how so sensitive a poet could write [in his autobiographies] so foolishly, so aggressively, about the affairs of mankind" (281). In Light on a Dark Horse, Campbell showed that,

> In the world of ideas [he] moved with great élan and no skill whatsoever. He called Calvin and Luther crooks, and thought his praise of Afrikanerdom would be apreciated by the Afrikaners, who were Calvinist almost to a man. He despised Jews and Quakers. He thought that the killing of bulls should be reserved for the aristocrats of mankind [...]. He despised democracy, egalitarianism and any kind of socialism.[39] He defended the virtues of illiteracy—he whose own literacy had opened to him so many doors. His hatred of communism and the communists amounted to a mania. He boasted of his own exploits [...]. (Paton, 281)

The fact is, few of the aspects to Campbell's "philosophy" outlined above

---

[37] Although readers are left in no doubt as to some of the major crises in the life of the Campbell family, it would appear that not every scandalous event is recounted. In these life narratives, as indeed in all life narratives, certain memories will be excluded, both due to tact (what right does a close family member have to reveal all of the secrets of another? Why should one satisfy the craving of readers to know all, when a sampling will give an idea of what occurred in life?) and, one can surmise, due to the frailties of memory.

[38] The essay was first published in the Christian Science Monitor 2(4) 1974. It is reproduced in Alan Paton, Knocking on the Door: Shorter Writings Ed. Colin Gardner. Cape Town: David Philip, 1975: 278–282.

[39] Alexander observes that RC associated socialism with the death of individuality (143).

by Paton were consistently held. As with most of us, opinions Campbell held at one time did not persist throughout his life. The South African poet, David Wright, notes that "nobody had a more catholic or contradictory assortment of friends of so many diverse races, colours, creeds, and political tenets, or from so many varying walks of life" (qtd in Pearce: 272).

In his "Foreword" to Light on a Dark Horse, Laurie Lee distances himself from most of Roy's "dottier prejudices", but adds that he nevertheless

> continued to cherish him through the years [...]: knowing that behind the arrogant chest-thumper there was a humble and kindly man capable of the most sensitive acts of friendship; that here was one whose natural heavens lay not in political ideologies but in the open sea and the veldt; and whose instinctive allegiance was to the inhabitants of the wilderness, and who had the words to celebrate them—their power, vulnerability and beauty—in a sort of poetry that will never be equalled.[40]

The memoirs of Roy Campbell's daughters remind us that their father lived in a world which was in turmoil; that he presciently challenged the "progress" that we can now see is destroying the earth; that he fought his own demons while struggling to cling to his ideals; and that, should we choose to write off this troubled poet and his poetry, we will be the poorer.

My Interest

Paul Valéry is oft quoted as saying that there is no theory that is not a fragment, carefully prepared, of some autobiography. The same can be said of the specialisations of literary critics: the desire to explore a particular period or writer can frequently be traced to some sort of personal investment. My own work on the poet and writer Roy Campbell, however, began via a rather less direct route: in my doctoral research into South African autobiographies published in English during the apartheid period between 1948 and 1994, I came across the two autobiographical texts by Campbell. The decision to focus analysis on Light on a Dark Horse (1951) was not because Campbell was a fellow Durbanite or even because I much liked the narrative or its rather opinionated narrator. Nor was I drawn to Campbell's poetry; indeed, like most South Africans I knew very little about his work, having encountered only a couple of Campbell's poems at school, but not after. Rather I wanted a text, published in the early years of apartheid (1948-1994), which explored a white

---

[40] Laurie Lee, "Foreword" (1969), Light on a Dark Horse (Harmondsworth: Penguin, 1971: 11).

South African's representation of self and history.

I was not looking for a typical autobiography. And, of course, Campbell was never a typical white South African—Campbell was arguably never a typical anything—and his autobiography is quite unlike the colourless, bland efforts seen in other autobiographies by white South Africans of the 1940s and '50s. In most autobiographies by whites published at the time, the writer tries to tell an interesting life story while strenuously avoiding giving too much away. Usually, conventional autobiographies by whites at the time are rather impersonal records of a career or hobby. Campbell's autobiographical narrator, on the other hand, while revealing precious little about his private life, nevertheless makes declarations unflinchingly, not shying away from race and gender politics which I was interested in exploring. So Campbell's autobiography—or "autobuggeroffery",[41] in his terms—received some prominence in my thesis.

Some endeavours are dead-ends but often one thing leads to another. Out of this dissertation, some years later, came a publication.[42] This attracted the attention of a fellow academic, Jean-Philippe Wade, and we decided to convene a colloquium in Campbell's birthplace to commemorate the centennial of his birth. Rather unexpectedly, there was considerable interest in Campbell amongst scholars from diverse disciplines, and, in addition to scholars from all over South Africa, we had participants from Portugal, Canada, England, Spain, Germany and Australia, including Campbell's two biographers, Peter Alexander and Joseph Pearce. Then, in 2004, we produced a CD entitled CAMPBELL IN CONTEXT.[43] Appropriately drawing on the considerable holdings of the Killie Campbell Africana Library[44]—Killie was Roy's aunt—the CD became a kind of omnibus, featuring a great many photographs and other personal artifacts such as Roy's handwritten letters and his drawings, selected poetry (including some early handwritten drafts) and scholarly essays on Campbell and his family. Tess and Anna's memoirs came to light when doing this research.

Anna, I learned, passed away in November 2002, but Tess was still living in Portugal. Correspondence with Tess and Francesca, Anna's daughter, began

---

[41] In a note, the editors say that Campbell described his autobiography thus in private letters (ROY CAMPBELL: COLLECTED WORKS VOL.III. Ed. Peter Alexander, Michael Chapman and Marcia Leveson. Craighall: Ad. Donker, 1985: 614).

[42] "The Race to be Hero: Race and Gender in Roy Campbell's LIGHT ON A DARK HORSE." SCRUTINY2, 6 (2), 2001.

[43] CAMPBELL IN CONTEXT. Compiled and edited by Judith Lütge Coullie and Jean-Philippe Wade. Durban: University of KwaZulu-Natal, Killie Campbell Africana Library Series, 2004.

[44] Part of the University of KwaZulu-Natal's library system.

in about 2001. Although very elderly and frail, Tess was a prompt correspondent and unswervingly encouraging and helpful. When it was discovered that Anna's memoirs had been published in a limited run of 150 and Tess's had never been published, it was proposed to Francesca and Tess that the memoirs be published together. It seemed to be a good idea to publish them together because the daughters' records throw light on different aspects of their lives with their parents. And even when there are overlaps, these are important because they provide verification of the information contained therein.[45]

The proposal for joint publication was enthusiastically received by Tess and her niece, and in 2005, on a visit to Tess in Estoril and Francesca in Sintra, they confirmed their support for this project.[46] They shared photographs, letters, handwritten snippets and answered what must have been tiresome questions.[47]

From that time on, the project was not only about a now growing interest in the writing and the writer, but also about my commitment to two wonderful, warm women. That commitment has grown, not lessened, since Tess's death on 13 December 2006.

Judith Lütge Coullie
University of KwaZulu-Natal

---

[45] Note about the editing: I have standardised and corrected spelling and punctuation. There were numerous errors in Anna's and Tess's quotations from their father's work which have been rectified.

Tess's memoirs required more extensive editing to improve the style. For example, I reduced instances of word repetition. For both memoirs, I sought to make the reader's grasp of events recounted easier by providing explanatory footnotes.

[46] All royalties go to Francisco and Francesca, Tess and Anna's children.

[47] The source of photographs and other illustrative material is indicated in brackets in the captions.

Acknowledgments

From the outset, Tess Campbell was unfailingly encouraging and helpful. When the idea of publishing together in one volume her own as yet unpublished memoirs and Anna's memoirs was put to her, she expressed her pleasure in the prospect. Thanks in part to funding provided by the National Research Foundation, I was able to travel to Portugal to meet Tess in 2005. Already an elderly and rather frail lady, Tess received me graciously and answered my questions. When I returned to South Africa, she continued to write many letters expressing her continued advocacy and answering further questions I put to her with frankness. She also gave me copies of some photographs of herself and her family.

Sadly, Tess passed away in 2006. Since then, her son, Francisco, has assisted in ensuring this publication comes to fruition.

I never met Anna. She had passed away in 2002. Attempts to find the copyright holder of her memoirs, which were first published in a limited print run of 150 by Typographeum (Francestown, N.H., 1986), led me to Terry Risk, who edited the manuscript. He suggested that Anna's only child would be heir to the copyright. I thus contacted Anna's daughter, Francesca Cavero de Carondelet Bento. Again, I encountered generosity and enthusiasm for the project. My husband and I visited Francesca and her husband, Filipe Bento, in their beautiful home in Sintra in 2005. Francesca and Filipe gave this project their blessing. Francesca's support for this publication has not wavered. She has kindly provided information and visual material, including the copy of the striking Bernard Meninsky portrait of Mary, her grandmother.

Thanks go to the staff of Campbell Collections. Campbell Collections has extensive holdings on Roy Campbell and other family members. The staff have generously allowed me to reproduce in this book selected photographs and letters that appear in the CAMPBELL IN CONTEXT CD (eds. Judith Lütge Coullie and Jean-Philippe Wade, Durban: Killie Campbell Africana Library Series, 2004).

Colleen Goldsworthy of the University of KwaZulu-Natal's DISA (Digital Innovation South Africa) unit who compiled the CD so superbly and with such calm good grace, stepped in to help yet again by making images from the CD available for use in the book. Colleen truly is worthy of her surname!

Anneke Schaafsma, of Special Collections at the University of Stellenbosch J.S. Gericke Library located the transcript of the Uys Krige piece on Campbell quoted (and misidentified) by Anna.

I am indebted to the editors of Campbell's four volume COLLECTED WORKS (Peter Alexander, Michael Chapman and Marcia Leveson) for their meticulous scholarship. I have relied on their work and that of both of Campbell's biographers, Peter Alexander and Joseph Pearce. In their biographies, Alexander and Pearce approach their subject with what seems to me to be just the right blend of sympathy and critical distance. Amongst other works, I also consulted THE RARE AND THE BEAUTIFUL, Cressida Connolly's intriguing biography of Mary, Kathleen, Lorna and Douglas Garman.

From the outset, many years back, when I first mooted the idea of publishing the memoirs, Michael Hanke commended the idea; his assistance and backing are much appreciated. He and Peter Alexander read the MS and made helpful suggestions and I thank them both.

Joseph Pearce is owed a huge debt of gratitude for his unfaltering encouragement and practical guidance in finding a suitable publisher for the memoirs. I am grateful, too, to the publisher, Robert Trexler, of Winged Lion Press.

A further grant from the National Research Foundation was crucial in the final stages of this project. The indexer, Frances Roberts, approached her task with enthusiasm and dedication; her contribution makes this book a richer resource for future researchers.

I thank my friends and family who have listened indulgently to my ramblings about Roy Campbell and his family. Ian, Charis and Benjamin have uncomplainingly shared their home with the spirit of the Campbells. They have now, as always, my love and gratitude.

POETIC JUSTICE:
A Memoir of My Father, Roy Campbell

by

Anna Campbell Lyle

Preface to Poetic Justice

ON the day, in fact at the very hour, that Father was dying in a car crash on a lonely road in Portugal, I was buying a black coat at Simpson's in Piccadilly. It was 3:30 in the afternoon of the 23rd of April 1957—the birthday and, according to tradition, also the deathday of Shakespeare.

The car my parents were travelling in, a small Fiat 600, had one very worn tyre. Mary, my mother, who did all the driving,[1] thought she had had this tyre put at the back, but the mechanic made a mistake when servicing the car, and put it in front on the right-hand side where Father sat. He was a big man and under his weight the tyre which had held out since Seville burst, and the car crashed into a tree on a lonely road near Setubal, south of Lisbon. Both my parents were knocked unconscious instantly. Father was driven to a hospital at Setubal by some people who passed shortly after the accident. He died on the way, after murmuring some words and giving two deep sighs. Mother recovered after a long convalescence, but she was never the same, brave optimist again; though she did retain her profound sense of humour and enchantment. Certainly a part of her died with Father and she blamed herself for his death. This was nonsense: fate had joined them; fate now separated them.

In many of Father's last poems he senses approaching death, and even that it was to come, indirectly, through Mary.

> *And best is my Muse this companion of mine*
> *Who has learned, like de Lenclos, to age like good wine*
> *And the scent of her hair is the wind in the pine*
> *As black as the future that looms in our way*
> *I like it that colour forbode what it may…*

And this from an unpublished poem:

---

[1] This memoir was originally published by Typograpeum (Francestown, N.H.: 1986). Notes supplied by the author in the original Typographeum publication are indicated by her initials, ACL. All other notes are by the editor, Judith Lütge Coullie.

Anna says later that Roy would not drive. See handwritten copy of poem by RC p.157; he is thought to be referring to this car.

Poetic Justice

Your hair my shroud, that was your black mantilla...

The first I knew of the accident was when a cousin of mine phoned early in the morning of the 24th, to say that Father's death had just been announced on the B.B.C. I had arrived in London two days before from Portugal. The shock was staggering. I could not collect my wits but sat in a chair as though stunned. At last I saw the black coat I had bought the day before and suddenly I realised that I had to get back to Portugal as fast as possible. Strangely enough, this black coat was a tremendous comfort to me, and after putting it on I rushed round to the Carmelites in Church Street and asked the monks there (who were old friends) to say a mass for Father. I then tried to book a place on a flight to Lisbon, but there were no seats available. Just as I was beginning to despair, Father's great friend, Rob Lyle,[2] rang up to ask if he could help in any way. It was with blessed relief that I left everything in his capable hands and in a couple of hours he had managed to find a roundabout route which got us to Lisbon at three am, on the 25th. We flew via Brussels and Paris and just managed to board the last flight to Lisbon. This was before the bridge over the Tagus had been built, so we still had to catch the ferry to Cacilhas and then go on by taxi to Setubal.

After booking into an hotel, we walked to the Misericordia hospital just as dawn was breaking. The nuns at the Misericordia took us straight to the chapel where Father's body was lying in a coffin surrounded by candles. He looked absolutely beautiful, and a look of transcendental peace, and even happiness, was visible on his marble-like face. Although his injuries had been terrible, neither his hands nor his face had been hurt. It was only when I bent to kiss his cheek, and felt its shocking coldness, that I realised that I would never be able to hear his dearly loved voice again. The tears started to pour down Rob's face and mine as we remembered all this very special man's gifts and how we would miss him forever. Father and I had been especially close in the last fifteen years of his life. What made his death at this time even more poignant, was that he and Mary had been having their very first house built and were returning, after Easter in Seville, for the house-warming.

The last time I had seen Father alive was at a picnic he gave when the roof was put up. All his family, his friends and the workmen joined in making this an occasion to remember. It was a great day and my sister Tess, my mother and

---

[2] Rob Lyle edited the journal Catacomb with RC. Partly as a result of RC's influence, he converted to Catholicism. RC was his godfather (Alexander, 216). In 1958, Rob Lyle, Richard Aldington, Lawrence Durrell, Alan Paton, Edith Sitwell and others published Hommage à Roy Campbell (F.-J. Temple et al. Trans. Armand Guibert. Montpellier: Societe Cevenole du Mercou). Lyle and Anna were married in 1982.

A Memoir of my Father, Roy Campbell

I and our children were thrilled that at last Father would have no more worries about rent. The house was set in the Sintra hills among pines, eucalyptus trees, myrtle bushes, camelias and mimosas of every variety, on the only piece of land that was not state-owned in that part of the Serra.

Father was only fifty-six when he died, but he was exhausted and suffering greatly from an old war injury in his hip which made him groan with pain at night. The two lecture tours he had made to the States and Canada in 1953 and 1955 had used up his nervous energy, and the continual imbecility of the West's policy vis-á-vis the Soviet Union added to his feeling of impotence and frustration in his lonely fight against Marxism; we therefore hoped that up at Casa da Serra he would recover his energies and be able to add further works to his already prolific output.

As I stood in the icy chapel that morning, all these thoughts disturbed me so deeply that I completely forgot to send for someone to do a death-mask or take a last photo. Utterly prostrated by grief and exhaustion I fell asleep fully clothed on a bed next door to the room in which Mary lay fighting for her life. When I woke some hours later, the coffin had been sealed, and I blamed myself for forgetting to do the most important things. Rob Lyle's state of shock equalled mine, and he also forgot to send for a photographer.

In the evening of the 25th I was allowed to see Mary. Her beautiful face had been badly injured by the steering wheel, but this completely cleared up after a few months, except for a nerve in her upper lip which made it quite numb and irritated her for the rest of her life. When I saw her that evening, she was half asleep with a drug which she later told me felt like gold flowing through her veins, and she hardly recognised me. The nuns of the Misericordia had told her of Father's death, and she had insisted on being taken on a stretcher to the chapel, to see his body, and spend some time there in prayer. This had been on the previous day. Mary was deeply religious and it was a great happiness to her to know that Father had died two days after receiving the Sacrament on Easter Sunday, so that he was in a state of grace when his soul left his body. Father was buried at the cemetery of Sao Pedro in Sintra (the Cintra of Byron's CHILDE HAROLD) on the 26th. I often go there to take flowers to his tomb in which Mary now also lies.

This is not to be their last resting place. The South Africans want their greatest poet to be buried in what was, when all is said, the part of this planet that he loved most.[3]

---

[3] Enquiries about this have drawn a blank. It is, however, unlikely to be a priority in post-apartheid South Africa.

Poetic Justice

Roy as a teenager, his last year at Durban High School, 1917
(from Campbell Collections, hereafter CC)

Chapter I

Roy was sent to Oxford when he was seventeen by his father Dr. Sam Campbell of Durban, but after three terms at Merton College he felt he was wasting his time there because the only thing he wanted to do—or, as he himself said in an early letter, could do—was to write poetry. He had wanted to be a poet from the age of twelve. But how was he to convince his parents of this fact? The struggle he sustained, because of this, severely undermined his health, as it went on for a long time. In the following letter to Dr. Sam, Roy stated his case quite clearly:

> *Dear Father, with regard to a degree I find that Oxford with its lectures interferes very much with my work. I cannot conscientiously apply valuable time to such a subject, as for instance Anglo-Saxon. If I were to take a degree and become a school master, can you imagine my giving out dogmas to a crowd of gaping students hour after hour, day after day? Could you imagine me being friendly with the type of person who does that kind of thing? I would be half way across the Pacific after two months of it. As far as money is concerned, I am sorry to be so expensive. It is unnecessary to tell you how grateful I am to you. I will try to reward your kindness by making my future as great as your past.*
>
> *Love to all Roy.*

It is a great pity that Dr. Sam took absolutely no notice of this letter. What is remarkable about it is that it shows Roy's absolute certainty in his vocation. This letter is undated as his letters always were, not through carelessness, but because he never knew the day of the week, let alone the date of the month. He was constitutionally incapable of keeping a calendar, note-book or any of the other things with which we order our lives. The only order he knew was the divine order of verse and of thought. He used his brain like a machine. How often have I seen him close the book he was reading and sit patting it rhythmically, as he digested its contents, so deep in thought that it was difficult to rouse him.

Poetic Justice

Both Philip Heseltine[4] and Rob Lyle have remarked on his "deeply intellectual imagination." Because he was inefficient about worldly matters, materialists made the mistake of thinking him simple-minded or "unintellectual," whereas he was merely lacking in cunning. Whether stern Dr. Sam was convinced by the above letter is a matter for conjecture. He probably got into one of his wrathful states at his young son's insubordination. All I know is that Roy left Oxford after his third term there.

Roy at seventeen was truly beautiful. Six feet two inches tall and broad-shouldered, with delicate, almost too sensitive features.

Dr S.G. Campbell, 1915 (Tess)

His always pale face was lit up by large, deep blue and luminous eyes surrounded by thick black lashes. The colour of his eyes (what Edith Sitwell[5] called his kingfisher eyes) changed with his moods from grey, through green to almost black when he was angry. Roy realised the importance that eyes have in one's battle through life and he could use them to good effect, to condemn or to praise. He was always gentle to me in my childhood, but if he was annoyed at some misdemeanor, it was his eyes I feared. Many people remarked on the power and beauty of his eyes. Osbert Sitwell[6] once said to Rob Lyle, "Have you ever seen eyes as luminous as Roy's?"

Immediately Roy arrived at Oxford, he was beset by homosexuals.[7] In his

---

[4] Anglo-Welsh composer and music critic (1894-1930). Composed under the pseudonym "Peter Warlock".

[5] Born of aristocratic parents, Dame Sitwell (1887-1964) was herself a poet of some renown and a loyal friend to the Campbells. She converted to Catholicism in 1955. Roy and Mary were her godparents.

[6] Brother of Edith and Sacheverell Sitwell, Sir Francis Osbert Sacheverell Sitwell (1892-1969) published poetry, fiction, journalism, art criticism and an autobiography in five volumes.

[7] When Campbell was at Oxford, there would have been few women. Women were not admitted to membership of the University until 1920, although they had been allowed to sit some University examinations and attend lectures for over forty years by that

LIGHT ON A DARK HORSE he says that he had nothing against homosexuality since he had been brought up since childhood among sailors and anyway he would never set himself up as a judge of other peoples' mores.[8] What he could not bear was the perpetual lamentations of homosexuals, and I know that secretly he hated the effect that homosexuality has eventually on peoples' characters. I personally think that Roy was completely innocent when he arrived in England, otherwise why should he have written, at the age of nineteen, in his FLAMING TERRAPIN:[9]

> *So dread Corruption, over human shoals,*
> *Instead of pearls, comes groping after souls,*
> *And the pure pearl of many a noble life*
> *Falls to the scraping of his rusty knife...*

Roy once told me that he had been stricken with remorse when at Oxford he cut a barmaid, with whom he had had an affair, because he was in the company of a snobbish homosexual. In later years he was haunted by this, to him, terrible behaviour, and he was always performing quixotic acts in reparation. For instance, when he was dining at the Tom Burnses one night, the Spanish maid tripped as she entered the dining-room with a dish of red mullet, whereupon Roy immediately got down on all fours and started throwing the fish up onto the table so that, in the general mêlée, the maid should be able to get over her embarrassment. This characteristic behaviour was a reflection of his deep concern for those in subservient positions. He was a practising democrat—never to be confused with being a socialist. At Oxford T.W. Earp[10] had a strong influence

---

date. By many accounts, homosexual practices were widespread at Oxford at the time. "Oxford Style" refers to a system by which upperclassmen helped new students assimilate to university life in exchange for sexual gratification, usually by means of intercrural sex. Students may have been imitating homosexual practices in ancient Greece, referenced by authors such as Plato and Aristotle.

[8] Published in 1952. In the autobiography and elsewhere, Campbell is scathing in his criticism of "the smug little Sunday School world of Bloomsbury 'queerness'" (Harmondsworth: Penguin, 1971: 263) but as mentioned in the Introduction, the contempt was for what he perceived as the self-satisfied smugness, the exclusiveness and joylessness of such practitioners of homosexuality.

[9] Published in 1924, this poem established Campbell as major poetic talent.

[10] (1892-1958) A critic, he edited several issues of OXFORD POETRY between 1915 and 1919. Anna seems to be alluding to Earp's literary guidance, but may also be hinting at a homosexual influence (in spite of her disavowals elsewhere). According to John Garth, the Tolkien scholar (Tolkien knew Earp), Earp (who was often described as odd, and was thus the inspiration for a new word in English, namely, twerp), was homosexual or

Poetic Justice

on Roy which extended over the next two years until he met Mary.

It was in those two years that Roy went through a sort of *saison en enfer* and what Baudelaire called "a deliberate derangement of all the senses."[11] It was not for nothing that Rimbaud[12] and Baudelaire[13] were two of Roy's greatest loves.

---

bisexual ("Tolkien, Exeter College and the Great War", 2006: 8. http://www.johngarth.co.uk/php/tolkein-exiter-great-war.php. Accessed 13.3.2010)

[11] It would seem that Anna is mistakenly attributing this to Baudelaire rather than Rimbaud.

[12] The poet Jean Nicholas Arthur Rimbaud (1854-1891) famously had a homosexual relationship with the poet Paul Verlaine. In an early letter to a friend, he wrote about his programme for achieving poetic heights by embracing the derangement of rational senses. UNE SAISON EN ENFER was self-published in 1873. Harold Nicolson claims that RC reminded him of Rimbaud (Alexander, 78). RC translated some of Rimbaud's poems.

[13] Charles Baudelaire (1821-1867), poet. His most famous collection of poems, LES FLEURS DU MAL, was first published 1857. The themes of his poems scandalised mainstream critics. With Stéphane Mallarmé and Paul Verlaine he formed the Decadents. He spent most of his life in debt and addicted to laudanum. RC's translations of Baudelaire are to be found in COLLECTED WORKS II.

Chapter II

Roy met my mother, Mary Garman, in October 1921. Mary was the eldest of Dr. Walter Garman's nine children. She was brought up in all the security of a long-established county family. They lived in a beautiful Elizabethan manor house, Oakeswell Hall, at Wednesbury, with the usual retinue of parlour-maids, gardeners, nannies, and governesses.

Mary went to a fashionable boarding-school where she passed her Higher School Certificate with Honours at the age of seventeen and where she fell in love with her beautiful art mistress.

In 1916 when Mary was eighteen, she learned to drive and used to chauffeur her father on his rounds. She also took piano and art lessons in neighbouring Birmingham, played golf with her father and tennis with the local curates and students; nevertheless, she found Wednesbury boring and depressing. The newspapers in those days seemed to consist entirely of long blacklists of the young men killed in the previous day's fighting, among which, inevitably, appeared from time to time the names of Mary's cousins and friends. It was altogether a gloomy time, and Mary longed to get away and meet interesting people and study painting seriously. She often told me how the eternally grey skies of the Midlands and the smog from factories and fires, which turned even the roses in the garden black by evening, drove her melancholy mad. Failing to get the consent of her father to go to London, she simply ran away, taking her younger sister, Kathleen (later Lady Epstein), with her.

She earned her living by driving a van for Lyon's Corner Houses—a very brave thing to do in those days. With the money she earned she paid for lessons at the Slade (School of Art) and attended concerts at the Queen's Hall. In fact, she became such an assiduous concert-goer that Bernard van Dieren[14] noticed her there and fell in love with her. I still have the very moving love letters he wrote to her at that time. At the Slade, Bernard Meninsky,[15] her drawing

---

[14] (1887-1936) Of Dutch birth, he moved to England in 1909 and is thus known as a British composer, critic, author and writer on music.
[15] (1891-1950) Artist, born in the Ukraine but raised in Liverpool. He was appointed

Poetic Justice

Roy, 1921, the year he and Mary met. (Francesca)

teacher, also fell in love with her, and I still have, hanging over my desk, the portrait he painted of her in 1920 when she was 22.[16]

Roy was living in Russell Square (Bloomsbury) at that time, so Mary often saw him wandering about that district where she also had a small studio. She thought he looked the most interesting of all the interesting people she was seeing and meeting in London. Sometimes she saw him in the company of Iris Tree,[17] at other times with Constant Lambert,[18] Augustus John,[19] and Wyndham Lewis[20] at the Café Royal. Then, one day, she realised that she had not seen him for some months; he seemed to have vanished from the scene. She wished then that she had made more of an effort to be introduced to him.

One very cold day in October, as she was walking down Charlotte Street, she

---

Official War Artist during WWI.

[16] Francesca, Anna's daughter, has the original. A copy which she kindly sent to the editor is reproduced in the "Illustrations" section of this volume.

[17] (1897-1968) English poet, actress and painter.

[18] (1905-1951) Leonard Constant Lambert: British composer and conductor.

[19] (1878 -1961) Welsh painter, draughtsman and etcher. He painted many famous people of his day including Thomas Hardy, George Bernard Shaw and Dylan Thomas. The two volumes of his autobiography were CHIAROSCURO (1952) and FINISHING TOUCHES (1964). Augustus John's portrait of RC appears on the cover of Peter Alexander's ROY CAMPBELL: A CRITICAL BIOGRAPHY (Oxford: Oxford University Press, 1982).

[20] (1882-1957) English painter and author and co-founder of the Vorticist movement in art. He wrote two volumes of autobiography: BLASTING AND BOMBARDIERING (1937) and RUDE ASSIGNMENT (1950). Once dismissed for his politics, there is now a revival of interest in his work.

was surprised to see him walking towards her. He wore no overcoat and looked extremely ill.

Roy could change from looking desperate to the opposite in the space of a few seconds. He had the most mercurial personality. Mary realised, with deep pity, that this young man needed help desperately, and without realising that she was breaking the conventions, she asked him whether he was ill. Coming out of a deep trance—he was writing poetry even in his sleep at that time—he saw before him the incarnation of his dreams, what he had been looking for from the age of twelve. He saw far more than a very beautiful young woman. Being highly intuitive he realised at once that this was his complementary self.

Mary Garman 1921 (CC)

He never tired of telling me what an extraordinary feeling overcame him when he first saw Mary. It was as though a painting, long-loved, had come to life. He never stopped loving Mary with the same passion as on that cold October morning. But then she was a very unusual person. Whole books could be written about her. In her were combined a fiery and passionate temperament, intelligence, originality and independence of mind, strength of will and of character, energy, a profound sense of humour and limitless courage, both physical and moral. Added to these was a deep understanding of poets and poetry. She was admired and portrayed by many gifted men, among them Busoni,[21] van Dieren, John, and Wyndham Lewis.

One of Mary's charms was that she could listen to what people said to her and give it thought and consideration. She took her beauty lightly which added to her attraction, and finally, as the Portuguese obituaries said of her, she had "authority" and "distinction": *alta distincao*. Of course, she had faults; one of these was her complete fearlessness which sometimes made her insensitive and

---

[21] (1866-1924) Ferruccio Busoni, composer, pianist, piano teacher and conductor.

Poetic Justice

led to all sorts of complications, as will be seen in this narrative.

Mary now asked Roy if he would like to come back to her studio for a meal. He accepted with alacrity, and for the next three days and nights he kept her and Kathleen in fits of laughter. They were enchanted with this very young (Roy was three years younger than Mary) unspoilt genius. A few weeks after that first meeting, Mary took Roy down to Oakswell to meet her parents.

Roy used to tell me how overwhelmed he felt sitting at the dining-room table with all Mary's brothers and sisters staring at him with their remarkable eyes. They were an exceptionally good-looking family. The five eldest took after Grandfather Garman: Mary, Sylvia, Douglas, Kathleen, and Rosalind were dark with very fair skins and greenish-brown eyes. The other four—Helen, Mavin, Ruth, and Lorna—were very faired-haired and blue-eyed like Grandmama. She, in turn, was so like Lord Grey of Falloden (of whom she was the illegitimate sister) that in the photos we have of them they are like twins. Grandmama was retiring and shy, whereas Grandfather Garman was very debonair, handsome, and a great favourite with his female patients.

Although Grandfather admired the as yet unpublished FLAMING TERRAPIN and liked Roy enormously, he did not want my parents to marry. He had been struck by the huge quantities of drink Roy had got through while he was at Oakswell in order to get over his shyness. Dr. Sam, in South Africa, was also seething with anger at what he considered further irresponsibility on his unpredictable son's part. Things were slightly smoothed over when the two old gentlemen discovered that they had both graduated from St. Andrews University. However, all their fussing was useless, because my parents already considered themselves eternal partners. I once asked Mary when Roy had proposed to her. She answered indignantly, "But he didn't propose! We took it for granted we would marry when we first spoke to each other."

On the 11th of February 1922 my parents were married from Oakswell. Mary wore a long black dress and a long golden veil—not to be eccentric but because she had nothing else suitable. Roy borrowed a frock-coat from one of the waiters at Stulick's restaurant. When Mary saw him in this get-up, she almost fainted, and begged him to get back into his old suit. When Roy knelt at the altar, the guests were shocked to see that he had holes in the soles of his shoes. And Mary's old nanny, Ada, said, "Oh, I always thought Miss Mary would marry a gentleman!" Roy was completely unconscious of what he wore, until quite late in life when he tried without much success to be *comme-il-faut*.[22] The only vanity he had was over hats. But this was more because of his baldness—which started

---

[22] Appropriate, fitting, fashionable.

when he was quite young, being a Campbell characteristic—than for any other reason. He did not like homburgs or berets very much, so he turned to wide-brimmed hats which suited his face.

After a rowdy party in London, wittily described by Wyndham Lewis in his BLASTING AND BOMBARDIERING, my parents retired to a lonely cottage near Aberdaron in Wales. Mary insisted on Roy having absolute quiet so that he could finish THE FLAMING TERRAPIN in peace. My sister, Teresa Mary, was born there on the 26th of November 1922. The birth was a difficult one, the cottage being more than rustic and the doctor arriving when it was all over. Luckily for Mary she had a brave Welsh woman who helped everything along and also coped with a nervous young husband.

Mary was very touched when the next morning Roy presented her with a quail, caught and cooked by himself, on a tray with a bunch of wild flowers. One of the things my parents remembered at Aberdaron was coming face to face with a small seal while bathing. It stayed and played with them for some time.

In 1924, when Roy was twenty-three[23], THE FLAMING TERRAPIN was published, and he found himself famous overnight. This epic poem received the most wonderful reviews from all the foremost critics of the day—both in Britain and in the United States—and letters from friends, relations, and total strangers poured in with congratulations. By this time Tess, Mary, and Roy were living in rooms in Charlotte Street in London.

Talking of reviews, reminds me of one of the many absurdities in Dr. Alexander's biography[24]: he claims that although Roy pretended not to care what the critics said about him, he carefully saved his reviews nonetheless. But in our nomadic existence it was hard to hold on to essentials, let alone lug trunks full of press-cuttings around the world. Even supposing that Roy had been able to hang on to some laudatory reviews, everything of that sort—letters from famous friends, manuscripts, Mary's drawings—were all used to light fires by the two armies which occupied our house during the Spanish Civil War. What Dr. Alexander did find among Roy's papers were the cuttings collected over many years by his mother, Mrs. Margaret Campbell, and which at her death, two years before his, were sent to us for safekeeping stuck neatly into three large albums.

---

[23] He was in his twenty third year.
[24] Alexander's ROY CAMPBELL: A CRITICAL BIOGRAPHY was published in 1982. He is co-editor (with Michael Chapman and Marcia Leveson) of the four volume COLLECTED WORKS and editor of SELECTED POETRY OF ROY CAMPBELL (1982). As mentioned in the Introduction, Alexander's biography met with Mary Campbell's approval (Alexander, 1982: viii).

Chapter III

My parents had been together day and night for four years when Roy decided to return "home," as he always called South Africa, to see how things stood between him and his father. His mother assured him that after the success of THE FLAMING TERRAPIN he would be welcomed home like a long-lost hero. But it did not take him long to find out that his father had not really forgiven him for leaving Oxford and for marrying while he was still under age, without a "proper" job. It would have been simplicity itself for Dr. Sam to give him a small house and a tiny income so that he could do his work in peace and look after Mary and his children with the minimum of strain. But it is quite clear that Dr. Sam never understood Roy. Instead of the warm welcome he expected, he was treated coldly and sternly. Roy's timidity had always exasperated his father.[25] He says as much in his book for children, THE MAMBA'S PRECIPICE,[26] a very revealing piece of autobiography. Because of this friction and combined with his longing to give Mary a home of her own, Roy's nerves began to give way. He became so ill that he almost died. In photos of him at that time he looks desperately unhappy.

Although Roy was often afflicted by imaginary diseases, he was genuinely acutely suffering from the dislocated vertebrae in his neck caused by a bad fall in 1920 when he did some stunt riding in a travelling circus. The strange sensations he felt in his head from what he called his "broken neck" exacerbated his fear of madness.[27] Out of all these tribulations and sufferings, however, came some of the greatest and most moving of Roy's poems.

When little Tess and Mary turned up in Durban, some three or four weeks

---

[25] Both of Campbell's biographers (Alexander and Pearce) comment on the difficulties of the father-son relationship.

[26] First published in 1953. Although clearly heavily autobiographical, it is published as a work of fiction.

[27] According to Alexander, RC was a hypochondriac his entire life, and took various drugs for diseases he thought he had, but "seldom mentioned his real illnesses. He would drink until his heart palpitated and then take sedatives to calm it, followed by powerful stimulants to even the balance" (234).

after Roy, Grandfather Campbell was torn between adoration for his first grandchild and indignation with Mary. He reduced this woman, who so seldom wept, to tears. What he should have done was to go down on his knees and thank her for taking such good care of his delicate son, under very spartan circumstances. Poor Mary must have wondered what on earth she had got herself into. Coming from a free and easy family, she was poorly equipped to put up with her martinet in-laws and the stultifying society of South Africa. When I asked her in later years what it had been like, she said, "I was very dreamy when I was young and although Dr. Sam was an irritable little man, I hardly remember him. He was already very near to death from exhaustion when I met him. But to tell you the truth the novelty of the country, the wild animals, and the picturesqueness of the Africans—like your nanny, for instance—made the Whites pale into insignificance." Mary was fond of Granny Campbell and also of Roy's brother, George, who was a good friend through thick and thin, but her best friends in South Africa were Paul and Anna von Schubert (my godmother)[28] and Katie Hewitt, the novelist.[29]

The magazine edited by Roy called VOORSLAG (Whiplash) started coming out in early 1926, but it only ran for three issues because the backers[30] got cold feet when they saw how outspoken it was and Roy resigned when they started to muzzle the contributions.

I was born on the 1st of February 1926, and Grandfather Campbell died in March.[31] He was widely respected, and his funeral was attended by 30,000 Africans by whom he was much loved, and by thousands of White Africans.

It was late November 1926 when my parents started making preparations to return to Europe. All their friends had left Natal at more or less the same time; among these were Laurens van der Post[32] and William Plomer.[33] From Roy's

---

[28] After whom Anna was named. In the Typographeum edition Anna misspells this as Shubert.
[29] Kathleen Hewitt wrote a series of detective novels as well as other novels, short stories and journalism. A satirical novel, DECORATION, was dedicated to Roy and Mary (Connolly, 117).
[30] Lewis Reynolds is the backer alluded to here.
[31] According to Alexander, RC was haunted all his life by the profound rift between himself and his father (53).
[32] (1906-1996) Afrikaner author, war hero, conservationist, philosopher and explorer. RC later fell out with him, telling Plomer that "the only reason he'd liked him was because the younger man believed everything he said" (Connolly, 68).
[33] (1903-1973) South African author, poet, literary editor and librettist. Alexander notes that Mary saw Plomer roughly every six months when she traveled to London, but the relationship cooled, in part because of Plomer's friendship with the Bloomsburies but

Poetic Justice

letters, one can see what a deep love and admiration he had for the latter. But their friendship gradually petered out when they were both back in Europe: Plomer was easily sucked into the Bloomsbury set for which Roy had a deep abhorrence. Writing to Lewis in 1928 he says, "... Plomer was supposed to have passed this way [Martigues] but was completely put off by SATIRE AND FICTION, about which he wrote me 17 pages of expostulation, advice and entreaty... .I don't know what has come over him, he writes like an anglican person—and I have treated him like one accordingly. He has become a proper Bloomsbury..."

Whereas Plomer was drawn to that little community of gossips, mutual congratulators, and what the Americans call "sick" people without any difficulty, Roy was drawn to—or was in love with—beauty, health, and, yes, goodness. But the following letter to Edmund Blunden[34] shows how ready he was to help Plomer before he joined the Bloomsburies:

28 Musgrave Road
Durban South Africa
1926

Dear Blunden,
I am taking advantage of my intimate knowledge of your poetry, rather than of our brief personal acquaintance at Oxford—to introduce you to my friend William Plomer, who is going to Japan. He has just written, at the age of twenty, a very fine novel TURBOT[T] WOLFE *which has been highly praised in* THE NATION *and* NEW STATESMAN. *His achievements as a writer are all the more remarkable when one considers that he has lived since childhood in the intellectually murderous atmosphere of Colonial South Africa. I have been involved with him in the extremely precarious business of trying to defend the native races out here from exploitation by the colonists—and he has behaved with a great deal of courage all through.*

It is in the hope that you and he will interest one another that I have told him to seek you out.
With kind regards to Mrs Blunden
Yours truly,
Roy Campbell

---

also because he was irritated that instead of giving the manuscript of ADAMASTOR to him as promised, RC gave it to Enslin du Plessis (Alexander, 113). The final nail in the coffin, in 1933, was Plomer's claim that Mary had made a pass at him (see Alexander, 114).

[34] Edmund Blunden (1896-1974), English poet, writer, teacher and critic for THE NATION and the TIMES LITERARY SUPPLEMENT, his work and life were shaped by his experience of the First World War.

One of the best friends Roy made in South Africa in those two years was C. J. Sibbett.³⁵ Sibbett was a South African living in Cape Town at the time of my parents' visit to Durban. He ran a magazine called THE OWL and was a great lover of the arts. He corresponded regularly until Roy's death and was a great help, morally. It was Sibbett who lent my parents £50 to get back to England, and over thirty years he gave them in all about £200.

The journey home was disastrous. It was a very rough crossing. Someone left the porthole open so that a wave inundated the cabin and soaked everything, including Roy's latest poems. I cried

William Plomer, Roy and Mary Campbell at Sezela, Natal, 1926 (CC)

without ceasing, so that Roy strapped my pram to the mast and my howls were buffeted into outer space by the wind, and little Tess was disturbed by one more upheaval in her young life. Mary hated the crossing as she suffered badly from sea-sickness. We arrived at Southampton in a snowstorm which, strangely enough, I can remember. I also distinctly recall being put into the arms of Mary's one-time governess, Miss Elizabeth Thomas, known as Tony. Tony was always coming to the rescue in our lives. A diminutive spinster with the face of a dove and the heart of a lion, she was always on hand at moments of crisis. I remember her with deep love and more than admiration. She was Grandmama's house-keeper and companion and went on helping the large Garman family to the end of her days.

---

[35] He was an advertising executive. It was he who, in 1926, suggested that RC read a translation of Camões's epic poem THE LUSIADS. Cecil Sibbett and RC were to remain friends, corresponding regularly over the years (see Alexander, 68).

Chapter IV

In the spring of 1927 my parents rented a cottage at Weald, in Kent. They were delighted to find, late in 1926, that Grandfather Campbell had left them a small income in his will, of £20 a month. They thought this would be enough to live on when supplemented by Mary's £100 a year[36] and what Roy could earn from his royalties and the reviews, essays etc., he contributed to different magazines and newspapers. They were young and hopeful, and they took the hardships such a life would entail in their stride. The luxury of not having to work at routine jobs was more important to them than a thousand possessions. Roy literally never noticed discomfort, but Mary, who had a sensual nature, sometimes found the spartan life she had to lead with her husband a bit too much. Yet, however broke my parents were, Mary managed, all through her life, to make our homes lovable and beautiful.

By the time we arrived at Weald, Mary had been living for six years without a home of her own. She had two young children to look after and a very ill husband and was near the end of her tether. It is not surprising, therefore, that when her neighbour, Vita Sackville-West,[37] offered her help, Mary accepted it with relief. I don't know what Roy's feelings were about moving into the gardener's cottage at Long Barn, but I think it would have been hard to find two people more uncongenial, to him personally, than Vita and Harold Nicolson.[38] I do know that Roy was very ill most of the time he spent at Long Barn even though he was glad to see that Mary was happy in Vita's company. Besides, he was just coming under the very strong influence of Wyndham Lewis and everything else paled into insignificance in comparison. He was dazzled by Lewis's brilliance and prolific output (he was at that time publishing one book a year

---

[36] It would seem that this was left to Mary in her late father's will.
[37] Victoria Mary Sackville-West (1892-1962): daughter of the third Baron of Sackville; English poet, novelist and gardener.
[38] Sir Harold Nicolson (1886-1968): British diplomat, author, diarist and politician. Vita and Harold each had many same-sex affairs but were, by all accounts, devoted to each other.

and sometimes two, or even three). The fertility of his imagination, his stringent and savage wit, were very appealing to Roy, especially at a time when he was finding it more and more of a strain to live in the hot-house atmosphere in which he found himself. In similar circumstances, Rimbaud would simply have shattered the conventionalities by general irreverence or worse, but Roy had to think of his wife and children, so he stayed on.

Everyone has had their say about what happened at Long Barn between the Campbells and the Nicolsons, about what prompted Roy to write THE GEORGIAD,[39] but no one has got it right—perhaps no one ever will. How can one unravel the complicated motivations of four different peoples' passions, egoisms, loves, and self-interests? But the point to be made about THE GEORGIAD (at one level anyway) is that it attacked a clique which exercised an influence on the literary world out of all proportion to the sum of its talents, abilities, or achievements. In other words THE GEORGIAD was written to destroy a "racket." What made Roy so indignant was that reputations were made or destroyed, not according to merit, but according to any passing whim or fashion, and much depended on the wearing of "the homosexual livery of the British Intelligentsia." One of the leading lights of the clique in question was Lytton Strachey.[40] In the margin of Roy's first edition of THE GEORGIAD, he records, in his own hand, the following conversation:

> Lytton Strachey: "Some people find expression like you Roy, in poetry, others in good works, others in heroism. But I look in a higher direction and find it in detachment."
> Roy Campbell: "Strachey, you are about as *detached* morally, physically and intellectually as the animal you most resemble."
> Lytton Strachey: "What is that?"
> Roy Campbell: "A tapeworm."

It has been suggested that THE GEORGIAD was written in a fit of jealousy about Mary's love for Vita. But the whole thing was far more complicated than that. If anything, it was Vita's cruelty to Mary, when she refused to satisfy Vita's physical demands, that made Roy angry.[41] He realised that his beloved wife had

---

[39] This long satirical poem in rhyming couplets is an attack on the Bloomsbury group.
[40] Giles Lytton Strachey (1880-1932), British biographer, writer and critic. Founder member of the Bloomsbury group and openly homosexual.
[41] Cressida Connolly, in THE RARE AND THE BEAUTIFUL: THE LIVES OF THE GARMANS (London: Fourth Estate, 2004), the biography of Mary and three other Garman siblings, interprets the reasons for the failure of the relationship very differently: Vita had other lovers (as Vita herself records in a poem about their relationship) (73-83) and this

Poetic Justice

been led into an emotional trap (from which he himself had many times successfully escaped) and was suffering all its consequences. My parents had an understanding of sorts about infidelities. Because Mary was lonely at the times when Roy spent weeks together shut away from the world writing, or went afterwards on long drinking sprees, it was tacitly understood that she should have other loves; but these were always platonic. The last thing Mary needed was more sex.[42] She always told me that Roy was a wonderful lover. What Mary was looking for in her friendship with Vita was a breathing space in which to renew her strength. Living with Roy was at times like living with a whirlwind.

On the other hand, one gathers from Harold Nicolson's diaries (to mention only one source) that Vita was dissatisfied sexually, morally, and artistically. In those endless pages of whining petulance, one is left with the impression of an infinitely dreary relationship, in which Harold's almost insane worship of Vita's superior lineage takes the place of love. I could not help wondering, after reading Harold's diaries, why the Nicolsons were so incensed by THE GEORGIAD; Roy only put more wittily what Harold writes.

As for the much vaunted Nicolson generosity, described in the latest Campbell biography[43] thus: "Their continued generosity...", "The Nicolsons' generosity...", "Her library, her wealth, her generosity...". "... so much generosity...", what did this wealth of generosity consist in? Lending a gardener's cottage to a young poet in ill health and seducing his wife into the bargain.

I think this sort of generosity is best forgotten.

There is no doubt that Vita used all the resources at her disposition to get Mary away from Roy. Because she was an exceptionally plain woman, Vita used her privileged position, her beautiful houses, her savoir faire, her jewels, and all the rest of it to dazzle and overwhelm Mary who had had a rough time of it since throwing in her lot with that of a poet. Roy often compared Mary to Sappho and St. Teresa of Avila because Mary could love men, women, and God with equal

---

was hurtful to Mary.

[42] Again, Connolly sees this differently. In an unreferenced note, she recounts "an apocryphal story" of the effects on Mary of Vita's "prodigious" sexual appetite (82). It would appear, however, that over the years Mary had many lovers. And Roy was not monogamous either. He avers that their marriage only became monogamous after they had converted to Catholicism (LIGHT ON A DARK HORSE, 1971: 325). Whether this was indeed so or whether this was "just complete nonsense"— as Anna (quoted in Pearce: 307) was to describe everything in the second part of that autobiography—remains to be seen.

[43] Anna is referring to Peter Alexander's CRITICAL BIOGRAPHY. Joseph Pearce has since published another entitled BLOOMSBURY AND BEYOND: THE FRIENDS AND ENEMIES OF ROY CAMPBELL (Harper Collins, 2001), published in the USA as UNAFRAID OF VIRGINIA WOOLF: THE FRIENDS AND ENEMIES OF ROY CAMPBELL (ISI Books, 2004).

intensity. But Mary was deeply moral by instinct as was proved after her conversion to the Catholic Church when she joined the very strict Order of Carmelite Tertiaries.[44] This did not stop her from having very deep loves all through her life. The two things are not incompatible.

What put the finishing touches to Roy's malaise at Long Barn was coming across Virginia Woolf[45] crawling about on all fours under the bushes. She raised to his, a face so ravaged by madness that Roy fled—like Tam O'Shanter pursued by the witches—to London and thence to Provence and never returned again. I think also, given Roy's almost too vivid imagination, that the thought of the poor old unkempt Woolf, in bed with Vita, was a bit too distasteful to him, if also very comical. He tended to associate Lesbianism with beautiful Sappho and the Golden Isles, rather than with two middle-aged English ladies, six feet tall and with enormous hands and feet.

It was this side of things that led inevitably to the wittier passages in THE GEORGIAD—which, I must stress here, was written to veritable gales of laughter, that I well remember, though understanding nothing.

---

[44] Both St John of the Cross and Teresa of Avila were members of the order and founders of the Discalced Camelites. The spiritual focus of the Carmelite Order is contemplative prayer. The First Order is the friars, the Second Order is the nuns and the Third Order consists of laypeople. To be a tertiary required strict observance of rules concerning the daily recitation of prayers, regular fasting, abstinence during Advent and Lent, as well as acts of mortification, devotion and charity. See THE ENCYCLOPEDIA BRITANNICA: A DICTIONARY OF ARTS, SCIENCE AND GENERAL LITERATURE Vol. V, 9th ed. Thomas Spencer Baynes (New York: Henry G. Allen, 1833: 116-7) and TRADITIONAL CATHOLIC RELIGIOUS ORDERS: LIVING IN COMMUNITY. Edward A. Wynne (New Brunswick, N.J.: Transaction, 1988: 207-210).

Once she had joined the order, on the advice of her spiritual advisor Mary destroyed all Vita's love letters (Pearce, 170).

[45] Cressida Connolly writes in some detail about the Virginia Woolf—Vita Sackville-West—Mary Campbell relationship in THE RARE AND THE BEAUTIFUL.

Chapter V

My first clear memory is of the sun trying to burst through the shutters of my room. I was two, and I remember watching the silver and gold motes doing an endless dance in the rays of the sun. Roy, very tall, was leaning over my cot and a little flaxen-haired girl, my sister Tess, was looking through its bars.

We lived at first in a small house shaded by giant umbrella pines, at a place called Tour de Vallier, some kilometres from Martigues.[46] In front of this house was a broad terrace with a low wall and beneath this terrace stretched two fields of olive trees that shivered into silver in the Mistral. Beyond these fields ran the road from Martigues to Istres which had once been a Roman highway. Roy said it was haunted and he sometimes heard the rhythmic marching of Roman legions through the screeches and booms of the Mistral. Among the tormented olives, grew slim almond trees which in January burst into bloom and lit up the grey olive orchards like delicate chandeliers. In the spring we found beneath these trees small, scarlet tulips among the short-lived green grass.

There was a stone well in the garden, half hidden by bay laurels. The colour of Provençal stone is unforgettable: our well, the arenas of Nimes and Arles, and the farmhouses and manors we frequented, were all made of this warm, grey stone.

Behind the house a meandering path led down through the woods to the Étang de Berre, not a lake at all but a miniature sea joined to the Mediterranean by four canals. In our day, before it was polluted by factory wastes, it teemed with marine life. There were ink-blue, rust, or sage-green sea-urchins, seaweed of every colour imaginable, shoals of darting fish, and one small solitary fish with the brilliant hues of a kingfisher.

This lake was our paradise, especially in the summer months when we spent whole days there. The pines went right down to its edge and were reflected in its

---

[46] Anna was by all accounts an exceptionally beautiful child. When Mary and the girls were to leave Kent and join RC in Martigues, Vita Sackville-West is reputed to have asked Mary if she could adopt Anna (Connolly, 80).

Roy, Mary and Grandpére (Marius Polge), Martigues, 1931 (Francesca)

cool, translucent waters. Tess and I would rise with the birds and after Serafine, our maid, had given us big bowls of café-au-lait, we were off, trotting happily through woods filled with giant bushes of pink and white rock-roses with eternally crumpled petals. Our hair and clothes were filled with the scent of crushed thyme, sage, rosemary and other herbs which grow wild all over Provence and are more pungent in that part of the world than anywhere else.

We thought the lake belonged to us because we never saw another soul there; only occasionally a motor-boat would putt-putt across the horizon. Gradually, as the sun rose higher and the pines began to creak in the heat, the cicadas, like so many tiny kettles, would begin to simmer and then boil, until the whole of Provence was softly roaring and we would be caught in its cruel, golden heat.

Roy's health seemed miraculously restored. He had received such a deep psychological shock at Long Barn that even his "broken neck" was no longer mentioned. We Campbells have these recuperative powers. Our over-active imaginations can make us ill, or well, in a matter of hours.[47]

When Roy was not going through a writing phase, he spent a great deal of his time with Tess and me, and, without being in the least boring, he would

---

[47] RC had indeed damaged one of the vertebrae in his neck when he was in his early twenties (see Pearce, 32).

Poetic Justice

constantly be instructing us, whether on walks, or when bathing, or at meals. His own interest in everything under the sun was so intense that he sometimes trembled with excitement when he was describing something to us. He passed on to us his love of birds, flowers, trees, fishes, stars and constellations, clouds, races, civilisations, Greek and Latin, French and English writers. Roy never seemed to tire of recounting to us stories which he adapted from Homer, Chaucer or Rabelais, and the anonymous Zulu servants of his youth.

It was Roy who taught us to ride—first bicycles and later horses. It was he too, who told us about the Courts of Love and the beautiful Queen Jeanne. He told us how Mistral had been born at Les Baux, among the ruins and the goats, and how, when he grew up, he got the French Government to re-house the peasants of that strangely haunted place, so that it became once more a center of pilgrimage.

We missed our Father sadly when he began to write. I got to know well an approaching spell of inspiration. He became abstracted and jumpy. He usually wrote all night because the silence was necessary to him. These phases could last for anything from two to six weeks. We hardly saw him during that time as he seemed to live entirely on coffee and cigarettes. Only occasionally would he wander in to a meal, stuff a few grapes into his mouth, his eyes bulging with concentration, and wander out again. Our house was so small that he worked in a sort of loft a few stairs up from my bedroom. How often I woke up in the night to hear him murmuring his poems to himself as he read out what he had just written. Once, out of curiosity, I crept to his door and looked in. He was lying on a mattress on the floor, propped up against the wall by pillows, his pad on his bent knees, a couple of candles in a saucer on a chair by his head, and his pen scratching away. There were books everywhere and spilt ink bottles. He would write a line of a poem on one page and then turn the page and start again until whole pads, or exercise books, would have one or two lines on each page gradually lengthening to complete poems. The only thing he fussed about was having the right sort of paper and nib.

Roy's manuscripts were often decorated with exquisite drawings of horses, antelopes, bulls, deer, and other animals. Drawing was Roy's *Violon d'Ingres*.[48] Next to poetry it was painting that filled him with what Byron called "enthusymusy." One of the first things he did on arriving in a new town was to visit the picture gallery.

As I stared at him that night, I was struck by his total absorption. Children understand these things—I would like to say "these sacred times," but Roy would have pulled my leg unmercifully if he had heard such a phrase. He had been so

---

[48] Hobby or avocation.

A Memoir of my Father, Roy Campbell

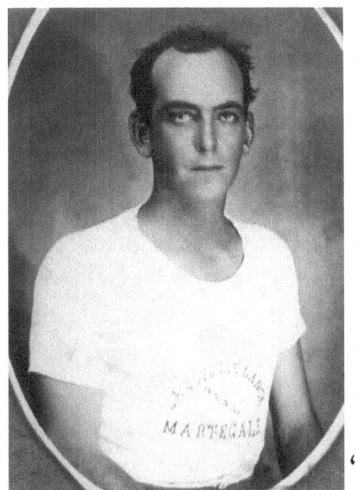

Roy in his shirt from the Club de la Joyeuse Lance Martégale, 1930 (Tess)

repelled by mediocre artists talking eternally about "my art" and pretending to be sensitive that he over-reacted in the opposite direction. Because in his heart of hearts he really believed art to be sacred, he could not bear phonies like S. Spender, for instance, posing as artists and talking about the art of poetry.[49] He did not think poetry should even be mentioned by such clumsy manipulators of verse. That is why, when anyone asked him how he had written such a perfectly formed poem as, for example, "The Palm," he answered, "With a steel nib"!

We always knew when at last one of Roy's writing phases was over, because he would start to sing early in the morning while he shaved his, by then, quite long beard. He would be very pale and emaciated, but his eyes would flash as he looked forward to a day of relaxation and freedom from his relentless muse. He always hung, on a nail outside the front door, a looking-glass, into which he peered as he shaved and sang away. He had a large repertoire of songs: English and Scots ballads, French sailing songs, American rag-time, and First World War comforters, of which the undoubted favourite was "Pack Up Your Troubles."

When he had finished shaving, he would fetch up a bucket of icy well-water and throw it over his head, always remarking, "That's better!" Then Serafine would rush out with a towel, grumbling, *"Mais il faut s'essuyer quand méme!"*[50]

Mary would now appear at her bedroom window, immediately above the front door. How I loved that mother of mine! Her serene beauty lightened and lit up my world. Mary was often compared to a rose, even by my school friends. Her skin had the same sort of inner glow that roses have. Roy used to say that you could see the red wine going down her throat, as Ronsard said of Diane de Poitiers.

Mary was rather remote in my early childhood. She was still in love with the "forlorn Georgiana and her gruff moustaches." This was still noticeable at Tour

---

[49] While we must guard against equating the autobiographical narrator with the living person (as RC's own embroidered autobiographies demonstrate), Spender's autobiography does not convey a pretentious attitude to his art. See Spender WORLD WITHIN WORLD (London: Faber and Faber (1951) 1997: 247-8 and elsewhere).

[50] But he must dry himself!

Poetic Justice

de Vallier. Because Mary had refused to sleep with her, Vita was punishing her by not writing and in fact behaving in a low and cruel way.[51]

Mary painted all through her life. At Tour, she had a studio in a small house next door to the one we lived in. Here she spent hours painting very beautiful landscapes. She also did portraits of Roy, Tess and me, and anyone else she could get to sit for her. She was very talented, but owing to our nomadic existence (brought on by money shortages) she frequently had to interrupt her work. Writers are lucky, they can pick up a pen and paper anywhere, but for a painter it is more complicated to be on the move: easels, canvases, oil paints, etc., are difficult to come by—especially for someone living far away in the country as we often did. Mary had to sell most of her paintings at the end of her life, because she was literally penniless. But I still have some good landscapes and a few portraits done by her.

On those summer mornings, when our shadows were long on the terrace, and the stillness gave promise of a perfect day, and after Mary had sent a shopping list fluttering down from her window, Roy would lift me on to his shoulder, take Tess by the hand, and in this way—somehow securing baskets and a *bonbonne*[52] for wine—we would set off for Martigues to do the shopping. It was a long walk there and back, but Roy never seemed to get tired. Mary always stayed at her window, waving, until we were out of sight beyond the olives.

Doing the shopping with Roy was a leisurely business. We stopped at Pouzol's for Roy's glass of "gros rouge"[53] and our "pins and needles" as we called lemonade. While Roy was talking to his various friends—Marius, Grandpére,[54] the Comte de Fremenville, Henri Samat, and Dr. Contensaint—we children played round the fountain in the plane-treed square outside. "Where the white quay is chequered by cool planes...." Roy loved the non-Riviera part of Provence so deeply—especially Martigues, Nimes, Arles, Port-de-Bouc, Sète, Marseilles, the Crau, and the Camargue—that all his poetry, of that time, is impregnated with the feel of those places.

---

[51] Other autobiographical and biographical accounts of this love affair do not express this view: the more commonly held opinion is that Vita had tired of Mary and had, much to Mary's distress, moved on to other lovers.
[52] A demijohn.
[53] Cheap red table wine.
[54] The punctuation here suggests that Anna is referring to two people though this might have been the publisher's amendment. (See also note 57.) Biographers Alexander (102) and Pearce, however, indicate this is the same person, namely, Marius Babtistin Polge, who later married Mary's sister, Helen (BLOOMSBURY AND BEYOND, 108). Connolly (119) concurs. Their daughter, Katherine (Kitty), married Laurie Lee (see LIGHT ON A DARK HORSE 1971: 268.)

In his unpublished biography of Roy, Rob Lyle writes: "Despite a turbulent under-current of suffering, life there was idyllic, and resulted in some of Roy's loveliest and serenest lyrics. It was the happiest period of his life…". But this is not really true. He did not have periods of unhappiness: he went so easily from deep gloom to almost rapturous joy, brought on variously by something he saw, or heard, or read, that he could not be either happy or sad for long. Both my parents were continually seeing beauty and pointing it out to each other and to us children. It was in this way that they taught us to see life. Nothing exasperated Roy more than complainers.[55] One of Mary's sisters came to see us at Martigues with her very rich husband,[56] and when they left Roy said, "Did you notice? They never mentioned the loveliness of the Berre, but talked all the time about the inadequacy of the lavatories!"

When it began to seem that we would never get home in time for lunch to be cooked, Tess would remind Roy that we still had to buy the fish, and then we would go over to the gorgeous fish-market where every fish was still alive so that Tess and I wanted to throw them all back into the sea. Here we bought the best ingredients for a bouillabaisse[57] and then armed with bread, garlic, saffron, fish, fruit, vegetables, and a thing called *"poutargue"* without which Roy could not live—it was a sort of dried caviar, very pungent—we would set off for home.

When I was old enough to walk by myself, Roy had to watch out for motor-bikes. I was in mortal dread of these noisy machines; I thought they were my personal enemies and would run off into the fields when I heard one coming. It was on one such occasion that I felt I was flying, as though I had wings on my feet: after running a few yards I would suddenly lose the feeling of gravity and speed along as though jet-propelled. Roy noticed this and said I was like a Mercury.

Although my love and loyalty to my mother would have made me die for her at any time, I did notice that she was an unusually unworried sort of parent. She never seemed to notice what we were eating: sometimes we would be given bread and milk, or sour milk, every night for our suppers, for weeks on end. Luckily, we always had neighbours who filled us up with brandied cherries, dried fish (which we liked eating raw), plenty of strong coffee with milk, and other delicacies of this sort. What we detested most were the inevitable fish soups which were the staple diet of the very poor in those days but have now become rechér-

---

[55] Of course, in this as in all things context is important: after WWII RC was to appreciate that grumbling was an important safety valve for post-war Britons. See text of RC's broadcast "Calling South Africa", reproduced in Tess's memoir, ch. 29.
[56] This was Lorna and Ernest Wishart.
[57] Bouillabaisse, in its classic form, includes a variety of fish and eel; it is garnished with garlicy croutons and rouille (a spicy red sauce made with garlic, olive oil and red peppers).

Poetic Justice

ché dishes all over the world. Mary was also capable of getting very annoyed if our hair needed washing, as though it had nothing to do with her. She was a past master at relegating her duties to others and making you feel guilty into the bargain. Sometimes we would be bathing in the lake in the first throes of some childhood illness, such as measles, and she would be quite oblivious about this until even the maids noticed and put us to bed.

Tess and I spent a lot of our time playing with the children of the neighbouring Chateau. They belonged to an aristocratic family who only came there in the summer months. Once when we had spent the whole previous week there, only returning to sleep, Mary suddenly noticed our absence and got very worried. When we got home, she made an awful fuss which seemed, under the circumstances, terribly unfair, and a bit late in the day. Certainly if she had known what we got up to with the *gosses* over there, her hair would have stood on end.[58] French children spend a lot of their time finding out about sex. It would be quite superfluous for a French father to take his son aside to tell him about the birds and the bees. I am sure that the healthy attitude towards sex of the French is due partly to this precocious education. Sex does not have to be a complicated mess. Parents have an extraordinarily difficult task in striking a happy medium about this subject. Therefore, if the children find out about it from each other it is more normal and saves a lot of trouble.

I remember friends of my first husband with whom I was staying in Paris, taking me to a typically French review. We sat in the front row of the stalls. M. de Montaigue promptly fell asleep, only waking once when a dazzling redhead walked on to the stage, stark naked, to answer the telephone. Then he leant across me and said to his wife, *"Elle n'est pas mal, la petite, heim?"* (i.e. "The little one is not bad looking, what?")

But to get back to my mother: she was so lovely in her long, white or scarlet dresses, that everyone forgave her anything she did. She had the disarming quality of laughing away her faults so that these seemed more like virtues.

The only time I noticed any underlying tensions between my parents was on account of Vita, when a bottle of "Cuir de Russie" scent came flying out of Mary's bedroom window. What could it mean? Why was Roy angry? Much later, Mary told me that this scent had been given to her by Vita. Mary retrieved the pretty little bottle and put it back on her dressing-table. But a cloud, heavier than its own very heavy fumes, hung about it for a long time. In any case, it was a perfume that did not suit Mary, though it might have been appropriate for a lesbian blue-stocking or a Russian commissar.

---

[58] Kids, young boys and girls.

Another thing I found inexplicable at Tour was Roy's exaggerated animosity towards the radio. True, he never did like radios (such a terrible waste of time). But at Tour, he only had to see one to become sad or angry. At that time I thought it was because the radio came into the same category as advertisements, magazines, films (except cow-boy films), murder mysteries, and other unaesthetic things about which Roy was very strict. Later Mary told me that his radiophobia was brought on because the "high priestess of funereal wits" gave weekly broadcasts about gardening and *married bliss.*

Mary returned several times to England, in order to see Vita, while we were living in Provence. On these trips she usually took Tess and me with her to stay at Grandmama Garman's house. Roy, who loved Mary more than himself, gave his reluctant consent to these absences. He knew too well the sufferings that passion entails to stop her from going.

Tess and I thoroughly enjoyed our stays at "Blackhall" as Grandmama's new house was called. Nothing could have been greater than the contrast between our way of life in Provence and that in England. The lavender-scented baths, after the salty bathes in the lake. The delicious cooking of Mrs. Beeton after *bouillabaisses* with *rouille* sauce. The soft green fields after the blazing forest fires. The dancing lessons in Hereford after fierce games of *cache-cache*[59] at the chateau. The nursery rhymes after such songs as "Lord Randall My Son." Even the contented paddling of ducks after the soaring of a thousand flamingoes—crimson in the setting sun. Of course Grandmama, and the ever faithful Tony, spoilt us and cosseted us. At Tour we suffered from an excess of freedom.

While Mary, Tess, and I were away, Roy would take the opportunity to take part in all sorts of sports which, after the confinement of writing, were essential to his well-being. It was important also that the sport should involved a certain amount of risk which, for some paradoxical reason, restored his nervous equanimity. It has been suggested that Roy only took part in bull-fighting and water jousting in order to show off. As he says in BROKEN RECORD:[60]

> I am so passionate a spectator of action that I have often found myself taking part in things which do not come the way of most other poets, and a series of disjointed, romantic adventures have been the result, some of

---

[59] Hide and seek.
[60] This "collection of reminiscences" (BROKEN RECORD, in COLLECTED WORKS III: 77) was first published in 1934 and reprinted in 1971. RC confessed to Wyndham Lewis that it was "stuffed full of lies" (Pearce, 155).

Poetic Justice

which project into my imagination, but for that I can make no excuse, as my memory and imagination work as one; by force of recounting them they have assumed more elegant shapes and I am not one to wish to bore you with a list of facts. Rather a manipulation of such facts into some sort of design. Looking back I see things in terms of places rather than in order of periods. But at the same time, this is far truer an autobiography than any written and passed off as truth by any one of my acquaintances (one of whom accounted for some months' disappearance in a lunatic asylum with a more hair-raising list of adventures than even Trelawney—but that is an extreme case). I am only letting my reader know that he is welcome to take anything with a pinch of salt. I shall be lucky if I can shake as many coppers out of the sack of experience as I have recklessly thrown into it...

Roy's two great friends, Marius and Grandpère,[61] introduced him to the Club de la Joyeuse Lance Martégale, and the three of them represented Martigues at the jousting contests which took place in the season at such places as Port-de-Bouc, Sète, Marseilles, Istres, and other towns east of the Côte d'Azur. Roy also took part in the French corrida which has none of the drama of the Spanish bullfight, but is a light-hearted affair requiring great skill and dexterity. The participants in this sport have to snatch a cockade from between the horns of the bull without getting tossed. Roy managed to do this on one occasion, and leaping over the barricade he ran up the steps of the arena and presented it to Mary on one knee. The whole arena stood up to applaud him. He was rewarded for this act of gallantry by receiving, some weeks later, a large prize in the form of money. This came as a complete surprise and was very welcome indeed.

It was while we were still at Tour de Vallier that Grandpère—a young blond giant, there was nothing grandfatherly about him—got married. His new wife became jealous when she found her husband clutching one of Mary's handkerchiefs to his breast as he lay asleep. The new wife made such a fuss about this that, in the end and without it being in any way Mary's fault, Roy and Grandpère were forced to have a fight. Tess and I were at a neighbouring house, when Sérafine came running to fetch us, shouting in a distraught way, "Thérèse, Anna come quickly! Grandpère is killing your father!" We rushed to the scene and saw with surprise, in a circle of bystanders (the peasants had an uncanny way of knowing when something interesting was going on *chez les Anglais*[62]), Grandpère sitting astride Roy's stomach and repeatedly lifting and banging his head

---

[61] Anna or her original publisher seems again to mistake Marius (nicknamed Grandpère) for two individuals.
[62] At the home of the English people.

on the ground. Without even knowing what I was doing, I rushed at Grandpère and sank my teeth into his large calf which was exposed between his trouser-leg and his espadrille. He jumped up with a roar of pain and started hopping about. I hated to have to do this, as I was very fond of Grandpère, but Roy had to be protected. I had felt his vulnerability in the very dawn of my existence, something which worried me terribly in my childhood, and was later carried on into adulthood. But what irritated me most was that this very gentle man should spend so much time and energy trying to prove that he was tough.

Chapter VI

While we were at Tour de Vallier, a steady stream of artists of all sorts came to see Roy. Among these gifted people Wyndham Lewis was a favourite with all our family. This very brilliant man has been much maligned by his contemporaries. It is true that he was complicated and more than eccentric—I am always amazed that true artists manage to do their difficult work despite the anomalies and complexities of their characters—but with my parents he seemed to be entirely at his ease. Roy warmed the cockles of Lewis's rather cold heart. He was attractive with his dark eyes and mocking smile, rather like an intellectual Clark Gable, if one can imagine such a thing. He and Roy were the same height, and they were equally well-matched intellectually. Both brilliant satirists, their conversation, in those halcyon days, must have been like a gorgeous display of fireworks. Long into the night they talked, drank, laughed and sang in Homeric feasts of wit. Roy's voice boomed up the stairs and competed with the Mistral in relentlessness. Towards dawn, when Tess and I were preparing to get up, there would descend a sudden silence: the poets had fallen asleep. But by about ten a.m. they were up again and ready to set off for Martigues.

In the evening my parents and Lewis would troop down to the lake to join Tess and me. All three swam out so far that their heads looked liked tiny dots bobbing about in the water. Later, fish was grilled by Roy over a fire of dried fennel and rosemary and, as the moon came up, dead centre, across the lake

> *We watched the moon as from the gilded mire*
> *Where the black river trails its reedy fringes.*
> *She fished her shadow with a line of fire...*

Mother would pick up her guitar and strum while all three sang "Nita Juanita" or some such melancholy song. This was too much for my small soul. Overwhelmed by emotion I would raise my voice in a howl of anguish. Then Roy or Lewis (strangely enough) would pick me up and rock me to sleep, and I would wake up the next morning safe in my bed, with the reassuring sun

A Memoir of my Father, Roy Campbell

Anna, Tess, Mary and Roy at Tour de Vallier, 1929/30 (Tess)

trying to burst through the shutters.

Roy used to complain that Lewis was always killing him off in his books.[63] He certainly does this in SNOOTY BARONET and THE REVENGE FOR LOVE.[64] Though it is difficult to know whether this last novel is about Roy and Mary Campbell or Mr. and Mrs. Lewis. Both probably.

Ever since leaving South Africa, Roy had been in thrall to Wyndham Lewis. The latter was at the height of his powers between 1920 and 1936. One masterpiece followed another in a really extraordinary spate of creativity. No sooner had Roy written to congratulate Lewis on one work than another appeared and he had to do it again.

These two men would sometimes have the same thought at the same time, and each of them would worry over the possibility of being regarded as a plagiarist by the other! But their thoughts *were* so simultaneous that at last they called it telepathy. For instance in a letter to Lewis, Roy says: "In case you should think I deliberately plagiarised your 'Engine Fight Talks,' Boriswood has had in his possession my 'Junction of the Rails' for several weeks and some of the phrases are almost identical. The theme is almost identical—but the puff-puff boys are all stuck in the waiting-room: scouts waiting for a 'Jamboree,' but waiting for a special that never arrives… on the whole One Way is a great treat—it made me laugh like hell. My 'Junction of the Rails' is not properly satirical but the similarity is striking and I must have been thinking in precisely the same way as you, since we last met, *my mental pendulum of course, having been given a swing by you*" (my italics). There is no doubt that Lewis's influence on Roy was very strong and not always, by any means, beneficial. It was Lewis who got Roy interested in politics, a soul-destroying business.

---

[63] In BROKEN RECORD, RC complains that "Already nine novels and stories have put me to violent and harrowing deaths" (in COLLECTED WORKS III: 77).

[64] SNOOTY BARONET (1932) is a satire of London's bohemia. THE REVENGE FOR LOVE (1937)—a novel which Lewis apparently thought of as his best—is set in Britain and Spain just before the Spanish Civil War.

Poetic Justice

Lewis was, it must be remembered, twenty years older than Roy. Although they must both have talked about THE APES OF GOD and THE GEORGIAD,[65] the idea for these two satires came to them simultaneously, but separately. Once the idea was conceived, they probably egged each other on to ever more daring flights of fantasy—the last thing Roy needed.

It was during Lewis's long visit to us in 1931 that he brought Roy a book about the extermination of the Kulaks in the Soviet Union. I remember how excited they both became when the strange words "Kulak" and "Dostoevsky" were mentioned. In fact I heard the name Dostoevsky so often that I called one of my kittens Dr. Evsky, much to Roy's amusement.

From things which Roy told me later, and from what I myself remember, THE POSSESSED had recently been translated into English (perhaps a new, and better version, had just appeared by Constance Garnett in 1931), and everyone was reading it. To Roy and Lewis it was such a strangely prophetic book about the Soviet Union that they were both deeply impressed and deeply disturbed. Neither man was bamboozled by Shaw's infamously misleading descriptions of the Workers' Paradise. They knew, through reading history, that there are no Utopias in this world; that the world becomes distorted and there is terrible *extra* suffering if and when *intellectuals* start to better the lot of mankind by force. I only wish that Lewis had not influenced Roy into thinking that because Stalin and Co. were evil, their enemies were therefore right; although it must be stressed that Roy only began to think dictatorships a solution after he had seen his dearest friends massacred in Toledo. He knew that a regime which allows freedom of religion is a thousand times better than one that murders you for believing in God.

What amazed and later disgusted both these men was that 90 per cent of Western artists, thinkers, and politicians seemed to suffer from collective amnesia where the Soviet Union was concerned. They could not understand whence this mass-blindness came, what induced it. Anything that happened in Soviet Russia, however grisly, obscene, unjust, terrifying, brutal, infinitely ghastly, or plain mad, was perfectly all right with those bigoted people. When one thinks back to that time, one cannot help thinking there was something almost supernatural about the *Great Amnesia*. Even stranger was the way the whole 90 per cent began to froth at the mouth and lose all trace of indifference when some brave soul had the courage to state the truth.

But has anything really changed? Dr. Alexander says (I quote from memory):

---

[65] THE APES OF GOD, Lewis's attack on the London literary scene, was published in 1930. Campbell's THE GEORGIAD, also an attack on the Bloomsbury group, was written in 1929 and '30 (see COLLECTED WORKS I: 640) and published in 1931.

"And then Campbell got on the wrong side of the left...". I pointed out to him that Roy could not get on the *wrong* side of the left since, after reading about the Kulaks, he was in perpetual confrontation with the left—if by left is meant the Soviet Union and its principles.

Although there were some writers like Yeats, Pound, D. H. Lawrence, Léon Daudet and others who were anti-marxist, it was only Roy who fought with all his strength against totalitarian marxism by writing the truth in his great poem FLOWERING RIFLE.[66] Pace, pace. Certainly it is repetitive and needs editing, but if one forgets about these faults and reads it with an open mind, one sees why Roy thought it contained some of his best verse.

Anna and Tess in Provence, 1931 (Tess)

Of course, Roy was labeled a "fascist." He was one of the few Western writers who was a militant anti-marxist. That is, he wrote *clearly* against all the satanical zombies, inhabited by seven devils, who have made rivers of blood and tears wherever they have appeared. Yes, Roy was one of the few who never compromised. He condemned Lenin and Stalin when it was literary lunacy and suicide to do so. Even now John Lehmann[67] claims that Roy was duped by Franco. But what does he mean? That it was perfectly fine to be taken in by Stalin and Co. but wrong to admire the only man who successfully defeated communism in the world?

That Roy's and Lewis's destinies were linked in some way is borne out by the fact that they died within weeks of each other; and even more strange, twenty years later, their respective wives also died within weeks of each other.

When Lewis lay dying in the arms of Ashley Dukes,[68] he said, "I really loved Roy..."—quite an admission from the man, who more than anyone else, prided himself on having no heart whatsoever. That was his great blemish. I believe it has affected the durability of his work.

---

[66] First published 1939, revised 1957. For information on the differences between the two versions, see note no. 1, COLLECTED WORKS I: 662-3.

[67] (1907-1987) English poet, writer (including three volumes of autobiography) and editor.

[68] Anna spells this incorrectly as Ashly Dukes. He was a dramatist, critic and theatre manager (1885-1959).

Poetic Justice

Augustus John and Roy had a long and stormy friendship. John came to Martigues, but strangely enough I remember him only very vaguely.[69] It was he who nicknamed Mary "Little Lord Fondleroy." I told this to my cousin, Michael Wishart,[70] but he missed the pun and went on to write that Mary dressed like the Little Lord. What can one do?

The person I do remember vividly is Aldous Huxley[71] when he came to Tour. His high-pitched, rather affected voice, his lanky and disjointed body, the thick glasses he wore because of his near blindness—all made a strong impression on me. Once after bathing in the lake, Mother and I were left behind. Aldous also, because of his sight, was lingering, and Mary was having difficulty in doing up the countless little buttons on the back of her dress. I tried to help, but my small hands were ineffectual (I was five at the time), so Aldous came over to see what he could do. He peered at the small buttons, and as he started to do them up he kept saying, "I hope I'm getting this right. If I get one wrong, I shall have to start all over again and we shall be here all night!"

The American poet, Hart Crane, stayed with us for several weeks. He looked more like a bank-clerk than a poet. Roy was surprised that he could use a typewriter to write his poetry—he thought the noise must be distracting. But he admired Hart Crane's poetry. In a letter to Lewis, Roy writes: "My wife had a post-card from Hart Crane from Brooklyn. Still begging our pardon! He said when he got back he was going to 'hurl' himself from Brooklyn bridge..." — which he did some months later.[72]

While Roy was under the influence of Lewis, he used to imitate the latter's cynical contempt for some people, I'm sorry to say. But in reality he had liked

---

[69] Augustus John had a big house in Martigues (Alexander, 110). The friendship wavered in 1931 when RC publicly supported Wyndham Lewis' THE APES OF GOD (Alexander, 118).

[70] John Michael Garman Wishart (1928-1996): painter and autobiographer (HIGH DIVER, 1978).

[71] (1894-1963) English writer and critic, he was at Oxford University a few years before RC. Huxley sometimes spent the weekend with the Campbells (Alexander, 110). As with RC's friendship with Augustus John, the friendship cooled when RC came out in support of Wyndham Lewis (Alexander, 118).

[72] (1899-1932) Hart Crane committed suicide by throwing himself off a steamship in the Gulf of Mexico. In LIGHT ON A DARK HORSE, RC describes his uncontrollable promiscuity (he made passes at sailors and fishermen when in Provence) and his inability to hold his drink: "He was charming when sober, which was seldom: he read his poems like an angel, and we were very fond of him, but he needed a keeper" (316).

and pitied Hart Crane. Once when we were walking back from the lake, we came to a field full of thyme. Roy threw himself on those aromatic tufts and rolled about on them. Hart Crane immediately followed suit and so did we children. The scent from all that crushed thyme was heavenly. Roy called this "getting scented before dinner."

Liam O'Flaherty[73] stayed at Pascal's for a time and dazzled us with his Irish beauty, but he was a bit too wild even for Roy. He brought his daughter, Pegueen, to stay at our house. She was a comical, rough child with a strong Irish brogue. We used to take it in turns to tell stories, and when Pegueen's turn came she said, "Once there was a waal [wall], and it went on and on and on..."—here we all joined in and roared "on and on and on" until we were speechless with laughter.

Nancy Cunard[74] arrived in a very grand car driven by a black chauffeur—very black and very jovial. She fascinated me. Her long bare arms were encased in bracelets from wrist to shoulder, and she spread a strong aroma around her of scent and dry martinis. She was like a beautiful, if over-stimulated, snake.

The charming adonis Tristram Hillier,[75] a very gifted painter, took a house near ours where he lived with his wife and twin sons, all of great beauty. He did a large painting of our family complete with our Pyrenean sheepdog, Sarah. Sarah had been given to Mary by a repentant Grandpère. This lovely dog was entirely black, hence her name. She turned out to be highly intelligent, and we all loved her, but she came to an untimely end in Spain.

---

[73] (1986-1984) Anglo-Irish novelist, short story writer, autobiographer.
[74] (1896-1965) English poet, writer, editor, publisher and political activist (against racism). Heiress to the Cunard shipping fortune, before being shunned by her family for her politics. Her "chauffeur" was the African-American pianist Henry Crowder (Pearce: 119). Cunard records that RC gave her and Crowder "a beautiful, friendly welcome" (quoted in Pearce, 119). This lack of race-consciousness is not conveyed when he refers to them decades later in LIGHT ON A DARK HORSE: "When superannuated English society tarts take up Negro lovers, it is generally a sort of perversion like the exaggerated feeling for dogs and cats." He explained to locals why he was "sitting at the same table with a Negro [...] by saying it was [... an aunt's] dear old faithful servant" (162-3).
Cunard published a volume of RC's poems in Paris (Hours Press, 1930). This "expensively produced" book was a financial success (Alexander, 117).
[75] (1905-1983) Anna spells it incorrectly as Tristam. He studied at the Slade and at the Westminster School of Art under Bernard Meninsky. RC wrote MARINE PROVENCE early in 1933, during a stay in Hillier's ruined Gascon castle (Alexander, 121; see also LIGHT ON A DARK HORSE, 318-9).

Chapter VII

In 1932, while Tess and I were on our third visit to Grandmama's, our parents moved to a lovely old house called "Figuerolles." Roy sent us an illustrated letter showing the house and a large cedar-tree with horizontal branches, in the middle of a lawn of sorts. He also drew the stone ornamental well, and the marble table under two huge ilex trees, and Sarah with her latest litter of puppies, and in the distance Mary painting under a large parasol. I remember this letter dearly because we were very excited by the thought of a new home. The letter disappeared in the Spanish holocaust.

We returned to Provence with our first governess, a young lady called Marie-Louise, whom Tess and I loathed. She looked like an over made-up pug. What gave her the idea of being a governess is inexplicable. She never taught us anything but drove every night to the casino at Foss, to dance. She flirted with everyone, including Roy, a thing we had never witnessed before and which thoroughly annoyed us and made Mary send her packing. She later married a banker with whom she lived happily ever after.

Marie-Louise was replaced by a young Afrikaaner [sic], the writer Uys Krige,[76] with whom we enjoyed doing our lessons and thanks to whom we made rapid progress. He stayed with us for almost two years.[77]

Cecil Grey[78] spent New Year's day with us at "Figuerolles," and later C.J. Sibbett came for a week. Unfortunately, his visit coincided with that of my God-

---

[76] (1910-1987) Mattheus Uys Krige: South African writer, poet, playwright, rugby player, translator (of French, Spanish and English works into Afrikaans). Like RC, he was awarded an honorary doctorate by the University of Natal (in 1958). He fought on the Republican side of the Spanish Civil War because, RC claimed in Light on a Dark Horse, he was "an incurable Calvinist" (321). The Way Out (1946) recounts his experiences as a prisoner of war in Italy, and his subsequent escape. Interestingly, a photo of Uys on the Stellenbosch University Special Collections Gallery webpage (http://erlsrv.sun.ac.za/Library/eng/about/Collections/gallery.html) shows a close resemblance between his wife, Lydia Lindeque, and Mary Campbell.

[77] Tess says he tutored them for nine months. See note 218.

[78] (1895-1951) British composer and music critic. RC met him at Oxford.

Mary, Roy and Anna von Schubert, Figuerolles, Provence, 1932
(Francesca)

mother, Anna von Schubert,[79] so he left rather sooner than he would otherwise have done. He liked to have Roy to himself.

Anna was an Estonian baroness of great charm, and she braved the *vie de Bohème* to see my parents. She was married to a Russo-German businessman from Petrograd, and they were now living in Shanghai from where she brought Tess and me two exquisite Chinese dolls. Mary and Anna spent long hours painting out of doors. Our new *bonne*,[80] Paulette, and her husband used to take camp-stools, easels, and oil-paints to some previously chosen "motif," and they would spend the day there, talking and working. Paulette and we children took them lunch and bottles of white wine. I can still remember the smell of turpentine and dried pine needles with which the air was redolent around them.

We have, in our albums, a photo of Roy, Mary and Anna, and the taxi-driver, Chaves, standing outside the front door at "Figuerolles" dressed to the nines before setting off for a bullfight at Arles. It is an amusing photo and infinitely nostalgic. The next time those three were to meet was in post-war, austerity London. Roy had by then been invalided out of the army, Anna released from a Japanese prisoner-of-war camp, and Mary was trying to run a house, 17

---

[79] She was "an amateur painter and wife of a wealthy expatriate Estonian" (COLLECTED WORKS III: 612, note 152). Anna misspells it as "von Shubert". In BROKEN RECORD, RC spells it as "von Schubert" and says that she was living in Durban when he, Mary and Tess were living on the south coast of Natal and that, since that time (1924-26), she had "done so much to stimulate and inspire us" (COLLECTED WORKS III: 143). As we see, the family's attitude to her changed when she was to stay with them in war-torn London.
[80] Maid.

Poetic Justice

Campden Grove, with the help of two paying guests. Rather sadly, the three old friends tried to pick up the threads. But it did not work out. Roy was working all day at the B.B.C., and the last thing he wanted was to come home and find Anna grumbling about the way the house was run. Mary was at her wits end to find reliable char-women and was overworked. Besides, this was at the height of Tess's illness which was a strain all round, but Anna never lifted a finger to help in any way whatsoever. Even to do some of the washing-up.

Still, those glorious days in Provence live on (in my memory) and in Roy's magnificent poem, "Choosing a Mast."

We took part in the *vendanges*[81] at "Figuerolles," helping our nearest neighbour to harvest his grapes. We worked as we wanted to, and drank endless glasses of unfermented grape juice. In the evenings, the lord of the manor, all his family, friends, and labourers would sit at long trestle tables and partake of a wonderful Provençal meal. The *vendanges* lasted about three weeks. The whole time was festive. It was one of our favourite rituals.

Although autumn is not dramatic in Provence, as it is in more northerly districts, it does have the same effect on one. There is perhaps less nostalgia and more relief when the first leaves start to fall because soon it will rain, and the immense thirst of that parched earth will be relieved. After the first rains the grass shoots up and many (always purple) autumnal flowers appear: crocuses, twin-flowers, and Belladonna lilies.

The winter we spent at "Figuerolles" was very cold. It even snowed a little which was wonderful for us children. Roy enjoyed Christmas as much as we did. He always disguised himself as Father Christmas. Tess was well taken in and once asked him whether he was made of "meat"!

By Christmas of 1932 we already knew that we were to leave "Figuerolles." The Pound had been devalued, and we could no longer afford to live in France.[82] We had grown more than attached to "Figuerolles" and wanted to live there forever.

---

[81] Tess explains that this is the picking of grapes for wine making.

[82] Britain abandoned the gold standard in 1931, causing the pound to devalue. This meant that the Campbell's income, converted to French francs, was reduced. RC's debt mounted (Alexander, 121). Of more immediate concern was the fact that Tess's pet goat had destroyed a number of the neighbour's valuable peach trees. The Campbells could not pay compensation, nor could they pay the considerable amount they were ordered to pay when sued (Connolly, 130).

A Memoir of my Father, Roy Campbell

One night, in the spring of 1933, we were all lying on the lawn gazing at the constellations, when suddenly the sky became filled with thousands upon thousands of shooting stars, thousands upon thousands of them going in all directions. It was like watching a totally silent display of fireworks. "There will be signs in the heavens and on earth...."

My parents and Uys were discussing where to go and live next. All sorts of places were considered, Spain being the most often suggested, especially by Mary who had read the autobiography of St. Teresa of Avila when she was at school and had a preconceived idea of everything Spanish. Roy also was predisposed to love the country of bullfighters and poets. My parents were already poised, like Stendhal's "christalysation," to fall in love with Spain and be blind to its faults.

I now call to mind that Freddy de Fremenville was also with us that night. This diminutive French count was our closest friend for all the years we lived near Martigues. He spent so much time at our house that he was more like one of the family than a friend. Whenever he went away on a trip, he would return with a present for one or other of my parents: a first edition of Rabelais, or a bottle of old wine, or a lump of rose-quartz. For Tess and me he brought the immortal works of the Comtesse de Ségur which we read and re-read so often that I can still remember the opening lines of LES VACANCES: *"Tout était en l'air au Chateau de Fleurville..."*.[83]

It was Freddy who taught Mary to dress. Until he did so, she tended to wear what Katie Hewitt called "arty Italian" clothes, but after Freddy had introduced Mary to a dressmaker in Martigues she became very smart. Roy loved her to dress in scarlet, his favourite colour, but I remember that white was her usual choice as it set off her dark hair and delicate complexion wonderfully.

Freddy was a sculptor; he had a bad limp having been born with a deformed leg; and he had a rather indistinct way of speaking and always illustrated what he was saying with the little finger of his right hand. We missed Freddy after leaving Provence as though a dearly loved brother had been left behind and yet he was my parents' age. But he had a childish simplicity about him and was equally at ease with grown-ups and children.

༺◎༻

My parents and Uys left for Barcelona in the autumn of 1933.[84] Tess and I stayed with our latest governess, a young French girl whom we both loved

---

[83] (1799-1874) Sophie Feodorovna Rostopchine, French writer of children's books.
[84] Alexander avers that Krige travelled with the children (131).

Poetic Justice

dearly. Thérèse took us to live with her aunts in their little chateau which had blue china elephants on the entrance gates. Thérèse was an orphan, but she was deeply loved by the two aunts who now proceeded to make our stay with them memorable. I find the French easy to get on with. I feel more at home with them than other races. They are, on the whole, more cultured and well-informed in general than other Europeans. I love their *very critical* appreciation of the arts, their broad-mindedness, and their subtle wit. The wit of Colette[85] rather than of Cocteau.[86]

About a month after our parents had gone, we received letters from them summoning us to Barcelona. We left Provence and the aunts with regret. Thérèse, Tess, Sarah, and I set off from Montpellier for Barcelona. On the way we had to change trains and spend the night in an hotel. Tess was terribly upset because Sarah was not allowed to stay in our bedroom. In the middle of the night we were woken up by the dog's distant howls. Tess did not hesitate. She rushed off in her nightgown, down winding staircases, along corridors until she located Sarah in a kennel in a courtyard. She stayed the rest of the night there, comforting her pet.

We arrived at Barcelona in October 1933. Our parents took us by taxi to the street of S. Pedro y S. Pablo where our pension was housed in the two top stories of a large lugubrious building. Roy clapped his hands to summon the *Sereno* (night-watchman), who ran up with his large bunch of keys to let us in by the main entrance. We entirely filled the two flats of which the pension consisted. We later got used to hearing people clapping their hands all through the night for the *Sereno*. He had the keys to all the front doors in our, and two adjacent streets.

At first we liked Barcelona. There were so many novelties, especially the Ramblas with its flower stalls; we had never seen so many flowers for such low prices, and our rooms at the pension were soon filled with tuberoses, carnations, roses, and violets. You could buy huge bunches of these flowers for very few pesetas. Another novelty was the food. We ate most of our meals at the pension, where they gave us five-course meals, twice a day. At lunch there were hors d'oeuvre, fried fish with salad, steak with potatoes, an omelet, fruit, wine, and coffee. The same for dinner except that the hors d'oeuvres were replaced by soup. The quantity of churches was also a surprise. The bells never ceased ringing. We loved them. I always miss Spanish bells when I am in other countries. Many of the bells in Barcelona rang every quarter of an hour. They

---

[85] French novelist Sidonie-Gabrielle Colette (1873-1954).
[86] Jean Maurice Eugène Clément Cocteau (1889- 1963). French poet, novelist, set designer, playwright, actor, artist, and filmmaker; associated with surrealism.

also rang for the Angelus, for mass, for the dead, for Benediction, and so on.

Despite pre-revolutionary tension, the whole town was full of *joie de vivre.* Life was comparatively easy for the Spanish at that time because of low taxation and the complete lack of inflation. People had plenty of time to sit in cafés to stroll up and down, to go to church, to see *"los toros,"* and to dance the Sardana in the park.

Roy's sketch of a bull (CC)

We children did lessons every morning with Thérèse and then took Sarah for a long walk in the park. After a few weeks we began to miss Provence and the real country painfully. Tess became so desperate that she threw herself on the grass and kissed it. Mary had enrolled at the local arts school. Every evening she brought some of her fellow-students or models back to supper at the pension. Most of these people were Jewish refugees from Hitler's Germany. Mary was the only one in our family to speak German, and we never understood what they were saying.

Roy was trying to finish his first book of reminiscences, BROKEN RECORD. He found this book a strain to write because of the noise and constant interruptions of one sort or another. It was hard to be shut up in front of a writing-pad all day when there were so many extraordinary things to see and do. He did not, in any case, take prose-writing seriously, and whereas he loved writing verse he found the other to be a chore. Because he and Mary and Uys went to hear the gypsies every night he was always sleepy in the day and accordingly did his writing standing up so as not to nod off.

We spent the Christmas of '33 at the pension. All the Jews came. A lot of them were half starved, and I saw one young lady put some chicken in her handbag. They sang "Stille Nacht" and "Tannenbaum." Uys brought his girl, Emilia, a handsome Catalán. I danced a *paso-doble*[87] on the table and realised that moving to that stirring rhythm was one of life's great pleasures.

Roy wrote the following letter to Freddy de Fremenville from Barcelona:

---

[87] Literally, double step.

Poetic Justice

28, Calle de San Pedro y San Pablo
Barcelona
Spain

1933

Dear de Fremenville, many thanks for your letter. Please give my reciprocal salutes to Sammat, and when you see them Grandpére, Chabrol, Contensaint and toute la bande.

This town is quite amazing. What vitality this race has. The cafés, two or three to every street, are always crowded. The town is dominated by the Tibidabo mountain on which shelters the ancient monastery of Monserrat which is reached by a terrifying funicular. It sometimes goes wrong and hangs suspended over the abysmal depths.

Besides the noise of trams, musical bands, church bells, street vendors, the Sereno who rushes about all night letting people into their houses—he acts as a night watchman and has an enormous bunch of keys—there is also the chatter of machine-guns and an occasional bomb. We appear to have arrived in the middle of a revolution.

Uys and Mary and I went last night to hear the gipsies sing. We all fell under the spell of Cante Hondo: I remember you telling me how much you liked Flamenco.

Mlle Thérèse, the children, Sarah, Mary and I fill this pension so that we have the whole top floor to ourselves.

How immensely rich Spanish literature is! I am reading Gongora, an extraordinarily modern poet though he lived between 1561 and 1612. He gave rise to the word Gongorismo, meaning, as far as I can make out, an accentuation of all the characteristics that distinguish Baroque art. He reminds me of Mallarmé but is far greater. And Quevado, what a satirist! Did you know that Cervantes was also a poet? I always thought he was one of us. We all miss you. When we are settled in our own house you must come and stay with us. I know you hate to travel, but one should see Spain before one's death. Let that be an added inducement. With love from us all. Toujours a toi.

Roi.

Chapter VIII

Sometime in January 1934 a bomb went off in our district. Catalonia had seen much unrest since Primo de Rivera had been replaced by the atheistic, masonic, liberaloid Republic, and the Soviet Union was not slow to take advantage of this state of affairs. Lenin had "prophesied" that Spain would be the next country after the U.S.S.R. to become marxist. He was almost right, but he had not reckoned with the Spanish temperament. In Russia slavery is part of tradition; in Spain everyone thinks he is a king. For instance, if you ask someone why he is not doing this or that, he will answer, *"Porque no me da la real gana"* (because it is not my royal wish). Everyone has tried to make out that the Civil War in Spain was a fight between Fascism and Communism, or, as romantics like Nancy Cunard would have it, between rich and poor. It was nothing of the sort. When the Civil War broke out, most of the riches in Spain were in the hands of the Republic. They had the huge gold reserves and the richest provinces and towns. To those of us who lived through three years of pre-Civil War anarchy, there was never any doubt as to what the Civil War in Spain was about. The only consistent strife, the only sustained fight, was between Christianity and atheism. That, into these two categories of belief, there entered all sorts of other interests and illusions is undoubtedly true as is shown by the many affiliations on both sides. On the left, there were Anarchists, Liberals, Communists, etc. On the right, there were Monarchists, Basques, Carlists, Falangists, etc. But each side was united by a common denominator: Christianity or Atheism.

As usual, the Intelligentsia was busily stirring up hatred and controversy:

> For some reason or other all poets (nearly all poets come of the middle class) consider it their duty to love workmen, and to incite workmen to fight against their own class; the more bourgeois they are, the more violent "bolshies" they become. The workman-abstract is conveniently removed from them and their middle-class incomes. They see a muscular sort of statue, a struggling Saint Sebastian; and like idiots they go and tell him how ill-treated he is.... If we look at our time after two centuries of

Poetic Justice

reform, progress, rights and freedom, we see how we have lost ground in all these points... . [S]ocialistic states have re-established a super-feudal serfdom, with no chance of appeal to the human instincts of a chief or an overlord, but only to a great, blind, inhuman mechanism, the State. (BROKEN RECORD, 1933)[88]

After the bomb blast, our party split up. Thérèse returned to the aunts, much to our sadness; Uys stayed on in Barcelona with his girl; and we went down to Valencia.

Because Uys Krige lived with us for eighteen months at "Figuerolles" and was a devoted friend to Roy for a quarter of a century, I would like to quote some passages from his DAUGHTER OF THE STORM: [89]

> Roy Campbell had the essential gaiety of the true poet. A son of the sun, life to him was something splendid, something to be rejoiced over... . He, more than any poet I have known, had an almost child-like sense of wonder at the beauty and abundance of life and nature... Without doubt his character as well as his poetry, had a definite Dionysiac quality. You always felt a little drunk in his company, but it was a mental drunkenness without a hangover.
>
> There were times when one asked oneself whether his gaiety wasn't "a gaiety transfiguring all dread", of which Yeats speaks, whether that spectacular beautifully executed dive into a shining sky did not come from a spring-board of sadness or of a fundamental loneliness of which he never spoke and to which there are few references in his poetry*... For me however Roy's ancient glittering eyes were always gay... but he could be quiet too, and as still and lucid as a mountain pool.
>
> Humour he had in plenty. And also wit. Suddenly in the midst of all that ebullient humour, he would pause and instantaneously with the sharp edge of his mind, cut a phrase, a sentence, an image or an epigram as clean as a whistle... . Several of our mutual friends gave me, in 1954, in Madrid, the following charming illustration of Roy's spontaneous imagination, his at times intensely poetical sense of humour.
>
> Roy had just finished his first lecture at the Ateneo, the most famous

---

[88] I have corrected several errors which occured in the Typographeum publication.
[89] It is unclear where Anna found this title. After much searching and with the help of Anneke Schaafsma of the University of Stellenbosch Library, the first part of this passage (up to *) was traced to a radio talk on RC given by Krige. The transcript of the talk (entitled "Roy Campbell: The Man and his humour"), held by the University of Stellenbosch Library, is dated 1 April 1963.

literary club, or society, in Spain. Among the audience was the cream of Spain's intellectuals, artists and aristocracy. At question time a priest-writer of great distinction asked to what he ascribed the extraordinary success of his verse translation of St. John of the Cross, one of the greatest mystic poets of world literature.... .

With a straight face Roy answered in his halting Spanish: "But the good saint helped me Father.... You see when I got tired, or my spirit flagged, or I got stuck, I would just look over my shoulder and there St. John would be sitting against the sky, smiling down at me. He would call out *"Arre burrico!"* ("Go little donkey!").

And here Roy paused a second to allow the suspense to pile up, the sketch to grow into a complete picture in his audience's mind before coming out with his climax of only four words that fairly brought the house down.... . "And I just went on trotting."

There is for me a touch of genius in this mixture of humility and ironical pride that is typical of the true poet; in this complete integration of the poet Campbell with the Spanish people and Spanish soil...

At Valencia my parents had a terrible row. There was always tension at home towards the end of the month, when the money from South Africa was late. I remember Roy lying in a stupor from drink, fully clothed on his bed while Mary railed at him and shook him. She was trying to make him go to the post, but he could not even stand up. This is the first time I remember them having a quarrel. It went on for several days. Roy, unused to Spanish wine, had got caught on one of those benders which are like riding a tiger, impossible to get off! Here again there was no question of my parents separating. Often, when Mary was desperate to stop him from drinking, she would threaten to leave him because it was the most effective means available to her. Dr. Alexander says many times, in his biography, that my parents were on the point of separating at different times in their lives. This, I really must stress, is absolute poppycock.[90] They were not only wedded by then, they were knitted together. There was no unravelling that garment!

After a few days the money turned up safely, and we went on to Alicante. Here it was suggested that we should go to Benidorm—which even in those days was a tourist resort. My parents took one look at it and decided against it, so we carried on in the little train that hurtles along the sea-coast to the next village, Altea. This place was so enchanting that we got off the train and stayed

---

[90] Tess recalls this row as the worst of their married life; she says her parents "nearly separated."

Poetic Justice

there for over a year.

Altea, named after the goddess Althea, had white-washed houses running up to a blue-domed church at the top of a hill. Great purple mountains rose up in the distance, making a jagged sky-line, parallel with the sea, but far inland. Everywhere there was the sound of running water. The streams that came down from the mountains made the whole place luscious and fertile, and acres and acres of orange groves stretched as far as the eye could see, filling the air with the scent of their blossoms for months on end.

The mixture of sea and mountains, of wildness and domestication, the cascades of flowers, the still landscape with columns of pale-blue smoke rising from the farmhouses, the temperate climate, and the diamond-clear air made this place seductive and inviting.

We rented one of the farmhouses, smothered in jasmine and heliotrope—even now, after all these years, I am transported back to that house when I smell either of these flowers. On feast days, the girls wore rosettes of jasmine flowers in their hair.

Our neighbours were very friendly and kept calling to bring us presents: vases of geraniums; baskets of oranges, tangerines, and almonds; great earthen jars of special drinking water from a healing well; newly baked loaves and baskets of artichokes which they cooked in a variety of inventive ways.

We were befriended by the Mayor of Altea, Don Jacinto, the parish priest, Don Gregorio, the local aristocrats and peasants, a Russian princess and her French husband with whom I spent many happy times, and by an American couple called Bone who seldom spoke but looked at us with grave approval.

In the summer the Norwegian playwright, Helge Krog,[91] his wife, and his best friend, Winsnes,[92] used to come every day with laden baskets which our maids, Paca and Anamaria, turned into fabulous paellas. The Krogs and Winsnes were even taller than Roy, and the four of them made an impressive sight walking through the narrow streets of Altea. Krog was a left-wing liberal and Wisnes a Nationalist with an ardent admiration of Hitler so that

---

[91] Campbell is generally credited with the translation of the Norwegian's plays. RC denied that he knew any Norwegian beyond "a few phrases and technical whaling terms" and said that he merely signed the English translation done by Krog's aunt or mother-in-law since the playwright thought RC's name "would help" (Light on a Dark Horse, 1971: 325). Alexander claims that RC rephrased the English translations done by Krog's wife (151).

[92] Norwegian publisher and writer (1893–1935). Anna gives this as "Vinceness" while Alexander incorrectly gives his name as Winsness (151). RC, it would seem, is correct: Erling Winsnes (Light on a Dark Horse, 325).

arguments between them were frequent and fierce, but this in no way affected their friendship.

Tess and I loved the expeditions we sometimes made to a distant *finca*,[93] a sort of Sleeping Beauty manor-house some ten kilometres up-stream from us. Antonio Fuster, the father of our two maids, and his two youngest daughters took us there about once a month. He was the *Capataz* (overseer) of an absentee landlord.

To get to Mandem, as it was called, we had to start at dawn. Antonio always took his two donkeys fitted with paniers into which he stuffed the large *cantaros* (earthen pots) for water. Those peasants' faith in the healing powers of the Holy Spring of St. Anne was very strong and we, also, thought it had the most marvellous taste and effects. The river, which we joined near our house, was a raging torrent in winter, but in the summer it became a meandering stream between sandbanks. Strange birds came and went along the river bed, including cranes and dazzling kingfishers. We used to paddle in the stream and when it became really hot we bathed in a sandy pool at the foot of a small water-fall. In the foothills of the mountains we found red and blue quartz crystals which we greatly prized. These pre-pollution excursions were like the day of Creation.

Once arrived at Mandem we would eat our lunch and our fill of whatever fruit was in season. There was so much fruit at that time in Spain that a law was passed allowing anyone to take as much as they wanted when travelling along the endless, deserted roads. I specially remember at Mandem the figs with purple skins and crimson hearts of an exceptional sweetness. We would sit on one tree until we had eaten it bare of fruit and then move on to the next one. We once became very ill from this gluttony. The golden orioles, called "fig-eaters" in Spain, flashed through the giant, dark fig-trees getting quite drunk on the fermented figs we left while uttering their strange, figure-of-eight cries.

After lunch we would fall asleep in one of the great shuttered rooms and wake up, after a two hour siesta, filled with animal vitality. On the way home we were intoxicated with well-being and shouted and sang while helping Antonio to gather rabbit food as we went. Peasants are chary of wasting time and like to combine walking with gathering something or other. At home again we would fall into bed without prompting.

My parents would take long hikes into the mountains. They were away for days at a time and became more enthusiastic about the country every day. Sometimes they would discover incredibly remote towns or villages, perched on steep hills and so inaccessible that time and changing customs hardly affected them. The children in these villages would run after them asking when the rest of the

---

[93] Farm.

Poetic Justice

circus was coming or shouting, *"Franceses! Franceses!"* They took all strangers to be French, a notion probably dating from the Napoleonic invasion.

The traditions which ordered these people's lives were absorbingly interesting to Roy. Spain was the first country he had visited which had not been under Protestant influence and its appeal lay in being a pastoral society long after other countries had become industrialised. His dislike of machinery was instinctive—he never learned to drive a car or use a typewriter. People often argued with him about this. He was not "progressive" they said; but industrialisation, as he saw it, was inimical to man. People pointed out that without the tractor, for instance, you could never feed the population of the world, to which he always answered, "You are putting the cart before the horse; it is only since the Industrial Revolution that the world has become over-crowded..." How can one say he was wrong when we see what progress has done to this small planet?

He thought that poets and scientists were equally important to the world, but that they had become, in some way, inimical to each other. He thought the great modern scientists lacked all integrity, preferring fame to man's well-being.

Chapter IX

Because, for our neighbours, religion was present in every action of the day, it inevitably affected us. Both my parents were absorbed in the works of St. John of the Cross and St. Teresa of Avila. They were profoundly moved by St. John's attitude to suffering: instead of thinking it something to be avoided at all costs, it was to be accepted as a strengthener of the soul.

Roy began to accept Christ's teaching; His wisdom seemed to lift a great weight from his shoulders.[94] Life suddenly had a deeper meaning than he had so far imagined. Life made sense instead of being a haphazard muddle. Roy had come under many influences since arriving at Oxford at seventeen, but this was the only one that went straight to his heart.

Now he began to heal spiritually as well as physically. All that he felt about these manifestations of the soul are to be found in FLOWERING RIFLE. This is one of the reasons I find it so baffling that that poem should be described as "fascist propaganda." If Roy was a fascist, then so was Christ!

Until 1935 we had lived like pagans, doing what the Spanish call *"nuestra real gana"* (our royal will), but now Mary had a conversion of the heart—a sort of road to Damascus conversion. When she announced her intention of joining the Catholic Church, Roy agreed, but with certain reservations. It was many years before he could reconcile his love of freedom with, for instance, obligatory mass on Sundays. He gave such deep sighs during the sermons that everyone turned round to stare. Also, when he went to confession, which he hated, his whisper was so loud that the people in the church started to cough or to scrape their feet in order to drown the list of his pecadillos. But over the years, his faith became strong and very humble. To him an atheistic poet was a contradiction in terms.

Tess was rather startled by this new turn. She said to me, "But only last year Daddy was calling priests black beetles, and now we are to revere them!" Later,

---

[94] Spain in the mid-1930s was probably the very worst time and place to become an ardent Catholic convert. The battle lines were drawn in Spain between Christians and non-believers. The Campbells' conversion to Catholicism thus inevitably placed them on the side that defended Christianity.

Poetic Justice

much later in life, she was to find her religion a great help. Tess's religion was that of the early Christians. To her the most important part of the *New Testament* message was love and forgiveness. I took to religion like a duck to water. I liked all its manifestations, dogmas, and mysteries. I even liked the catechism, but this was probably due to the fact that I memorised it more quickly than my fellow catechumens. I still had a very long way to go...

We were received into the Church by Don Gregorio, the gentle parish-priest of Altea. This man, who was deeply loved by all the Alteanos, was shot outside his house a year later by militiamen from Valencia.

We were impressed by our first Holy Week in Spain. The whole of the village and its neighbourhood lived through the Passion of Our Lord. The very beautiful statue of Our Lady of Sorrows was borne through the streets between rows of barefoot penitents carrying candles. Then came the figure of Christ with his cross. The drums were beating; someone howled a *saeta*—this word means arrow and sounds like a heart being pierced by the arrow of pain. It was all incredibly moving and we were transported back to the greatest drama of all time. A side of Christianity that Nietzsche never discovered.

Next came the glorious Sunday of Resurrection—this after forty days of real fasting—was indeed a day for rejoicing. All was music, flowers, bells, sung masses, and the wearing of new dresses for Easter. Even the poorest peasant girl was able to *estrenar* a new dress for Easter. This word, *estrenar*, is in constant use in Spain; it means to wear, or use, for the first time. Every feast is good for *estrenar*-ing something. Easter-week was dedicated to pilgrimages into the country to indulge in bucolic merry-making. The sweet air was full of laughter, songs, the ripple of a guitar. Groups ate and drank beneath the trees.

It was at about this time (the spring of 1935) that strict Granny Campbell came to pay us a visit. She did not approve of our easy-going way of life and set about disciplining us in a variety of ways. I, who took after her, was rather pleased by her ordered way of life, but my parents and Tess could not bear it. Granny came of a distinguished Highland family, the Dunnachies. She met Dr. Sam when he was at St. Andrews as a medical student. They were married after his graduation, and immediately after the wedding the young wife went out to Durban with her new, and probably unknown, husband. After two years she left him to return home to Scotland which she missed dreadfully, but her parents reasoned with her and so she returned to her wifely duties. She bore Dr. Sam a daughter, my aunt Ethel,[95] and fifteen years later five boys in succession of which Roy

---

95 For a photo of Ethel semaphoring ships in Durban Harbour in WWI see CAMPBELL IN CONTEXT, Coullie and Wade: 690.

was the third,⁹⁶ so that she was far older than most mothers are, when he was born. In fact when she came to stay with us, he was thirty-three and she in her seventies.

Granny produced from her innumerable trunks and suitcases (she was on the last laps of a world tour and had recently been in China) exquisite Chinese linen beautifully embroidered, and reams of coloured folding-paper which she taught us to make into frogs, palm trees, kangeroos, and even a kettle that boiled water when held over a candle. She later wrote and illustrated a book for children about this pastime.⁹⁷

Studio photograph of Mary in Toledo circa 1935 (Tess)

Granny also managed, in the short time she was with us, to instil in my heart a burning admiration for everything Scottish. She gave me that inspiring book THE SCOTTISH CHIEFTANS by Anne Porter which made me fall in love with William Wallace and Robert Burns. From her fathomless trunks she also produced kilts for Tess and me in the Campbell tartan and all sorts of Campbell insignia such as silver brooches of wild boars' heads, thistles, etc.

Granny was, after Mary, the great love of Roy's life. When she was with us,

---

96 Sam Campbell and Margaret Dunnachie had six children. Their names and dates of birth are as follows: Ethel (1887), Archie (1892), George Gordon (1894), Royston Dunnachie (1901), William Neil (1904), Bruce Patrick (1907). Anna thus seems to be confused. There were fourteen years between Ethel and RC, but Archie and George were born in the intervening years.

97 Margaret W. Campbell's book, PAPER TOY MAKING (London: Pitman, 1937; rpt in paperback, New York: Dover, 1975) has a Preface by RC (see COLLECTED WORKS IV: 276).

In contemporary origami circles, Margaret Campbell is credited as one of the first to develop the idea of paperfolding bases through her "Foundation Folds".

Poetic Justice

he was like a small boy. "Yes, mother. No, mother." He even gave up drinking red wine during her stay.[98]

Strict Granny did not approve of our easy-going way of life; neither was she impressed by our schooling in spite of the fact that we now spoke, read, and wrote (after a fashion) in three different languages—which have been far more of a blessing in life than any other education; certainly more useful than knowing how much coal Britain exported each year! But she did not see things this way, and so it was decided that Tess should accompany Granny to England on her return to South Africa. She was to stay with Grandmama Garman and attend a day school in order to avoid the trauma of boarding-school. In the event, our English cousins, one in particular, were to be just as cruel as school girls would have been, and Tess's complexes and traumas date from that time.[99]

Tess and I were appalled at the thought of being separated, and, in fact, it did turn out to be a disastrous decision. When she returned a year later, she had become complex and bitter. This was due in part to adolescence but also to the ridicule to which she had been subjected. Tess was a gauche child, very trusting and open. She had always been treated by Roy with special love and care. He saw that she was a bit slow, but he also saw that she made up for this by her shining virtues. She was diligent, kind, generous, and deeply thoughtful. Had she not had this "rude awakening," I am sure she would have overcome the complexities of early life with ease. But under the circumstances, the treatment she received in England was to cause us all years of deep suffering. In Tess, Roy saw a special kind of soul. She was always more of a Campbell than a Garman. And in her, all the steadfast qualities of his own family were present, whereas in me there was a great deal of frivolous Garman blood.[100]

Granny took Roy to a tailor in Alicante who fitted him out with a beautiful green tweed suit—he even wore a waistcoat. He looked very dashing in this outfit, but he far preferred his usual clothes: blue cotton trousers and a fisherman's shirt.

---

[98] Alexander avers that RC's "mother's unwavering love provided the boy throughout his nervous, delicate childhood (he suffered much from asthma) with the security he needed. His love for her was as great as his admiration for his father. Her unshakeable calm provided the still center around which the family moved. Campbell thought of her always as a haven from the storm". He adds in a footnote that, "All his life Campbell seems to have needed the security of a dominant woman's love in order to produce his best work" (6).

[99] Anna seems to be referring to Kitty, illegitimate daughter of Mary's sister Kathleen and Jacob Epstein. In conversation, Tess denied that her cousin was cruel, saying she was just a brusque person.

[100] Nevertheless, Anna says on the previous page that she took to her Dunnachie Campbell grandmother's strictness.

Paca and Anamaria were fond of the *Abuelita* (little grandmother), and she in turn was delighted when they introduced her to the weekly ritual of bread-making. Every house in that part of the world has its own out-door oven like a giant ant-heap attached to it. Once a week this was filled with kindling wood which, when burnt down to ashes, left the oven burning hot; the large dough loaves were then pushed in on long spatulas, and, after the alloted time, the doors were opened and the crisp, golden loaves taken out, wrapped in spotless linen cloths and stored away in the carved wooden bread-chests which every family possessed and in which they took great pride. In those days bread was of primal importance in Spain. If a piece fell to the floor, it was kissed when retrieved and I never remember a new loaf being cut without having sign of the cross made over it first.

Granny Campbell was rather taken aback by our conversion to the Catholic Church, although she was charmed by some of the devotions that took place in our district. For example, the Holy Family was taken in a glass case from house to house staying a week in each. The house that was to receive the Holy Family took great pains to prepare an altar for its reception. The best linen and the prettiest flowers were arranged and the whole family gathered there every evening to say the Rosary and sing hymns.

I think Granny was deeply shocked when we alluded to the glass case as though we were talking about the real Holy Family. I once said to her, shortly after her arrival, "The Holy Family is coming to stay tonight." "What, child? What are you talking about?!"

Granny's farewell gift to Roy was the collected works of Calderón de la Barca. Roy had recently discovered this dramatist and could talk of little else. She had this copy bound in a beautiful, thick cretonne knowing Roy's habit of almost eating any new book he admired—by which I mean that he would take it everywhere with him; to the pub, to bed, to table, so that it soon became stained and rumpled. This book disappeared on our journey to Toledo.

We all left Altea together. Tess and Granny were to leave for England from Madrid, and we other three were bound for Toledo. The parting from all our friends at the station in Altea was prolonged (the train being late as usual) and tearful. Roy was in a thunderous mood; he detested changes and upheavals. This mood was exacerbated when Paca and Anamaria came running up at the last minute with vases of geraniums, old flit machines,[101] and some vast china chamber-pots, all of which had been carefully discarded by Mary; the maids now tried to thrust these into our compartment. At last, order was restored and

---

[101] An insecticide spray-gun.

Poetic Justice

the train pulled out of the station to the waving of handkerchiefs and shouts of *Adios! Hasta la Vista! Hasta siempre!*[102]

A cross-country journey through Spain in those days was a complicated business, but I was blessedly in another world. This went unnoticed until Mary felt my burning body next to hers and put a worried hand to my forehead. A kindly old gentleman, sitting opposite us in one of the many trains we took that day, diagnosed my illness as *gripe;* I had a fearful fever, and I remember him saying, "Give her plenty of rest and boiled fish." It seemed the last straw. All the rest is oblivion: parting from Tess and Granny, arriving at Toledo—all has gone.

The next I remember is Roy coming into my room at the Hotel Lino in Toledo, where Mary was sitting, and saying, "Good Lord, Kid (he often called Mary, Kid), this town is fabulous. I never realised it would be so marvellous! Let's stay here for the rest of our lives...". The gods must have heard that remark, for they got to work about fifteen months later when we were forced to leave in sadness and in tears.

---

[102] Roughly translated as Goodbye. Until we meet again. So long!

Chapter X

For centuries a centre of learning, Toledo was also laden with history. The great fortress of the Alcázar (of which the reconstructed version is a feeble imitation), built by the Emperor Charles V, was a military academy so that the town was full of cadets in smart uniforms, top-boots, and jingling spurs. There were also innumerable monasteries, convents, seminaries, schools, churches (72), shrines, and two cathedrals, one called *El Cristo de los Reyes* (The Christ of Kings) was still not quite finished, but the other in the centre of the town was a gothic building of great beauty. It contained cloistered gardens with orange trees, and attached to it by a bridge over the street was the palace of the Cardinal Archbishop, the Primate of Spain. There was a strong atmosphere in Toledo of religious and military discipline. Every other person one met was either a priest, monk, nun, or soldier of every hierarchy and rank. Although now it is a provincial town since Madrid replaced it as the capital, it still has an air of sophistication such as university-garrison towns have all over the world: Edinburgh, Crakow, Kiev in old Russia, and so on. Reading Michael Bulgakov's WHITE GUARD some time ago, I was vividly reminded of Toledo, although Kiev was far larger. But its cadets, its Dnieper—green like the Tagus—its endless monasteries and churches, its steep hills, and finally its Civil War and the way the two towns were so tragically fought over, made such a comparison inevitable.

Roy, at first so enthusiastic about Toledo, sometimes came to the same conclusions as Rilke about that town. The latter says in one of his letters, "My God how many things I have loved because they tried to be like this, because they had a drop of this blood in their hearts... Can I bear it?" Perhaps the atmosphere of the place is too much, at first, for people of sensitivity and imagination. The fact is that for the first two or three months we were there, Roy swooned about in a state of mental and physical intoxication. I had never seen him drink like he did in Toledo except for that one time in Valencia. I think also that he was suffering from the unrelenting war of hatred unleashed by the Nicolsons after the publication of THE GEORGIAD. What sort of democracy

Poetic Justice

is it, in which a handful of powerful, but mediocre writers, can dictate the literary trends of two countries—the United States and Britain—to whole generations of readers? Roy used to say that the power of the press was so great in the Democracies that they dictated as though they were the government and that they did not care what happened to the general conscience as long as they increased their hoard of gold.

I was very worried about my father at that time, but as Mary seemed to think he was all right, I decided that no harm could come to him. But in this I was mistaken.

So many things happened during our first stay in Toledo, that looking back I often feel we were there far longer than the fifteen months which actually elapsed until the outbreak of the Civil War. Mary was on another plane. The ardour of her conversion was fanned by the spiritual heritage of Toledo. It was in this town that St. John of the Cross was imprisoned by the Inquisition and here St. Teresa of Avila founded one of her Discalced Carmelite Convents.

There were services going on all the time at one place or another, and the smell of incense percolated from the churches into the street.

We soon moved from the Hotel Lino to a house in the Street of Cardinal Cisneros which half circles the Cathedral. From the top story of this house you could see the gargoyles and griffins across the way only too clearly. Our dwelling was almost bare of furniture, and while Mary was at church and Roy at the tavern, our sad maid, who drank vinegar all day, spent much time talking to the Ranero. This ghastly looking Frog-Man carried wherever he went, strung on reeds from the river, the lower halves of innumerable skinned frogs reminiscent of the buttocks and legs of naked babies. The Ranero was always telling the sad maid what he was going to do when the revolution came, drawing a finger across his throat. And, later, he was responsible for the murder of many clergymen whom he took to be his personal enemies.

We used to go every evening to the Plaza de Zocodover, the main square in Toledo, where I had an ice-cream and my parents their aperitifs. At that hour of the evening the whole square came to life. The girls in their best dresses strolled back and forth, arm-in-arm, as they received complicated *piropos* (compliments) from the youths who strolled in the opposite direction. "Long live your mother," they whispered, "now I can die content" or *"Adios guapisima!"* ("Hello beautiful!"), and so on. Many courtships were started in this way which eventually led to marriages. The watchful parents, in the meantime, sat at adjoining café tables. The cadets stood about in groups like so many Vronskies[103] or sat in armchairs

---

[103] Count Alexei Kirillovich Vronsky is the character in Tolstoy's ANNA KARENINA with

having their boots polished by skillful boot-blacks, until they shone as brightly as their eyes under their peaked caps. Gypsy women strolled about in their voluminous skirts swaying haughtily with their graceful, barefooted walk while their menfolk, with long moustaches, leaned on tall walking sticks watching everything with narrowed eyes.

It was on one such evening that Laurie Lee[104] made his debut in Toledan society. He startled the animated gathering by standing up and playing on, of all things, the violin, the more sentimental tunes from Schubert's songs. After a polite silence lasting a full minute, the conversations were resumed, drowning any sound from the violin. Nevertheless, we could see that he was still sawing away. When he was satisfied, he began going from table to table holding out his hat. When he reached our table, Roy, seeing his long red nose and blistered skin, felt sorry for him and asked him to sit down. After listening to his hard luck story, Roy invited him back to Cisneros where Laurie stayed for some time. He later described Roy as a *burnt out eagle*. However, there was nothing burnt out about Roy's kindness. Still, to be quite fair, it must be admitted that Roy was drinking like a madman at that time and that his nerves could not stand the onslaught of alcohol with which they were being bombarded.

Gradually, after a melodramatic sunset, the sky would turn green. This was a relief after those blood-red skies which seemed to reflect the carnage and fires of the approaching Civil War. I never remember the sunsets being so violent after the hostilities were over. In the darkening skies the first star would appear and then, suddenly, all the lights would come on in the town and it was time for dinner. As we walked slowly home, we could feel the heat pressing on us from both sides because the walls of the houses stayed warm long after dark. Those Castillian summers used to be terribly, satisfyingly hot.

Mary and I often took long walks through the town, always discovering some treasure such as El Greco's BURIAL OF THE CONDE DE ORGAZ, which hung in the old church of San Tomé without any protection in spite of the ever increasing anarchy in Spain. But works of art had not become major currency in those days.

It was on one of these walks that we discovered our new home, 13 Airosas. We were returning from the Vega where we had been trying to get a breath of

---

whom the heroine falls in love.

[104] (1914-1997) Laurence Edward Alan "Laurie" Lee, English poet, novelist and screenwriter. He fell in love with Anna's aunt, Lorna Wishart (née Garman), and fathered a daughter, Yasmin, with her. After his affair with Lorna ended he had an affair with her niece, Kitty (the daughter of Kathleen and Jacob Epstein). He later married another of Lorna's nieces, Katherine Polge (daughter of her sister Helen and the French fisherman, Marius Polge) (Pearce: 267).

Poetic Justice

air under the trees, for it was forty degrees centigrade or more, and had just come through the old Moorish gate when we found ourselves in a sort of courtyard in one corner of which was an imposing carriage entrance covered in cobwebs and trailing vines. At right angles to it, in the very high walls, was a small green door. Curious to see what lay behind the walls we pushed this door open and a bell jangled over our heads. We found ourselves in an enchanting garden, rising in terraces to a low, stone Renaissance house shaded by a thick trellis of grape-vines. The whole place was encircled by the Moorish battlements which in some places were forty feet high. You could walk along those battlements on the worn sentinel's parapet, from one tower to another. The lower part of the garden, where we were, was full of every variety of rose. In the centre was a crystal-clear fountain surrounded by a group of tall trees. The terraces were joined by double flights of steps surmounted by stone urns from which cascaded ivy-leaved geraniums. This place had been designed on the golden section,[105] by a cardinal for his summer residence. Here he had entertained some of Spain's greatest writers, including Lope de Vega and Quevado. It was incredibly grand and silent. We opened the garden door several times to attract attention with the bell, and at last a tall man came running from one of the greenhouses at the other end of the garden. This was Don Bonifacio, the owner of this paradise. Mary, after remarking on the beauty of the place, asked if it was occupied—but no, no one lived there. Don Bonifacio proceeded to show us over the house. When we arrived at the top terrace we stopped in wonder, for the view over the battlements brought tears to our eyes; it was literally breathtaking. The vast golden plain stretched away for miles to the hazy, ghost-blue snow mountains of the Gredos on one side and the Guadarramas to the north.

Don Bonifacio was delighted to rent us this place for a ridiculous sum since he wanted it lived in. We were struck by the coolness of the house when we entered it because its walls were very thick. It was furnished throughout with Spanish Empire furniture, heavy but attractive dark wooden chairs, tables, beds, etc. At the back of the house were stables and a large corral.

Roy was very taken with 13 Airosas and when he saw the stables he immediately set about acquiring some horses. He was attracted to people in the horse trade and had already made friends among the gypsies, cowpunchers, and other horsy people who throng the markets of Toledo and nearby Talavera, both cen-

---

[105] The golden ratio or golden section is a mathematical relationship identified by Euclid that exists in art, shapes, nature and patterns. This ratio is thought to be aesthetically pleasing and beneficial to the objects that possess them. The golden ratio states that the proportion of a geometric figure is such that the smaller dimension is to the greater as the greater is to the whole. It works out to about 1.61803.

tres of equestrian lore and trade. Soon the corral was thronged with every sort of person wanting to sell horses. They came down the hill at the back of the house and made their way into the corral by a rear entrance.

At one time it seemed to be crowded with the whole tribe of Toledan gypsies: Flamenco dancers and singers included. When Roy's back was turned, they pulled down their lower eyelids as much as to say, "This one should be easy to cheat." I began to loathe them from that time. But they were cunning in a simple sort of way and were so sharp that they cut themselves more often than others. Gypsies are stuck somewhere in history; they never seem to move forward. And now, although they used all their tricks, they sold us two perfectly good horses, and one that was above average. They did manage to trick Roy over a splendid mule which turned out to be deaf, but it is probable that the gypsies themselves did not know this since all mules seem to be deaf at one time or another.

At last the corral became so crowded, the original traders being joined by sellers of oats, alfalfa, beans, and hay, that our two maids, Flora and the beautiful Eugenia, lost all patience—they had the peasants' mistrust and loathing of gypsies—and they set about clearing the corral once and for all by attacking the mob verbally and with their brooms until peace was restored.

It took some time to get over my fear of riding, but Roy was very patient with me, and once he had helped me to overcome my fear, there was nothing I liked better than to gallop across the plain accompanied by our groom Rodrigo and my large dog Blanca, which raced beside my horse. The plain was full of rollers, so blue that they were indistinguishable from the sky, and every here and there one of their feathers lay in the burnt grass like a flash of sky. Partridges, in their thousands, rose at the last minute, startling the horse and rider out of their wits.

We soon settled into a routine. Mary was completely engrossed in her new religion. Because she was so devoted to John and Teresa, she used to attend mass at the Carmelite monastery and benediction at the Carmelite convent. She became, at that time, a Carmelite tertiary which meant abandoning make-up, cigarettes, trousers, wine except at meals, and going to daily mass and communion and reciting the Office. This left little time for anything else, and I became desperately lonely. I loved going to Benediction at the Carmelite convent. I tried to imagine what the ever-hidden nuns' lives were like so surrounded by mystery. Although they were a strictly enclosed order, you could speak to one of the nuns on duty through a sort of revolving cupboard. People went to this cupboard with their troubles, problems, or news. You could also place things on the shelf in the cupboard such as a piece of linen to be embroidered or collected. I have never seen such exquisite needle work since.

Poetic Justice

Although Roy now had the horses to ride and look after, he still seemed to spend a lot of time drinking. It was really suicidal behaviour. Once, when the maids were out and Mary was at church, they sent from the local tavern to ask someone to come and fetch Roy home as he was too drunk to walk. There was only me—I know that this is beginning to sound like Little Nell and her grandfather—so I went to fetch him. It was a frightful shock. He was insensible. He sat at a table with only the whites of his eyes showing and piss all over his trousers. The taverner pulled him to his feet and, somehow, we managed to get him home to bed, having run the gauntlet of a thousand stares from curious watchers in the street of Airosas.

Despite the horses, the lovely house, the dear, good maids, my dog, and my great friend Angelita, I was often lonely. I missed Tess desperately. It was only then that I realised what a buffer she had been between me and the world. I tried to make Mary a substitute by clinging to her like a limpet, but she had her own life to lead. Every time I was apart from her I was in mortal dread that something awful would happen to her, that she would be run over by a car or simply disappear into one more church and never be seen again. Trying to ensure this did not happen was an exhausting business; it meant spending hours in worship or pretended worship. Mother was delighted by what she took to be genuine devotion, not even realising that all I wanted was to be with her. I tried to explain my fears to her, but she simply laughed them away as fantasies. Of course, they *were* fantasies but only too real to me.

Darling Mary, she really did everything to make life pleasant for me. How could I expect her to understand what I was going through?

It was Roy who eventually realised there was something wrong. I was so thin by then that it was noticed even by the maids, and so my parents decided that I should attend the Ursuline Convent, in the approaching autumn.

When the first day of school came, in October, I climbed the hill to the Ursulines escorted by my private maid, Dolores. She was a tiny woman, very ugly indeed, very neat with little gold [earrings] in her small white ears and wearing a dignified black dress. On the way to school we stopped to buy green liquorice sticks from the old widows who sold bananas, bobby pins, peanuts, etc., and almost every day we met coming down the hill towards us, a stern-looking officer with dark glasses and a moustache. This was Colonel Moscardó who, a year later, was to show such outstanding heroism in the siege of the Alcázar.[106]

Unfortunately, attending the Ursulines only increased my anxiety about

---

[106] He was military governor of Toledo Province and then commandant of the citadel. A religious man, he defiantly held the Alcázar for the 70 days it was under siege by the Republican forces.

Mary. The fear that something would happen to her was quite irrational and obsessive. But she now had a whole day in which to fall off her horse, get lost, etc. I became, if anything, more nervous, and Dolores added to my troubles by being an old-fashioned tippler. She never had a hair out of place, but occasionally she lurched and she sometimes smelled like an open brandy bottle. This weakness of hers made her late in fetching me from school. I watched the classroom gradually empty as one more maid came for one more pupil with no sign of mine. Sometimes she was so late that it was almost dark. At last, when she did arrive, I would race home, down the narrow, poorly lit streets, ignoring Dolores' cries, only to find the house in darkness: Roy at the tavern, the maids out with their fiancés, and Mary at Benediction.

I think the nuns must have been rather un-imaginative. Instead of making me feel at home, they were perpetually surprised at my oddness. They did not understand that a little girl of nine, a foreigner, was bound to feel a bit out of her depths at the novelty of everything: the instruction, the other girls, the intense religion, and so on. It was the amazement that I and my parents caused them that I found exhausting. "Why did I ride?" "Why did Mother ride?" "Was Dolores my grandmother?" (This suggestion filled me with indignation.) "Why had we come to Toledo?" I think one of the things that muddled the nuns most was that by then I was speaking Spanish like a native and, because of my avid reading, I spelt in that language far better than the other girls of my age. Perhaps, if I had spoken Spanish with a strong English accent, they would have found it easier to place me. As it was, I remained a puzzle.

There were, however, two things at school which I loved: one was a gambling game with bobby-pins for currency, the other a girl, nicknamed La Revoltosa, a born satirist who saw far more than most grown-ups at that establishment. She made everyone laugh, and the nuns wisely allowed her imagination free rein.

There was another thing about going to school, however, that filled me with distress. On our way to and from the Ursulines, Dolores and I often met a haggard woman with long grey curls down to her waist. Sometimes she was asleep in one of the shadowy corners of the cathedral; at others she would be followed by young boys who pelted her with dead cats or old tins. She usually clutched to her bosom, or raised to her lips, a black bottle which inevitably drove the boys to jeers and howls. The sight used to fill me with deep depression and anguish every time we came across it. I probably thought that Roy might end up like this. It was so like a scene from Goya's drawings, that later when I saw these in the Prado, I was instantly reminded of Maria la Borracha, poor old Mary the drunk.

To show how morbid I had become and how differently Roy was seeing

Poetic Justice

things I include this letter he wrote to Tess at that time.

> 13 Airosas
> Toledo
> *1935*
>
> *Darling Teresita mia,*
>
> *thanks for your letter. Don't ever feel homesick. In our thoughts you are always with us, my paloma.*[107] *We never sit down to lunch or supper without saying, I wonder what Tess is doing now. Neil*[108] *wrote to say what a sweet girl you are. I am glad you liked him. He may be small as you say but he is as strong as a panther. You should see him playing rugby. You go on being as good as you can, and try to help Tony and Grandmama by being as tidy as you can—because you are not in your place now like at Altea—and I'm sure you will get on well. Your school report was very good. Well done!*
>
> *I have tried to draw a map of our new house. Oh! it is lovely. And I put in the little dog I am keeping for you (No 4 on the map). He is like a tiny lion with a black nose and tip to his tail. He is as clever as a monkey, but kind: and he never seems to bark. From the deep sound of his growl, I should think he will grow as big as the kitchen table at Altea. Also he is a very doggy sort of dog, whenever I call him he runs away but he comes to everyone else and when he wags his tail it looks like this,*[109] *like the old wheel that drives an aeroplane.*
>
> *Your painting of a donkey was beautiful. Especially the algaroba*[110] *tree. How did you remember so well? The hind legs of the donkey are nearly right now. Send us more drawings.*
>
> *I am saving up for you to come here for Xmas.*[111] *We shall have a grand time: and you and I shall fish in the Tagus and take our lunch into the high cliffs where the hawks nest and go and sit by the roaring, flashing waters; and watch the big fish jumping. Anna and Mum are looking lovely. Write often to Mum, she is always, always thinking about you: and you needn't write to me, because I get it all from your letters to her. You must write to Anna too. She loves you and you are going to see the lovely book she is sending you soon.*
>
> *Your loving Dad.*

---

[107] "My dove". (ACL)

[108] Neil, Roy's youngest brother. Three of the Campbell brothers were quite small like Dr. Sam, but Roy and George were over six feet tall. (ACL)

[109] Here there is a drawing of a propeller. (ACL)

[110] Carob tree. Altea was full of donkeys and these trees, and Tess had, in a fit of homesickness, drawn them both. (ACL)

[111] In the event, Tess only returned in June after being in England for a year. (ACL)

A Memoir of my Father, Roy Campbell

Chapter XI

Spain itself was becoming more and more unstable and turbulent. Roy was out riding one day in the late autumn, by the distant hermitage of the Bastida, when he was stopped at gun point by two Guardias de Asalco (the new police instituted by the Republic), who told him to dismount and when he had done so proceeded to beat him up, especially his poor dear face. He was then ordered to walk back with them to headquarters.

The first we knew of this was when a friend came to the corral to say he had just seen Roy being marched up the hill by two guards. I went cold with fear. Mary flung a shawl round her shoulders and set off immediately for the police station. She tried to make me stay at home, but I insisted on going with her. We found Roy lying on some straw in a police cell. His face was terribly swollen, and blood was oozing from a cut on his cheek. He looked like one of the crucifixes before which Mary spent so many hours praying.

Mother was furious. She rounded on the horrible policemen and, in her comical Spanish, proceeded to tell them what she thought of them and their ways. They looked nonplussed. I think they understood little of what she was saying because of her strong English accent, but they became effusively apologetic and said Roy had been mistaken for someone else—a stupid excuse: Roy was so definitely not to be mistaken for anyone else. There was a strongly hostile atmosphere in that place, but they let us take Roy home with us.

We never found out why he was treated in this barbarous way. Our Spanish friends seemed to think it was all in the day's work. There was so much anarchy and confusion everywhere that one more beating made little difference. In Madrid, for instance, the Sunday sport of the Anarchists was called the *juerga*, which in the normal course of events means having fun but which they used to describe the murder of someone they had taken a dislike to, or with whom they wanted to settle a score.

Whatever the reason for Roy's beating-up, it left us very apprehensive. For the first time we realised how dangerous the situation was becoming. Roy began to urge Mary to leave Spain "while the going was good," but she had become so attached to her lovely home, and to Toledo, that she would not hear of leaving. She kept assuring Roy that everything would blow over very soon.

Because Toledo is as cold in the winter as it is hot in the summer and the Cardinal, the original owner of the house, had only used it in the latter season, we had to install large wood-burning stoves in order to keep out the cold. Because of what happened later, these stoves always remind me of the two Carmelite fathers, Fr. Eusebio and Fr. Evaristo, both cultured and intelligent men, who came occasionally to our house and had a deep influence on my parents.

Fr. Eusebio, the younger of the two, was Roy's confessor and spiritual director. It was he who reconciled the latter to confession. Fr. Eusebio's saintliness was noticed by everyone, and it was his wisdom and kindness that helped Roy to fight against the nervousness that made him drink. He celebrated mass with extraordinary holiness. With him this sacrifice took on a new dimension. His feet, bare except for sandals in the icy Castillian winter, seemed to float rather than walk across the freezing flagstones. We did not know then that he had only a few more months to live, but I'm sure he did. It was he who kept up the spirits of his fellow monks when they were all dragged out to be shot. They died heroically—a friend of ours who was with them to the end said that Fr. Eusebio was smiling when he fell, and shouting, "Long live Christ the King! Long live Spain!"

After Christmas of 1935 the country was in a fever of excitement because elections were to be held in February. This had come about because even the rotten Republic was getting frightened at the rising tide of provocation and terror. As the election date drew near, most of the clergy went into hiding because of the ferocious threats made against them on the radio, in the press, in popular songs, in Parliament, and at what the Reds called Mitins. *"Gran Mitin General"*[112] we read on all the hoardings.

Three young postulants and the elderly Fr. Evaristo took refuge in our house. Fr. Evaristo had a slightly pock-marked face and a great sense of humour. They stayed with us for about a week and looked very sad in their borrowed civilian clothes. They said mass at an improvised altar and read their breviaries as they strolled to and fro in the sitting-room. I remember it being so cold, they had to keep their overcoats on most of the time.

The monks brought with them, from their famous library, the precious MSS of St. John and St. Teresa of Avila. These enormous yellow parchment volumes were difficult to hide, so Roy decided to leave them lying about as he thought, correctly, that they would draw less attention than if hidden away. This turned

---

[112] That is, big general meeting.

out to be a psychologically wise decision, for when the house was searched later on, these great archives were completely overlooked. After our escape, our house was occupied by two separate armies, and although the soldiers must often have sat on the archives or knocked into them, they suffered no harm, and it was with pride that Roy was able to return them to the monastery after the Civil War—the only remnants of a once fabulous library.

Although the elections did not resolve anything since they took place amid such violence that it could never be determined who had won, the monks decided to return to their monastery. The Republic stayed in power but was weakened, and at least the Opposition was now led by a brilliant parliamentarian of great integrity, Calvo Sotelo.[113] Had this very intelligent and brave man not been murdered, it is quite probable that all the devastation and horror of the Civil War could have been avoided. But Calvo Sotelo was too outspoken for the left to stomach, and the Pasionaria[114] called for his death every day in the Cortes. In the five months before his murder, we continued to ride, to write and paint, and to go to school. Roy had become calmer since his horrible experience with the guards. He was writing the poems for MITHRAIC EMBLEMS[115] and had more or less given up drinking.

In April I became very ill indeed with what appeared to be typhoid fever. I think Roy's arrest had been the last straw on a camel's back of fears and worries. But it was Roy who made my convalescence a delight. Every morning he and I would climb the hill to the little museum of San Vicente where one of El Greco's most beautiful paintings of the Assumption of Our Lady was hung. We would sit before it for half an hour or so. I remember thinking how like my father's were the feet of the angels—very long and narrow. There were all sorts of other things in the museum of interest to a ten year old child, but what I liked best was listening to my father talking about El Greco. After this we always went to Zocodover for ice-cream and tapas: small delicacies served on saucers, of great variety.

Sometimes on these walks we would meet the Prior of the Carmelites, a very different man from Eusebio and Evaristo. He was fat and bad-tempered

---

[113] (1893-1936) A monarchist and conservative who opposed the Republican government. His death, in retaliation for the assassination the previous day of José Costillo, precipitated the start of the Spanish Civil War.
[114] Dolores Ibárruri (1895-1989), Communist leader.
[115] Published in 1936. The editors of the COLLECTED WORKS 1 note: "RC had become interested in the dead and mysterious worship of Mithras in Provence. [... It] gave to his work that framework of personal mythology which Yeats sought and found in the occult" (643). Alexander notes that the volume met with "almost complete silence" probably due to a boycott of his work in England at the time (168).

Poetic Justice

and in wet weather of which there was a lot that April, he would lift his habit above his knees exposing white, plump calves. I went in dread of him because he was the children's confessor, and he often seemed to find something ludicrous about my small sins. Once when I had used the word "damn" rather often, I told him I had "blasphemed". He jumped out of the confessional and, literally, grabbed me by the scruff of the neck and made me kneel before him to say a special act of contrition. I forgave him from the depths of my heart because I knew only too well what a strain the clergy were going through. My friend, Angelita, had taught me a song about teaching the monks and nuns to go up to the choir singing liberty, liberty, liberty. This wretched song had a catchy tune and often came to my mind, but I sometimes wondered whether the Prior would consider this as bad as "blaspheming."

Tess returned from England in May. At first I thought we should be able to go on having the same relationship of love and trust we had had before, but we never really became intimate again until we were both grown up. As I said earlier, Tess had changed. It seems to me that all her mental troubles started in that year away from home. These were to come and go for many years causing us all a great deal of suffering.

A Memoir of my Father, Roy Campbell

Chapter XII

The unrestrained anarchy that followed the elections culminated on the 13th of July in the brutal murder of Calvo Sotelo. His brilliance and integrity were a continual provocation to *The Possessed*. He was arrested by the Guardias de Asalto and was shot in cold-blood by them soon afterwards. This was too much for the armed forces. They could not stand by while one after another of the democratically elected members of Parliament were "liquidated." The army realised that either law and order were to be restored in Spain or that country would become a Soviet satellite. What the West has never realised is that the same tactics used in Spain before the Civil War are now being used in almost every country which has a democratic government and that the police are having to become more and more tough so that the populations of these countries can go about their business unmolested.

A week after Calvo Sotelo's murder General Franco landed in the south of Spain. This was the signal for the *Movimiento*—the movement that was to oust all atheists, anarchists, communists, Russian advisors, and interfering do-gooders from the seats of power in Spain, so that for some generations peace and prosperity reigned in that country.

We, in Toledo, were woken at dawn on the 19th of July by the most fearful cacophony I ever hope to hear. The battle for Toledo had begun. We were all fast asleep, when three artillery batteries, under General Riquelme (loyal to the Republic), 6,000 militiamen and many armoured cars, all from Madrid, opened fire on the town. Toledo was defended by a handful of officers from the Academy (the cadets had all gone home for the holidays) and the army-trained Civil Guard, numbering 1,105 men all told.

Toledo was a pro-Franco island in a sea of Red.

The battle for the town lasted three days and nights without a single break. Heavily outnumbered, the defenders slowly retreated up the hill to the Alcázar where 520 wives of the Civil Guard and their children were already assembled. The siege lasted for 70 days, but not a single civilian was wounded in that time.

In the very first days of the siege the son of Colonel Moscardó, the inspired leader of the defenders, was taken prisoner by the militia in Madrid. They made him speak to his father over the telephone. The conversation was brief.

"Father, they say they will shoot me if the Alcázar does not surrender. But don't worry about me."

"If it be true, commend your soul to God, shout Long Live Spain, and die like a hero. Good-bye my son, a last kiss."

"Good-bye father, a very big kiss."

How is one to explain the resistance of the Alcázar to the overwhelming attacks of every kind by superior forces that it sustained? Eventually, when the enemy was at the end of its tether, three enormous mines were detonated immediately beneath the fortress, producing such a blast that some of its huge stones were blown to a distance of two kilometres. Nevertheless, the survivors were still able to repulse the last great attack. Deafened by the explosion, covered with falling plaster, choking and blinded by dust, they answered the call to action stations and sent the 11,000 militiamen reeling back, panic-stricken at what they believed must be supernatural tactics.

Two days later, amid scenes of indescribable rejoicing, when General Varela lifted the siege, Colonel Moscardó, emaciated, skeletal, still dusty, bloody but unbowed, emerged from the ruins, stood to attention, and said, *"Mi general, sin novedad en el Alcázar."* ("Nothing to report in the Alcázar, Sir.")

In the meantime, we Campbells and the faithful Flora were locked into our thick-walled house, hungry and thirsty. I do not recall my sister or my parents being frightened—I suppose they were putting on a brave front for my sake—but I was absolutely petrified with terror. It was the noise which for 72 hours had been a concert of machine-guns, zooming shells, rifles and hand-grenades, and what I took to be falling masonry, that unnerved me most.

Of course the water was cut off, but we managed to fill some earthen jars from a spring in the garden. There was a truce on the third day, and I remember going down to a lower terrace to fetch some cucumbers with Flora. These were so hot from the sun that they had begun to turn yellow; nevertheless, Flora managed to make a *gazpacho* with them. We felt very daring walking in the garden, but it was not the bullets that drove us back into the house, it was the overwhelming heat.

Now with Toledo in the hands of the enemy, everything had become much more dangerous, and we did not know what to expect. The truce lasted for a day or two. In this time Roy decided to go into the town to reconnoitre. When I saw him leaving the relative safety of our walled garden, I felt the most unspeakable anguish. I was convinced we would never see him again. But he returned late that evening looking very drawn and pale. I cannot remember a single face that was not that terrible colour during all the time we were in Civil War Spain. Roy's news was appalling: all the Carmelites had been shot (there is now a plaque on the wall near where they fell); the Maristas, another order of priests, were still lying where they had been shot and scrawled in their blood on the wall was written: "Thus strikes the Cheka,"[116] there were also search parties going from house to house looking for "priests, fascists, and other enemies of the people." That hackneyed phrase was quite new to us at the time and filled everyone with foreboding. It was worrying also to us personally, as can be imagined. Another worry was that the banks were closed so that even had we been allowed to, there was no way for us to leave. Roy also told us that the Carmelite library had been set on fire. We went to the back of the house from where we could see the monastery clearly and saw billows of smoke and flames pouring from the building. It went on smouldering all the time we were in Toledo but the great wrought-iron cross which all along was silhouetted against the flames is still standing to this day.

There was further news: in the square of the *Ayuntamiento*,[117] bonfires had been lit by the militia from Madrid and were being continually re-stocked with crucifixes, vestments, missals, and other loot from churches and private houses. We were all in tears by this time, but Roy consoled us by telling us that our friends were in heaven at that very moment—something we believed with all our hearts—and that we still had a chance to save the Archives for posterity.

There was nothing for us to do but wait in a state of stress and apprehension. Soon the firing and shelling started up again. Shells zoomed over the house with monotonous regularity and the machine-guns never stopped their maddening chatter. All this gunfire was aimed at the Alcázar, but sometimes it fell short of the mark and crashed into the hill behind our house. One shell went right into the house and exploded in the room where we always took refuge, but by then we had left.

During siesta time all the firing stopped; the heat, which that year reached 42 degrees centigrade, was too much even for the tough Spanish soldiers, and it was during this interval that the civilians got things done, going for water and whatever food was to be found and trying to find out what was happening in the rest of Spain. It was during one of these lulls that an old man was sent to requisition our horses. We were naturally sad to part with them, but it was also a relief as we were running short of fodder.

---

[116] Created in 1917 in Russia, its function was to liquidate counter-revolutionary movements. The Spanish communists used the same name.
[117] Town Hall.

Poetic Justice

Some months before the Civil War, Granny Campbell had sent us two Union Jacks. Mary thought the time had come to hang these up. With some difficulty this was done, but half an hour later, when they were hanging limply in the heat, a girl called Pepa, daughter of one of the chief Reds in the district, came running up with a message from the militiamen to say that if we did not take down that "fascist" flag at once the house would be blown to smithereens. They also ordered us to fly the *real* flag, the red one.

"But," Mary protested furiously, "we haven't got a red *flag*. The only red thing in the house is my silk pyjamas!"

"We'll fly those, Kid," Roy said, "though I should have thought there was enough red in the Union Jack to satisfy the most fanatical bolshy." He burst out laughing.

We all tried to help in hanging up the pyjamas, but every time we got them up they fell down again until we were speechless with laughter. We rolled about with tears pouring down our faces. In the end it became a sort of game, but at last with one final fling of contempt the wretched Red Flag stayed in the topmost branches of a tree looking utterly incongruous. What a marvellous relief that laughter was. For the first time in days my small body stopped being shaken by spasms of trembling which utterly exhausted me.

Flora left at about this time. Her faithful fiancé, now an involuntary recruit in the Militia, called to take her back to her village. We were all in tears when she strapped her possessions to the inevitable donkey.

The worst part of our ordeal was still to come in the form of a search party. This took place some time after Flora had gone. I was on the terrace with Blanca during one of the lulls in the fighting, when I heard the tinkle of the garden bell and looking down saw a file of militiamen entering the garden and coming up the steps. They had cartridge belts around their chests, and their rifles bobbed up and down as they walked. All my fear returned and I started to shiver again. I ran to warn my parents. Roy went to the entrance hall and waited for them very calmly. Since the first day of fighting he had become someone quite new. All his habitual nervousness disappeared. He kept up our spirits and, once the shock of realising we were caught in a Terror was over, he behaved with complete sang-froid. I often noticed this in Roy's life because I saw him in grave danger quite a lot of times. It was the apprehension of danger, when his imagination ran riot, that made him fearful. Once the thing actually happened, he felt a release and realised it was not so bad after all.

The leader of the search party said that we had been denounced as priest-harbourers and they had come to arrest those we were protecting, and any

A Memoir of my Father, Roy Campbell

other "fascists" there might be in the house. Roy told them to look wherever they wanted, and they dispersed through the house. One young man stayed behind to do up his rope-soled *alpargatas*.[118] To do so he sat on one of the stacks of St. John's works. Mary, who was standing next to me, gave me a steadying look and squeezed my hand. I must have made a nervous gesture to try and get him away from the precious MSS. We both watched this extraordinary sight in stunned silence, until the young man got up and hurried after his companions.

In the meantime, the other men, after looking rather desultorily under beds and behind cupboards, gradually foregathered in the sitting-room where there were rows and rows of bookcases. They pulled the books off the shelves and began looking at the illustrations. Some of them were holding the books upside down. I have always been touched by the passion for learning shown by so many simple-minded, politically muddled men. It was Roy who taught me to feel like this. It was obvious to him that much of the chaotic state of the world was due to "a little learning...". Marxist teachers and professors the world over have a lot to answer for. They are so good at fostering negative feelings in their pupils but never give them any foundation for living. It is so much simpler to teach people to hate than it is to teach them to love! Roy thought that Marx was anti-Christ because Christ taught that love could save the world, whereas Marx really believed that hate would level things down into equality.

The militiamen asked Roy all sorts of questions. It was good to see these young men gradually relax under his influence. When he wanted to, he could charm anyone. He looked particularly handsome that day. Not having laid hands on a single glass of wine since the hostilities began, he had the alert, fine-drawn look which was natural to him and which under the influence of drink became blurred and made him look sleepy. That day he looked clear-cut and very noble.

The leader, or chief, or whatever he was, who had some authority over the other *milicianos,* was holding a thick volume of the Divina Commedia. He was staring with fascination at Doré's drawings of hell, and he asked, "What is this one about?"

"Ah, that is a great Italian poet, Dante."

"Italian? All Italians are fascists."

"Well, perhaps, but here we have Gogol, Dostoevsky, Tolstoy—you see, all Russians."

"Ah, Russians..."

Immediately they heard that word, they all looked up with broad smiles. They never tired of hearing about the "Workers' Paradise" where "justice, brotherly

---

[118] Sandals.

Poetic Justice

love, and freedom reigned." What irony, at the time of Stalin's worst atrocities!

"Yes,' Roy went on. 'You see this heavy book here? This is Karl Marx's DAS KAPITAL."

"Who is that?"

"That, my friends, was the first theoretical Marxist."

Now there was real excitement. "Marxista, Marxista… are you a Marxist?"

"I, Senores, am a poet."

This was equally interesting. A poet in Spain was, at that time, as important as he had always been in pastoral societies since the beginning of history. And, thank goodness, it was the right thing to have said at that moment. A sudden look of respect was reflected on all those faces, the age-old veneration for the poet, the *singer*.

Knowing that the man they had come to arrest for harbouring priests was a poet suddenly made these men come to their senses and they became self-conscious and human. In the customary way of simple people, they began to get ready for departure. They sighed, coughed, and shook hands, one after another as they went, using the new substitute for "Go with God," "Health Comrade!". Then they filed out never to return.

I noticed that all our faces had a little colour in them except for Mary who was looking rather strained, "I did not have time to hide the crucifix round my neck, and I've been trying to cover it with my hand all the time they were here." Roy told us that we had had a lucky escape. He said the *milicianos* were trigger-happy and that he had seen a dog shot, while he was in town, just because it had frightened one of these men. He begged Mary to stop wearing anything that could lead to our arrest.

There was such an orgy of massacres going on that even the most squeamish militiamen were becoming quite blasé about murder. In the Madrid gaols they even had a macabre parody of the evening *Paseo*.[119] The militia were allowed into the prisons every evening to walk round and round while the prisoners were taking their exercise. They would stop someone they did not like the look of and say, "This one is mine," and drag the wretched man off to be shot to the jeers and laughter of the comrades. But if I were to recount all the terrible things, the obscene babooneries of the Reds, it would take an eternity and fill whole books; suffice it to say that they went on for three years and were very terrible.

Some days after the search party had been and gone, a young poet, a friend of Roy's, came to see us in a great state of excitement to tell the following story.[120]

---

[119] Walk, stroll.
[120] Alexander says he was carrying 3000 pesetas and a dead child (165).

Angel, as he was called, said that after the army entered the town and everyone was rushing about in a fever to know what was happening, he left his house to fetch water. In the corner of the Puerta Visagra,[121] the main entrance to Toledo, he saw a militiaman robbing a badly wounded man who was lying on the ground, groaning. The militiaman, seeing that he had been observed by Angel, hastily divided the enormous quantity of bank notes with the latter, saying, "Keep quiet." He then disappeared. Angel had just knelt to ask the wounded man who he was, when he died. Angel knew that we would be in difficulties about getting out of Toledo, and he now suggested that as we could not get our own money from the bank, we should use this for the journey to England taking him with us. After some discussion my parents believed the money was an answer to their prayers, and they decided to accept it. For "God moves in mysterious ways...".

A few days later, Roy and Angel were able to procure some "safe-conducts," and we were all set to leave. They had been told that the buses were running normally to Madrid, though not the trains, for the station was within range of the guns of the Alcázar. Our only worry now was what to take with us. Since we could only take what we could carry, the choice was limited and in the end we took the usual rubbish one decides on, on such occasions. All paper work or anything of value would have been confiscated anyway, so we left the most important things behind. Blanca was left with Mr. Boniface, and our two budgerigars were let out of their cage. I do not know what the date was when we finally left the house, but it could have been the 9th or 10th of August. We set off for the bus stop at 9 a.m. At that hour it was still reasonably cool, but as that awful day dragged on, the temperature rose from about 25 degrees centigrade to 40 degrees or over.

We only had a short walk to the bus stop which was just outside the Puerta Visagra, but even so the sporadic firing was scary. I was amazed when we got outside the great garden walls to see that everything was more or less intact. After all that noise I had imagined everything to be in ruins. At the bus stop we sat on our luggage waiting for the 9:30 bus to Madrid. We were immediately surrounded by a large group of militiamen, armed to the teeth and dressed mostly in dungarees. They all gave conflicting reports about the buses, the Alcázar, the progress of the Civil War, and so on. They also began to ask innumerable and dangerous questions. Luckily for us as the sun got hotter and hotter, they gradually dispersed, until there were only two left to guard the great gates of Visagra. By that time we had been waiting nearly three hours. It was getting on for

---

[121] Some tourist guides give this as Puerta de Bisagra. This Moorish gate was once the main entrance to Toledo.

Poetic Justice

midday, and the heat was quite literally unendurable. At last we heard the familiar hooting of the bus as it swept down from Zocodover. It was with a feeling of vast relief that we began to gather our bags together; but, to our horror, two buses went by laden to the roofs with singing and waving men and women of the militia. They did not even stop to have their papers examined, and we were left in despair amid the swirling dust.

My parents could not decide whether to wait for the evening bus or go home for the night and try again the next day. The two militiamen, who had been showing Roy photos of their wives and children in Madrid, and who kept bemoaning their fate, the stupidity of the fighting and other things, advised us to wait: some of their friends drove lorries between Toledo and a place called Algodor, where the trains still ran.

The wait took on the proportions of eternity, a sort of ante-chamber to hell. Besides the heat we were tormented by flies, thirst, hunger—it was many days since we had had anything to eat but cucumbers—and, of course, the fear which had become nightmarish. One of the militiamen shared his ration of water with Mary and us children, while Roy and Angel shared their cigarettes with him.

At last an army lorry, painted all over with skulls and cross bones, stopped and our militiamen asked the corporal to drive us to Algodor for which they were bound anyway. He adamantly refused until the bribe was big enough; then with a bad grace he asked his men to move over so that we could sit on the floor of the lorry with them. We were appalled at having to travel in that heat in an uncovered truck with all those bad-tempered soldiers, who, we found out later, were the people responsible for gathering up the bodies of murdered men and women and burying them. Still, anything was better than sitting waiting for death. The grumbling soldiers made room for us, and we piled into the back of their truck. It was a little cooler driving, which was a relief. When we got to the part of the road directly exposed to the firing from the Alcázar, we had to lie flat on the floor of the truck as the bullets whined overhead.

The soldiers kept falling asleep, and their rifles fell from their nerveless hands alarmingly. We were bumping along doing good time when an alarm clock in one of our bags began to ring. One of the soldiers, who had dozed over that bag, jumped up in real agitation and aimed his gun at each of us in turn until he realised what had happened because the clock rang on and on. We could not help laughing and even some of the soldiers joined in, but most of them glared furiously. There was one other incident on that ride: we stopped at a farmhouse for some water, and the kind peasant women gave Tess and me the two halves of a juicy pear; it was absolutely delicious.

A Memoir of my Father, Roy Campbell

At last towards evening we reached Algodor and trooped into the station restaurant. Our driver ordered ham and eggs. The owner tried to pretend there was no food to be had, but he changed his mind when the Corporal told him what his fate would be if he did not serve us immediately. After that I remember nothing until we arrived in Madrid. It was dark, and as we drove from the station to the British Embassy, we passed church after church in flames. Even now, as I shut my eyes, I can see the flames running up one steeple as though I had only just seen it. It was around midnight when we finally arrived at the blessed Embassy and real security. We rang the bell and a voice said, "Is that Roy Campbell? Thank God!" Many other refugees were there, but it appeared we had been in the greatest danger because of the battle for Toledo. We all sat on the floor and drank iced water. The next morning we were driven to the station for a train to Valencia where the hospital ship, the MAINE, was picking up British refugees. It was Major Lance who drove us; he acted as a Scarlet Pimpernel, saving many people's lives.

It was awful to be loose again among the *canaille*.[122] At the station before being allowed onto the train, we were subjected to a thorough search by the first really frightening person we had come across so far. This was a militia *woman* with death in her eyes. They do say that some of these women were far worse than the men in their fury.

It was as we were getting into the train for Valencia that Mary, who until then had been a model of silent suffering, now lost her temper for the first time. The porter, who was installing us in our places, was not pleased with his tip so Mary suddenly emptied her handbag over his head. Yes, I think we were all at the end of our tethers.

That evening we puffed into Valencia. The train went right down to the quay, and there the Captain of the MAINE (once Jennie Churchill's hospital ship) was awaiting us. He was a vision of civilisation in his immaculate whites. After what we had been through he looked like something from a different part of the Universe. Unfortunately, the expression on his face did not match his uniform. He looked at us in a supercilious and forbidding way. After all, we did not resemble Vogue mannequins. We were dishevelled, grimy from the train, exhausted, and still unnerved, partly from lack of sustenance. And it had been a long time since any of us had been able to have a bath.

We realised at once that in part because of our frightful appearance there was no hope of Angel being allowed onto the MAINE. Roy pleaded, Mary begged, but that cold face was adamant. Only British passport holders were

---

[122] Rabble; riff-raff.

Poetic Justice

permitted onto the ship. We turned to Angel, our saviour, and burst into tears. Poor Angel, he had been so full of hope. He believed so whole-heartedly in the justice of the English. Now he put his arm up to his face to hide his tears, and when I saw how shabby his sleeve was, I thought my heart would break. Had it not been for this detail I would have thought of him as a biblical angel, sent straight from God to lead us out of danger. Perhaps after all he was a real angel because after that no one ever saw or heard of him again. We left him still hiding his head in his arm, sobbing.

The next thing in this series of pictures was, I remember, being picked up by a comforting British sailor who carried me on deck and said, "There darling, all safe now"—so compassionate compared with the Captain.

Children are very resilient (though they pay later for their early sufferings). There were two little English girls playing on deck. Very prim and proper. They and their parents had boarded the ship at Majorca so they had seen no fighting. I went up to them in my dishevelled condition, dying to make friends. The younger one started to talk to me, but her sister said, "No, Jane, don't talk to her. She is poor." My God, how this hurt. It was worse than the terror of Toledo. I felt a deep, dark pain round my heart.

This rather terrible incident was redressed in the end, however. When we steamed into Victoria, all the journalists rushed onto the platform shouting, "Is Roy Campbell on this train?" Just then I saw Jane and her sister and shouted back, "Yes, he is my father!" and made a hideous face at those embryonic bourgeoises. By then we were all smartened up and looking fine, and the two girls gazed at us in admiration—we were, after all, an unusually good-looking family. The next day many newspapers had photos of Roy on their front pages, and also of Tess and me riding in the bullring,[123] along with rather lurid descriptions of our escape. Thus I felt compensated for the cruelty of the little girl. But it made me see, in later years, that Marxism-Leninism is still attractive to many people because those in the positions of power are callous or brutal about the feelings of the ones they should protect and help.

When Roy had been taken off to be interviewed by the press, we were enveloped once more in the loving, lavender-scented embrace of Grandmama and the ever-faithful Tony.

End of Part 1

---

[123] Tess describes this event in more detail in ch. 17.

A Memoir of my Father, Roy Campbell

The Fight[124]

One silver-white and one of scarlet hue,
Storm-hornets humming in the wind of death,
Two aeroplanes were fighting in the blue
Above our town; and if I held my breath,
It was because my youth was in the Red
While in the White an unknown pilot flew—
And that the White had risen overhead.

From time to time the crackle of a gun
Far into flawless ether faintly railed,
And now, mosquito-thin, into the Sun,
And now like mating dragonflies they sailed:
And, when like eagles near the earth they drove,
The Red, still losing what the White had won,
The harder for each lost advantage strove.

So lovely lay the land—the towns and trees
Taking the seaward counsel of the stream:
The city seemed, above the far-off seas,
The crest and turret of a Jacob's dream,
And those two gun-birds in their frantic spire
At death-grips for its ultimate regime—
Less to be whirled by anger than desire.

Till (Glory!) from his chrysalis of steel
The Red flung wide the fatal fans of fire:
I saw the long flames, ribboning, unreel,
And slow bitumen trawling from his pyre.
I knew the ecstasy, the fearful throes,
And the white phoenix from his scarlet sire,
As silver in the Solitude he rose.

---

[124] Pearce notes that this poem was composed at Altea. In this poem, Campbell "pours out the fervour of his Christian conversion […] 'the fight' is being waged for the poet's soul […]. Clearly the struggle is not merely between belief and unbelief, but between the poet's new and previous self. His youth, scarlet with sinfulness and red with the political atheism he had rejected, was at war with a new force in his life—the 'white', symbolic of the Mithraic unity of the spectral colours and also of the dimly discerned purity of Christ, the 'unknown pilot'." (165)

Poetic Justice

The towers and trees were lifted hymns of praise,
The city was a prayer, the land a nun:
The noonday azure strumming all its rays
Sang that a famous battle had been won,
As signing his white Cross, the very Sun,
The Solar Christ and captain of my days
Zoomed in the azure; and his will was done.[125]

Roy Campbell, 1934

---

[125] The last line of the version of this poem in COLLECTED WORKS I reads: "Zoomed to the zenith; and his will was done."

Chapter XIII

The "*money from South Africa*" having got stuck in our bank in Toledo, we found ourselves broke in a London hotel, the only income being what Roy was able to earn from articles he managed to place in certain papers and magazines. We stayed in London for about two weeks. After that Mary's sister, the beautiful Lorna Garman, offered us her house for a fortnight while she and her family were away at the seaside.

Marsh Farm was one of those ancient English houses that do so much to soothe the spirit. I remember with gratitude the time we spent there. The orchards were laden with apples and Victoria plums, the shrubberies were filled with birds, the stalls with cows, the ponds with geese and ducks, and the garages with Bentleys. In front of the house a wide lawn stretched away to a poplared stream in the distance.

This delightful respite was short-lived. Hardly recovered from the traumas we had received in Spain, we were plunged once again into civil strife. My parents were completely unaware that Marsh Farm was the centre of a Stalinist cult, and had they been forewarned of this state of affairs nothing in the world would have induced them to go near the place. The Squire of Binstead, Mary's brother-in-law, was a fervent admirer of Soviet Russia. Much of the Wishart fortune had gone to subsidise Soviet propaganda, and the attics of Marsh Farm are still stacked with the unsellable works of their master, Lenin.

Directly Ernest Wishart[126] returned, Binstead was divided into two factions. The one on the left was composed of Wishart himself, Dr. Drury, the parson who was also an atheist, Douglas Garman, Mary's brother and a militant communist, and Peggy Guggenheim, the millionairess.[127] On the right were my par-

---

[126] Ernest Wishart (1902-1987) was a socialist publisher and gentleman farmer. He was married to Lorna (when she was 16), the youngest of the Garman children. He joined the Communist Party of Great Britain in 1935.

[127] It was Douglas Garman (1903-1969) who introduced Ernest Wishart to his sister, Lorna. According to Connolly, fourteen year old Lorna seduced the much older Wishart in a hayrick (49). Douglas was to work for Wishart's publishing company. Douglas was married to Jeanne Hewitt (who, in 1932, had an affair with Mary while her sister, Lisa,

ents, a hesitant Lorna Wishart, Lady Wishart (the Squire's mother), and the two chauffeurs: Cook, who drove Lady Wishart, and Floyd, who drove the Squire. When these two teams gathered at Marsh Farm, the rafters rang with their outraged cries. Tess and I, lying upstairs trying to sleep, agreed that it was almost as bad as the battle for Toledo, and we were heartily relieved when Lady Wishart offered us her Glebe House some two miles away.

After we moved, Wishart and Roy hardly ever met, but they only had to see each other to start up again—a bit like those dogs one sees who seem to have forgotten their quarrel but at some given moment start up again as though demented. I remember a tea-party before which my parents had made a vow not to mention politics because Wish was coming. Everything went along smoothly for a bit, until Wish announced something he had read in THE DAILY WORKER: about it being all lies that the Reds were murdering people without trial. Roy, his face ashen with indignation, stood over Wish and said fiercely, "You mutt! You mutt!" and then walked out of the room, horrified at the credulity of these people. Mary, who felt as he did, said nothing but looked infinitely sad.

It was too much to bear and made the hideous things that were happening in Spain far worse. That the horripilant[128] *Brigadas del Amanecer* (Dawn Brigades) killed 16,000 people without trial during the first month of the war—the wall against which they stood their victims had a deep trench, heart high—the salon communists would not believe. It was too inconvenient for their ideals to face what was really happening.

I shall never forget the morning when the Alcázar was mined. We were at breakfast as Mary returned from mass with the papers. On the front pages were photos of the mountain of rubble to which the fortress had been reduced. There were also photos of the town being evacuated and jolly snapshots of the Pasionaria, Margarita Nelken,[129] Malraux,[130] Largo Caballero,[131] Russian advisors, and other Red stars picnicking beside their expensive cars as they waited in delighted expectation for the blasting of the garrison to begin.

---

became Roy's lover). Douglas Garman and Peggy Guggenheim became lovers after her partner, John Holms, died. He joined the Communist Party of GB in 1934.
[128] French, meaning insupportable, exasperating.
[129] (1896-1968) Art critic, literary critic and feminist. A socialist, she was one of a small number of women elected to the Spanish Parliament during the Republic (1931-36). (Katharina M. Wilson, AN ENCYCLOPEDIA OF CONTINENTAL WOMEN WRITERS, Vol. II. London: Routledge, 1991: 911.)
[130] (1901-1976) French author and adventuror, André Malraux joined the Republican forces in Spain.
[131] (1869-1946) Francisco Largo Caballero, Spanish socialist and trade unionist. In 1936-7 he was Prime Minister of the Spanish Republic.

All was gloom at Glebe House that day. But there was great rejoicing in the other faction. The resistance or surrender of the fortress had become a matter of extreme importance to both sides. Then the next morning the rejoicing was reversed. It was announced on the radio that the garrison was still holding out. We were elated: the ill and wounded men in the ruins of the Alcázar had not been overcome by the militia hordes.

Our knees had become bruised while praying for the deliverance of that gallant band of men. The whole Catholic world had prayed with the defenders, and when our prayers were answered we were overcome and overawed. You had to be stony-hearted indeed not to be moved by so much heroism. But nothing seemed to move the Binsted Reds, and when the siege was lifted by General Varela[132] two days later, they were simply livid with anger.

Roy wrote to Wyndham Lewis at that time:

> *I'm delighted you like those boys in the Alcázar. Everybody here was gloating at the news of the mine. But it turned out the other way. Western Europeans, especially Latins and Celts, are not Russians. If they think anyone wants to get at their throats, they strike terrible quick and hard first. The Alcázar was proof of West versus East. I think I told you my faith in those men, they are heroes and saints. That steel wedge, the Christian and Classical mind, can now drive right into the materialists. It was a victory of the spirit over avoirdupoid.[133] It shows that spiritual people are even better as materialists, and 50 times braver... For years you have been the prophet of something like this miracle. If you look at my new book [*MITHRAIC EMBLEMS*] you will see that spooring you I became a small prophet myself, a local one. The battle of the aeroplanes* ["The Fight"] *was written in 1934, before I ever saw Toledo and it was printed in* TIME AND TIDE *before there was any Civil War. All the work in this book prefigures what is happening now—and the victory of Christ....*

About this time a young Spanish girl, who was stranded at her finishing school in London on the outbreak of the Civil War, was introduced to my parents through mutual friends. She had not heard a word from her family who were in hiding in a Republican-held area, and she feared greatly for their lives. To make things worse her school fees had not been paid for the last term. So it was decided that she should come and live with us until she could return home to Barcelona. Josephine Bosch became a wonderful addition to the family. She

---

132 (1891-1951) José Enrique Varela Iglesias: Spanish military commander who, during the Civil War, organised the Carlists' militia, the Requetés, into a formidable military organisation.

133 Meaning excess weight, heaviness.

Poetic Justice

had immense tact and was always good-tempered and sunny; she shared our sense of humour and got on with us all equally well. Tess and I did our lessons with her. We were soon such good friends that we shared everything together; it was like having a rather sophisticated elder sister. She taught us a lot.

My parents were lonely among British intellectuals. Except for Yeats, Wyndham Lewis, Edmund Blunden, and one or two others, everyone was drunk with enthusiasm for the other side.[134] Gradually the idea of going to another country became stronger.

One day in the autumn of 1936 Lewis rang up to ask Roy to go up to London because he had arranged a meeting with Sir Oswald Mosley.[135] He thought these two men would be on the same wave length. I sometimes wonder whether Lewis even began to understand Roy. Lewis had been singing Mosley's praises for so long that Roy went off expecting great things. When he returned that evening, he looked tired and wan, and to Mary's questions he answered, "It's no good, Kid. He's as bad as the others." I do not think he had taken a personal dislike to Mosley, but I do know that politicians in general were the only people for whom he felt an automatic dislike. He distrusted the whole world of politics and thought this planet could easily get on without it.

In his memoirs Sir Oswald Mosley says, "I found [Wyndham Lewis] agreeable but touchy. Roy Campbell was an altogether more robust character.... These gifted men will undoubtedly get the recognition they deserve when their opinions cease to be unpopular...". Of course, Roy agreed with Mosley about certain things. I remember from my earliest years hearing him groaning over Britain's disarmament policy. "What idiots," he used to say, "even the Romans knew that an unprotected country leads to war." He was quoting Vegetius:[136] "Let him who desires peace, prepare for war." And when Hitler invaded Czechoslovakia, Roy tended to think the British Empire was safe as long as the Germans went on advancing eastwards. He hoped, as did a great many right-thinking people at the time, that Germany and Russia would fight each other without dragging in the rest of the world. They could at least weaken each other to such an extent that neither was a threat to civilisation. He knew, with his prophetic gifts,

---

134 Spender says that it was Fascism—and the rejection thereof—that created "a new political class—the anti-Fascists" (WORLD WITHIN WORLD, London: Faber and Faber, 1997: xiii). This movement, made up of individuals of diverse persuasions, appealed to "the conscience of each individual" (Spender, xv).

135 (1896-1980) British politician, founder of the anti-communist British Union of Fascists in 1932. His autobiography, MY LIFE, was published in 1968.

136 Flavius Vegetius Renatus, the 4th century Roman military expert who wrote an influential military treatise.

that to help Russia in any way would be disastrous. He and Lewis and Mosley, because they had brains and instincts and perhaps even more because they knew their history backwards, so to speak, concurred on these points. But they can not be branded as fellow-fascists. On the contrary, Roy detested fascism, especially after reading MEIN KAMPF. "No good can come from a teetotalitarian vegetarian," he said. And this was in the early Thirties.

Roy and Lady Wishart had become great friends. She kept his photo on her desk until her death. She used to send Cook over once or twice a week to fetch us all for luncheon at her Brighton mansion. At other times she would have fresh lobsters and apple jelly delivered to Glebe House.

At last, because of its proximity to Spain, my parents decided to go to Portugal. By this time, December, my Aunt Lorna had chosen to become a Catholic following Mary's example. The two sisters often went riding on the Downs together, and Lorna would drive Mary to the Cathedral at Arundel. They remained good friends until Mary's death in 1979. Lorna is now the one who goes to daily mass. She must be well into her seventies, but she still has the most beautiful cornflower blue eyes. She must have been one of the great beauties of this century.[137]

---

[137] Born in 1911, she was the youngest of the Garman children. Peggy Guggenheim described her as "the most beautiful creature I had ever seen" (Connolly, 136) and her friend, Pauline Tennant, said that with her "profoundly blue eyes" she was "*remarkably* beautiful" (Connolly 151). While married to Ernest Wishart, she had a child by Laurie Lee, and then an affair with Lucien Freud. She later converted to Catholicism. Lorna died in 2000.

Poetic Justice

Chapter XIV

In the middle of January 1937, after saying goodbye to the innumerable friends and enemies we had made, we were driven by Grandmama and Tony to Southampton where we boarded a German boat, the NIASSA, which used to go every week to and from Lisbon. It was snowing as we stood on deck waving to our dear old ladies. As the NIASSA steamed out of the port, the band struck up, and we went down to our cabins. That night we sailed into one of the worst cyclones ever to tear up the coast of Portugal. The cyclone and the NIASSA entered the Bay of Biscay at the same time. Mary, Josephine, Tess, and I became so sea-sick that we did not fully realise what was happening: although the juddering and creaking and plunging of the boat was at times really terrifying. The ship behind us, which was the same size as the NIASSA, went down with no survivors.

Roy was in his element: he never suffered from sea-sickness; the rougher the sea the more he enjoyed it. He came to see us every half-hour or so to try to console us. On the second day we were allowed to go on deck. The waves were unrecognisable, more like gigantic walls of water sweeping towards us. I felt, every time one of those walls reached our ship, that we would be engulfed, but miraculously it managed to surmount the mass of water while only a huge fountain of spray dashed over the prow. We were able to sit on deck drinking beef tea as the stewards tucked blankets snugly around us. The Nazi flag was at half-mast, and this was when we were told that our accompanying ship had gone down. When we arrived at Lisbon, the Tagus was flooded, and the masts of many sunken ships stuck up out of the water.

In Lisbon we stayed at the Pensao Lis in the Avenida da Liberdade. The town was so romantic then, very foreign and full of delightful surprises, as though it had turned its back on Europe and opened itself to the many influences of Portugal's various colonies, especially those in China. Even the houses had turned-up roofs, like pagodas. In the streets we would hear the fishwives, still wearing their traditional dresses of green and blue, shouting their wares in raucous voices as they ran nimbly up and down carrying shallow baskets of gleamingly fresh fish on their heads. Round their necks they wore all their worldly wealth: thick, golden necklaces from which hung golden filigree hearts.

We did not stay long in Lisbon. Estoril was recommended to us, "where all the English go." "God forbid," said my parents, "we shall travel in the opposite direction." And so we ended up in the fishing village of Sesimbra, where we stayed for about nine months, living at first in the Pensao Chic and later in a house on the beach.

Josephine, Tess, and I made friends with practically the whole village. Josephine was a great flirt and soon had the chemist, the tubercular student from Coimbra, the mayor, the doctor, and the owner of the biggest shop in love with her. She was marvellous in that, without giving an inch to any of them, she managed to keep them all happy and in thrall. Tess was adored by the sacristan of the church, a handsome youth, but going to mass became a self-conscious business. Even I had a *faiblesse*[138] for a boy with black curls and green eyes who winked at me every time we passed each other in the street. Josephine was taken to the Town Hall dance every Saturday where she was a *succés fou*.[139] She was neither pretty nor beautiful, but she bubbled over with love for everyone and was full of charm.

Mary painted and helped the Sisters of Charity to look after the many cases of tuberculosis there were in the village.

In the meantime Roy was preparing to go to Spain to join up. I could not stop him from doing this, since I was only eleven at the time. In any event, I had reached saturation point in being preoccupied about him. I was beginning to realise that he got on just as well whether I was worried about him or not. So I decided to put him out of my mind as much as possible. Also, one of his most acute pre-composition periods was upon him, and this made his moods difficult to bear.

I remember going for a picnic with him just before he left for Spain. Tess and Josephine took it in turns to prepare these *dejeuners sur l'herbe*[140] and that day was Josephine's. We climbed the steep hill to the Moorish castle at the top. It was already quite hot although we were only in March, and the climb was not easy. When we had everything spread out on the grass, it was discovered that the wine had been forgotten. Roy immediately went into a deep sulk, and Josephine was upset that she had forgotten this essential part of the meal. She was moodily peeling an orange, when, by mistake, she threw a large piece straight into his eye. There was a moment of awed silence, and then he began to laugh. He

---

[138] Weakness.
[139] Mad, wild success.
[140] Picnics.

laughed and laughed and so did we all. "What a horrible person I am," he said. "I'm so sorry, Josephine, but I must say that your tactics for getting someone out of a bad mood are marvellous." Then he kissed her hand.

And shortly after this Roy went off Spain to join up. The whole summer passed without our seeing him. He wrote the following letter while on his way:

> Dearest,
> I am writing in the train—we have gone about 1/3rd of the way to the border. I am very comfy as I squared the guard to give me a first-class seat. I hope you are not very tired after your trip. Tell Tessy and Anna that I expect them to look after you for me.[141]
>
> I feel very calm on the train, not at all as though I were going on an "adventure."…This is the Porto train and we change engines in about an hour—I'm afraid we don't pass through the Sierra de Gredos: but I shall on my way to Toledo.
>
> God bless you my darling. I hope you keep fit. Don't worry about me as it will be worrying about nothing at all. I am reading Gringoire's book—it makes me laugh like anything—all about Blooms.[142] St. Audaire's book is brilliant. You ought to read that book of Daudet's "PARIS VÉCU" which I left in my room. Coimbra looks a lovely place—with a great big river streaming in forks among islands of white sand and poplar trees. We have just left it. I wish I had brought a map to see how we get nearer to Spain as I am longing to get there.… All my dearest love to you and to Tess and Anna and my best wishes to Josephine. Roy

And Roy wrote this letter on the train as his journey took him from one town to another:

> Darling Tessy and Anna, I shall write from Salamanca and Toledo. I miss you all very much even in the first three hours. Pray for Spain and for Franco, love from Dad. I have got to Salamanca, it is wonderful. The troops look splendid. I have just met a Carmelite Father who knows Fr. Evaristo[143] and says Fr. Felipe is here in Salamanca. He thinks Evaristo is in Toledo. I have spent most of my time chasing after safe-conducts etc. I shall write later. Don't worry about me.… God bless you all. R.

Later came this letter for Mary:

Salamanca

1937

> Dearest one,

---

[141] Mary had been very run down since we arrived in Portugal. (ACL)
[142] The Bloomsburites (sic). (ACL)
[143] Fr. Evaristo escaped the massacre in Toledo as he was in Avila. (ACL)

A Memoir of my Father, Roy Campbell

Señor Merry del Val[144] was very kind to me indeed and has given me letters for Seville—for Queipo de Llano[145] and others.

We have had rain and storms ever since I came here. I am in a good Hotel pension, 10 ptas a day. I dare say I shall be off to the Madrid front as soon as my salvo-conducto[146] is ready. Señor Merry del Val seems to be a charming man. I feel I must see as much of Salamanca as possible before I go. I am being very economical. I have your photo on my table as I write so I am not as lonely as I might be.

I have done a lot of work by night since I came here and have nearly finished that thing about the Toledo Carmelites. It is very quiet here at night but the central square is extremely lively until about 11 P.M.

I went to the Carmelite church here for mass. One of the fathers here knew all about us which he had heard from Padre Evaristo. I shall keep all the news until I come back. It is all good news and will improve for being kept. I have just seen a horse which I nearly mistook for Gaona but he did not have that white mark. What fun it would be if I managed to find Gaona and Moro[147] in Toledo!... Love to Tess and Anna and Josephine and most of all to yourself. You promised not to worry about me, remember! And you won't have any cause. God bless you my darling one. Roy.

I know that Roy was very disappointed not to be allowed to join up. In a letter written to his mother he says he tried hard to get into the Legión but had been turned down for not being fit enough. It was one of the toughest branches of the Army. He has been criticised for saying that he actually fought in the Spanish Army, but I find nothing wrong with this. It was Poetic Justice.[148] He did his best to get in and that was equivalent, for him, with having done so. The courage needed was the same. He really longed to fight the communists physically, but since he was unable to do so *he fought for Christianity and against Communism with his pen.*

When he came back in September, it was obvious he had been through a very tough time; the limp, which he was to have for the rest of his life, started while he was away. Upon returning he wrote "A Letter from the San Mateo Front."[149] He had spent the last month at San Mateo, north of Madrid, and it

---

[144] Head of Ministry of Culture. (ACL)
[145] General Queipo de Llano who liberated Seville. (ACL)
[146] Safe conduct.
[147] Our horses requisitioned by the militia. (ACL)
[148] Title of Anna's memoirs. For more on this see "Introduction".
[149] The editors of the COLLECTED WORKS where a version of the poem appears, note that the poem was originally the first book of FLOWERING RIFLE (1939), but was altered

Poetic Justice

was there that he witnessed the surrender of a battalion of the International Brigade. The men had wanted to capitulate to the Italians because they had heard such tall stories of what the Nationalists did to their prisoners. They thought they might be eaten or skinned alive. As a matter of fact Franco never used anything but the firing squad to avenge the outrages of the anarchists and communists in their three-year reign of terror.

If one reads "San Mateo Front" and "Flowering Rifle," one can see what Roy meant by fighting for Franco. Everything he says in these two poems was true: that during the war the Democracies sent so much food to Red Spain the crops were constantly neglected and that locusts kept coming over to eat the crops on the Nationalist side. Then after Franco's victory and despite the great famine that came once the fighting was over, the same Democracies ceased to provide anything for the Spanish poor. Roy has been criticised for using the collective "we" when writing "Flowering Rifle," as though referring to himself as a Spaniard; in fact he was simply identifying himself as a fellow-Catholic.

Mary was sad all the time that Roy was in Spain. She not only missed him but also her home in Toledo and all the friends who had been shot. She suffered too from the fallow time that succeeds the heady fertility of conversion.

We younger ones were tired of suffering and sought pleasure, now that the summer holidays had started, wherever we could. In the summer Sesimbra became a family seaside resort. The tragedy-laden atmosphere of the winter, when fishermen quite often lost their lives, was put aside for a few months of sun. The usual sight of fishermen bravely trying to get their boats over the gigantic Atlantic breakers was replaced by a vista of bathing huts and ice-cream vendors.

We spent the whole day and much of the night on the beach. From Coimbra came many students in their romantic black capes and with the inevitable guitar or mandolin under their arms. By then we had formed a large group of young people, and we used to sail away for the day to beaches inaccessible by land owing to the steep cliffs. The fishermen, bronzed and salty as the sea in winter,[150] grilled sardines; then we ate watermelons by the light of the moon, to the sound of the mournful *fados*[151] which so delight the Lusitanians.

Towards the end of August, on the recommendation of our good friends the Caupers, an Anglo-Portuguese family of great charm, Mary decided to go south to the Algarve where the coming winter would be much milder.

---

and published as an integral poem in COLLECTED POEMS (Vol. I: 655-6).

[150] The original has "the sea in wit". This seems to be a typo.

[151] Music, characterised by melancholic tunes and lyrics.

Chapter XV

The Algarve, in those days, was unspoilt and had such strong characteristics that it was like a little country on its own—in fact Portugal used to be called The Kingdom of Portugal and the Algarves.

We rented a pretty house in the village of Estombar, near Portimao. Roy bought three horses, and when we all went on excursions together, we rented two donkeys as well.

We made many friends among the Portuguese and the foreigners who came to Praia da Rocha, one of the most beautiful beaches in the world. Among these was an American woman, Baroness Zglinitsky,[152] who had just published a book called DEATH IN THE MORNING about her experiences in the Civil War. She became a life-long friend. Then Roy's French translator, Armand Guibert,[153] came, amazing the Estombarese with his party of chic Parisian women in bright-coloured slacks.

The winter in the Algarve was a delight because of the miles and miles of almond blossom stretching in every direction. Roy loved to wander off into this sea of blossom on his black mare, Garota, whose delicate hooves trod on a carpet of miniature iris of intense blue.

As usual, Roy wrote FLOWERING RIFLE at one go. For six weeks or so we hardly saw him, and when it was finished Mary took him to the sanctuary of Fatima, north of Lisbon, where the Virgin Mary appeared to three shepherd children in May, 1917, and predicted the Russian Revolution and that the whole world would become communist if people did not mend their ways.

After leaving the sanctuary, my parents stopped to get some provisions to eat on their way home. Roy had his *bota,* or wine-skin, filled at the same time. But when they stopped for lunch and he took a sip, he found the wine had turned to water. Since he had watched the taverner pour the wine in, there was no question of having been cheated; anyway, wine is more plentiful in the

---

152 Helen Nicholson, Baroness De Zglinitzki, DEATH IN THE MORNING: A WOMAN'S EXPERIENCES OF THE CIVIL WAR IN SPAIN. London: Lovat Dickinson, 1937.
153 HOMMAGE À ROY CAMPBELL: CHOIX DE POEMES (1958).

Poetic Justice

Iberian Peninsula, very often, than water. Roy took it to be an indication that he should abstain from strong drink until the end of the Civil War. He took a vow on the spot to this effect and kept it so well that, when Franco won the war in 1939, he was almost dead from anaemia.

In the spring of 1938 Josephine returned to her parents who had managed to escape to France from their hideout in Barcelona and were now back in Spain, at Burgos, Franco's capital. My parents made plans to return to Toledo at the same time. Then we were to go to Italy for six months and there Granny Campbell would join us at Christmas.

Tess and I spent the summer with friends in Portugal while my parents went to Toledo. We all met up again at Seville in September, 1938. Mary was rejuvenated by her stay in Spain and looked particularly beautiful. We spent two nights in Seville and then went on by bus to Gibraltar where we boarded the Italian liner, IL REX. While we were on deck waiting to sail, we saw, looming through the mist, the great bulk of the British battleship, the HOOD. Roy pointed it out to us with great emotion, his eyes full of tears: he was thinking of Trafalgar and the glories of the Royal Navy and of his great hero, Nelson.

As we sailed into the Bay of Naples and saw Vesuvius smoking peacefully in the sun, we were told about de Lisle Adam saying, *"Les coussins de ma mere sont plus pareilles..."* meaning, no doubt, that the embroidery on the cushions of his mother (of Vesuvius) were better proportioned than the original.

In Rome we lived in the Via Donatello in the top floor flat of a pretty, three-storied house, owned by a doctor. Roy was lionized. Mrs. Strong, the then leader of Roman society, introduced my parents to King Alfonso XIII of Spain and his court. They had all been reading FLOWERING RIFLE, which they much admired, and the King embraced Roy who was delighted. He loved Royalty. My parents were also introduced to Prince and Princess Rospigliosi who became their good friends, and the Maxwell-Scotts, who headed the British Institute at that time.[154]

Granny stayed a month in Rome, at the old Hotel de Russie in the Piazza del Popolo. In January she took us to Venice and we said goodbye to her. We then went on to Florence where, at the Uffizi Galleries, Roy burst into tears on seeing Botticelli's PRIMAVERA. We left him standing there for about an hour.

We were in Rome between October, 1938 and April, 1939. It was the time when Pius XI died and Cardinal Pacelli was elected Pope as Pius XII of saintly memory. My parents attended his coronation in St. Peter's. Another, and unforgettable, experience for me personally was that Roy introduced me to the works of Dick-

---

[154] In her own copy of the Typographeum publication, Anna wrote in the margin: "Also the Sforza family were good friends."

ens.¹⁵⁵ But then we said goodbye to glamorous Rome—I at least, for reasons of my own, with a heavy heart.

When Franco's troops finally defeated the communists at Barcelona, we packed our bags and walked open-eyed into one of the worst famines of all time. Arriving at Irún with its blackened ruins was profoundly depressing. We stood on the station platform in the pouring rain waiting for our train to Madrid amid a crowd of soldiers in every degree of exhaustion. They lay about on their knapsacks oblivious to the cold and wet. When the train arrived, we all stumbled into it pell-mell. All semblance of comfort had long since disappeared. Every carriage window was missing, and the once red velvet seats were now greasy with dirt. This train had been used by the opposing armies for most of the war. We watched in horror as a sleek procession of bedbugs came and went, like large ants, into the upholstery. The soldiers had slumped down wherever there was room and gone to sleep. Roy stood all the way to Madrid so that at least one soldier could travel in relative comfort. Every house we passed was either burnt or machine-gunned because each inch of the territory had been fought over fiercely. It was only when we reached Avila, a town that had never known the Red occupation, that things began to look like the Spain we remembered from before the Civil War.

---

¹⁵⁵ On the same page referred to in note 150, Anna added:
"One day he walked into my room with a little green second-hand book in his hand, he threw it onto my bed, remarking: 'Here darling you may like this.' It was OLIVER TWIST. Like it! My passion for Dickens has never abated. I have re-read M.CHUZZLEWIT & D. COPPERFIELD 3 times."

Chapter XVI

We took a taxi from the station at Toledo, which is right outside the town, to 13 Airosas. On the way we were surprised to see what we took to be make-up round the eyes of the skeletal children who stood about outside their houses; later we realised that the dark lines were made by flies which the children were too apathetic to shoo away. They were starving.

In a few days so were we.

Gradually we managed to find some food, but for the next two years I, perhaps because I was still growing, never had enough to satisfy my hunger. Sometimes we could get things on the black-market at outrageous prices. At other times a rumour would go round Toledo that there was to be a distribution of rice or cocoa or black bread at a certain shop, and immediately everyone would come rushing from their houses and form a queue which was soon winding through the streets.

The families in the two little Toledo slums, however, were too far gone and too poor to partake in these activities. So the first time we got a sack of potatoes, we took it down to the poorer houses and made soup for the wretched mothers and children who lay starving on their beds. But this did not go far, and Mary, with the help of Catholic Action, and by bullying the Bishop, started a soup kitchen in the poorest district of all. She worked so devotedly and tirelessly that in six months she made the families reasonably contented. She sacrificed her last pieces of jewelry to get funds, and she had the church there re-built. She also put on a Nativity play by Lope de Vega,[156] having trained the children in their various parts. She had had good practice in this sort of work after taking care of the slum children in her native Wednesbury when she was young.

Tess seemed to me to be terribly peculiar during that rather sad summer.

---

[156] (1562-1635) He is considered by many to be Spain's finest playwright. Pearce notes that RC translated plays by Lope de Vega in the summer of 1954 when he was bedridden due to recurring malaria. The translation of FUENTE OVENJUNA by RC appears in THE CLASSIC THEATRE. VOLUME III: SIX SPANISH PLAYS. Ed. Eric Bentley. N.Y.: Doubleday (Anchor Books), 1959.

She was thrilled by the famine because she could diet drastically without anyone fussing. She seemed to have a passion for getting thinner and thinner. She had, she told me in Rome, days of terrible depression when nothing seemed worthwhile. All the time we had been in Portugal she had been perfectly normal and a great success with the young men who loved her golden hair and her lovely figure, so I was not too worried about her. But now as the days passed, she became ever more introspective. The change in her was so gradual that our parents took some time to notice it, and when they did they made her carry on with her guitar lessons and her painting, at both of which she was extremely talented. Her guitar professor in Rome had said she should never give up playing because it came naturally to her. So now she went twice a week to Madrid to carry on her studies. She became better for a time.

Roy was dreadfully bored that summer. He and I spent hours reading Dickens: he read aloud to me, impersonating the different characters brilliantly. But I could see that he was restless. He was going through a fallow time; it would soon be two years since he had finished FLOWERING RIFLE and had written nothing since.

On the 19th of May, 1939, my parents went to the Victory Parade in Madrid. Such was the poverty in the town that the Victors did not even have a rostrum to stand on. Francisco Franco was decorated with Spain's highest accolade, the Cross of San Fernando. As he stood for the march past, he was flanked by his generals: Varela, the hero of a thousand battles, Queipo de Llano,[157] whose sense of humour and wit had kept the Nationalists going through the war with his daily radio broadcasts, Yagüe,[158] the new head of the Falange, the bearded Moscardó, who was in slight disgrace for not rescuing the Italians at some time, and many others.

The parade was led by El Mizzian,[159] the Moroccan commander who had sided with the Nationalists when he heard they were fighting the atheists: "For God and for Spain." His Muslim troops were followed by the Italians under General Gambara;[160]

---

[157] (1875-1951) He was party to the military revolt that led to the Spanish Civil War. He made propaganda broadcasts during the war. There were occasions when both Queipo de Llano and Yagüe were critical of Franco (THE POLITICS OF REVENGE: FASCISM AND THE MILITARY IN TWENTIETH-CENTURY SPAIN, Paul Preston, London: Routledge, 1995: 86).

[158] (1891-1952) Under the direction of the army officer, Yuan Yagüe, thousands of prisoners and civilians were executed at Badajoz.

[159] (1897-1975) A museum dedicated to Mohamed ben Mizzian was opened in 2006.

[160] (1890-1962) Gastone Gambara, Fascist Italian general; the "most successful Italian commander of the Spanish Civil War" and later Italian ambassador to Spain (MUSSOLINI UNLEASHED, 1939-1941: POLITICS AND STRATEGY IN FASCIST ITALY'S LAST WAR, MacGregor Knox, Cambridge: Cambridge University Press, 1999 (1982): 100).

Poetic Justice

then came the Condor Legion under von Richthofen,[161] two battalions of Falange and Requeté troops in their red berets, the Foreign Legion, and the great and most popular "Conjunto de Infantes" with its glorious history. The rear was brought up by the cavalry, now entirely mechanised.

A solemn *Te Deum* was sung in the Church of Santa Barbara, and then the charismatic General Franco made his famous speech: "Lord God: accept we humbly beg you, the effort of this people, always yours, who with me, in your name, defeated with heroism the enemy of Truth in this century...".

Roy's FLOWERING RIFLE had caused a new scandal in Britain which was quickly followed by a conspiracy of silence. One of the few people to stand up for it was Edmund Blunden, the poet, to whom he wrote the following letter:

13, Airosas,
Toledo,
Spain
May 30th
1939

> *My dear Blunden,*
>
> *I was highly delighted to see that* FLOWERING RIFLE *had received your fraternal blessing. It was extremely noble and generous of you at a time like this when it is so likely to redound to your unpopularity. I am sure that this spontaneous gesture of yours has helped (more than anything inside the covers) to launch the book so successfully: I have been more than compensated by seeing it fulfilled by history as exactly as if I had written it in retrospect. I take it as an excellent omen that you should have been the only English poet to welcome it, as you are the only one who has in your blood that wisdom and those virtues whose victory it celebrates....*
>
> *The Eldorado of the British Book Trade, fell through inward putrefaction. Red Madrid was an unbelievably Hellish sight of Filth, Famine and Moral degradation and General Baboonery. The countryside had more or less reverted to locust-breeding bushveld. We are afraid of getting locusts from their side.... We have a really lovely place here. In the garden we have two fountains under huge mulberry trees and two pairs of hopoes [sic]. The craters of the Alcázar are on the hill above us. But from the rhythm of life here you would never think that this had been a front-line town through most of the war. The garden is one battlefield of roses with a twenty horse-power nightingale fusillading overhead.... To*

---

[161] (1895–1945) Wolfram Freiherr von Richthofen, cousin of the famous fighter pilot, the "Red Baron". The Condor Legion comprised volunteers from the German Air Force. They were responsible for the bombing of Guernica.

have shared in some of the moments of divine madness of these people was worth having lived for, and it was worth writing about to have aroused the spontaneous sympathy which you have so kindly shown

Dios se lo pagará[162]
Roy Campbell

When war was declared in September, Roy rushed off to Madrid to join up at the British Embassy, but since he was over age it was suggested that he should join an Intelligence Unit in Spain instead. He was terribly disappointed that he could not immediately become a soldier, a life-long ambition that kept getting thwarted. I never knew what he was doing in Intelligence, but he did seem more contented than before. He always refused to talk about his work, except to say he was helping to catch some bandits in the Sierra Nevada. It was only after his death that I knew he had worked for British Intelligence at all. He was very conscientious about this job, and I very much doubt that he ever talked to anyone else about it, as Dr. Alexander reports.

I now lost touch with my family, except during the holidays, because I spent the next two years at two different schools. The first year was with the Teresianas, and I did not enjoy that at all. The girls, mostly daughters of provincial shop-keepers, were ugly and uneducated; the teachers (nuns in lay clothes) were bigoted and most of them seemed to me to be mad; and the school itself was monstrously ugly and uncomfortable and freezingly cold. The plumbing was a nightmare. But at least there was enough to eat, if only just enough; we were never given meat, eggs, fish, or cheese, though we had plenty of lentils and potatoes, bread and oranges and an occasional piece of chocolate.

Except for Roy, whose strange job kept him continually on the alert in Toledo, we spent the summer of 1940 at Altea. But this was little better than being in devastated Toledo. Much of its charm was gone, and it was full of ghosts. There had been three years in which to execute "enemies of the people," and the *milicianos* had profited to the full. The beautiful little church too had been sacked and looted so that only the shell remained.

Because of the continuing food shortage it was decided that Tess and I should become boarders at the School of the Assumption in Madrid. After we got back to Toledo in September, the rest of the holidays was spent in preparing the endless list of things we would need: dresses, stockings, gloves, veils, sheets, blankets, cutlery, books, etc. All these had to be numbered and were meant to last for the eight years girls usually stayed at that establishment. In the event we were there for barely a year.

---

[162] Meaning, God will repay.

Poetic Justice

I loved the Assumption. I loved the nuns in their beautiful habits, the other girls, the teaching, the large, airy class-rooms, the neat little maids in their starched uniforms, and the cedar trees in the courtyard, round which the school was built and in which nested many blackbirds whose beautiful song we could hear during Benediction when the chapel windows were open. Oh, that chapel! The parents of the boarders used to send daily baskets of carnations, not just a dozen but hundreds, and the multi-coloured flowers filled the chapel with their intoxicating scent.

The great fly in this wonderful ointment was my sister's illness which became worse at the Assumption. Tess was so brave. She taught English to the older girls, took a secretarial course, and learnt German. But on the rare occasions when we met, she told me how she suffered from the cold. For her this was exacerbated because she had virtually given up eating. Goodness knows, there was little enough to eat at that school; we lived on half-cooked rice for lunch and pancakes in the evening. The other girls received large parcels of food from their families so they did not bother with what was served at the school. But Tess and I, knowing what sacrifices our parents were making in sending us to the Assumption, could not possibly worry them by telling them that we were slowly starving to death. Tess used to put her own food onto my plate which amused the other girls who watched us ironically.

The Refectory was the only place where the 500 girls gathered every day at the same time. At one end of this enormous room was a pulpit in which a sarcastic, but well-intentioned, nun always stood to see that we all behaved. She used to call attention to Tess's strangeness, which was a terrible mortification to me, though Tess herself did not mind at all. The girls invented a little rhyme which is branded on my memory. It went: *"Anita, Anita, no comas croquetas que tu pobre hermanita se queda esqueleta!"* ("Annie, Annie, don't eat rissoles; your poor little sister is becoming a skeleton!")

Gradually, what with being half starved and seeing my dearly loved sister made ever more a subject for mockery, I began to be frightened of other people. It was a slow process and only became really bothersome when I was eighteen.

I loved the schooling I was getting. Always first in my class, I found the lessons of enthralling interest. French, which had stayed in my mind since Provençal days, came back and I was asked to read Hugo and Lamartine to the whole class. My parents used to come once or twice a month to see us and take us out to lunch at the British Legation with Professor Starkie[163] and his beautiful Italian

---

[163] (1894-1976) Walter Starkie, Irish scholar, Hispanist, author and musician; founder of the British Institute in Madrid. He was married to Italia Augusta Porchietti.

wife. At other times we went to the only restaurant in Madrid that appeared to have any food. It was a modern, German place all made of glass. Here you could get beefsteaks, bread and butter, and cakes. It was frightfully expensive, and we were really put off our food, starving though we were, because of the people who, even less well off, pressed their faces against the huge plate-glass windows watching every mouthful we took.

I began to be very worried about my sister. I overheard some girls saying that she was becoming more eccentric every day. She had a way of putting her finger to her lips and keeping it there as though she were saying "hush" all the time. On top of that she fell in love with the head girl, Sonsoles, a beautiful aristocrat with green eyes and golden hair. This was embarrassing because she sometimes fainted when Sonsoles spoke to her. Finally, as well as being painfully thin, she became desperately ill with pneumonia. The nuns were casual about Tess's illness; she was not even put in the Infirmary. But I could see that she was dying. I sent our parents a telegram, and they came posthaste. They got a specialist, who prescribed M and B, a forerunner of penicillin, and Tess went back to Toledo to convalesce.

Roy was unhappy because Mary would not let him go back to England to join up. She did not like the idea of being alone in Spain. I think she was unwise about this. It would have been far better to let him get away from us all for a while. He sometimes found family life a bit of a strain. Really he could get no peace until he actually enlisted to fight Hitler, and this was a heaven sent opportunity to fulfill his lifelong ambition to become a soldier. Also, he thought he was giving his political enemies an opportunity to attack him. Later, while he was on active service in East Africa, he read in the MANCHESTER GUARDIAN: "Where has the fascist bully, Roy Campbell, got to now?" They had not even bothered to find out. I am always surprised when he is referred to as a "bully." No one had less of that characteristic than he; he was gentle to a fault, as all the people who knew him well have so often testified. What was strange about my father was that he always made light of his gifts as a poet, but exaggerated his prowess in the fields of action. I used to feel about him that he was on such a different plane from other people that he often suffered from loneliness, as though he was not really in this world, but came down to it from time to time.

It was, of course, inevitable that we should go back to England. All my parents' dormant patriotism began to stir when they thought Britain was in real

Poetic Justice

danger. But I knew nothing about their decision to return until I went home for the summer holidays.

We left at the end of June, 1941. We had never been to Segovia before, so we took our leave of Spain—my parents thought they would never see it again—by going there for a week. Then we took the train from Atocha, in Madrid, to Lisbon. The journey took twelve hours, and from the train we gazed with fascination at that lovely, wild part of Spain full of cork-trees and giant grey rocks. The birds, especially bee-eaters, partridges, and rollers, were in their thousands all along the line and perched on the telegraph wires like notes of music. But the thing that filled us with most wonder was the bread. Small, fresh loaves of white bread. And butter! It was two years since we had had our fill of these delicacies.

We were met at the station in Lisbon by our old friends, the Caupers, who took us to their lovely home in the Estrada da Luz. These kind people put the top story of their house at our disposal.

Roy stayed only three days and then left us to sail on a small ship to Gibraltar where he joined a convoy going to England. So many ships were being sunk by U-boats at the time, it was decided that Mary, Tess, and I should go on later when there was room on a clipper. There was a six months waiting-list, so we simply idled away our time, which was the worst possible thing for me just then. I was frankly in despair and began to have neurotic fears. I remember waking one night and sitting up in bed with a terrible start as I heard, or imagined, a voice saying, "You will die too. It is not only other people who die." This realisation, which was very strong, haunted me for days afterwards and was followed by a pantheistic ecstasy when I saw some raindrops hanging from a leaf. Then I was gripped by the most terrible bouts of recurring depression which at times were so bad I felt suicidal.

Mary—darling Mother!—became so very worried about me. How much she did for Roy and Tess and me! And how often her plans went wrong. The trouble was she would belatedly realise that one of us was not getting the right tuition or was doing something of which she disapproved as a Catholic; then she would use all her will-power to correct this state of affairs. It would have been far better if she had either done things at the right time or neglected us completely: one or the other. As it was, every time we were just becoming independent, she would interfere and muddle us all up again.[164]

---

[164] One example of what Anna's cousin Kitty remembers as Mary's harshness was to occur when Mary stopped Anna's dancing lessons as she said she could not afford the fees. Anna also recalls that Mary preferred that she tour the UK rather than continue to train. "Why did I allow Mary to make destructive decisions for me? She had a very strong will and she used to blackmail very subtly so that I was trapped. [...] She never,

And yet to put all the blame on her is very unjust. It was also my complete dedication to her as a person that was wrong. Until I was about twenty-five years old, Mary could do no wrong in my eyes, so that I often followed her when my own instincts told me to do the contrary. She herself was, perhaps, suffering at that time more than any other member of the family. She fell in love, in Lisbon, with a very handsome Irish priest who kept her busy helping him in his poor parish. He was very good to Mary and made those days of doldrums quite bearable.

In September I was taken to the Algarve by the Caupers. This helped my melancholia temporarily, but on our return to Lisbon it was as bad as ever.

Once, we were asked by the Repatriation Officer whether we were prepared to go to England on a certain ship. After some deliberation we decided to hang on until there was room aboard a clipper. The ship we might have taken was torpedoed, and there were only four survivors.

At last, in December, we were ordered to pack, and it was with great relief that we did so. The Caupers drove us to the quay where the flying-boat was moored, and we said goodbye to those kind people. What a blessing it was to get away! We flew many hours through the starlit night and arrived at Foyles in southern Ireland at dawn. The day became sunny and the Irish countryside looked its loveliest as we went by bus up to Dublin. After spending the night in a gloriously comfortable hotel, we flew to Bristol in a small aeroplane that dipped, leaving our stomachs behind us until we were all violently sick. We arrived at Paddington at night in the blackout for which we were quite unprepared. We got a taxi to Fitzroy Square, where we looked for Roy. But because the post was so delayed in those days, owing to the censorship, the letter with his new address had not reached us. At last we found him at Eve Kirk's flat which was also in Bloomsbury.[165]

Neither was expecting us. Eve seemed a bit odd: it was only later that she told us she had been blown from one end of Charlotte Street to the other by a bomb blast and was still in a state of shock. Roy, hearing voices but not realising they were ours, did not come out of his room, so we found him, the dear darling, on a mattress on the floor, leaning against the wall, and writing, writing. He looked sober and diligent and very neat in his A.R.P. uniform.[166] When he saw us, he went wild with joy and started to tremble and kiss us and so on. He was overjoyed to have Mary back. The letters he had written during this separation were full of love, along with some items of news: the death of Virginia Woolf and the

---

until I had a breakdown [in 1948], realized how fragile I was" (qtd in Connolly, 216).
[165] (1900-1969) Eve Kirk, British artist.
[166] Air Raid Precautions, volunteers.

Poetic Justice

disgraceful behaviour of that poor ninny, Nancy Cunard, who, when her companion shouted "fascist" at Roy, turned away as though she did not know him.

Roy told us that there had not been a single air-raid since he had come to London. But just as he was saying this, as hard as it is to believe, we heard the terrible wail of the sirens. He insisted on taking us straight down to his A.R.P. station. I was only too willing, as the old Civil War trembling had started up again at that fearful sound. Once there, we met Roy's boss, a small Cockney, whom he referred to as "my great friend, Mr. King." While we were chatting to Mr. King the "All Clear" went, and we returned to Eve's flat.

The next morning we went down to Hampshire where Grandmama lived. Roy stayed on in London doing his job until he was called up early in 1942. We stayed at Vine Cottage until we found a small house to rent, at six miles from Petersfield.

Grandmama lived in exactly the same way as she had in her previous homes, although she now had far less money than before. Tony still ran the house with all her old smoothness and harmony. Vine Cottage was always crowded. Our Epstein cousins, Theodore, Esther, and Kitty, were there most of the time because their own house in London had been bombed.

A Memoir of my Father, Roy Campbell

Chapter XVII

We spent the Christmas of 1941 with Grandmama and then moved to a house some miles away. It was draughty, but so English, that I loved it. The greatest hardship there was trying to get to the nearest Catholic Church which entailed a two mile walk to the bus stop, then a six mile bus ride, and all this on an empty stomach. Mary made the journey every day.

We did not stay long at Penn Farm, as it was called, because after our unwilling delay in Lisbon we owed the Repatriation Office a large sum of money. Tess and Mary went to Petersfield where an old lady, named Mrs. Brideson, let them have a flat in her large Victorian mansion, "White Reddins," in return for "light housework."

I became a full-time student with Miss Saul, a Cecchetti teacher of ballet in London. I boarded with a family, friends of hers, in Chiswick whence I took a bus daily to Kensington High Street, where Miss Saul's modest little studio was.

I went down every weekend to visit Tess and Mary. I found them deep in bondage. Mrs. Brideson had turned out to be a bit of a termagant, and the "light housework" was mere slavery. She insisted on living as though there were no war going on. The ten or so lounging-rooms and the eleven bedrooms had to be cleaned as a large staff would have done. This task fell to Tess who did not mind too much because she was waiting to go into the W.R.N.S.[167] and because she was going through a very good patch at that time. Mary did the cooking, and since she had to prepare the food in plenty, I loved my weekend trips so that I could eat my fill of roasts and every sort of pudding. It amazed me, after being in famine-stricken Spain, to see how much food there still was in war-time England, although, of course, over the years the rationing became more and more severe and by 1947 we were subsisting on the barest minimum.

We did not see much of Roy at this time, although he managed to get the odd weekend away from his job. In the spring of 1942 he was drafted into the Army and sent to Brecon, in Wales, from where he sent Mary the following letter:

---

[167] Women's Royal Naval Service, formed in WWI then revived in 1939.

Poetic Justice

My own beloved girl,

I am writing this alone in the barrack room after having a lovely picnic with your parcel down by the Usk. It was really sweet of you to send me all those lovely things. The tin and the jam bottle will be very useful for keeping my sewing tackle etc. I nearly went to spend this week end at Bristol but I thought you might turn up by chance. Some of my pals lent me £2 so I had quite a nice jaunt on Friday and Saturday up in the Beacons by bus but I telephoned about every three hours to see if you had turned up. I ended up Saturday with a mild pub-crawl when I met our G.S.M. in his cups and he has let me spend my leave in the barracks which saves no end of money since I'd have to pay for lodgings and meals. After early mass today I cleared off as I told you by the river and spent a very happy day reading Shakespeare and Ibanez's SANGRE Y ARENA *which is an extremely well written book and made me terribly homesick for Spain*[168] *(I picked it up for a [song?]).*[169] *He wrote it before he became a demagogue....*

One of our N.C.Os got a squint at my "history sheets" and told me on the quiet that the Intelligence Corps have me marked down as "Special"; apparently only one other has this distinction in our Platoon—I think it's Pearson. I have [found?] too that I can do almost anything with the C.S.M the Q.S.M and the Officers and they don't look at my buttons or my kit since O'Donovan left. And they let me eat in the cookhouse....

We have the big Archpampano of the Intelligence Corps coming up next week to interview us all personally....

When we changed into this barrack room Mobles and Weaver were reshuffled to the other end of the room and my neighbours are now Pearson and Sinclair. We change friends here according to circumstances just as birds mate. These two are much more hidalgo[170] *than Mobles and Weaver who are decent cockneys, a bit on the tradesman side. But these two other ones seem easier to get on with as they like each other very much. M and W were always jealous of each other and I had to be a sort of umpire. Pearson and Sinclair have both been promoted to a stripe but they are entirely different from each other. Sinclair is an MA at nineteen: he has "advanced" ideas: he considers soldiering a relic of barbarism, though he is the best soldier in the platoon. But he is a very natural, unspoilt, and intelligent kid. Pearson is an ex-Palestine policeman and Scotland Yard man. He writes tremendous erotic thrillers about valiant British soldiers saving distressed*

---

[168] Alexander notes that Spain really captured Roy's heart. He longed to live in Spain, even as he and Mary were at last building their own house on their own land in Portugal.

[169] This and the other question marks indicating unclear writing are in Anna's original publication. The suggestions are the editor's.

[170] Upper class. An hidalgo is a member of the lower nobility in Spain.

A Memoir of my Father, Roy Campbell

damsels from [?]. So far he has not been able to find a publisher, so as usual I have detailed myself to try and find him one. He is a charming fellow, courteous, generous, sincere, very brave and [?]. Both these fellows have the most [?] ginger hair I have ever seen except on some bay horses that have been curry-combed and shined up. So I am always calling Sinclair Pearson & vice versa. Front view it is all right since Pearson has a moustache and white eyebrows and Sinclair has neither moustache nor eyebrows. But back view it is quite hard. "Who said so, Campbell?" someone will ask me. "Pearson said so," I reply. "Did you say so-and-so, Pearson?" "I'm damned if I said anything of the kind—who told you I said so?" "Campbell told me." "Campbell, did you tell Longgaffe that I said so and so?" says Pearson. "No, Sinclair it was Pearson who said it, Longstaffe must be off his chump," I reply. "Well I'm Pearson." "Of course you are Sinclair, Pearson, I mean Sinclair. Of course I made a mistake it was Pearson who said it"—and so on. Funnily enough my confusion is contagious and everyone mixes them up now, though they have different accents and voices....

We have all sorts of inspections this week so I had better get cracking on some of my kit. I forgot to take my pencil out today by the river so I could not write you my usual Sunday letter—but there is so little time to wait now beloved that it doesn't matter does it. I had a perfectly sweet letter from my darling Tessy and shall write to her during some break this week.....Love to all and a big hug

Your loving husband

Roy

P.S. Thank Tess for reminding me of my Saint's Day.

This P.S. dates the letter at approximately the end of July, 1942.[171]

Mary went to Brecon for a week at this time which made Roy rapturously happy. I think she took Grandmama with her, though I am not certain.

Sometime in August, 1942 Roy's platoon was moved to Winchester, where he had to learn rough-riding on motorcycles. He used to refer to his motorcycle as though it were alive in some way, and they seemed to have a running battle in which the bike often came out the winner.[172] The training was very hard, but in the end he became quite enthusiastic about it. While he was at Winchester, he often came over to "White Reddins" for weekend leave. And Tess and I went to see him at Winchester. He took us to look at the Cathedral with those who must have been the Sinclair and Pearson mentioned above. They were very young,

---

[171] Roy's patron saint was St. Ignatius of Loyola, founder of the Jesuits. The saint's day is on 31 July. St Ignatius and St Teresa were both reformers who sought to emphasise faith and undermine material and political aspects of the Christian church.

[172] RC uses these experiences to good effect in THE MAMBA'S PRECIPICE.

but Roy treated them with the same consideration he would have shown to men of his own age and culture.

In November he was moved to Wentworth Woodhouse in Yorkshire to await embarcation to some unknown destination.

Chapter XVIII

Roy was unable to spend the Christmas of 1943 with us. But the following March he came to "White Reddins" on embarcation leave, and we had a great farewell feast. Then he and Mary and a new friend, Fr. Murphy, spent some days at the Mitre Hotel in Midhurst, which they all three greatly preferred to Petersfield. Tess was already in the W.R.N.S., and Roy was delighted to see her looking happy and very chic in her navy-blue uniform.

Two weeks after we had said goodbye to him and thought him well on his way overseas, he suddenly turned up again. His transport ship had been torpedoed and set on fire, but it managed to limp back to Greanoch. He has described this experience in his poem "One Transport Lost."[173] He was then given an extra two weeks' leave while waiting for his next ship. None of us had the faintest idea of his destination, but in a letter written some time after his second departure he made a cryptic remark about going "home" so we gathered that he was bound for South Africa. Our assumption was correct, and the then Governor General, Roy's brother-in-law, Sir Patrick Duncan,[174] pulled strings so that he was able to get a fortnight's leave from his unit which he spent at his mother's beautiful house in Pietermaritzburg; there he thoroughly enjoyed himself, being wined and dined as a celebrity. In order to rejoin his unit, now in Kenya, he travelled across country seeing every variety of wild bird and animal which was a great thrill to him.

Roy's first letter from Kenya is full of hope and happy expectations of going to the Far East with his original command but gradually these were replaced by a mounting despair as he realises he is going to be stuck in the bush, far from the active service for which he so longed. He was more frightened of boredom than

---

[173] Written in February 1943. First published in the South African magazine THE OUTSPAN in 1944 (COLLECTED WORKS, Vol. 1: 649), and included in TALKING BRONCO (1946).
[174] Sir Patrick Duncan (1870-1943) was the sixth Governor-General of the Union of South Africa, holding office from 1937 to 1943. He married Alice Dold in 1916. Her sister, Agnes, was married to RC's brother, Dr. George Campbell (PATRICK DUNCAN: SOUTH AFRICAN AND PAN-AFRICAN, C. J. Driver and Anthony Sampson. Oxford and Claremont: James Currey and David Philip, 2000: 4).

Poetic Justice

anything else in life, and the thought of being without books, friends, drink or Mary was infinitely depressing.

In a letter to Tess written in September, 1943,[175] he says:

> *My beloved Tess*
>
> *Many many happy returns of the Day! —just a scribble from my new post to send you my love and a picture of Robinson Campbell and Friday Abdullah in their clearing in the jungle. In front is Coconut Manor [here is a drawing of a small hut] and, behind the cookhouse and water tank, you can see a specimen of our poultry resting in the baobab over it. I think you would quite like it for a week or so....*
>
> *You and Anna would have a good time making sweets with coconuts and sugar and eggs which abound here. You said you tried to imagine what I was looking like, and how I was feeling, and what I was thinking of, well this drawing will give you a rough idea of my surroundings. When I get a touch of fever I think of the most amazing things, half in a kind of dream but it is mostly about Mum and you and Anita. But I never mope or let it get me down since that would do no good to anyone.... Well beloved girl it will soon be your twenty-first birthday. I sent back my last cheque from Jonathan Cape[176] to him and have asked him to make out both my royalties from last June and next November and send them to you for a birthday present. It won't be much since the book was published 20 years ago but perhaps enough to buy you a few books or some things to paint with—you must not give up drawing—ever, but keep slogging at it....*

There are three more pages to this letter, all with exquisite drawings. One is entirely of zebras and giraffes, and another is of Roy: you can just see his legs, as he is drawing from a lying down position on his bunk; beyond is a shelf with photos of Mary, Tess, and me, a rosary, a bunch of flowers, and a large King's African Rifles hat hanging on the wall.[177]

Roy made many friends while he was in East Africa, one of whom, S. C. Mason,[178] wrote an article about him after his death, and I would like to quote it at length because there is much in it that is revealing and that confutes many of his enemies' asseverations.

---

[175] Tess's birthday was 26 November; if this date is correct it would seem that RC waas writing early so as to ensure that the letter reached Tess in time.
[176] British publisher.
[177] See the additional illustrations section.
[178] The poem, "Heartbreak Camp" (in TALKING BRONCO), is dedicated "To Major S.C. Mason of the Nigerian Regiment". The editors of the COLLECTED WORKS 1 describe him as "a minor poet" (650).

A Memoir of my Father, Roy Campbell

Roy's drawing of the camp in Kenya, 1943 (CC)

We sat and talked. The conversation was good. It always was when Roy was one of the party. His voice at first sounded harsh to me, and oddly accented. Later when he was working at the B.B.C., he told me philosophically that he knew his voice was un-melodious. But he did not try to refine it, and it suited him. Sometimes his more scholarly expressions gained from the contrast of the tone in which they were uttered. One could not be with him for long without hearing him speak of his wife: and he always did so with love and pride. His religion too was something he often referred to; he carried it with him in his daily life.

I never served with him in the same unit and since the army was the last thing that most of us wanted to discuss—I did not learn what fighting he had done—far too little I am sure for his ardent spirit. He had recently been in hospital for a spell and there he had written some lyrics for Jambo, a periodical published for soldiers serving in East Africa. One of these pieces was 'Heartbreak Camp,' a nostalgic poem, unlike most of his work. But I think there is no mystery about its mood. It must have been composed while Roy was homesick and depressed as the keenest warrior may be when he is engulfed in the routine of soldiering—as opposed to fighting... He was fit again at the time we met, and was stationed in Nairobi. Once I saw him when he was in charge of the guard at Command Headquarters. The Commander-in-Chief was about to pass on his way to his office, and Roy's guard was turning out to him. Roy played his part in the ceremony very well, and with an aplomb that would have done credit to a veteran regular soldier... He passed along the ranks carrying out a preliminary inspection. He straightened a bayonet here, did up a button there, checked a large pair of feet elsewhere. The effect was rather like a hen fussing over her chicks. Then Roy took up his position to the right of the guard, confident that they would do him credit when they paid their well-drilled compliment to the general. On that glimpse of him at work, I classified him as a keen and efficient N.C.O.

He was often free in the evenings, and in the month or so that followed a group of us gathered round him for informal discussions, usually after dinner. My contribution was to name him "maestro"—a title that certainly suited him. Apart from Roy and me this group was formed entirely of Jews. I would not stress this fact if I had not seen it stated, by at least one critic since his death, that Roy hated the Jews. Certainly I did not find it so. He may have hated some Jews, perhaps for reasons unconnected with their Jewishness. We can be certain that he did not hate *all* Jews. Nothing could have been kinder or more cordial than the relations between him and the clever young people who sat, literally, at his feet on those tropical nights in Kenya... I see him as I look back, sitting like a benevolent patriarch in the midst of that group of keen and intelligent young critics. He was confident, courteous and good-humoured, and he kept on scoring points. I began to understand what a great scholar he was. He seldom spoke of his own work and never of poetic technique...

At some point during this exile Roy realised that Luis de Camões,[179] the Portuguese epic poet and lyricist, had been banished to a place very near to his own and that he, also, had contracted malaria and almost died of sadness in the jungle. This knowledge consoled him, and it prompted him to write his moving sonnet to Camões:

---

[179] (c 1524-1580) He is considered to be Portugal's greatest poet. RC also translated many of his poems. See ROY CAMPBELL: COLLECTED WORKS II (Ed. Peter Alexander, Michael Chapman and Marcia Leveson. Craighall: AD. Donker, 1985).

A Memoir of my Father, Roy Campbell

Luis de Camões

Camões, alone, of all the lyric race,
Born in the black aurora of disaster,
Can look a common soldier in the face:
I find a comrade where I sought a master:
For daily, while the stinking crocodiles
Glide from the mangroves on the swampy shore,
He shares my awning on the dhow, he smiles,
And tells me that he lived it all before.
Through fire and shipwreck, pestilence and loss,
Led by the ignis fatuus of duty
To a dog's death—yet of his sorrows king—
He shouldered high his voluntary Cross,
Wrestled his hardships into forms of beauty,
And taught his gorgon destinies to sing.

Jube River, 1944

Poetic Justice

Chapter XIX

While he was far away in Africa, Roy was blissfully unaware of the dramas that were happening to his family.

Because Tess was now in the W.R.N.S., I in London, and Roy abroad, Mary no longer had to stay at "White Reddins," so she moved to a small cottage between South Harting and Petersfield. This was a primitive place when she first went there, but with her usual skill she soon transformed it into a little paradise. I loved going there for weekends, partly to get away from the air raids and partly because Mary had sown the garden with green peas, potatoes, and string beans of which there was a great dearth in London.

No sooner had she made this place habitable, than Tess, after ten successful months in the W.R.N.S., was invalided out with a severe nervous breakdown. Mary realised that she needed extensive psychiatric treatment. At the cottage she would wander off into the fields, throw herself on the ground, and sob her heart out for hours on end.

Mary resolved to put Tess in the psychiatric ward at Guy's Hospital in London, so she gave up her cottage for a house in the city where she could be near Tess and at the same time let rooms in order to make some sort of income. While still at "White Reddins" she had befriended Robin Kenny, a nephew of Mrs. Brideson who was an ardent Catholic. They both found it an ordeal getting to morning mass in Protestant England, and so they decided to look together for a house in London as near to a Catholic church as possible. Robin was one of those souls immortalised by Dostoevsky in THE IDIOT. He wasn't exactly simple-minded; rather he was of such purity of heart and of such gaucheness that he reminded me strongly of Prince Myushkin. Being with him was a mixed pleasure.

With great ease, because of the bombing, Mary and Robin found a three-story house at 17, Campden Grove, off Church Street Kensington, just around the corner from the Carmelite Monastery and Church. Mary took a ninety-nine year lease, and our whole family and many friends lived there on and off, for the next eleven years. Robin, who helped with the rent, occupied two rooms on the ground floor, and the rest of the house was used by us, as and when we wanted to.

A Memoir of my Father, Roy Campbell

By the summer of 1944 Roy had lost so much weight and was limping so badly because the old injury to his leg had been exacerbated when a case of hand-grenades exploded near him, that he was given a long leave in South Africa. In Durban a medical board pronounced him unfit for army life, and after spending some time with his relations he was invalided back to Britain.

For some weeks he was detained at a hospital in Southport. Then he received his discharge. He left the Army with a cheap blue suit, a couple of medals, permanently recurring malaria, a badly disabled leg, a walking stick, two months back pay (roughly £2), and a pat on the back. He was allowed to keep his wide-brimmed King's African Rifles hat. He realised that he was entering a grim

Anna, in ENSA uniform, 1945 (Tess)

stretch in his life, but he was so ecstatic to be back with his beloved Mary that much of what he now had to face was attenuated.

However, we had kept him in the dark about the seriousness of Tess's illness and that she had had to have electric-shock treatment at Guy's, the fees for which had been very steep. But worst of all was finding how emaciated his dearest daughter had become. So the truth, when he learned it, was especially bitter.

Our family's reunion took place in Oxford, where Mary and Tess were living temporarily with friends because the house at 17, Campden Grove had been badly blasted by a land mine in the next street. I was there as well. By a coincidence my ballet company was performing for two weeks at the New Theatre. Thus, when Roy turned up, we were all reunited for a short time.

Roy did not like ballet, but to please me he did attend one of our performances in Oxford, that of LES SYPHIDES. Afterwards he told me how much he had liked it. "But who," he asked, "was the spavined old horse who took the man's part?" It was true: all the fit male dancers had been called up by then, and the few who remained really did look like tired old horses.

In the autumn of 1944 my parents and Tess were able to return to Campden Grove, although the house was still full of carpenters and plumbers. The top

Poetic Justice

Anna dancing Les Sylphides in Oxford, 1944 (Francesca)

two rooms and the kitchen were serviceable. Tess, however, could not stay there. The ceaseless hammering got on her fragile nerves. In fact she became so ill at the time that she was sent to a lunatic asylum in Epsom. To pay for her treatment, Roy got a job with the War Damage Commission as a clerk. He shared an office with an old gentleman called Major Milner who also had a neurotic child. Roy and he became good friends; in fact he was only able to bear the monotony of his job thanks to this friendship.

Once when I was on holiday from my company, Roy and I went down to Epsom to see Tess. She seemed perfectly normal but in low spirits. On the way home my heart bled for Roy who was pale and silent. The doctors at Epsom suggested that Tess be certified and confined for life, but my parents were horrified at this idea and decided to bring her home again. So just before Christmas, 1944 we prepared a room for her. She stayed there lying in bed, not eating or speaking for months. The slightest noise was painful to her, and gradually all our nerves were in shreds trying to keep ourselves and our frequent callers quiet. Later, thanks to the generosity of some friends, we were able to move her to a cottage at Winchelsea where we took it in turns to nurse her.

In January, 1945 my company was called up by E.N.S.A.,[180] and after some hectic preparations we embarked for Italy where we spent a thrilling three months dancing for the Allied Armies. It was marvellous to be out of war-drab England and to see the sun and mimosa trees again.

---

[180] According to Paul Addison, whereas the reputation of CEMA, the Council for the Encouragement of Music and the Arts, was highbrow, that of the Entertainments National Service Association (ENSA) was decidedly "lowbrow". The purpose of ENSA, which had been set up at the outbreak of war, was to recruit performers of all kinds to entertain the armed forces. Although it attracted the services of a number of major stars, including Gracie Fields and George Formby, it paid poor fees and, as Angus Calder explains, "relied heavily on low-grade and near amateur talent". (Paul Addison, "Home front, 1939-1945", OXFORD DICTIONARY OF NATIONAL BIOGRAPHY, Oxford University Press, Sept 2004; online edn, Jan 2007 [http://www.oxforddnb.com/view/theme/92741, accessed 15 Jan 2007]. See also CONTINUUM COMPANION TO TWENTIETH CENTURY THEATRE, Colin Chambers. London and New York: Continuum, 2002: 179; 252.)

We arrived back in England in April, and Victory in Europe was in May. By then I was dancing at the Prince of Wales Theatre in a show called STRIKE A NEW NOTE. Roy came to see it and very much enjoyed the sketches by that great comedian, Sid Field, and a syncopated version of THE ODYSSEY which ended with the immortal words: "But see on the horizon there's a cloud of dust; Ulysses has come home in time, but only just!"

On my way home after one of the shows I remember watching from the top of a number 9 bus as the crowd rejoiced in Picadilly. I could not help wondering what they were so happy about. True, the endless bombardments were over, but we had lost an Empire, and in the circles my family moved in, it was common knowledge that there were thousands of fellow-travellers waiting eagerly in the West to hand over the secrets of the atom bomb to our worst enemies. Roy had tried to warn MacSpaunday—his portmanteau name for MacNeice,[181] Spender,[182] Auden,[183] and Day-Lewis[184]—but their only response was to call him a fascist. They were so smug in their homosexual club. Now they are even being knighted.

In the autumn of 1945 Mary realised that I was at the limit of my endurance—I had been touring Britain and Italy for three years by then, subsisting on the most meagre rations—so she used her annual £100 to take us both to Switzerland.[185]

It was quite extraordinary to wake up in Geneva. It was the first city we had been in since 1939, except for our stay in Lisbon, that had not been touched by the war. I think we had both forgotten what normal life really was. The sun was pouring through our window, which overlooked Lac Léman. Our breakfast table was set with real coffee, cherry jam, and hot croissants. But I was too

---

[181] Louis MacNeice (1907-1963) born in Belfast; at Oxford he became friends with Auden and Spender. It is not clear on what grounds (unless by association with Auden and Spender) Anna bases the innuendo that he was homosexual.

[182] Stephen Spender (1909-1995), English poet, writer and academic. In his autobiography, WORLD WITHIN WORLD (1966), Spender alludes to a homosexual relationship with "Jimmy Younger". There would seem to have been others, but Spender also had relationships with women, and was twice married. He was knighted in 1983.

[183] Wystan Hugh Auden (1907-1973) is the only one of these poets who was unambiguously homosexual. He left England for America in January 1939.

[184] Cecil Day-Lewis (1904-1972), Irish born, but English educated poet and novelist (under the pseudonym, Nicholas Blake). He was Poet Laureate for Britain from 1968-1972. As with MacNeice, the homosexual jibe seems unwarranted.

[185] In a letter to the editor (17 April 2005), Francesca, Anna's daughter, says the dancers, who were "dancing non stop", were plied with alcohol to warm them up and make them forget their hunger. Anna "became very ill and suffered a stroke" in London.

Poetic Justice

tired even to take much notice; I only craved sleep and more sleep. Mary, on the other hand, wanted to see as much of Switzerland as possible. In the end we compromised: I slept for three days and then we toured the country starting at St-Cergue and then going on to Vevey, Montreux, Gstaad, and Saanen, and so back to Geneva. Mary kept buying bottles of champagne which she opened in the most unlikely public places, thus startling the people around us. But it was all great fun, and it set us both up for another two years: of dancing on my part and running a house on Mary's.

Roy had been working for sixteen months at the War Damage Commission, a job he detested but did with the greatest abnegation and patience. In fact, during the fifteen years that elapsed between his leaving the Army and his death, he often came near to saintliness. Finally, though, T.S. Eliot[186] and especially Desmond MacCarthy[187] heard that one of England's greatest poets was earning a pittance at a soul-destroying job, so they pulled strings and got him employed at the B.B.C.

Rob Lyle has written of this episode in his still unpublished biography of my father, HERDSMAN OF APOLLO:

> From this deadly existence (the W.D. Commission) he was rescued by Desmond (later Sir Desmond) MacCarthy who besides sending him a cheque for £40, offered him a job on the B.B.C. Roy presented himself in uniform—plus medals—and was surprised to learn that he was being called upon to act as Talks Producer. "Why are you dressed like this?" he was asked. "I'm sorry I thought I was wanted as commissionaire" was the reply.

This story was always told by Roy with the deepest irony. It was not meant to be believed; he simply wanted to underline the way the best artists are sometimes treated in the modern world, especially those who will not toady for their bread. Rob Lyle continues:

> When I met him he had been there some time and was to be there some time longer, acquiring in the process, a life-long dislike of the "higher" ranks of that institution and an equally warm admiration for its executives—the engineers, electricians and secretaries upon whose shoulders, in fact, the Royal Charter reposes.

---

[186] RC met T.S. Eliot (1888-1965) not long after he had left South Africa and entered Oxford. Eliot was to prove a loyal supporter over the years and (under the Faber imprint) published several volumes of RC's work.

[187] (1878-1952) English journalist and literary critic; one of the original Bloomsbury group.

To the foregoing strictures there were of course exceptions: Sir Desmond MacCarthy, obviously, was one and Sir William Haley[188] another. Despite his exasperation, Roy felt a certain sympathy for this man, so much a fish out of water, so clearly unable—for one could not suppose him unwilling—to deal with an infiltration with which he was, to his credit, unsympathetic... .

While Roy was at the B.B.C., as also before and after to a lesser extent, many young writers wrote or visited him to ask his advice or for help with their work, or simply to prevail on him, as Talks Producer, to have their stories or poems read over the microphone. Among those who benefited from Roy's kindness were Charles David Ley,[189] John Heath-Stubbs,[190] Charles Causley,[191] John Russell, Angel Garcia, Henri Chabrol,[192] Alister Kershaw,[193] and Rob Lyle.

Rob Lyle and Roy in Campden Grove, London, circa 1947 (Francesca)

---

[188] (1901-1987) British newspaper editor and broadcasting administrator.
[189] Editor, writer and translator of Spanish, Portuguese, English.
[190] (1918-2006) English poet and translator.
[191] (1917-2003) Cornish poet and writer.
[192] A contributor to Alister Kershaw's SALUTE TO ROY CAMPBELL.
[193] Of Australian birth. Author, biographer and poet. Close friend and literary executor of Richard Aldington. Editor and translator of SALUTE TO ROY CAMPBELL (Francestown: Typographeum, 1984), the revised and expanded version of HOMMAGE À ROY CAMPBELL. Other contributors include Uys Krige, Alan Paton, Dylan Thomas, Laurie Lee, Lawrence Durrell and Wyndham Lewis.

Poetic Justice

Chapter XX

In 1946 Roy's collection of poems TALKING BRONCO[194] appeared. Desmond MacCarthy reviewed it for THE SUNDAY TIMES (a newspaper of distinction in those days) under the title "A Tragic Poet":[195]

> The best way to review poetry not already familiarly known—and especially good new poetry—is to quote it, and that is the way I propose to review Mr. Roy Campbell's new volume of verse. But first let me remind readers of the spirit of his work and his position among contemporary poets.
>
> Roy Campbell is a tragic poet, and to say that implies that he is either a very considerable one or a pretentious nonentity. It is impossible to be a rather good little *tragic* poet. Both Beddoes[196] and Housman[197] are either very remarkable poets or they are negligible... If a man is mainly inspired by a tragic sense of life, and has written beautifully—though, of course, he may write better at one time than another—he is a poet of the first consequence. Not a few today put Roy Campbell among the first three living poets, and at his best second to none. His most characteristic sense of beauty as a poet accepts pain, death and, as far as the world goes, despair; indeed, what he values most of all in life seems to be a joy that is wrung from them.
>
> The virtues, the glow of which he best transmits, are courage and unconscious humility. Of all modern poets I have read he is the most democratic, not—Heavens, no!—not in his politics but in his feeling for the common man and here the common soldier. There is something almost akin to Whitman[198] sometimes, or perhaps it is really Christian, in the passion and pity

---

[194] The editors of the COLLECTED WORKS note that, "The title is taken from a derogatory phrase in a review of FLOWERING RIFLE by Stephen Spender" (I: 648).
[195] Printed by kind permission of THE SUNDAY TIMES. (ACL)
[196] Thomas Lovell Beddoes (1803-1849), English poet and dramatist.
[197] A.E. Housman (1859-1936), Classical scholar and poet.
[198] Walt Whitman (1819-1892), American poet, essayist, journalist. Often called the father of free verse.

A Memoir of my Father, Roy Campbell

with which he is on the side of average, coarse, faithful, stupid humanity as against the superior sort of man. And yet he adores in pagan wise whatever is grand and glorious.

He is a tragic poet who laughs, and he laughs more often than he grieves... He loves being angry—sometimes over much, and he can't keep his anger on ice as the most formidable satirists of all can do. He sometimes reminds me of Belloc,[199] a poet by the way whose work is likely to be remembered after many who are perpetually praised and discussed today are forgotten or almost forgotten... Roy Campbell writes sound, copious and sonorous English; his images are visible, and to him metre is an inspiration not a hindrance—not something to be wriggled past or through somehow. (MacCarthy then goes on to quote the poems at length.)

On our return from Switzerland, Mary let the spare rooms to two Polish students who had escaped from Russia with General Anders' army. Robin Kenny had come home after the Armistice. I went on touring with a new ballet company, just formed, called, rather grandly for such an amateur gathering, The Anglo-Russian Ballet.

It was on one of my leaves in 1946 (my memory may be at fault over this date) that Roy and I bumped into Wyndham Lewis as we were walking along Notting Hill Gate. Lewis had spent the war years, miserably, in Canada. Mary had been in correspondence with him for some time before the end of the war. She had written to tell Roy, then in East Africa, that Lewis was still in action. This news excited Roy as he had heard practically nothing of him since 1939. That day in Notting Hill Gate Lewis looked very pale and emaciated. Nevertheless, the old electricity passed between the two tall men. They began talking about the peace and were soon so deeply engrossed they did not notice when I steered them into a tea-shop.

Both were indignant over Churchill's flirtation with "Uncle Joe." They referred to the "blood, sweat and tears" speech, in which at one point Churchill spoke of waging war "against the most monstrous tyranny never surpassed in the dark, lamentable history of human crime..."—while ensuring that a far worse tyranny, that of Lenin, Stalin, should be perpetuated until our time. Lewis and my father agreed that the radicalism of such "conservatives" as Churchill and Duff-Cooper made them blind to the sufferings of the Russian people. They said how much nobler and less devious were such Labourites as Ernest Bevin in comparison with Anthony Eden. They were in tears when they

---

199 Hilaire Belloc (1870-1953), French-born, naturalised British poet, writer and politician. Ardent Catholic.

Poetic Justice

talked about all the lives that had been sacrificed to defend Poland, only to hand it over *once more* to the Russians. They asked why, if the Nuremberg trials were just, Eden had not been hanged for handing back to Stalin thousands and thousands of Cossacks to be butchered.[200]

They were both indignant at descriptions given in the press of Winnie's and Clemmie's junkets with Uncle Joe. It boggled the mind to read that at one, a party given for President Truman, Stalin had arrived in a fleet of cars full of admirers. His costume for the evening's masquerade was his famous white cloth jacket blazing with insignia, *all self-awarded*. The affair was a great success, and afterwards cuddly Uncle Joe went around getting autographs. Everyone went home from this jamboree with memories of great merriment and goodwill! It was grim Lewis Carroll material.

Lewis and Roy went on meeting from time to time. Lewis protected his privacy even more assiduously than heretofore and only allowed a few chosen people to visit him at his flat in what he called "Rotting Hill."

Some time during 1947 Rob Lyle came into my father's life. While on active service in North Africa as a captain in the Queen's Bays, Rob came across a copy of ADAMASTOR,[201] which made him into a fervent Campbell fan. On being demobilised he wrote to Roy telling him how much he admired his poetry. Roy rang up to thank him, and they arranged to meet that same evening at the Catherine Wheel in Kensington Church Street, a pub that Roy had turned into a sort of club where he and his growing circle of friends met whenever they had a free night. This meeting was a memorable occasion and started a friendship that only ended with Roy's death ten years later. These two men, so utterly different in every way, became virtually inseparable, and Rob was like a blessing from God, both morally and materially, in the last decade of Roy's life.

It saddened Rob (who is a gifted poet in his own right) to see Roy wasting his time at the B.B.C., and after some time and thought he came up with the idea of starting a magazine of which Roy would be the nominal editor—nominal, in order to let him have as much free time as possible in which to write. The magazine was called THE CATACOMB, and most of the work was done by Mary,

---

[200] In her own copy of the Typographeum publication, Francesca showed me that Anna had crossed out "Eden had not been hanged for handing back to Stalin thousands and thousands of Cossacks to be butchered" and had written in the margin: "those responsible for 'saturation bombing' were not tried also."

[201] First published in 1930.

Rob, and Tess when she was well enough. This also enabled Rob to give Roy an income without embarrassing either of them, and he did it with the greatest delicacy and generosity.[202]

Roy wrote some parodies of other poets for the magazine. One of the best was of Gerard Manley Hopkins. I quote again from HERDSMAN OF APOLLO:

> The funniest parody, as well as the most serious criticism, was directed at Gerard Manley Hopkins, a poet who, to his lasting credit, himself never sought publicity or publication but who, as a result of Bridges' intervention,[203] has exercised a more pernicious influence, technically, on 20th century verse than any other single writer: for he encouraged the young and aspiring to match their wayward and often perverse introspection with a floundering technical obscurity.

But I will leave this subject with a few stanzas of Roy's parody, "The Drummer Boy's Catechism":

> *Comes he to learn. Ah! visit now the tenth this is*
> *To me, unworth. But in the mean parenthesis*
> *Ah how ecstatic is m-*
> *-y waiting soul with gust[204] to hear his catechism!*
>
> *His camp lies yonder. Yonder. His Camp-Commandant*
> *Caught him and brought him. Nay! no false mahommedan t—*
> *-o blight this bud, or canker (chief*
> *Server he is at mass). His pocket handkerchief*
>
> *He into-wept, beseeching me to train him*
> *In Godways, straitways, and his soul de-paynim.*
> *(Deep pain him it would bring*
> *Should soldier-budlet not with angels sing)[…].*
>
> *Youth-speckled, apple-freaked, dappled and peppered*

---

[202] Alexander notes that RC worked on his autobiography rather than on new poetry as Lyle had hoped he would. This was probably because "he had never been able to write well in England" and also because "poetry had always been 'the sweat of other activities' for him—and he had fewer and fewer activities" due to his problems with his leg (which, in turn, made him gain weight) and also his deteriorating eyesight (217).
[203] The poetry of Gerald Manley Hopkins (1844-1889) remained largely unpublished during his lifetime. Robert Bridges (1844-1930) with whom he became friends at Oxford published the first collection of his poems in 1918.
[204] The errors which occur in the Typographeum edition have been corrected here.

Poetic Justice

With pimple, dimple, and freckle. Of beauty spots he's the leopard.
(Old Age, Ah blood-fierce hag you are,
Spare, spare, not deface, this galaxy-pimple-jaguar)

Of apricot splotches and birds-egg blotches. O spare 'im!
Egg of an angel, perhaps, is this harum scarum,
Wagwanton, weechappy—,
Spare him, and both myself and Commandant make happy.

Bumfluff on cheeks, like peach-down or penicillin
Blooms plushwise, 'twixt the pimples, space to fill in
With microscopic bristles
Finer, more fine (ah!) than silver tuft of thistles.

Due Overseas... Wilt roam (ah me!) redcoatlet?
Salvation I'll launch thee, which like a life-boatlet
I'll caulk. Yes! Fore and aft let
No bilge soak in to sink thy spirit's raftlet [...].

    The two Poles to whom we let our rooms were charming, amusing, warm-hearted, and a great help in the house. They told us appalling stories of Russia, which they had had to cross with General Anders' army. The towns, they said, were full of roving bands of starving children who did not hesitate to kill for a pair of shoes. The two young men, however, after being with us for some eleven months, had to move to be nearer their places of work. Not long thereafter Anna von Schubert suddenly turned up in London having been freed from a Japanese prison camp in China. She took a liking to Campden Grove and with Mary arranged the two spare rooms for her to live in while her husband stayed at his club. Roy and I watched the installation of this bossy woman with grave misgivings. Recently I had been in two different ballet companies and was now on holiday from Les Ballets des Champs Elysée. I was longing for the peace of our home without intruders. Roy, also, after a day at the B.B.C. needed quiet in which to do his own work. With the arrival of my godmother all tranquillity left the house. It never occurred to her that she was a nuisance. Like a lot of middle-Europeans she was a total egoist. To keep 17, Campden Grove—three stories and a large basement—clean with no outside help but a slovenly au-pair was backbreaking work. Mary once was so tired she had to climb the stairs on all fours. To get food, which was extremely scarce, even in 1948, one had to queue for hours and then lug the heavy bags up the hill from Kensington High Street.[205] Anna never

---

[205] Alexander says that the occasional food parcels to supplement rations sent from

lifted a finger, even to help with the washing-up. She took tranquillizers and sipped gin in her room, went out to see her friends, and came back with gossip that helped no one. She was utterly exasperating. One day when Roy was deep in translating Baudelaire[206] and needed complete concentration, her nagging voice asking why the fridge had not been cleaned made him lose his temper. He told her to clean it herself and stop bullying his wife. He also told her she was a self-centered egoist. She could not accept these home truths, and from then on she tried to put not only our friends but also members of the family against him. I do not find it easy to write about her, since she was directly responsible for a serious nervous breakdown I suffered at that time. Shortly after this she moved away to America for a while which was an indescribable relief.

Roy forgot all about Anna after she left. He was writing a great deal besides doing his tedious work. Between 1946 and 1950 he translated the whole of Garcia Lorca's ROMANCERO GITANO as well as all his plays.[207] One of them, BLOOD WEDDING, was performed in London for one night with Maxine Audley in the role of the mother. It was a strange production. Almost everything went wrong including the sound of an approaching horse which sounded instead as if it were galloping away into the distance. So rather than being tragic, the whole thing was just improbable, and Roy and I fell into fits of laughter.

In addition Roy translated LES FLEURS DU MAL; he wrote and published a book for children, THE MAMBA'S PRECIPICE, which is partly autobiographical; he wrote a critical study of Lorca for Bowes and Bowes;[208] he translated THE SURGEON OF HIS HONOUR by Calderón de la Barca;[209] he wrote many poems, among which was "The Rhapsody of the Man in Hospital Blues"; he started his autobiography, LIGHT ON A DARK HORSE;[210] and finally he translated the poems of St. John of the Cross for which he was awarded the Foyle literary

---

South Africa by RC's faithful friend, C.J.Sibbett, were greatly appreciated (211).
[206] RC's translations of LES FLEURS DU MAL appear in the Alexander, Chapman, Leveson COLLECTED WORKS II: 61-257.
[207] See COLLECTED WORKS II, Alexander, Chapman and Leveson. Lorca (1898-1936)—poet, dramatist and theatre director—disappeared during the Spanish Civil War, thought to be have been executed by the Nationalists.
[208] Alexander, Chapman and Leveson (COLLECTED WORKS III: 627) note that the Bowes and Bowes edition of LORCA: AN APPRECIATION OF HIS POETRY was published in 1952, as was a Yale University Press edition. A paperback edition was published in 1959 (Burns and McEachern, Canada) and reprinted in 1961 (Unwin, London) and in 1971 (Haskell House, NY).
[209] Published in 1960 by the University of Wisconsin Press, and republished in 1978 by Greenwood Press.
[210] According to Alexander, Rob Lyle suggested the title (216).

Poetic Justice

prize.[211] A large luncheon was given in his honour at the Dorchester to celebrate this event. Mary was away at the time, so I substituted for her and took her place at the rostrum. The whole banqueting room, which is very large, was filled with literary celebrities, but I only remember Lord David Cecil[212] on whose right I sat. Roy looked every inch a poet as he stood up to receive the prize from (oh, ironies of life) S. Spender. What a contrast those two men made. I was filled with pride for Roy, who looked very fine and rather shy. It was a great day for us.

Of LIGHT ON A DARK HORSE Rob Lyle wrote:

> The original biography was destined never to see the light of day; it was treated with extraordinary levity, obtuseness and want of imagination. First the author was asked to alter the whole plan of the book, and then to alter the detail... The manuscript was handed to a school-mistress to correct the prose. She also took it on herself to delete anything of which she did not approve; including two anecdotes on the grounds that they were "too cruel"; and to an actor, who presumably was to correct everything else. Among other things he deleted all reference to persons he did not himself want mentioned; but his general suitability for the job is best illustrated by one example. Roy wrote of "whale sounding"; against this in the margin, this master of English, commented: "What sound did it make?"....[213]

I had hoped to leave out of this memoir any reference to the so-called "fight" between S. Spender and my father, but because of all the nonsense that has

---

[211] R.C's translation of the poems of the Spanish mystic (1542-1592) was first published as a collection in 1951. Sales soon surpassed those of any other of RC's works. A Penguin edition appeared in 1960.

[212] Edward Christian David Gascoyne Cecil (1902-1986), scholar, educator, writer. He was Professor of English Literature at Oxford from 1948-1969.

[213] RC "complained that Lewis Hastings had bowdlerized the book" (Alexander, 222).
Campbell referred to this as his "autobuggeroffery" (COLLECTED WORKS III: 614 note 1). Alexander says this second autobiography contained even more fabrication than BROKEN RECORD and that not even a credulous reader could believe his boasting (217).
In his MEMOIRS OF A DISSIDENT PUBLISHER, Henry Regnery notes that LIGHT ON A DARK HORSE was first published in England in 1951 and then in the US under his company's imprint in 1952. It is a good read, he says, in spite of "its uneven quality and some obvious padding, consisting mostly of accounts of various brawls and physical exploits" (Lake Bluff IL: Regnery Books, 1985:196). Regnery recalls that when he first met RC he was "terribly drunk", having been plied with alcohol by two men who were loath to part from him since, as they told Regnery, "We will never have a chance to meet such a man again as long as we live" (195).

been written about it, by one person or another, I find I have to put the record straight. I will do this by reproducing Roy's defence against defamation and slander, of which there has been far too much since his death:

17 Campden Grove
London W.8.
2nd May 1949

Dear Ross Nichols,[214]

no doubt you will wonder at my reason for disturbing your session the other night.[215] *There was no option left me by the speaker's own announcement that he was going to denounce me from every platform as a "fascist, coward and liar"—merely because I called attention to his war-record. As I volunteered when over age, and when my own country, S. Africa, was still neutral, to fight against fascism which is merely another form of communism—and spent most of my time in the Secret Service and in Wingate's 12th East African Deception Unit, till permanently disabled on active service,—as a wearer of the King's Medals, I could not allow myself to be called a coward by one who during the struggle against fascism had employed no weapon more formidable to the adversary than his own Knife and Fork and his highly lucrative but innocuous pen—while I was on ranker's pay suffering malaria in the jungle.*[216] *By a couple of wide passes in the direction of your speaker, I was forced to demonstrate the unmanliness of my accuser. And having caused him to cower, I required no further chastisement of his person, and am now quite satisfied. I am only sorry to have disturbed the comfort of your audience though some have thanked me for providing a mild diversion, to those who were not diverted I offer my sincere apologies for this unfortunate but necessary demonstration.*

I can, whenever you like, show you the letter wherein he promises to denounce me and impugn my patriotism. It no more constitutes fascism to drive the communists out of Spain, than it constitutes communism to have fought the nazis. Both are equally unsympathetic to me. I hope you will tender my explanations along with my apologies, the latter being strictly conditioned by the former.

Yours ever
Roy Campbell.

---

[214] Philip Peter Ross Nichols (1902-1975), Cambridge academic, poet, artist, historian and founder of the Order of Bards, Ovates and Druids.

[215] Referring to a poetry reading at a chapel in Bayswater. (ACL)

[216] In the 1994 preface to his autobiography, Spender merely notes that the fact that his generation "did not fight and perhaps get killed" in the Spanish Civil War "can perhaps be felt as a reproach" (1997: xv). He does not mention, here, his failure to enlist during WWII.

Poetic Justice

Chapter XXI

In 1949 Roy went with Rob Lyle to Barcelona where he gave some talks at the University of Catalonia. At the press conference afterwards he said, to the surprise of the journalists, that Dylan Thomas[217] was the greatest living English poet and that he was always drunk. "Always?" the journalists asked. "Always," my father answered.

In 1950 Mary and I went to Rome for the Holy Year. While we were there, Roy sent me the following letter:

>
> 17 Campden Grove
> London W.8.,
> *May 1950*
>
> *My darling Anita, thank you for the article about me in* Il Messagiero. *I shall write and thank San Lazzaro for writing it when you let me have his address.*
>
> *You and Mary will have had your private audience with the Holy Father by now. I was very amused by your account of your tea-party with Cardinal Canary.*
>
> *I had lunch at the Sesame Club yesterday with Edith and Osbert [Sitwell]. Sachy*[218] *was also there. He and Arthur Waley*[219] *were enthusing about your beauty.*
>
> *I have decided to spend two weeks at St Jacut with Tess before meeting you in Toulon. I have to go over the proofs of* LOADH [Light on a Dark Horse] *with my editor. Charles*[220] *and Sylvia Mulvey have asked us to stay with them there. Tess is much better, I took her for a picnic on Winchelsea beach last week.*

---

[217] (1914-1953) Welsh poet, with whom RC became friends when RC returned to England from Spain in 1941. According to Guy Butler (South African literary critic and poet), the Thomases lived in the same lodgings as RC. When both were battling financially, RC and Dylan Thomas had together gone begging from fellow poets and publishers (A Local Habitation: An Autobiography, 1945-1990. Cape Town: David Philip, 1991:207-8).

[218] Sacheverall Sitwell, brother of Edith.

[219] (1889-1966) English Orientalist and translator of Chinese and Japanese.

[220] A Canadian soldier and hunter; one of RC's most faithful drinking companions (Alexander, 214).

I am so glad you and Mum are able to be in Rome for the Holy Year and I hope your holiday on Lake Garda did a lot to restore your health. Remember that breakdowns are all part of growing up and you must accept yours in that spirit. I have written some good articles for THE CAT[ACOMB].
Lots of love my darling from your old Dad
P.S. Won't it be lovely to be in France together again?

Actually, Roy was rather annoyed with me for refusing nineteen proposals of marriage. In fact, he was right; I should have accepted my first suitor and saved myself and my parents a lot of suffering. I was under the silly illusion that one had to be deeply in love to make a success of marriage, but this is another story and there is no room for it here. [221]

For some two years Roy had been in correspondence with Richard Aldington[222] whom he was longing to meet as he admired his poetry and his wonderful DEATH OF A HERO. He felt they had much to talk over and wanted to live as near him as possible. So at the beginning of summer Mary and I travelled by train from Rome to Nice where we were to look for a house. But because we had left it rather late, before the French exodus to the beaches, we only managed to find a flat of sorts over a garage, in the picturesque village of Bormes les Mimosas. Aldington lived down below near Le Lavandou. Mary stayed for about ten days then went back to London to take over the running of THE CATACOMB. Thus it was I who met Tess and Roy when they came from Brittany. As they got off the Paris train, they looked unworldly to the point of eccentricity, and everyone stared at them when we walked through the station. Tess was skeletal, and Roy, taller than anyone else, was wearing his large, broad-brimmed hat. It was wonderful to be with them again. I had not seen either for six months because I had been convalescing with relations who lived at Torn del Benaco on Lake Garda.

The next two months sped by. Roy walked almost every day down the long,

---

[221] In a letter to his mother, RC says that Anna is engaged to Alister Kershaw, the Australian, but that he does not expect the betrothal to "come to anything" since "he is always showing himself up as an empty headed braggart in front of her English friends". Whether there were other engagements or not is unclear.

[222] (1892-1962) Christened Edward Godfree, Richard Aldington was an English writer, critic and poet. His novel, DEATH OF A HERO (1929), was thought by some to be the best evocation of WWI. On R.C.'s death, he wrote in a letter to H.D.: "I loved and admired the man, a real hero, a real poet. I wish I could believe that the 'holy angels' of his faith did really receive him, as the Catholic burial service proclaims. If they did they'll have to make some changes in Heaven!" (RICHARD ALDINGTON AND H.D.: THEIR LIVES IN LETTERS, by Richard Aldington and H.D. (Hilda Doolittle) and Caroline Zilboorg. Manchester: Manchester University Press, 2003: 380).

Poetic Justice

Mary and Roy, Bochechos summer 1953 (Francesca)

winding path to Le Lavandou and then on to Aldington's house, and many times I went with him. It was a delight to be with those two tall, handsome, erudite, and very witty men and with Aldington's great friend, Alister Kershaw. The hospitality was lavish, for Aldington loved good food and good wine, and we often went there to lunch. Or else they would drive up to Bormes, and we would eat in a restaurant as the Bormese danced under the plane-trees in the village square.

I tried to protect Roy, on this rare holiday, from being importuned by publishers, editors, and other nuisances, so that he could really relax and get fit for another year of hard work in rainy London. But this was not easy.

Roy could not bear to be near the sea without fishing, and soon he and Tess and I were spending many mornings on the rocky shore waiting for bites. These times together enabled me to know him better than ever before. He was very understanding about my breakdown, having had something similar when he was at same age.

One of the best things about that holiday was to see Tess returning to normal. She began to eat again and to help with the cooking and shopping. I had not seen her so relaxed for many, many years. To Roy it was like a benediction from Heaven. He became really light-hearted, and this inspired him so that his conversation was better than ever.

But these happy days came to an end, and we all returned to our various tasks.

I could no longer dance, so I got a job looking after children at a place called Universal Aunts. Roy tried to sort out the mess his autobiography had been reduced to by two "genteel" editors. At THE CATACOMB Tess helped by typing manuscripts

Roy, Bochechos 1953 (Francesca)

while Mary ran it with Rob Lyle who had just published his first book of poems called GUITAR.

In 1951 Roy took Tess to Madrid where they stayed for two months. He gave several lectures at the Ateneo in Madrid and at the University of Salamanca. Tess became engaged to a Spanish poet but thought better of it when she got home. [223]

Late in 1951 my parents and the Lyles went for a holiday to Portugal. They had all decided they could no longer endure austerity London and its terrible climate, and when they found an old farmhouse in Sintra (the Cintra of Byron's CHILDE HAROLD) they made up their minds to move there lock, stock, and barrel as soon as it was expedient, which was in the spring of 1952.

In 1954 Roy went to South Africa to receive his Doctorate Honoris Causa from the Natal University. For the occasion he gave a polemical speech, which the South African intelligentsia called "trotting out his hobby-horses and dropping bricks." Among other things he said:

> Simplification and streamlining to suggest ease and grace are the hardest things in poetry. You know how easy it is to stir up a muddy pool with a stick so that you cannot see the bottom. Much of the obscurity, mistaken for profundity, in modern poetry, is obtained by similar means—Brown Study. It is far harder to make a deep river transparent

---

[223] Anna does not mention that in 1951 she met Viscount Jaime Cavero de Carondelet in Paris. They returned to England and were married. "The marriage was unhappy from the start, and caused Campbell great anxiety, but he was delighted by [Francesca] the first of his grandchildren" (Alexander, 224).

Poetic Justice

than to render a shallow one visually impenetrable. The popularity of obscure verse is due to the fact that the public, or the reader, wishes to participate in the construction and interpretation of a work of art, as when amateurs jump into the arena or the bullring and spoil the show. The arts begin to deteriorate when amateurs cease to be spectators and become clumsy participators. The Greek drama died when the audience began to join in the choruses.

The reader always becomes cross-word happy in an age of decadence, as in the Alexandria of Lecophoron, which gave us the most impenetrable literary jungles.

"Difficult" poetry confers a spurious importance on interpreters, and go-betweens; on the kind of literary pimp who aspires to totalitarian and ministerial authority. That is why a famous academic pedant recently insisted on having his poetry difficult, as much as to say, "I like my eggs hardboiled." What such pedants like is utterly beside the point. Much of the most difficult poetry *is* good poetry, but it was not written to the order of such pedants—not with a view to being difficult. Its difficulty is accidental, or the result of some idiosyncracy comparable to a lisp or a stammer which can be found in even the greatest poets. It reminds one of Alcibiades with his lisp, which all the youth in Athens could imitate but not his victories...

Here is Roy's description of the D. Litt. ceremony in a letter to Mary:

"Cardonagh"
Hilton Road
Natal, South Africa
May 1954

My dearest One, the doctoring went off well with a tremendous bang in the Pietermaritzburg Town Hall—it was like a bullfight with the gold and scarlet gowns, like "Capas de Paseo." My own was placed on me by George,[224] as President— he had to do it to three doctors and about 200 MAs and BAs. The whole Campbell family was there with heaven knows who else. There were seven thousand at the Capping and Gowning at the Town Hall and 1,000 at

---

[224] Dr. George Campbell, Roy's older brother. (ACL) He was in medical practice for over 50 years. Chancellor of the University of Natal from 1966-1973 and later Chairman of the University Council, in 1953 he was the recipient of the Coronation Medal for his contribution to education and the preservation of wildlife. He played a leading role in the establishment in 1952 of the South African Association of Marine Biological Research and, in 1959, established the Oceanographic Research Institute. (From Maritzburg College Old Boys' webpage: http://www.collegeoldboys.co.za).

A Memoir of my Father, Roy Campbell

the banquet. The papers are full of nothing else but the Campbell family and they had George and Killie[225] and me on the air too. Bill Payn[226] and Geoff and Nin Dutton[227] were also at the banquet. They go off on their trans-Africa trip tomorrow without me. You see how much I love you—that I'll turn down the last chance of an adventure in my life for you! The whole week has been a whirl of popularity—my people out here absolutely love me and it is very exciting. For no one but you would I give up the chance of being the leader of my people. So never say I don't [sic] love you. I am writing on Mother's verandah looking over Maritzburg, Table Mountain and the Valley of a Thousand Hills. From the back verendah [sic] there is an absolutely peerless view of the Drakenburg [sic], the Karkloaf [sic] and the Ithlona mountains with rivers, cascades, peaks—everything is wonderfully green but the distance is all colours ranging from sapphire to cobalt to indigo. Even Spain cannot equal it for sheer landscape (without architecture of course!)

Of the three doctors, I was the one chosen to make the Town Hall speech—and I made a good deal of Spanish propaganda on the sly.[228]

Everybody sends love... Mother and Ethel are no longer "TT".[229] They lay on dozens of bottles of beer, whiskey and sherry for all my guests.

I want to spend one last week with Mother, her memory has almost gone,[230] and Ethel[231] is very near her end though lucid and even at times brilliant. Mother cannot remember conversations of one minute ago.... Edith and Osbert [Sitwell] sent me a wire which arrived at the ceremony itself:

"Love and deepest congratulations on new Doctor," wasn't it sweet of them to remember?

>Your loving and adoring and devoted husband
>Roy

---

[225] Miss Killie Campbell, Roy's cousin, who founded the Africana Library in Durban (now part of the Campbell Collections of the Library of the University of KwaZulu-Natal). (ACL)
[226] Once Roy's schoolmaster and a life-long friend, RC paid homage to him in a short poem (COLLECTED WORKS I: 473). (ACL) In BROKEN RECORD, RC credits him with contributing to THE WAYZGOOSE: "Payn shared with me the joy of THE WAYZGOOSE—which was mainly written in 48 hours—and suggested some of the best lines" (COLLECTED WORKS III: 96). Gillian Tatham, RC's niece, recalls that when he was informed of RC's death, Bill Payn's toast was, "To Roy, who never messed around in the shallow end".
[227] Australian friends. (ACL)
[228] Roy's support for Franco had shocked the Marxist-minded intellectuals.
[229] Dr. Sam and Mrs. Margaret Campbell, RC's parents, had always been teetotallers.
[230] She was 93 at the time.
[231] Roy's sister. She had been mentally ill for years and was to die a week later.

Poetic Justice

On her death in 1956 Granny Campbell left a few thousand pounds in her will. With this and five thousand pounds given to my parents by Rob Lyle, they bought a piece of land in the Sintra Mountains, the only piece in that district that was not State-owned, and there they started to build a house. It was to be their first property. Mary had the Casa da Serra, as it was called, constructed by builders from the village and arranged all the details herself. The view from the house stretched away to distant Lisbon and the Arrabida Mountain across the Tagus.

Casa da Serra, building in progress, 1957 (Francesca)

Roy had recently made friends with the Marquesa de Cardaval who had a large farm on the other side of the Tagus, the sort of place he loved, with wild bulls herded by *campinos*[232] on horse-back and a small private bull-ring. She invited my parents there where they met her brother, the aviator Count Robilant, and his beautiful daughter, Olguina. Roy immediately got a strong crush on this lovely Italian girl who resembled Simonetta Vespucci, Botticelli's model for the BIRTH OF VENUS. It was an attraction she shared, for Roy became, as he grew older, yet more handsome and noble-looking.

But in those years he had already begun to have premonitions of his early death. While on his first lecture tour of the United States in 1953, he heard of Dylan Thomas's last illness and the terrible ordeal he suffered in hospital. Then on his return, just before Christmas, he got a letter from Marquesita Tschiffely saying that Aimé,[233] whom he loved dearly, was in hospital with kidney failure; two weeks later he was dead. This was a great blow. A little later he heard also of Charles Mulvey's death. It is clear in many of his last letters that mortality

---

[232] Peasant farmer, rural worker.

[233] Aimé Tschiffely (1895-1954), Swiss born author and lecturer, famous for his three year long solo ride from Buenos Aires (leaving in 1925) to New York. Campbell dedicated several poems to him.

was in his thoughts. But even much earlier there is a foretelling of the way he would die. It is in the last verse of "To Mary after the Red Terror":[234]

> *And that is why I do not simper,*
> *Nor sigh, nor whine in my harangue.*
> *Instead of ending with a whimper,*
> *My life will finish with a bang!*

My parents gave a picnic when the roof of their house was put up. They wanted to see all their friends together before leaving for Spain where they were going to spend Easter in Seville. But Roy was to know no real security in this life, and he died before he could say, "my house, my home…". Perhaps for such an anti-materialist this was a blessing.

However, his death at that time was in every way a tragedy. I am glad he died without suffering, but I am sorry that just as he was becoming well-known by a larger public, he had to go. His political enemies were frightened of his pen while he was alive, but once he was silenced they went to work with a will.

May God rest his noble soul; though I know he has gone long since to the Paradise of truly great poets, for he was one who risked poverty and unpopularity for the sake of the Truth.

---

[234] Alexander, Chapman and Leveson (eds. COLLECTED WORKS I: 646) note that the poem first appeared in MITHRAIC EMBLEMS (1936) as "To Mary". The poem appears in the COLLECTED WORKS I (311).

Poetic Justice

Chapter XXII

Mary moved into Casa da Serra about three months after the accident. In 1957 she was fifty-nine years old, but she looked much younger. Once she had recovered from her fractures, she set about making the garden beautiful. The house was built on solid rock, but it also had a very rich soil in which she planted, among many other things, red, white, and the palest pink camellias. These gave her much happiness over the years.

The drive to Casa da Serra is steep and winding, through an avenue of eucalyptus trees. The house itself is surrounded by pines, myrtle bushes, cork-trees, and mimosa. During Salazar's time these woods were carefully looked after by foresters. The trees were pruned and the thick undergrowth was cleared away every year. After his death, however, the mountain was neglected, and one summer when there was a high wind the forest was set on fire in three separate places by arsonists. For days it was devoured by gigantic flames that gradually came closer and closer to the house. At last the fire was so near, despite the heroic efforts of the fire-fighters, that Mary had to leave. We all watched from a safe distance as the property was surrounded by the flames, but just as all seemed lost the whole thing suddenly died down. It was quite uncanny, and that evening Mary returned to the house, although every summer thereafter she was haunted by a fear of the fires starting again.

When Roy died, Mary was quite well off and could afford a chauffeur-gardener and a cook-housekeeper. But as the years went by her income grew smaller and smaller as inflation devastated the economy. She was given a private pension by the Queen and another for the needy widows of poets, though it was never enough and she had to sell every scrap of Roy's beautiful manuscripts and most of her paintings.

Her last great love was for Pope Paul VI. She had three private audiences with that very cultured man, and we have a photograph of her presenting copies of Roy's works to him.

Mary had and treasured the friendship of many people in her later years, among them R. G. Montgomery, the South African ambassador, Joaquim Paco d'Arcos,[235] Nelly Millington-Drake, Jean Pontet, and our much loved Fr. Terence McLoughlin, prior of the Dominicans in Lisbon. She received many proposals of marriage after Roy's death, but she never seriously considered re-marrying.[236] She went on looking after the poor, especially in the parish of Ribeira where there was much poverty. She continued to attend morning mass every day until about six months before her death, and then the Sacrament was brought to her. She found consolation during the final year by listening to Mozart and warming her tired heart with a glass of whiskey at luncheon and another at dinner. In fact she developed such a love for Mozart that friends gave her records, a portrait, a life, and two volumes of his letters in a beautifully illustrated edition.

Tess had one son, Francis, from her marriage to a Portuguese shepherd[237] and I one daughter, Frances, by my marriage to a Spanish viscount. There was nothing our two children enjoyed better than going to stay with their grandmother. They both worshipped her, for she retained her beauty and her love of laughter right to the end.

I saw Mary the day before her death. I had just gotten back from England, and when I arrived at Casa da Serra, she was putting the laundry away in a cupboard. One side of her face seemed to me slightly different from the other, although no one else had noticed, perhaps because they saw her every day. I guessed that she had had a slight stroke, so I asked the parish priest to come over, which he did the following morning. She confessed and received the Last Sacrament. Her maid told me later that after Extreme Unction she looked like a young bride. In the afternoon Tess heard her fall and ran into her room. Mary died in her arms. There was no struggle; she simply sighed her soul out of her faithful body. It was the 27th of February 1979.

She was buried with my father in the cemetery of San Pedro.

---

[235] RC had published his translation of Paco D'Arcos' collection of poems entitled NOSTALGIA in 1960 (London: Sylvan Press). RC also translated poems by six other Portuguese poets. (See THE PRESENCE OF PESSOA: ENGLISH, AMERICAN AND SOUTHERN AFRICAN LITERARY RESPONSES, George Monteiro, University Press of Kentucky, 1998).

[236] The American publisher, Henry Regnery, had visited the Campbells in Portugal in the early fall of 1955. He describes Mary (who would have been 57 years old) as "striking, wonderfully loyal, strong-willed [with] black hair and flashing eyes" (MEMOIRS OF A DISSIDENT PUBLISHER, Lake Bluff IL: Regnery Books, 1985:198).

[237] Tess and Ignatius Custudio married when Tess was already pregnant. "Within two weeks he had deserted her for a wealthy Swiss woman, although he resumed contact following the birth of their son the following year" (Pearce, 320).

Poetic Justice

Anna and baby Francesca, 1952 (Francesca)

The Flower[238]

Let no light word your silence mar:
This one red flame be all you say,
Between the old and new desire
A solitary point of fire,
The hesitation of a star
Between the twilight and the day.

So rich the pollen of your breath
It is sufficient to be dumb,
Foreknowing, as the moment slips,
That in the parting of our lips
The hour has slain a rose whose death
Will colour all our days to come.

Roy Campbell

---

[238] This was first published in FLOWERING REEDS (1933).

Additional Illustrations

Additional Illustrations

Archie McKenzie and Roy's father, Sam Campbell, as students at Edinburgh University (CC)

Margaret Dunnachie Campbell with her three sons, Neil, Bruce and Roy (L-R) (CC)

Additional Illustrations

Roy as a teenager in Durban (Tess/Francisco)

Portrait of Roy by Mary (CC)

Additional Illustraions

Portrait of Mary by Bernard Meninsky, painted circa 1921 (Francesca)

Durban, 1926: Back row, L-R: Bruce, George, Roy; Front row: Mrs Campbell, Dr Campbell holding Tessa, Mary (CC)

Additional Illustrations

William Plomer, Roy Campbell and Laurens van der Post on the beach at Sezela (CC)

Roy, William Plomer and Tess in South Africa, year 1926 (Tess)

Additional Illustraions

Mary and Roy, 1929 (Tess)

Additional Illustrations

Mary and Jeanne Hewitt Garman, 1932, Provence (Francesca)

Laurie Lee, Mary and Roy in Toledo, with the Alcázar in the background (Tess)

Additional Illustraions

Mary, Roy and Mrs S.G. Campbell, Alicante, 1935 (Tess)

Anna and Tess in *alguaciles* regalia for bullring in Toledo, 1936 (Tess)

Additional Illustrations

Tess as a teenager in Lisbon, year 1937 (Tess)

Additional Illustraions

Anna, 1950 (Tess)

Additional Illustrations

Roy in King's African Rifles 1944 (Tess)

Handwritten letter (13 Sept. 1943) to Tess, with drawings of camp (below), wild game (p. 151, and Roy himself on his bed (p. 152) (CC)

Additional Illustraions

Against a reed hurdle, a very original 'Still Life'
I had a nice journey from Mombasa down through the game
reserve & through the game country, of which I've made you
a scribble here, of wildebeeste, zebra, giraffe, gazelle & guinea
fowl, with an eland and a reedbuck; and some hartebeeste
in the foreground. Though never so crowded as this, they
just stand and watch the train, or the truck,
go past, and often hardly even lift their
heads from grazing. I have
no rubber and only one horrible
nib and I'm doing the sketch
by hurricane lamp so it
isn't very encouraging
but I think you'll be able
to recognise the outlines —
with Kilimanjaro 200 miles
away on the skyline. If you
rub it with a rubber you'll
be able to see it better.
Well things and sights of
unusual things help to pass
the time during my absence
from you dear ones.
I have been writing a good
deal and should have another
book ready for Faber & Faber
shortly. I seem to be unable
to remember some of the things
I'm going to reprint from "Georgia"
the Tablet and other places but
I dare say I'll be able to find
them after the war.
I have a very nice companion
here, Private Paul Duponsel
from Madagascar but he is
going soon — so I shall
be all by myself — with
6 black fellows who rejoice in Akullas
the names of Mburuku, Mugandi,
Edie, Solomon, and Mwangi so
I'll be all right for cultured
society. I feel already like
a missionary who has been
eaten, swallowed, and digested
about six times over by
cannibals. But they're cheerful
and easy to get on with
if you know how to handle
them properly. Still they're
not a patch on the Zulus
or the Hausas. Well my
beloved little girl you'd
probably be a grown up
lady of 21 by the time you
get this. God bless you my
love and shower a thousand happinesses on you. Many,
many, many happy returns. Ever your own loving
Dad.

Additional Illustrations

Additional Illustrations

Roy with friends; in bowtie Enslin du Plessis in London, 1950 (Tess)

(L-R): Alan Paton, Laurens van der Post, Enslin du Plessis, Roy Campbell, Uys Krige, London, 1952 (CC)

Additional Illustrations

Roy in America with the children of Henry Regnery,
his American publisher, 1953 (Francesca)

Mary, Bochechos 1953 (Francesca)

Additional Illustraions

Roy and friends, Salamanca 1953 (Francesca)

George Campbell, Roy Campbell and Bill Payn
(at Honorary Doctorate graduation 1954) (CC)

Additional Illustrations

Tess with Frankie, 1954
(Francesca)

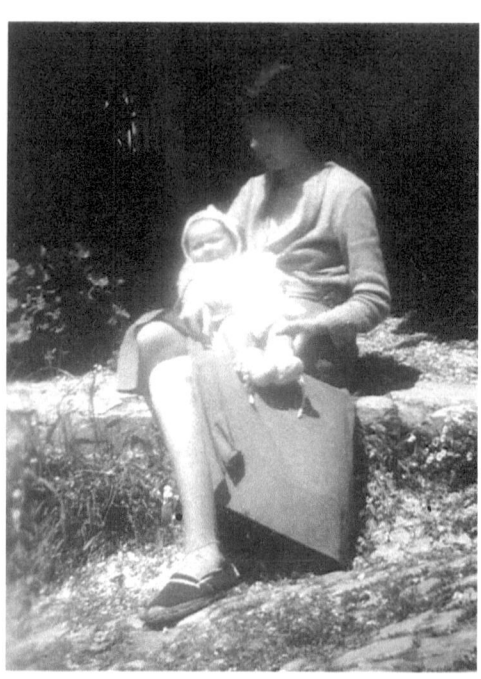

Anna and her daughter, Frances, 1957 (Francesca)

Additional Illustrations

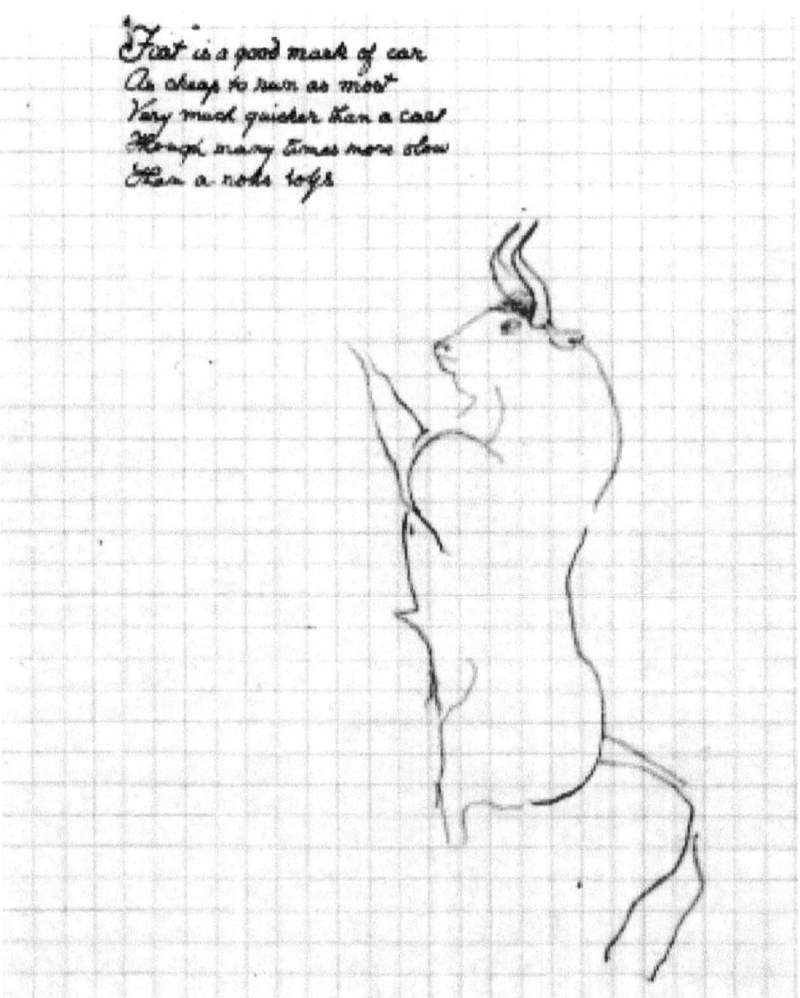

Unpublished poem fragment, found in Roy's notebooks. Believed to refer to the Fiat motorcar in which Roy was killed. (CC)

Additional Illustrations

RC's last drafts of poems (Tess)

Sunless must learn of silence how to
                                    sound
And live a generation underground
Before the sun can fill the fledged
                                cry

As it can fill a

Of all the trees the strongest and the
                                    proudest
The poplar sighs the loudest and
                              the longest
He has more sorrows to lament
more joy
To celebrate

My love will keep you young
When women were girls at school
With you
Are wrinkled you are lonely ah

Stone marks our miles. From stone we
                    take our bullions —
From tombs our lives, from termini our
                                lands
I'll spend my old age in the public
                    gardens
While into stone my own sclerosis
                        hardens
A statue mounted on a marble
                    statue
When of identity I've washed my
                    hands
Reading my name upon the bronze
                    medallion

A billion times (to keep from going
                            crackers)
I'll read my birth name and
                birth date to reclaim
My Pegasus
Has shared petrifaction

Additional Illustraions

Roy and Mary's headstone inscription (Francesca)

ROY CAMPBELL
1901 – 1957
POET
AND HIS BELOVED WIFE
MARY
1898 – 1979

Roy and Mary's grave in cemetery of Sao Pedro, near Sintra (Francesca)

Additional Illustrations

Francesca and Filipe Bento, Sintra 2005 (Editor's photo)

Tess with Judith Coullie, Estoril 2005 (Editor's photo)

IN THE SHADOW OF A POET:
Memoirs

by

Teresa Campbell

Ty-Corn (Tess)

Chapter 1
Born in a Stable

When people ask me where I was born, I say North Wales, and they look puzzled. Even the British don't seem to know where that is, but here in Portugal, my second homeland, where I live, they have never heard of Wales, let alone the North. To my more intimate friends, I say I was born in a stable—then, there is a puzzled and amused look.

I was born in a stable for good reasons, the strongest being that at the time my parents were married, they hadn't a penny between them—they were broke. They went to Wales on five pounds my mother's old governess generously offered them. There, they had to live as frugally as possible and a stable was cheaper than a house. The second reason was that they wanted peace and seclusion, and there they found it. My father had to make a living. He had since childhood had a great propensity for reading. Literature was the motivation of his life. Since he had decided to abandon his studies at Oxford, he was free to dedicate himself to poetry, which had been his enduring ambition.

My father and mother had fled the Bloomsbury atmosphere of London, the conventional life of their families and everything that they had been born and bred into, to start something quite new. Having got so far— wedded and with a roof over their heads—they settled down to married life. There was a complete absence of anything in the stable. As for money, it had to be made. There was no means of producing anything except perhaps with a pen and ink, so my father got down to writing. Up in the loft of the stable, he had to light a candle to enable him to see his pen and paper as there was no other light. The air was thick with poetry. I know this from my mother's accounts of the times about their equal passion for poetry and the way my father was overflowing with inspiration.

THE FLAMING TERRAPIN was written there, all except a few parts which my father had started before meeting my mother and which he had composed when he had first been struck with the theme of the poem during his lonely wanderings. This first published work[239] of my father's is a long mystical poem involving

---

[239] This was the first major work of Campbell's to be published. He had published individual poems prior to this in the OXFORD CHRONICLE. See Tony Voss, "Roy Campbell, Before the Terrapin", CAMPBELL IN CONTEXT (Coullie and Wade, Campbell Collections,

In the Shadow of a Poet

the incongruous Almighty that animates creation and stalks the earth, together with superlative descriptions of nature on this planet, taken most likely from his African memories which must have returned to him powerfully in this grey retirement. It is also a mystical poem in the sense that it was first inspired by the silent devastation and gloom after the First World War, the Terrapin symbolising the ever-determined spirit of the universe to make good, over the ruins left.

In the middle of this intense artistic and intellectual fertility, I was conceived. My mother's entire pregnancy with me was at the stable, at the same time as my father was composing THE FLAMING TERRAPIN. The atmosphere was charged with the constant flow of poetry, both that which was being created and that which was read aloud, as my father always read his finished work to my mother. They also had sessions of reading aloud from the cream of British poetry: Marlowe, Shakespeare, Keats, Shelley, Burns and so on.

My having been born in this unusual ambiance of material bareness conjoined with highly intellectual concentration may have contributed to my unbalanced make-up, as I have tended to be a bit barmy, with my head in the clouds.

After nine full months, a midwife was called for my mother and I was born on 26 November 1922.[240] I weighed ten pounds, and my mother nearly died having me as I was so big. After a year at Ty-Corn (the name of the village nearby)[241] we alternated our stays between London and Herefordshire, where my maternal grandmother lived. During this time THE FLAMING TERRAPIN was published. It exploded like a bomb on the English literary world to great acclaim as it was something quite different on the poetry scene.

During the years preceding this my father had had a wandering existence, and therefore was unsettled and unsure. But now, with the success of his first book, he gained more confidence and decided to go back to his native country, South Africa, not only because he was badly homesick but also because he felt there was more of a future for him there than in England. So in June 1924 he set sail for South Africa, leaving my mother and me with my grandmother. We followed in December.

2004: 600-650).

[240] It is interesting that Tess was named after St Teresa of Avila (Alexander, 150), given the importance that the saint—as a nun of the Carmelite Order—was to have later in Mary's life.

[241] Ty-Corn is the name of the cottage. A colleague, John Hart, who visited the current inhabitants of cottage and spoke to locals, says that it was not originally a stable: the building was part cottage, part animal keep. Locals informed him that Ty-Corn means chimney house. Aberdaron is the name of the nearest village. Readers may find interest in Gwyn Neale's "Love in a Hut" at Rhiw.com http://.rhiw.com/pobol/campbell/love_in_a_hut.htm.

Chapter 2
Two Rebels Converge in London

My parents had come together in London after the Great War, in November 1921. They were both searching for something. They were both runaways. My father had abandoned his studies at Oxford and my mother had run away from home with a younger sister. In their different ways they were trying to escape convention. As my mother often said when she was about eighty: "Roy and I were the first Hippies," and she seemed especially proud of the fact.

It seems to have been love at first sight between them but it was my mother who first noticed my father and followed him off a bus. He was an unusual type, and my mother and her sister were equally intrigued by him. No meeting took place then but it did shortly after when Augustus John, the painter, introduced them to each other.[242] After that they were united until the end of their lives.

My father was fortunate in meeting my mother because in her he found a nature complementary to his own. She was calm and stable in her habits, and for most of her life religion was her anchor. She brought a much-needed steadying influence to his rather nervous temperament. At the same time he found in her a companion who shared his love of adventure. She was unorthodox—it was apparent in every aspect of her life—from the way she dressed, to the occupations she dedicated her life to. She was quite perfect physically. She had a kind of exotic beauty which my father liked in women. She was cultured and came from the same background socially as he did. She was a great enthusiast of poetry and was highly artistic. What made her even more intriguing was her inexhaustible vitality and remarkably controversial mind, so that wherever she was, things were never dull. It was this combination of endowments that my father, through the many years of their married life, learnt so fully to appreciate.

Here is an extract from an account of their first meeting in London, from the only page recording her memories that my mother ever wrote:[243]

---

[242] See note 19 above.
[243] I asked Tess about Mary's memoirs; she no longer had them or knew of their whereabouts.

In the Shadow of a Poet

My sister Kathleen (who looked rather like an Egyptian princess and still does) and I, were riding on the top of a bus in Tottenham Court Road, on our way to the Eiffel Tower Restaurant when we saw Roy for the first time. He got off the bus when we did and made for the Eiffel Tower Restaurant in Charlotte Street. We were quite intrigued, he was so good-looking, so foreign, who could he be? Once inside the restaurant he went straight to a table where a golden-haired girl, Iris Tree, was sitting alone, evidently waiting for him. We still did not know who he was, but a few nights later we were in the Old Café Royal having a drink with Augustus John, when John suddenly started up and said,

"Ah, here is Roy, you must be introduced to him."

Now I really saw what Roy looked like and was shocked by his pallor and emaciation and the trembling of his hands.

At about midnight we decided to ask Roy where he lived. He said "nowhere", so we asked him to come to our studio in Regent's Square thinking we would try and feed him up.

This must have been about November 1921. Anyway, Roy came back with us, and quite a lot of interesting things happened at Regent's Square in the next few months.

I said that my mother was unique. One mark of her distinctiveness springs from a vision she had at the age of twelve; she saw clearly a venerable old man with a beard and a scroll. This old man, one of the archetypes, is said to symbolise the sage or the poet in psychology. Subconsciously, she was either poetry-struck or poet-struck, but when she met my father she must have been satisfied either way.

Even at an early age she used to read poetry avidly. Of this my mother writes:

> I suppose it was my love of poetry that was the main cause of our marriage, the marriage of Roy and myself. At twelve years old I was in love with poetry. I remember reading Blake and Shelley with the greatest delight. When I met Roy he seemed to me the personification of poetry, and when he recited couplets from THE FLAMING TERRAPIN, which he had just begun to write, I realised that I had met a poet in flesh and blood.

In the early 'twenties when my parents met, they must have been a captivating couple—at least from what one gathers from the description of them and the photos of the time. My father had a delicate face, the proportions of what one would call a poet's head with a larger top part, small chin, high forehead, and large mystical eyes which could change suddenly to down-to-earth concentration or, if provoked, to sudden attack. He was six foot two inches and slim. I remember as a child he had a magnetic effect on women, they were immediately responsive when he approached as he was extraordinarily handsome and seductive looking. He had a particularly easy way with them which put them at their ease.

My mother was small in comparison. She had curly, dark hair, which stuck out round her face with a strange electricity. Her hair was special, perhaps it showed a bit of her inner fire. She had brown eyes, with a contrastingly light skin, a perfectly chiselled nose, a rather masculine mouth, a broad but slender figure and large beautiful hands. She used to wear trousers at this time—and declared that she was the first woman in England to do so. This was so different from the woman she was to become fifteen years later when she took the habit of the Third Order of the Carmelites and wore a sombre, brown dress for more or less the rest of her life.

Chapter 3
Natal

My mother and I joined my father in South Africa in December 1924. I was two years old then, and my child's mind started to register things which to this day remain as clear as if they had happened yesterday.

One of the earliest impressions was the sound of the Indian Ocean[244]—a mysterious, thundering, curiously nostalgic vibration which filled me with consternation and wonderment, it was so prodigious. I recall the seething motion of the sea, the spray-covered waves crashing in onto the damp sand of the beach where shells of every colour of the rainbow lay, and between each crashing thud, that same humming reverberation came, surging up from the echoing canyons of the ocean. This memory must have been formed after a heavy storm because the sea was savage and the sounds booming.

Another unforgettable scene was a thunderstorm one summer night, one of those vicious ones. My father became wild and intent, he was pale and trembling and dripping with sweat. He was reciting lines from Goethe:[245]

> *Und Stürme brausen um die Wette,*
> *Vom Meer aufs Land, vom Land aufs Meer,*
> *Und bilden wütend eine Kette*
> *Der tiefsten Wirkung rings umher.*
> *Da flammt ein blitzendes Verheeren*
> *Dem Pfade vor des Donnerschlags;*

---

[244] The Campbells were living in a cottage belonging to Lewis Reynolds at Sezela, on the south coast of Natal. Reynolds had invested £1000 in VOORSLAG. Alarmed at the anti-colonial and anti-racist opinions expressed therein by RC, Reynolds insisted on curbing RC's editorial control. RC refused and resigned immediately. Reynolds then asked them to vacate the beach cottage (see Pearce 63-71).

[245] My thanks to Michael Hanke for pointing out certain errors in Tess's version. He says the lines are spoken by the Archangel Michael in the "Prolog im Himmel" in "Faust" (ll. 259-266). Quoted from GOETHES WERKE, vol. III (Hamburger Ausgabe), ed. Erich Trunz, 16th rev. ed. 1996:16.

Michael Hanke has edited a collection of new critical essays on RC: ROY CAMPBELL AND THE ROMANCE COUNTRIES (Trier: WVT—Wissenschaftlicher Verlag Trier, 2006).

> *Doch deine Boten, Herr, verehren*
> *Das sanfte Wandeln deines Tags.*[246]

He emphasised the words "blitzendes" and "Donnerschlag", repeating the lines over and over again, as he leapt into bed and out, his resounding voice accompanying the flashes and blasts. The strange German words, mixed with his fantastic behaviour were like an echo of the tumultuous goings-on outside. Our hair was almost standing on end with the electricity generated. To me it was uproarious; by instinct I knew it was poetry he was reciting and in spirit we all joined in the mood of high exultation. It was a memorable scene—the vigorous words, the rhyme, the sweat, the pallor, the trembling, the heat, the downpour, the flashes, the loud sounds, together combined to give it a metaphysical charge.

There were also nights when I was put on the veranda to sleep, and immense black cats from the forest near used to come and fight under my cot and send out loud agonised peals of emotion like witches' shrieks. I lay in complete bewilderment and amazement at the pandemonium and fighting, but soon learnt they were not concerned with me, so I got to quite like the feeling that such fearsome creatures were so near but didn't wish me any harm.

---

[246] My thanks to Peter Strauss for his translation of the lines as follows:

> And storms rage in competition
> From the sea on to the land, from the land on to the sea,
> And, furious, create a chain
> Of the deepest turbulence (influence) all around.
> A flashing destruction flames there
> Along the path ahead of the stroke of thunder;
> But your messengers, Lord, revere
> The gentle passage of your day.

An earlier translation (1870-71) by Bayard Taylor renders the lines thus:

> And rival storms abroad are surging
> From sea to land, from land to sea.
> A chain of deepest action forging
> Round all, in wrathful energy.
> There flames a desolation, blazing
> Before the Thunder's crashing way:
> Yet, Lord, Thy messengers are praising
> The gentle movement of Thy Day.

Cleveland, Ohio: World Publishing Company. Date of publication not listed on copyright page. Rpt. Boston: Houghton Mifflin and Company, 1906. Available from http://www.gutenberg.org/files/14551/14591/14591-h/14591-h.htm

My thanks to Thomas Olver for bringing this version to my attention.

In the Shadow of a Poet

(L-R): George, Roy, Mrs Campbell, Dr Sam Campbell, Neil at the Musgrave Road home (Tess/Francisco)

The scenes that produced panic in me were the periodical Hindu ritual dances. Tall dancers came towards the house in slow motion, with crowns and clanking metals, feathers and jewellery adorning their naked bodies, their faces painted white. They danced and leapt to the sound of drums. It wasn't the dancers themselves that frightened me, it was more the spirit of the thing—there was an otherworldly air about it, a cold detachment from anything or anyone around. Even when they were far-off, the sight of them sent me into hysterics and I would shoot off and hide my face in my black nurse's lap.

These memories are uppermost in my mind because they were the most striking, but they were set off against a background of glorious light, shade and colour in everyday life, by enticing attractions like the pools among the rocks where I used to bathe, full of little fish and curious things from the sea. I can still recall the air, redolent with the strong scents of curry and boiled rice from the Hindus' cooking. Then there were the

Roy, Mary and Tess in South Africa (Tess)

luscious fruit. Being by nature greedy, I remember each fruit distinctly with its breathtaking flavour: mangoes, paw-paws, guavas, litchis, granadillas, avocado pears, bananas, tangerines. My love for South African fruit was such that I was constantly found up the guava trees and had to be spanked before I gave up. Most of these experiences took place at Sezela, a railway junction not far from the sea, where my father was lent a bungalow for a few months. With these memories Africa fades away, and new ones begin of England and the south of France.

During this last year in South Africa (1926) my father edited a magazine called VOORSLAG (which in Dutch means whiplash).[247] In it he expressed his philosophical conclusions and savagely attacked the colour-bar and South Africa in general. This was just after he had been welcomed back home, after the success of THE FLAMING TERRAPIN in England. Later he condensed these ideas in THE WAYZGOOSE, a satire published in 1928.

My mother was not happy with this primitive life. She never managed to integrate herself into the Campbell family. Colonial life seemed vapid and pedestrian compared to England's highly cultured life. However, she did relish with my father the physical fascination of Africa. She used to go for long walks alone into the forests—she was fearless in this way—and she had quite a few adventures and narrow escapes. Once she nearly stepped on a green mamba, and another time, when she was pregnant with my sister, she was chased by a male baboon and she had to run for her life.[248]

During our last year in South Africa my sister was born. She was the most delicate, perfect little baby imaginable. This was a great consolation to my mother, but not wholly, as she had wanted a son and no daughters. In this way she was never fully satisfied.

At that time my parents were a sort of mixture of pagan-Christians. My mother baptised my sister in the sea, with the water of the Indian Ocean. She was named Anna after a great painter friend of theirs who lived near by.[249]

After three years in South Africa—with my father becoming more and more unpopular because of his politics and my mother becoming more and more homesick for Europe—early in 1927 we set sail for Southampton.[250]

---

[247] The three issues that RC edited (with William Plower and Lourens van der Post) are included in full on the CD CAMPBELL IN CONTEXT (ed. Judith Lütge Coullie and Jean-Philippe Wade. Durban: Killie Campbell Africana Library, 2004).
[248] Alexander says they also killed a cobra and a deadly black mamba. The animal that chased Mary was, he notes, a large monkey (45).
[249] Anna von Schubert was Anna's godmother.
[250] Pearce gives the date as 22 December 1926. Anna and Tess never visited South Africa again yet Francesca, Anna's daughter, told me that Anna always said she was South

In the Shadow of a Poet

The sea voyage back to England was horribly rough. My mother was seasick nearly all the way, and my father took full charge of my sister who was about a year old at the time. According to my mother he was excellent in baby-care; he had great knowledge which came to him quite naturally as he had an immense pride in his two little daughters.

African and that she only changed her nationality to British when she married Rob Lyle in 1985.

Chapter 4
The Weald, Kent

After leaving South Africa and arriving in England my parents were invited by Harold Nicolson, the MP, and his wife, Vita Sackville-West, whom they had met in London, to stay at Long Barn, a property of theirs in Kent, and they were lent a cottage on the premises which they soon left, moving to a bungalow in the nearest village of Weald.

As neighbours everything went well at first, until one night I recall waking up at about four in the morning and crying out for Mother or for Father. There was no answer and the house looked as if a wild wind had passed through it. I remember the anguish and fear, with my sister standing up in her cot and yelling her head off. It was dreadful for us because nothing like that had ever happened to us, and I was outraged at such neglect. I don't know how long this fearful panic lasted, but by next day we were reunited, and although my parents' disappearance from home left a bad taste in my mouth, it gradually faded in intensity. This was when the seeds of THE GEORGIAD, my father's second satire, were sown, and this acquaintance with the Nicolsons had serious repercussions.[251]

During this difficult period I remember being cussedly rebellious. On one occasion I wanted to go out with two older girls. They were twins, Joan and Peggy, but my father didn't want me to associate with them because I was getting a proper cockney accent, and it did not fit in with his aesthetic tastes. After a battle of wills, I forced my way and physically fought him and kicked him. He wouldn't have any nonsense and gave me a sound hiding. He did this three or four times during my childhood, when justly worked up. He was quick tempered and settled our punishments on the spot. On the whole, though, we

---

[251] In his autobiography, WORLD WITHIN WORLD, Stephen Spender refrains from mentioning Roy's name, but it seems clear, in a conversation with Virginia Woolf that he records, that Woolf was referring to Roy when she commented about, "a poet, later to become a supporter of Franco, who had written a satire directed at friends, viz., the Nicolsons" (Spender, London: Faber and Faber: 1997 (1951): 148-9). The soured relationship is mentioned also in ORLANDO.

In the Shadow of a Poet

were treated with such love and freedom by both our parents that we were good naturally.

But to go back to our stay at the cottage at Long Barn, the property of the Nicolsons. It was in the orderly, rambling garden at Long Barn, with its myriad flowers and neat lawns that I first tasted the gentle magic of England. It must have been early summer for the flower-beds were mosaics of forget-me-nots, pansies, wall flowers and sweet peas, all the collection of usual English garden flowers with their gentle colours and subtle smells. Even now when I come across these flowers, I get a thrill and am taken back to the first impressions at Weald. It wasn't only the civilised side of England which seduced me, it was the peaceful Kentish country-side with its quiet fields and cuckoos calling. I remember coming suddenly close up on a thrush's nest in a sunny thicket in the woods: the eggs were a wonderful blue with brown spots. It was a treasure, and after gazing at it in delight, I walked stealthily away.

At Long Barn, although we were not actually living that typical sumptuous life of the English upper classes, we got glimpses of it. While I was thoroughly enjoying the new surroundings, British society was beginning to worry my father. He was beginning to get restless. I was not conscious of the things that disturbed him. I was only vaguely aware of something terrific—the immense riches, the dazzling luxury and endless glories of the British Empire at its best.

Probably the prospect of having to settle in England affected my father; he took to drinking and used to disappear up to London.[252] He was probably wondering how he was going to write poetry in this atmosphere because, as he said, with him, poetry was the perspiration of his experiences. His drinking disturbed my mother who felt alienated from him, and she fell back on Harold Nicolson's wife for consolation. An extraordinary friendship grew between them. I think the secret of this sudden and passionate relationship lay in the fact that they were born under the constellation of Pisces, and this created an intense affinity, an unusual combination which probably lent to their understanding of each other. They almost shared a birthday, as Vita was born on the ninth of March and my mother on the tenth. The strange thing is that it was my father who interested Vita at first, but I expect he put a quick end to that attraction.

It has been said that the affair between my mother and Vita Sackville-West caused wretchedness and heart-ache for my father, and that he never got over it. It was deeply felt, but did not last so long; my father knew well that he and my mother were equally to be blamed for what had happened. He was in great difficulties at the time; having chosen a rare and risky profession, he was too

---

[252] Tess told me that her father never felt at home in England.

disturbed to write and had no hope of producing funds from anywhere. He was desperate, his only escape was drink. As my mother said later, he drank as he had never drunk before or after. Of course, they forgave each other and it was after having re-united that my father wrote two of his most famous poems, dedicated to my mother. Both my mother and father renounced any strange behaviour, and lived a married life ever after.[253]

After a few months our stay at Weald ended in an inevitable split with the Nicolsons. My father was too much of a rough diamond to settle in that refined and sophisticated atmosphere; he was a complete outsider.[254] This was when he got the name of "Zulu" from the "blue stockings". He remembered the South of France where he had been a few years before, and in April 1928 he went back there. Two months later, my mother packed our belongings and we joined him.

We set out for Martigues in Provence, and this was where one of the happiest childhoods imaginable started for me. Everything unfolded favourably for it. My sister's childhood was not so happy because her health was more delicate, and the impressionable years did not coincide with the best times; but mine, those seemingly long years between five and ten, were lived in the most peaceful, idyllic surroundings and circumstances.[255]

---

[253] Although Tess here denies that her mother and Vita were lovers, in a letter dated 11 September 2003 she acknowledges that "it is no good" to try to "minimise their relationship" since it features so prominently in the Pearce biography.
  Connolly, the biographer of four of the Garmans (including Mary), interprets Campbell's references to Mary's reputation as a "man-hater" as "a veiled way of implying lesbianism" (29). She devotes a chapter to Mary and Vita's love affair, noting that it "had a number of literary consequences", including Woolf's novel ORLANDO (81). When Roy died, Mary asked Vita to destroy her letters to her; Vita did not do this, nor did she destroy Mary's journal recording their affair (221). According to Connolly, this was not Mary's only lesbian experience. She also refers to a *ménage à quatre* when, in 1932, it seems that Mary and her sister-in-law, Jeanne Hewitt Garman, became lovers at the same time as Roy and Jeanne's sister, Lisa, had a rather longer lasting affair (122). As has been seen in Anna's account and editorial notes, both Roy and Mary also had heterosexual affairs in subsequent years.
  Although Roy does not give details about extra-marital affairs in his autobiography, LIGHT ON A DARK HORSE, he does say that it was only once he and Mary had converted to Catholicism and were remarried in the Catholic Church that they became "monogamous" (325).

[254] Antony Akerman's biographical play on RC is entitled DARK OUTSIDER (Johannesburg: Wits University Press, 2000)—a phrase RC used to describe himself.

[255] Tess told me that although they were always short of money, this was not hard on the children because they didn't know anything else and they were happy. They had a wonderful life with horses and travelling to many countries. It was, she says, fantastic, and they were "very, very, very loved".

In the Shadow of a Poet

Martigues was a fascinating fishing town. I say *was* because it has changed greatly since. There was something about that first blazing Provençal summer when we arrived that was exhilarating and captivating, everything about it was hot and welcoming. The people were so warm-hearted and attentive to the right things—at least the things which seemed most important to me, and we soon got on well with them.

Before settling in the country, we rented a ground floor apartment in the Rue St. Mitre, which was the beginning of the road which led to our next home. The new surroundings seemed to galvanise my mother. Here for some reason or other she picked on me to sit for a portrait. I suppose it was my suntan, as I turned a lovely apricot colour when sunburnt. She did an inspired little picture, rather impressionistic; it must have been her first attempt at painting since she had left the academy in London seven years earlier. The painting was done under pressure because I did not want to pose. Through the shutters behind me I could feel the heat coming in and I could hear my friends playing in the street. I so wanted to be with them. Although painted in a stormy atmosphere, the portrait ended up a great success and earned praise from Augustus John who, when he saw it, told my mother she should never leave off painting. After this she painted throughout our stay in Provence but never touched a brush again until we went to Portugal in 1952, and there, with us children having grown up and with servants to help with housework, she managed through the many hazards of life to start again and did some particularly accomplished work.[256]

During our stay at Rue St. Mitre, my father was busy making friends in the town while at the same time searching for a home for us. In the end my mother set her heart on a dream of a place set in a background of pine woods near the Étang de Berre. Here we settled for a few years. The name of the place was Tour de Vallier.[257]

---

[256] Tess said that her son, Francisco Campbell, has Mary's most perfect paintings.

[257] Tess spells this as "Tours de Valliers". Martin Garrett, who has a chapter on Roy Campbell's sojourn in the region in PROVENCE: A CULTURAL HISTORY (New York: OUP, 2006) uses the same spelling as Anna (and, for that matter, as Pearce) i.e. without the s.

Chapter 5
Provence

One of the first remembrances I have of our new home was one night, with the dark woods round, when something mysterious was going on, something which was upsetting my mother. There was a tussle going on behind the house; my mother was holding an empty bottle. How a bottle could cause such commotion was beyond me and I wondered what it was about, but it seemed my father should not drink wine. The bottle was empty and it had been hidden, and that was bad. That was as far as I got that night. It was puzzling, and my father didn't seem to be himself. This was the first I knew of my father's drinking. My awakening to the fact that my father drank was gradual because at Martigues it was not conspicuous. There he had a strong sense of fulfilment which satisfied his aspirations, so he did not drink heavily, and even later, when he had a crisis, I learnt to take it for granted. If he drank, it seemed quite natural, so much so that if he had been a teetotaller, *that* would have surprised me. His drinking never shocked or disturbed me. As a matter of fact, he was more mellow and less strict when he was drinking, which naturally suited me. Throughout our lives the brunt of the trouble fell on my mother, who was perpetually apprehensive about it and tried by every means to stop him overdoing it, partly for his health but also for her protection and for us children.

This rather disturbing incident was still an aftermath of the English influence which took some time to pass before the Latin sway took over and an idyllic life began for our family: sadness and mysteries were washed away and life took on a new meaning.

Our life in Provence, especially for me, was spent imbibing creation to the fullest and although we said the Our Father and Hail Mary at night, ours was really a pantheistic existence: the sun, the shade, the woods, the lake, the fruit, the seafood, the wine, the moonlight, the stars, our games, our friends and nature as a whole were the source of our inspiration and happiness. For our parents there were also poetry and painting, which reflected on us children. But above all we were free, utterly free, to enjoy these pleasures to the utmost. Our time passed so happily and harmoniously, we welcomed each booming

In the Shadow of a Poet

day with its liberty, adventures and contrasts.

Part of this unusual independence came from the fact that we did not have to go to school. We did easy lessons at home. My father used to teach me maths. He was fascinated by the square root and tried to show me the wonder of it but I was dull where maths was concerned and never got the hang of it. Funnily enough, my father was a brilliant student of maths and physics at school.[258] Besides maths he sent to Bumpus, the booksellers, for an atlas and with this laid before us, we had riveting lessons in geography. He also taught us astronomy from this book and sometimes gave us lessons about this with the night sky spread above us. Even now when I see Sirius sending out red and green flashes it reminds me of the nights on our way back from Martigues when the icy mistral in our faces brought tears to our eyes so that they magnified the stars, and my father would then point out to us the different constellations and planets. My mother used to gave us half an hour's gym in a clearing near the woods. She also taught us English and history; she was an expert, having passed these subjects with honours at school. We soaked up a lot about literature from my parents' conversation, and general knowledge we learnt every day as my father was an ambulating encyclopaedia. We assimilated most of this because it was so enthralling. He also taught us practical things, like how to fish, to row and to swim.

Anna, Mary and Tess in Provence (Tour de Vallier) (Tess)

For sheer worship of nature and life, the summers were the best. Then we even left off our easy lessons at home and romped through the long hot days, drenched with sun and the scents and scenes of harvest, when the shade was as delectable as the scorching sun rays, when the parched mid-days reverberated with the sound of cicadas. We would play all day on the threshing grounds, around the threshing machines on our neighbours' farms, sliding in the straw and making houses and tunnels with the bundles. These threshing machines used to go round to each farm in turn. The farm children were our friends and we would join them, their families and harvesters in their customs, festivities

---

[258] In 1913, RC obtained 87% for English, 35% for Algebra, 49% for Geometry and 26% for Science. See CAMPBELL IN CONTEXT (Coullie and Wade, 2004: 714).

and dancing and meals. The meals were laid on long tables in the shade of the plane trees and we would relish the carefully prepared food. There was plenty of red wine and everyone was very merry, and for dessert they would bring out melons and watermelons, cutting them into cool, juicy slices. There was the real flavour of Mistral's MIREILLE about it and our lives were bound up in it. After a few years we had deep roots here. As a child of eight I had already felt that my life was there.

All of us experienced that resplendent, passionate, absorbing life of the people of Provence. I think we believed it would always be ours, at least I did.

At the end of the summer there were the *vendanges*, the picking of grapes for the wine making. We picked grapes from sunrise to sunset, bunch after bunch of golden and black grapes and put more into our tummies than into the baskets. For about three days we ate nothing other than grapes. Some years we joined in the wine making and drank the grape juice in handfuls from the gutters where it flowed. We invariably got fat in the summer because of the grapes.

All the times of the year had their fascination. The spring was distinct, vivid. After the winter rains, the earth oozed water and many crystalline pools appeared in the woods, so clear they made one thirsty. Near our house, the lush, emerald cornfields were full of poppies and tulips. As spring advanced and the days grew hotter, some giant bushes of broom turned into masses of burning flowers and as one passed the heady scent nearly made one swoon and every year the pomegranate flowers burst flame-red against the cerulean sky.

Besides the summers and springs, there were the winters, too. We would go *en famille* to Martigues, usually to a café where groups of men played "Loto". They played for game they brought back from the hunt. My father was keen on raffles, games of luck and lotteries. He never missed one if he could help it and often won. One night he won a large pheasant which we triumphantly took home. After these outings we used to trail home with a howling wind against us. Some Sunday nights we would go to the cinema at the far end of Martigues, then, on our way back, we would pass through the deserted streets swept by the Mistral which came from the snowy Ventous. The cold was biting as we walked the length of the town, passing through the three divisions, Jonquieres, l'Ile and Ferriéres, and then doing another three kilometres on the road. My sister was seldom able to manage the long walk, and my father would carry her, fast asleep, on his shoulders with her head resting on his.

There were amusing things to do year round, such as collecting wild asparagus with our friends. The asparagus grew near two long hedges below the house that separated the fields. After searching the hedges, we would bring back big

In the Shadow of a Poet

bundles of them, enough for the whole family.

Another custom among the children was to search for crickets in holes in the fields. We would each have a fine blade of grass and poke their holes gently until a cricket hopped to the surface. Then we would catch it and pop it into a minute wire cage and take it home and feed it on lettuce leaves, and it would sing to us at night.

There were also wild animals of some kind or another to make pets of, such as hedgehogs, wild rabbits, tortoises and magpies. One day, I encountered the strangest sight on the rubbish heap: a creature which was all head, ribs and an enormous swollen tummy; it was grotesque and I thought, at first, that I'd seen a corpse, but it began mewing piteously. Once I had realised that it was a kitten, I took him home and fed him up and he turned into one of our most gorgeous pets. As a child this sort of transformation never ceased to amaze me.

At this time I had a large collection of cats—altogether, with kittens, about fifteen. Sometimes in the morning they would come round the corner and mew. My father had weird days and every now and again he would become formidable and volatile, and then my cats were damned and chased. He would appear brandishing anything he could lay his hands on and throw it at them so as to have some peace to be able to write.

While my sister and I were busy with our pets and roaming around occupied with so many pastimes—it would take a whole book to describe them—our mother was absorbed in her paintings. She made a studio of an old house next door. Here she painted some inspired pictures, the most famous being a portrait of my father which is now in the Killie Campbell Africana Museum in Durban.[259] She did landscapes of the lake and country around us and many striking portraits of the family and friends. Sadly, most of this work was lost during our travels, but we did manage to keep the best.

This existence satisfied each of us, my mother included, although only temporarily, because in her was the yearning for religion which, after the long lapse, resurged even more vigorously a few years later. She was a mystic by nature, and this pleasurable existence satisfied her only superficially.

---

[259] See Illustrations, p 142.

Chapter 6
Tour de Vallier

It was at about this time that my father started doing pen and ink drawings to illustrate his work. His drawings resembled his handwriting in that they were small, clear and compact. If they did not come right at the first effort, he would do them over and over again until he was satisfied and they were quite perfect. His concentration and patience were amazing. When they were finished, I would look at them in wonderment as they were so exact in movement, proportion and shape. He would spend a whole morning illustrating some poem like "Choosing a Mast", trying to get the precise slant of the boat in the wind, or doing a detailed map of Arles with its houses and bullring to illustrate his book TAURINE PROVENCE.[260] He was a superb draughtsman and when illustrating his work he captured much of the magic of the writing. His drawings were fine and his way of drawing precise and direct; he had a clear vision of the subject which he put straight onto paper with deliberate lines. He took immense pleasure in drawing which was an outlet for his abundant artistic talent. Funnily enough, before becoming a writer, his intention had been to be a painter. His two favourite painters were Tintoretto and Giorgio de Chirico.

Wherever my father was he interacted easily with the local people. Here at Martigues he had a spontaneous, exuberant zest for life. He seemed to be inebriated with the love of it. This, of course, affected and infected us all. He joined up with the fishermen of Martigues; he used to go out with them whole nights, fishing sardines and tunny fish and then when he came back home he would sleep through the day. Sometimes he would bring the fishermen back to the house and cook an outdoor bouillabaisse with them under the pine trees. He was also drawn to the bullfighting of Provence. He played some amateurish part, like taking the *cocarde*[261] off the bull's horns. He was healthy and strong, and this outdoor life made him even more so. It was when mixing with the fisher-

---

[260] Published in 1932, RC told Lewis he had "had to get drunk to write it" and referred to it as "a bloody potboiler". Early in 1933, RC wrote a companion volume, MARINE PROVENCE; the book was never published and the manuscript was lost (Alexander 121).
[261] Cockade or rosette, a little red ribbon attached between the horns of the bull.

In the Shadow of a Poet

men that he met Grandpère, his inseparable friend who was in the French navy at the time and was later to become one of the family by marrying one of my mother's sisters.[262] He was a lovable and original uncle.

Although much of my father's time was spent in these extravagant activities, he found time to be a first-class nurse to us. He was a wonderful story-teller as many people who knew him know. Mixed up in his repertoire were Zulu stories that were richly poetical and he told them with much embellishment.

He also used to take us for walks when he went to town for a drink and to meet friends. On these occasions when we arrived at the café, I would have my drink which might have been white, green, orange, yellow or red, depending on whether I was on almond syrup, peppermint, orange, lemon or pomegranate syrup at the time. Then I would make my way to the public fountain which was down in a hollow. At the bottom was a large stone basin with water that seeped down into the ground. I would sit on the worn steps that led down to the basin and stare down into the clear water to the clean gravel at the bottom. The taps were made of heavy brass, bright and shiny from use, which, in the strong sunlight, made dancing reflections on the water. This spot was enchanting. The water fascinated me, as it does most children. The fountain was also the centre where the locals had to come to fetch water. These people were captivating in their different ways and I used to spend hours studying them and the water. It was a way of really getting in touch with humanity and abundant water, and it gave me intense pleasure. The setting and mood were better than any story or film. Then, when we had finished with our activities in the evening, we would return home and my father would cook spinach mixed with milk and butter or boiled potatoes in their jackets and mash them up with butter and mint. These things he did with such gusto and absorption, our lives were filled with happiness.

My sister and I were also exceptionally lucky as children because my father loved to read to us in loud, clear tones. Among our children's literature, the stories that impressed me most were: Andersen's "The Skylark and the Daisy", "The Little Match Girl", "Aladdin and his Lamp", and Lear's Nonsense Stories, especially the "Yongi Bongi-Bo". My father knew Lear by heart. Sometimes, on winter nights, he would bring out a large tome of Robert Burns' works and read us hair-raising passages from "Tam O'Shanter" while we looked on, horrified at the graphic engravings that illustrated the poem.

When I was about nine, he decided to take me to a bullfight. It was the first big treat he gave me. He was beginning to feel proud of me because I was grow-

---

[262] See note 54 above.

ing up and he felt I was old enough to appreciate it. So we set out early in the morning and got the bus at Martigues. We arrived in Marseille about an hour later. After taking a motorboat to see the Chateau d'Ife, Napoleon's prison in the bay, and telling me about his history, we sailed back in the spray to the port and went to have a *panaché* at a café on the boulevard. A *panaché* is a large plate of various shellfish: oysters, mussels, clams, shrimps, sea urchins and others, decorated with slices of lemon to flavour it. It was the most delicious meal I had ever had. From there, we walked to have a proper meal at a restaurant and met Tristram Hillier, an English painter who was our neighbour at Martigues, who was also going to the bullfight. My expectation of the bullfight was fully satisfied because there was a marvellous horseman riding that day. From out of nowhere, it seemed, a romantic figure entered the arena, dressed in black and white lace and a three-cornered hat with an ostrich feather in it and a pig-tail behind. Riding a superb white horse, he was so gallant and agile, I fell quite in love with him. The rest of the bullfight had not much meaning for me, but the slim, black figure of Simao da Veiga left a lasting memory. After this exhilarating day we drove back towards the sunset to Martigues.

Another outing which took place every year was on the 14th of July, the national fête of France. For this the whole family went to town, all in their Sunday best. During the day there were the jousting contests, which my father took part in, and at night there were fireworks over the canals. At the far end of Martigues was the fair which lasted days. There were many different stalls for shooting, most fascinating of which were the bird stalls with little birds of every description. At night on the wide promenade, the cafés spread under the plane trees were crowded with people having drinks and dancing. The first year we went the merry-go-round enthralled me. I remember walking back to my father at least ten times to ask for pennies to mount the horses, such was my enchantment. To my great relief he never refused, and I rode over and over until I had had enough. The strange thing is, I never went on a merry-go-round again as far as I can remember, and never wanted to. It just goes to show there is a time for everything in life.

During these leisurely times at Martigues, when we went on our walks or when we were playing around, my father would sit down to rest and say, "Well, Tess, one day you will marry a duke or a prince". I felt so awkward when he said this as it sounded strange, like something out of the fairy stories he read us. I would look at him doubtfully and answer "yes" to comfort him. I don't know whether he said it because he thought I deserved a duke or prince or because he was anxious about me; he had good reason to be because I loved

In the Shadow of a Poet

my freedom and independence too much to cherish that idea. I felt fortunate that for some time I would be spared this frightening fate, as it couldn't happen for years to come.

Two of the not so agreeable occurrences that happened at Tour de Vallier were the sunstroke I suffered and a vision I had. Sunstroke is an uncommon affliction but in Provence it is quite usual. The heroine in Mistral's MIREILLE gets sunstroke, and so did I. It happened during one of the glorious summers at Tour de Vallier and it was a horrible experience. Usually, the sun was beneficial to our health and spirits, but as is well known, too much of a good thing can be prejudicial. I was playing with my little friends at one of our favourite spots where there were three old olive trees with spreading branches, so that we could sit, swing or hang on them as we pleased. I had been sitting on a branch of one of these trees, in the scanty shade, without a hat, at about two in the afternoon, on a sweltering July day, when I started feeling odd, so I went back home. The maid put me into a shaded room and I started seeing luminous coloured balloons floating across the walls and here, there and everywhere. After a session of these peculiar sensations my head felt as though it would crack with a pain so violent as only the devil knows, followed by a loud sound of rushing water before this awful experience ended. This experience of sunstroke was sudden and passed quickly, but it certainly taught me a lesson for life.

It must have been just about half-way through our stay at Tour de Vallier that I had another frightening experience, and it was much more horrifying and uncanny than having sunstroke. I was lying in bed, in our only bedroom, with a slight temperature perhaps. I was alone in the room (my sister was in England at the time) when in the doorway stood a little figure of a man with a cap on. He looked at me directly and intently. I gave a yell from the depths of my soul and the sprite disappeared; my mother rushed up the stairs and through the same door, as if nothing had happened, and asked me what was the matter. I was beside myself and tried to explain what I had seen. The worst part was the sprite had winked at me with one of his large eyes before disappearing. I had imagined it was someone from the woods around. This haunted me for days.

Three of us in the family had visions of strange spirits: my mother, myself and my son, and we were all three about the same age when we had them.

Chapter 7
Visitors and Friends

In spite of our primitive way of life, my sister and I were born into a highly intellectual atmosphere; nevertheless, although I have done a bit of painting,[263] I haven't ever been able to write a line of verse and wouldn't be able to, even if it were to save my life, and I am a lazy reader. The Spanish saying, "The shoemaker's children go barefoot" was, in my case, true. Because my parents shed this highly artistic aura, they were much sought after by the writers and artists of the time. Some stayed in a spare room we had outside, others were too swanky and used to stay at the luxury hotel in Martigues.

Of these people Wyndham Lewis left the clearest memories, perhaps because he was the most striking. He had a mysterious mien, accentuated by his dark appearance and black hat. His visits were rare but very precious to my father. It was not difficult to see they had a profound understanding and affinity. They could talk concentratedly in low voices for nights on end. This attachment lasted for years until Lewis turned "pink" and their friendship cooled off.

Hart Crane, the American poet, also paid us a visit. He was a generous and expansive man but suffered greatly, so much so that it was as if he were perpetually treading on hot coals. He was an extremely desperate character, in a typically American fashion.

Liam O'Flaherty, the novelist and short-story writer, Aldous Huxley, Augustus John, Armand Guibert, the French critic Pierre Maillot (one of the leaders of the French Resistance), Uys Krige, the Afrikaans poet and playwright, and the strangest mixture of people of all kinds and nationalities came and went.

The gayer and more adaptable ones, my father took on excursions to enjoy with him the most typical side of Provençal life—the bullfights at Arles and Nimes, the cowboy life of the Camargue, the religious gathering of the gypsies at Les Saintes Maries, the jousting championships and the many recreational pastimes and sports he loved so much.

---

[263] When I visited Tess in Estoril, she showed me many watercolours she had done, including a painting of leaping springbok based on a drawing of her father's. See p. 301.

In the Shadow of a Poet

Anna, Tess and Sarah the dog (Tess/Francisco)

What added diversity and appeal to our life at Martigues were the friends we made there. There were a few French intellectuals and their families. Anna and I used to play with the children. One lot lived on the other side of the lake, so we visited them by boat. Our greatest friend was Frederique, Comte de Fremenville. Coming from the French aristocracy he was a Catholic, although he did not practice the religion. He had a rich personality, was cultured, had a large heart, big mind, great soul, and he was a considerable sculptor. He had a magnificent studio in Martigues where we used to visit him, and he would spend whole days with us. My parents and he were, for a time, constant companions.

A person quite different from the rest who was with us a lot was Grandpère, our uncle. He brought countless happy moments to our lives. My father and he were like two six foot two twins. Grandpère had blond hair and bright blue eyes; he was just like a Norwegian. My father and he were firm friends and went about everywhere together. Grandpère was a jovial character and full of fun. At bedtime he would come up and sit on our bed and tease us about our boyfriends and bring us fascinating little rings to put on our fingers. One day he turned up with a fluffy black ball of a puppy which he laid on the bed; my mother promptly named her Sarah, after the Sarah of the Bible. From that day on, Sarah was a member of the family for many years. She grew into an attractive Pyrenean sheep dog.

As I said before, Grandpère and my father got on like a house on fire, but to our great surprise they did have a row one day which I think was caused by women's intrigues. It was a funny scene that we witnessed. One late afternoon we children and the maid were returning from a washing day at the public *lavoir*[264] when, to our astonishment, we saw a crowd assembled in front of the house and a big man with a straw hat was lying on top of my father, trying to strangle him. I anxiously imagined the worst: I saw a gang of robbers trying to kill my father, but as we peered more closely we saw it was Grandpère fighting my father; he had him pinned to the ground and was at his throat. I was horrified but my sister, who was only five years old then, seeing my father being beaten, rushed at Grandpère from behind and caught hold of one of his legs and bit it hard. Grandpère got such a surprise, he let go of my father and the fight ended. Everyone looked at each other in astonishment and my father and Grandpère made it up after my sister's courageous and loyal act.

Among the visitors who came to visit us from abroad were famous women writers and painters, and some of them, the more intimate ones, were drawn to us children. My sister was the perfect example of the highly-bred child. She was well proportioned, delicate, with soft brown hair. Her face was enchanting and at the same time slightly bizarre because of her large eyes, which at that age were slowly turning green. Her eyes had an extraordinary facility for producing tears. She never failed to captivate anyone who saw her.

I had a broad face, covered with freckles, and everyone said I was the spitting image of my father.

Kathleen Hewitt, the authoress, in her book THE ONLY PARADISE[265] says of us: "Anna and Tess were children when I was at Martigues. When Roy and Mary and I went out for the evening, they would roll up their nightgowns and walk solemnly to a neighbouring farm and spend the night with a Spanish family." I loved these absences of our parents because we could be with other children and stay up late and have big dinners with the entire family—about twenty people—under the pine trees at night.

Also, in another passage, she gives a good description of our life at that time:

> By the day the sun blazed gloriously and in the evening we cooked meals over a fire of sticks in an open hearth, and drank the local vin rosé tipped from a wicker flagon. Roy made wonderful mussel stews that we ate from bowls, with yards of French bread, and—possibly excited by numerous varieties of cheese—we talked a lot, arguing, laughing, boasting and contradicting, shamelessly. Roy would reduce Mary and me to tears with his violent re-enactions of comic incidents.

---

[264] Place in the village where washing is done.
[265] This is her autobiography; it was first published in London: Jarrolds, 1945. A revised edition was published in 2000 by Forehorse Press.

Chapter 8
The Lake

At Tour de Vallier we were not well off and had only the bare necessities of life. When we went to Martigues, we walked there and back; it was about three kilometres away. My sister was small and my father carried her on his shoulders, one leg on each side of his head. Later, when my father made more money from his work, we were each fixed up with bicycles, except my sister who used to go sometimes on the bar of my father's bike or sit in a basket chair fixed onto my mother's handlebars. I was the first to have a bike. The morning I received it I took it triumphantly up to a bare field above the house. The fever was such that I never let go of it once, the entire day. I came back in the evening with bloody knees but I had learnt to ride a bike.

It was a tremendous joy to my father when he got sums of money from his publishers. We would go out and celebrate. On these occasions we used to have a slap-up dinner at the Restaurant du Canal, one of the best in Martigues. We would sit outside in the balmy air as the evening sky swarmed with swifts flying in all directions, diving wildly and screeching loudly. On these occasions my sister and I invariably chose our favourite dish, steak and chips.

My father had a great love of the sea. The greatest treat and joy for him was a sea voyage, the longer the better, and if there was a storm, the more he loved it. Many times on his long voyages to South Africa and back, especially in the storms, he was the only passenger on board not to feel sick. He just didn't know what sea-sickness was. He loved sailing of any kind. One of the first things he did at Martigues when he had money was to buy a fishing boat. On summer evenings he would take the family and friends in his boat to the jetty out in the lake, and there we would bathe until it was dark and the moon came up, and my father and my uncle Grandpère would dive for mussels and bring them up in handfuls. My sister and I got a taste for shellfish at an early age. By the time we had bathed and swum, we were ravenous and besides the mussels we would have an assorted picnic. As the stars appeared and the lights came on, we rowed slowly back in the moonlight and moored the boats on our little beach and walked over the hill— my sister and I to our beds while the grown-ups would

(Back L–R): Mary, Helen (her sister); Front (L–R): Comte Freddy de Fremenville, Tess, Grandpére (Marius Polge), Anna, in Provence (Francesca)

gather together and sing. As long as I can remember, my mother always had a guitar. On nights like this, she would accompany my father's songs on the guitar, then everyone would join in and there would be a long singsong, far into the night.

The best description of my father at this time was written by Uys Krige, the South African playwright I mentioned earlier. He first visited us when he was a rugby player for Marseilles. The sketch of my father was written about twenty years later, after my father and he had got to know each other well. It is an excellent description of everything except the nightingales singing in October—here he is wrong. I remember them hard at it in the shady, midday summers and hot (summer) nights, but not in October. He must have got the month wrong in his calculations—it must have been July or August. Still, here are a few excerpts from this article which was written for a South African magazine:

> I shall never forget my first meeting with Roy Campbell. It was on a perfect autumn day in October 1932. In the picturesque Provençal fishing village of Martigues, I got off the bus from Marseilles. At the post office I almost came to blows with the Postmaster who, invoking the majestic dignity of the law, flatly refused to tell me where *Monsieur* Campbell lived. So I walked straight out of Martigues, due East in the direction of Spain, through a wonderful avenue of huge plane trees in whose branches a dozen nightingales were singing, at half past ten in the morning, as if with the express purpose of fluting me along on the last stage of my forty mile journey to my poet.
>
> I knocked on the open door. A sturdy black-eyed wild-looking young woman seemed to surge up out of the room's darkness. I backed down two steps. *Non, non, Monsieur*—she almost screamed at me in a thick Provençal accent—she wasn't *Madame* Campbell, she was Simone, the *bonne*. The Master was still asleep, but she would go and wake him, it

In the Shadow of a Poet

was time he got up, she wanted to get on with her work, do the room ... And she was off, bounding up the stairs two at a time.

I stood on the doorstep listening to the nightingales. The sunlight lay like a golden patina on that classic Mediterranean scene; and suddenly I was aware that countless cicadas were now shrilling a vibrant accompaniment to the nightingales' cool silvery effortless song.

Through the open window above me there floated the expostulating, raucous voice of Simone. And I could hear a man muttering sleepily. And then a door slammed.

A tall figure came stumbling down the rickety staircase. He wore a rough pair of sailor's trousers and a dark blue jersey. It was obvious that he had slept in his clothes. The next moment he was standing on the doorstep, blinking his large greenish-blue eyes in the sudden sharp sunlight and shaking, vigorously, my hand.

Something big and generous seemed to flow out of the man in that firm clasp, that forthright look and Roy's whole intensely alive, eager bearing. Touched by this warm reception from a famous poet who had never heard of me and to whom my coming was a complete surprise, I took a closer look at him.

It was a striking head, almost bald in front and in the middle, carried high on broad shoulders. The face—long, pointed and finely modelled—was unusual; but the most arresting feature of this young man of thirty-one was undoubtedly his eyes. They were both clear and mysterious, seemed innocent as well as sophisticated; there was something elusive, almost detached and inscrutable, yet at the same time friendly and intimate about them.

But it was when he spoke that I got my biggest surprise. He'd had a night out with some Martigues fishermen, he said, he had one hell of a thirst, and would I mind walking fifty yards to the well with him? It wasn't this brusque opening statement that astonished me, but his accent. It was even worse than my own, so broadly South African that you could cut it with a Knysna notch-saw. It made me feel quite nostalgic as I stood there beside him in that calm sun-drenched Virgilian landscape—reminding me at one and the same time of flinty old Table Mountain, the Aughrabies Falls and the Valley of a Thousand Hills.

The large dented bucket rattled to the bottom of the well, shattering our two images on its still, greenish surface. Back wheezed the bucket. Grabbing it in both hands, Roy emptied it over his head in a single abrupt gesture. Straightening up, he shook his head ponderously a couple of times, as if to scatter with the glittering drops the last cobwebs from his brain.

"That's better!" he boomed at me. "Much better, come on! Let's get going! It's getting late!"

I must have looked puzzled for: "I've got a bicycle," he continued. "It's strong enough for the two of us. You hop on to the crossbar and we'll go to Martigues. There's a very pleasant café under the plane trees by the canal. The *vin ordinaire* is not bad and the fishermen are good company. You'll like them. Come on, man!"

A few minutes later I was perched on the crossbar holding a huge demijohn in my arms. Roy vaulted into the saddle, jamming me against the handlebars as he leant forward to get up speed—and suddenly that calm landscape was no longer static; it came rushing at me and there was a roaring as of the Mistral wind in my ears; we were whizzing down that mile-long hill with me clinging for dear life to the demijohn and Roy shouting a running conversation into my left ear. It was a relief to glide along, some time later on, on that last long cool level under the tall planes and hear the nightingales again.[266]

After spending the day together down in Martigues, Uys says that they returned at night to find Mary, Anna and myself at home. Then they spent that night talking together until dawn. Uys goes on to say that although South Africa owes a lot to my father, my father owes a lot to South Africa, too—the magnificent scenery, colours, scents and sounds of that country had a lasting impact on my father and were the inspiration for some of his best poetry. That is true. He also mentions his stay with us for nine months as tutor to Anna and I.[267] Then, like most of the intellectuals of that time, he ends up pitying my father for being on the wrong side in politics. Still, he redeems himself at the end:

> Many might wonder how I could be so strongly attracted to a man who scorns so much that I respect and revere; who loves his "proud horseman" and hates the "shuffling, pedestrian Charlie"; who extols therefore, the aristocratic and feudal tradition, while he has nothing but contempt for my democratic or plebeian ideal; and who time and again has written such:

---

[266] From "First Meeting with Roy Campbell", THEORIA (12), 1954.
[267] Alexander (120) gives the duration of Krige's stay as eight months. Anna says he was with them for almost two years. Perhaps the discrepancy can be explained if Krige tutored the girls for less than a year but remained with the family for almost two.

In the Shadow of a Poet

> *Do they too have their loves, and with these clods*
> *Of bodies do they dare in their abodes*
> *To parody our dalliance, or the gods,*
> *By coupling in the chilly sport of toads?*
> *Do they too feel and hate—under our wheels*
> *Could they be crushed the deeper in the slime*
> *When forth we ride elate with bloody heels,*
> *Or jingle in the silver spurs of rhyme?*
> *("A Song for the People")*

I have two short comments to make on this. Although Campbell and I did not correspond for ten years because of our conflicting views on the Spanish Civil War, I no longer—now that I am a little older—take his politics seriously. (This, by the way, is the attitude of not a few to such politics as I myself profess.)

The second comment is this: I've been around quite a lot, but I have met few people so richly endowed as Roy Campbell with what is commonly called the common touch.

I was always astonished at the attraction he had for good, simple people. In Provence, Spain, wherever we were together, ordinary workmen, fishermen or peasants were immediately drawn to him. It was the basic simplicity of his highly complicated make-up, I concluded, that drew these simple people to him. To women he is chivalry itself. Gentle with children, he is kind and considerate to the old and infirm. Indeed, in his actions he is more of a Socialist than quite a number of Socialists I know.

Chapter 9
Italian Neighbors

During our last year at Tour de Vallier we had some Italian neighbours. They were a large family of immigrants to Provence, in search of a better life. There were quite a few of these Italian families there at that time. As a child I found them foreign and mysterious. They were superstitious and at every turn and corner there was some foreboding of bad luck; there was never an omen of good luck. Ursula, one of the members of the family nearby, was our maid for a time. One of the great attractions about these neighbours was that they had a gigantic fig tree which in summer was laden with soft, ripe figs—the branches forked on all sides and hung low down, so we could perch on them and eat the fruit. It also pleased us because we could play and swing on them and do acrobatic tricks.

I said these Italians were superstitious—this was the sad side of them. One day I opened our umbrella in front of our house and started twirling it round. Someone from the family told me to stop because it meant a member of the family was going to die. For weeks I was anxious, wandering around as though in a dream, wondering which member of the family would be leaving us. Some time later the old father of the family was ill and took to his bed. Owls were also bad omens and, at this time, an owl appeared and perched near the house for a few days. The old man died a short while later. My father said that was natural as owls are birds of prey and it probably smelt death.

Ursula used to take us to another Italian family further away. We had to cross a clearing in the woods, behind which was a little white house where other Italians lived. Here we passed with great trepidation as the Italian husband had shot his wife. My father always had matter-of-fact answers to these strange occurrences. He said Italians are trigger-happy, which observation seems true when one thinks of the way the Mafia have behaved in the last decades.

It happened during a three day stay with the Italians, while our parents went to sail with friends on a yacht, that a fierce thunderstorm broke out at about mid-day—the longest, fiercest thunderstorm I could remember, loud and bright. It lasted three full days. We children escaped into an enormous

In the Shadow of a Poet

wide bed and hid to try and escape the loud noise. We would go to the door every now and again to see if the storm had subsided but it seemed to never end. While we played in this bed, someone brought out a book, well illustrated, about the various ways our world could end. This was new to me and it got me really worried. It could end with never-ending floods, or showers of stars from the heavens falling onto the earth, or with the inhabitants of the earth getting a general paralysis, and so on. We began to fear that this special thunderstorm was the end. As far as I can remember, late on the third day the lightning got mixed up with the sunset, so the flashes were intensely red, which made it look like the end of the world. Of course, it was simply the end of the storm, much to our relief.

Chapter 10
Herefordshire

While at Martigues my sister and I went several times to stay in Herefordshire. It was a place where we spent joyous times.[268]

If ever my sister and I were under par or run-down, there was an exchange of letters between my mother and grandmother and we were soon on our way to England to stay with our maternal grandmother. These periods of change between England and Provence were part of the strongest glamour of our childhood. We lived that inspired world of *Saudade*.[269] I was perpetually drawn between the two worlds—when in France I longed for the chance to see frost and snow, cows and green fields. When in England, I longed for the late starry nights, when we, full of exuberance and wild freedom, raced the streets of Martigues with our little friends. So besides having a fabulous real life, there was this other one, even more vivid and vibrant in the imagination.

In England, some weeks of early bed (we went to bed at six) and plenty of English milk restored us and we were one hundred percent fit to start fantasising about the other world. Fortunately, there wasn't much time to dream of what we were missing in our alternate life since the sensations of the real world were, most of the time, too enthralling.

When we went to stay with our grandmother we enjoyed everything that was best of English life on a farm. It was a proper working farm, with cows, a bull with a ring in its nose, pigs, cart horses and carts, barns full of hay and straw and the best of farm produce: fresh creamy milk, butter and eggs. There were servants and a cook who created assorted English puddings and a stable boy who cleaned and polished the Wellingtons and shoes.

There was the prosperity of British civilisation. I was struck by the ceremonious meals, the never-ending breakfasts and teas, served on elegantly

---

[268] Anna says many of the visits to England enabled Mary to visit Vita. I asked Tess about it. She said she was unaware of this, if indeed it was so; she was just thrilled to be back in England.

[269] *Saudade* is a Portuguese word for a feeling of longing for something that one is fond of, which is gone, but might return in a distant future. It often carries a fatalist tone and a repressed knowledge that the object of longing might really never return.

In the Shadow of a Poet

detailed ornamented cups and saucers: some with perfect little roses, some with flowers, others with delicate patterns, some in pinks and gold, some in greens, all so perfect. Each time we sat down to tea or breakfast there was this renewed pleasure in seeing this beautiful crockery laid on immaculate, starched lace tablecloths. When the meal did begin, if it was tea, everything else was forgotten with the endless varieties of coloured jams, jellies, marmalades, honeys and the different crumpets, buns, breads and cakes. It seems that never again will there be so much peace and plenty.

And when the sound of the church bells came across the fields of Herefordshire—then the essence of England flowed and flowed, re-animating all that is most English in life and legend.

It was a marvellously health-giving existence. Three or four of us, usually accompanied by some baby cousin in a pram, took daily long walks along peaceful country roads which brought us back relaxed and ready for a long night's sleep. Sometimes we walked for two or more hours, it did not matter whether it was sunny or rainy. In springtime, we would gather an assortment of wild flowers: bluebells from the woods, violets and snowdrops from the hedges, cowslips from the fields. And when we returned with our bunches of flowers we would arrange them in vases.

A wonderful woman took care of every detail of our life: Tony, whom I mentioned before, was a kind of genius who had been my mother's governess. She knew all the ins and outs of childcare. I think she taught nearly every member of the old and the new generation to read and write.

Among my mother's six sisters, there was one I especially loved. She was uncommonly tall and lanky with beautiful eyes, full of overflowing variety and sweetness. Her name was Ruth. I loved her because she was so lively and refreshing. Particularly when things got a bit too strict and proper, she would break the stiff monotony. She used to teach me the Charleston, a step we danced to a song called "Black Bottom". Everything with her was different and enchanting. She would send me on errands with heavy silver half crown pieces to buy her cigarettes. I loved the heavy money and the beautifully painted picture of the British sailor on the packets of Gold Flakes. The half crown pieces seemed to be a great deal of money and the packets of cigarettes seemed awfully expensive compared to French money and cigarettes. Going on these errands gave me unusual independence and a good opportunity to see the village and look over the sweet shop which was like a very full Beatrix Potter one.

Chapter 11
Figuerolles

From Tour de Vallier in the pine woods we moved, in 1933, to Figuerolles, further in the woods, an old pink farm house with a large spreading cedar in the garden.

My sister and I were first introduced to Figuerolles by a detailed drawing done by my father. It was a map of the whole farm, with the cedar and its surroundings. My sister and I were spending the winter with our maternal grandmother in Herefordshire. One early morning, when the window-panes were covered with frost patterns, the postman brought this intriguing letter with the drawing. What pangs of longing I felt. Although I loved being where I was, I was desperate to see this wonderful looking place my parents had found. In this map one could even see Sarah, the dog, walking on one of the paths. This map was a treasure, and for the remainder of the stay I used to bring it out and study it with passion—it brought back the vivid flavours of that warm Mediterranean country. No one else in that company knew the delight of my soul, and it was no good trying to communicate it as they could never experience it, never having lived there.

When we did see Figuerolles later, it was a dream of a place. Behind the house there were huge cork trees. On one side there were olive groves with a path leading down to the lake, just ten minutes away. In front was a spacious garden with laurel bushes and a vast cedar which gave character to the place. There were endless sheds, stables, chicken-runs, just the sort of place I loved. Here I could have animals to my heart's content. I got a whole crowd together—some giant, rust coloured pigeons, that were always flying back to their home in Martigues, rabbits, chickens and a white goat called Blanchette. Apart from my lessons I used to spend my day feeding and attending them. I would milk the goat, and we had a lot of milk when she didn't put her foot in it and upset it all. With the milk I made cheeses and put them in the sun to dry, covered with thyme and rosemary, in the proper Provençal manner. This goat used to provide us with milk and cheese but was nearly the death of me. She used to gallop away with me hanging on to her chain and drag me to the places

In the Shadow of a Poet

she wanted to feed. One day she almost killed me by running round me and a tree so that I was bound to the trunk. For some time I was helpless, but, after a great struggle, I eventually managed to free myself. Later on she ran away and got into somebody else's peach orchard and ate the new shoots there, so that we were given a heavy fine, but we never paid it because it happened just as we were planning to leave for Spain.[270] I have always loved farming but learnt early its disappointments.

It was here at Figuerolles that life seemed abruptly to change for me. I was just eleven when we left for Spain, and life was no longer entirely happy. I no longer saw life through a child's eyes, and this is where a free and easy travelling childhood and adolescence like mine has its drawbacks, because at the age when one needs reassurance and security most, there is no firm foundation and there are no real friends. I was also at the age of serious lessons, and a governess from England had been sent for. We used to learn weird, modern poems about gardens and nature by heart, and what a distorted nature it seemed.

After this we were privileged in having as our tutor Uys Krige, the Afrikaans playwright, who came to live with us.[271] His lessons were sensible and fascinating, but he was rather dreamy when young and one day he could not remember whether cows had horns. As I only saw cows when I was in England, my memory was a bit hazy, and I became more confused because he was doubtful. Still, my sister put us right by telling us that they did have horns, and then we remembered that of course cows have horns. My father had a high opinion of Uys as a poet and said he was the greatest South African poet.

It was about this time that my father was compiling FLOWERING REEDS, a book of lyrical poems.[272] I remember him coming up to my mother at about five in the morning and reading her what he had written during the night. I used to listen to him reading verse after verse from some poem like "A Jug of

---

[270] Pearce and Connolly interpret this event rather differently. It was because they were unable to pay damages that they were forced to leave. "When the neighbour won his suit for compensation against the Campbells, they—being unable to pay—fled in the dead of night, leaving everything but their clothes and books behind" (Connolly, 130).

[271] Krige was to stay with the Campbells for almost two years. Tess mentioned that he was engaged as tutor because they couldn't attend the local school because of the language difficulties. Krige taught her and Anna everything, as if they were at school. I asked whether Krige and Roy spoke Afrikaans to each other, but Tess said they did not. Although he and Mary and Roy got on so well, Tess says the families did not later keep in touch.

Mary painted a picture of Krige in the nude. According to Connolly (129), Mary and Uys were lovers.

[272] The volume was ignored by many reviewers. RC believed this was a boycott due to THE GEORGIAD and his defence of Lewis' THE APES OF GOD (Alexander, 130).

Water", and I was entranced. Although I did not understand much, I was conscious of the condensed language and to hear these exquisite poems read by candlelight before dawn was quite an experience.

At Figuerolles my father sometimes took us to the little village of St. Mitre for a walk. It was in the opposite direction from Martigues, and nearer. On the way he would stop to show us that the cobbled path we were walking on was the remains of a Roman road. He used to tell us about the Romans and how they made roads like this one across Europe, and he reminded us that perhaps Julius Caesar had passed on this one. He had a colossal and innate admiration for the Romans and their civilisation; he was haunted by them, soaked in their literature and he never tired of reading about them in history, and from their experience and example he gathered many of his ideas and theories.

There were lovely walks in these parts. On other occasions we used to go with our mother to the Caderau, a hill about a mile away behind the house, and on its slopes search for quartzes. We often found lovely pink ones.

It was the whole set-up at Figuerolles, with its atmosphere and seclusion and peace, that provided such a wonderful background for writing poetry. Here my father wrote some of his best lyrical work.

Chapter 12
Spain

Our sojourn at Figuerolles was too short. It was in 1933 that the sterling was devalued; life in France became too expensive for us. Apart from a book of poems, my father published at irregular intervals and there was only one reliable source of income, the 20 pounds that came from South Africa every month. These sources of income together were not enough to sustain a family of four. In Spain the cost of living was cheaper.

This departure for Spain was decided on almost overnight. For once I did not welcome adventure or novelty, and the future seemed uncertain. From what we had heard of the Spaniards, they were a barbarous people; the French hadn't a good word to say of them. Compared to English and French standards they seemed backward and savage. Still there was nothing to be done, so we moved to our next destination.

It is useless to generalise about nations, although certain characteristics can be marked.[273] Our apprehensions about the Spanish people proved wrong. After being there some time we found them remarkably generous, frank and human, and in some ways gayer, more fascinating than other peoples, and their country perhaps the most gorgeous in Europe. After the nightmare of the Spanish Civil War the mass of the people did seem to deteriorate with the hatred, suffering, epidemics, starvations, illnesses and tortures they had endured, but that was inevitable. Now there are signs of recovery of their old selves.

At that time the move to Spain may not have been to my taste but it was just what was needed for my father. The different life and unfamiliar horizons brought new blood and inspiration to his work, and fresh ideas orientated his life. We did not feel the change too abruptly because we stayed in Catalonia for the first few months before entering the real Spain.

---

[273] RC has no such difficulty. For instance, in his autobiography, Light on a Dark Horse, Campbell pronounces freely on a variety of nationalities: the French are thrifty yet given to extreme avarice; the Spanish are "at once the hardest-working and also the laziest people in the world", (271); the Germans are castigated for preferring "animals, especially dogs, to their own species and exult[ing] in the killing of men" (310).

My father was intent and wholly wrapped up in the new life about him. As usual he set on making the best of everything. He soon found second-hand bookstalls and bought books to learn Spanish. My sister and I were given Rubén Darío's poems to learn by heart.[274] It was through his simple language and poems full of music and magic that we learnt our first Spanish, although he was a South American from Nicaragua.

From Catalonia, we stayed for a short time in a pension in Barcelona, within a stone's throw from the Barrio Chino (the bad quarter of the town) —the whole family, governess and Sarah included. We stayed here long enough to make me almost die of yearning for the countryside; we who had for so long stepped from the front door into the woods felt the harshness of this city life, with its myriad restrictions and discomforts. After three months I felt a violent and desperate nostalgia; I felt as if I was being smothered. I used to drag our poor governess miles across the city to a hill where wild grass grew, not lawn grass like in the parks. I used to pick tufts of it and in ecstasy rub it against my face; Sarah felt the same. We rolled in it and ran about as if we had gone mad, to the consternation of my sister and governess.

There was a cheerful gentleman in the pension who used to go for weekends into the country and bring back branches of orange trees with oranges still on them. What a joy it was to know that those orange branches had come from the deep country, somewhere. Also it was a novelty to see oranges on a branch.

Barcelona is a fascinating town but as I say, I had had my fill in the first two months. We enjoyed many things about it: we walked the Ramblas and never tired of looking at the profusion of flowers and birds exhibited there; every day it was a new source of pleasure and interest, but town life seemed oppressive and restricted after our free country life, and I was glad when we left.

From here we went to Valencia in search of a place to settle. This town left only sad memories for us because it was here my parents had the worst row of their married life and nearly separated. My mother was not a convert yet, life was unsettled, money was scarce and the Spanish wine was telling on my father. My mother had not the stability religion gave her later. The crisis came to a head and my parents were deciding to separate. A piercing sorrow and hopelessness came over me—no home and not even unity between our parents. I remember that after thinking a lot, I decided that if there was a separation and I could choose, I would stay with my mother. I loved both of them but decided that way, I suppose, because my mother was my mother and

---

[274] (1867-1916) Known as the Father of Spanish Modernism. RC met him in a bar in the Barrio. He helped the family learn Spanish and RC made adaptations of at least two of his poems (Alexander, 133).

In the Shadow of a Poet

of a calm and unchangeable disposition; that was her most wonderful quality as a mother; she had no moods, and this was reassuring and gave one complete confidence. After a desperate few days the crisis passed, my father left off drinking, and everything went back to normal to the great relief of my sister and I. But in the depth of our misery a wonderful thing happened—my father had bought a lottery ticket in the street and he had one of his strokes of luck. He won 17 pounds, which cheered us up.

Then we moved further south to Alicante.

This east side of Spain is permeated by Arab influence. One can see it in the methods of irrigation, in the symmetrical rows of the orange groves and many other aspects of life. The Moors entrenched themselves and they must have felt in clover in this rich and fertile land, where jasmine grows like a weed and the whole country is like a garden.

Strangely, it was not this flourishing and luxuriant Spain that was going to foment inspiration and impress my father. It was the desiccated, barren, parched, frugal, severe Castile that was to give such stimulus to his work and have such a deep influence on his life and mind.

Chapter 13
Altea

*A*ltea, the village we settled at after Alicante, was built on a hill beside the sea, with ranges of mountains around. Our first day here was at the Fonda-Ronda (a pension). It was a damp, stormy night when we arrived, the waves were breaking wildly on the pebbled beach outside and almost reached the pension's dining-room which went right to the edge of the sea.

At this stage in our wanderings, Sarah and I sensed that the country was not far off now, and we were right because, not long after, we moved into a little house set among some olive trees in the country. It had one large room, with a loft above where we slept. It was pretty primitive but it was heaven after our recent adventures and we all enjoyed it. It was not long before we got a maid to help, and everything fell into place. Later we found a larger and more comfortable house and gradually assembled a few commodities and a donkey to carry the water.

The most memorable events at Altea were the autumn rains. I remember, after the parched, dry summer, looking towards the sierras for signs of rain which would refresh everything, our spirits included. But the few clouds seemed always to evaporate and the dry weather to continue. Still, one autumn day my wish was granted and it rained cats and dogs for three whole days and the wide river bed, which was about a mile across, was filled with rushing, billowing water; it was where the best gardens of the district were—everything, huts, gardens, animals were washed away to sea. It was a breathtaking spectacle: the deep, swirling, red water carrying everything before it, while we sat on the high banks in wonderment. The rush of the water was so great because it came down from the nearby sierras.

Some of the most enjoyable occupations at Altea were our periodical visits to Altea la Vieja (the old Altea). Altea is surrounded, except on the coast side, by rocky sierras. On one side there is a sheer rock of a mountain, rising straight up like a wall. In those days if one looked carefully, one could see from far off two or three little huts where shepherds slept when they took their flocks up there. Altea la Vieja is beneath—almost identical to the new Altea, but much

In the Shadow of a Poet

smaller and older; it is a gem of antiquity, also built on a hill. We used to go there on pilgrimages to get special water to drink.

The spring was beyond the village, it came straight out of the rock at the foot of the mountain. From here one looked up and saw the mountain go straight up into the sky; the effect was quite surreal. The rock was grey with big tufts of grass and olive trees hanging on it; they looked as if they might fall straight on top of one. We went to get this water because it was renowned for its goodness. To get there we had to cross the wide river-bed full of pink oleander bushes; down this bed, over the sand, trickled a shallow stream of warm water. Where it was deep enough among the boulders, we used to stop to bathe. We children especially loved it because the water was warm and clear, having run over the sand so far. After this we went through the vineyards, along the winding paths, over rocks until we got to the spring. It was a day's expedition.

The whole family went, with the maid and her relations, and our donkeys laden with water pots. After getting to the spring we would unload our picnic baskets and decanters and put the donkeys to graze. Then we would make a camp fire and roast *boboches* (a Zulu word), which consists of mutton grilled with bacon, for our lunch.[275] After this, some of the grown-ups would have a nap, but we children would roam about; it was one of those delightful places where nothing has been except the sun, the wind and the rain. We would climb the olive trees, roll in the big tufts of grass and wash our feet and faces at the spring. Then we would fill the decanters with the good water. While riding home our maid would teach us a little rhyme in Valencian (which is a mixture of French, Provençal and Spanish) about Altea la Vieja which sounded as old as the mountains around us.

It was in the minute village church here that my father noticed a little statue of Our Lady of the Sorrows. It was this statue with the many swords in her heart that inspired the seven sword poems of his book, MITHRAIC EMBLEMS.

On one of these occasions after our excursion to Altea la Vieja, after parting from our parents and some other members of the party on the way, the maid, Anna and I ended up by having a fierce race. It was started by the donkeys. We were coming back on our donkeys from fetching the good water. The maid and Anna were mounted on the maid's huge she-donkey, loaded with four water pots, full of water. I was mounted on our donkey, alone. At that time I had a passion for playing at cowboys and I used to pretend that Snowball, our donkey, was a horse. Snowball was dark brown all over, except for a white patch on his

---

[275] Zulu academic, Noleen Turner, could not find any evidence of this word. Moreover, she added that Zulus seldom eat mutton. (Alexander, 152, spells this as *boboches*. This is not the way Tess spells it here, nor is it the way she pronounced it in conversation.)

nose. This passion for playing at cowboys came about from a Western trailer that went on for months at the Altea cinema. We used to go and see it every Sunday. Not that Snowball was anything like a horse—he was small and savage, but handsome. One couldn't get anywhere near his head because he would snap and bite fiercely, and he had large, sharp teeth. Still, I used to make do.

This day when we were coming back from the spring, the she-donkey carrying the maid and Anna, riding side-saddle, comfortably settled among the full water-pots. Without provocation, she started first to trot, then to gallop. They passed us who weren't expecting anything, until suddenly Snowball got excited and started galloping after the she-donkey. Then I also got worked up and really thought the cowboy life had begun at last. We started a race, full speed ahead, but this didn't last long because just as we were catching the others up, I went shooting over Snowball's head onto the stony path. I landed painfully on my head and let out a long, piercing yell. Snowball went racing on until he reached the others. Snowball won in the end, but without me; I was left alone on the path, nursing my head.

A few months before leaving Altea we were admitted into the Catholic Church. In this strong Spanish setting, my mother moved swiftly towards her decision to become a Catholic. Until then we had practised no particular religion. My father's family were strict Presbyterians, and my mother was an Anglo-Catholic. What teaching was not instilled into us children against the Catholic Church, wasn't worth mentioning! I remember the heated discussions my sister and I had with the French and Spanish children about their sinful priests and superstitious ways. We were champion Protestants against the corrupt Catholic Church. Still the change came when our mother led us gently into the Catholic Church, just a few months after our damning and slanging it. Thanks to ecumenism, that great enmity between Protestants and Catholics has since calmed down somewhat.

This move had a profound influence on our lives and filled an abysmal vacuum. After my mother's decision Anna and I managed the tremendous task of learning the whole catechism and all the prayers in Spanish. To do this we attended the village catechisms for about a year with the other village children. After being well catechised, confessed and baptised, we were ready for the Church.

As I said before, my mother's life had been deficient spiritually; in joining the Catholic Church she found infinite satisfaction and consolation. She had already got the notion of her conversion years before in France, when she had read St. Teresa of Avila's autobiography.

Towards the end of our stay at Altea our grandmother Campbell came to

In the Shadow of a Poet

visit us. She was about seventy and in the last few years had been round the world three times. She was surprisingly up-to-date and Americanified; she had gadgets for everything. She was used to elevators, telephones, cars and a variety of modern conveniences. Our house didn't even have a tap! We had to fetch water in decanters by donkey. There were no roads to the house; the paths were just wide enough for the donkey to walk on. My grandmother was rather critical of me, at my age, not wearing stockings, so she immediately fixed me up with a suspender belt and stockings. She seemed wonderful to my sister and me because she had no end of money. She bought suits for my father and clothes for my sister and me. She was remarkably energetic for her age and insisted on going for walks. One day, when out walking on a narrow path, she lost her balance and went toppling over into an orange grove—much to our consternation—but she wasn't a bit ruffled and just lay there and laughed hysterically until we managed to heave her onto the path again. She ever after recalled her fall as a great joke. The simplicity and poverty of our life completely baffled her. She was kind-hearted and introduced many innovations to help us. We used to go on shopping expeditions to Alicante but she seldom found what she wanted. She was a superb cook, dressmaker and needlewoman. During her travels in Japan she had studied the art of paper-folding and she would shape birds, animals, boats and aeroplanes with coloured squares of paper folded in different ways. With her we had long sessions of paper folding. It was amazing how with these squares of paper she shaped all sorts of objects—even a little kettle to put water in and make it boil over a candle. She was such an expert at this that she later compiled a book about paper-folding which was a success in many countries in the world.

Mrs Margaret Campbell, Roy and Mary in Alicante, Spain (CC)

At the end of her visit, on our train journey to Madrid, the family feasted on a *Cordon Bleu* apple tart which she baked in the peasant's bread oven.

We all went together on this train journey, but split up in Madrid. My grandmother and I were going to England: me, for a year's schooling there, my parents and Anna were going to explore Toledo to see if it would be a suitable place for us to settle. So for the move to Toledo I was absent, but from what I could gather later, from the letters, drawings and photographs I received, it seemed an uncommonly homely and fascinating place.

Chapter 14
One Year in England

After parting with the family in Madrid, my grandmother and I boarded the night train at Santander. We had a first class compartment, with beds and every comfort imaginable. Next morning we sped through the province of Leon, one of the central counties of Spain, a vast, desolate country, all orange rock and empty villages, abandoned supposedly for the large towns. The deserted villages seemed to come out of the rock and go back to the Stone Age. They were entirely uninhabited, one didn't see a soul anywhere. How these villages were ever inhabited surpassed one's imagination, as there didn't seem to be any earth anywhere to plant anything. From Santander we again travelled first class, on a ship to England. On this journey my grandmother enjoyed introducing me to the luxuries of our first class suite—the bathroom with hot and cold water, our opulent cabin. The meals were sumptuous with all the ice cream one wanted, and even breakfast comprised of three courses.

Once in London, my grandmother took me to Swan and Edgar's to buy me a collection of summer frocks; then she chose a film for us to see which impressed us both. It was THE MOVING OF THE THIRD FLOOR BACK, with Conrad Veit, about an overworked servant girl who ends up having a nervous breakdown. The story, concerning justice and the relationship between employer and employee, was so forceful and subtle that its effects remained with me for life.

A few days later, I was left with my other grandmother.

After our wanderings as a family, at the age of twelve I was longing for a more settled and disciplined life. In England I certainly found it. Coming out of the wilds of Spain, the strict and exacting life of an English school was just what I craved. My schooling had been planned months before by my mother. I was supposed to stay quite a few years but because of unexpected circumstances I only stayed a year.

My maternal grandmother had become considerably less well off in the last few years. She no longer had the home and servants she had had in the Herefordshire days. She had moved to Sussex. We were just four people in this little cottage in South Harting: my grandmother, Tony, Kitty, my cousin, and myself. Kitty and I got on well, although we were totally different in every way.[276] She had curly hair, I had straight; she was delicate, I was strong; she was the purest intellectual. A real book-worm, she spent nearly all her time reading: at nine years old she had read all of Dickens; she sped through books at an astonishing pace. One couldn't mention a child's book or a grown-up's that she hadn't read. In painting she astounded us by finding out, by herself, special ways to mix the water-colours. Her drawing, too, had a kind of magic. I don't know how she did it, it was so expressive. Any painting she did was lovely and full of sensitivity.

In these areas I was only groping still, and as for reading I was not enthused. My interests lay more in exploring and experiencing real life. At that age I was really strong, and the world about me thrilled me.

With Kitty and me, in every respect, our tastes were different, from the ice-creams we chose to the laxatives we took at night. The only thing we were alike in was that we both suffered from chronic constipation, and that was the fault of the Victorian diet we were on and which made of the English of that time, of all nations, the people who depended most on laxatives.

For me everything was a novelty. The spring with its wild flowers, carpeting the woods and studding the fields; the summer with the shade of the beech woods and the fairy patterns of the branches and leaves, like green lace against the blue sky; the beech woods in autumn, with their fiery colours; and then the ice, frost and snow of the winter which I never saw in Latin countries.

I was also totally engrossed with the Petersfield High School which I attended along with three hundred girls of all ages. Some of the subjects we studied, like maths, algebra, geometry, were far above my level. I could never understand anything but did my best. Geography was my strongest subject and French, of course, as I knew it fluently.

My English grandmother was a cultured woman, and from her nine children ended up with twenty-five grandchildren. I was the eldest. She came up with the wonderful idea of a magazine for us which she edited. We all contributed, even the toddlers did their bit. It was called the MOUNT OLYMPUS MAGAZINE. For this we could write stories, poems and do paintings.[277] Even grown-ups

---

[276] It would appear that Tess is referring to Kitty Epstein, the daughter of Jacob and Kathleen.

Anna says that one of their cousins (presumably Kitty) was cruel to Tess and that Tess' psychological ailments began at this time. I asked Tess about this but she denied that her cousin was unkind or a bully; she was, she said, merely brusque with Tess.

[277] For one of Tess's paintings in the magazine, see ch. 21, p. 236.

In the Shadow of a Poet

could join, and my father contributed. Each contributor had a god or goddess's name. Mine was Diana, Kitty's Ariadne and so on; my father chose Eros.

We all loved doing our bit. It was a gratifying project, as we were a naturally gifted family. It was altogether successful and went on for years. In the end, it attained such a high standard that my grandmother had all the numbers bound.

This year in England helped me in life. Although it was not sufficient for my schooling, it helped my English which I got to know quite well, and I was in later years able to teach English in Portugal where I needed to earn a living.

So during the Easter holidays of that year I returned to the family, accompanied by my grandmother, Tony and Kitty who were coming to spend the Easter holidays with us.

But my schooling in England came to an abrupt end because my sister missed me so much. She was becoming a sickly child, and my parents were afraid she might become chronically ill, so I was called back.

Chapter 15
Castile

When I had left for England with my grandmother, my parents and Anna went to Toledo hoping to find a permanent place to settle. They were totally captivated by Toledo and after their visit moved with our belongings from Altea to a house in one of Toledo's main streets. That was how Toledo, so unknown and so phenomenal, came into our lives.

The Spanish poet Bécquer[278] gave the best description of Toledo when he said: *"Tolède, est comme un crie dans le desert."* She is unexpected, arresting and startling—rising abruptly, with her many battlements, churches, convents, palaces, castles, bridges, cathedral and Alcázar, on an endless plain. It is this unexpected abundance soaring out of nothing that confounds the beholder. To really be able to appreciate the description, *"un crie dans le desert",* one has to see Toledo from the distance as one rounds one of the corners on the south west entrance to the town. Then one gets the essential picture: she is like a gem lost in an immense desert of plains. She is truly like *"un crie dans le desert",* not only from her physical appearance in the distance but also inside the town. There is a kind of mystery and depth in her dark and narrow streets, endless riches and meaning in her ancient buildings and walls. Everything seems to breathe wise, wild, fascinating and fantastic stories from time immemorial.

All sorts of peoples and races have left their traces.

Castile, the province Toledo belongs to, is also full of surprises and exotic in many ways. It seems parched and dead, but just for this reason everything is more concentrated and purified. As can be imagined, all that is left after the passing of the sun (in summer the thermometer rises to 35 to 40 centigrade every day) is burnished and refined. In contrast, in winter the air is freezing, frosty but sunny. Being high above sea level, the atmosphere is extraordinarily lucid, giving the impression that the sky is higher than in other places and

---

[278] (1836-1870) Gustavo Adolfo Domínguez Bastida, better known as Gustavo Adolfo Bécquer, was an Andalusian poet and short story writer, now considered one of the most important figures in Spanish literature. The words, in English, are "Toledo is like a cry, a shout in the desert".

In the Shadow of a Poet

producing the most marvellous changes of light. In summer, especially in the evening, the light changes from magenta to amethyst and gradually melts into darkness. The sunsets and sunrises are spectacular, and one can see the full expanse over the plains. There is a riches of birds: bee-eaters, rollers, lories, orioles and hoopoes in summer, fill the parched landscape with touches of turquoise, violet, orange, gold and all the most fiery colours. Fat partridges, buzzards, owls, hawks and, in the mountains, eagles abound. The fruit is much sweeter and more delectable than in other places, everything being ripened and blessed by the sun. Being on this high plateau gives one the sensation of being nearer heaven, and time slows down. It must have been this light and rare atmosphere that helped to inspire a poem like "Songs between the Soul and the Bridegroom" of St. John of the Cross.

Water here becomes particularly important, too. The swift Tagus, encircling Toledo and watering the plains, enhances the extravagance of the panorama. The gardens on the river banks are full of lilies, nards and jasmine, which contrast strongly with the rock around.

However, this is just the physical and tangible side of Castile; the spirit of its people is just as surprising—their severity, their frugality, their endurance and their whole outlook on life is different from ours. As they have very little material comfort and few distractions, they find their interests in a spiritual sphere. The cult in the churches, chapels and convents is very alive; religious life is vibrant. Evidence of this can be seen in the flaming candles, altar lights and profusion of flowers—all symbols of heat and love. Even a few years ago, when motoring through Castile one saw no signs or notices up for restaurants, hotels or cafés, like in other countries, but solitary notices everywhere giving the times of masses in the churches on the road. For the Castilian, this is paramount.

After much wandering and searching, it was in this rare atmosphere that my parents found the place to settle. It was after some time and getting to know this land and its people that they felt that at last they had reached the ideal site for the fulfilment of their aspirations. Here they found the source to quench their spiritual thirst.

For my father a tremendous flow of inspiration followed this first experience of Castile, a strong pulse of the surreal and exotic side of Spain is evident in his work. His style became more concentrated and compact than hitherto. His poetry of this time was a stepping stone from the more pagan world to the Roman Catholic. His poems are full of religious symbolism. The poems "Faith" and "The Fight" are examples of this. From this splendour of light and religion, the sun and Christ are often mentioned. MITHRAIC EMBLEMS (published in 1936) was the outcome.

This very intense religious awakening also affected my mother, though in a different way. She felt she must work for the Church. By the time I came back from England, she was working in Catholic Action.

Chapter 16
Chance Meeting

After deciding to settle in Toledo my parents rented a house in Calle Cardenal Cisnero, a street in the shadow of the Cathedral and the archbishop's palace. This was significant because it was archbishop Goma who confirmed my father, mother and sister and received them with great ceremony into the Church a second time.

Calle Cardenal Cisneros was a wide street. At one end there are narrow streets that lead to the Zocodover Square which was the central square of Toledo, where all sorts of people assembled for drinks in the evenings. There were the officers from the Military Academy as well as the opulent gypsy families, tourists and the common people of Toledo.

By chance one evening a young Englishman who was touring Spain with a guitar got acquainted with my parents.[279] After his pavement performance he went to them to collect tips, so they introduced themselves. It turned out later that this young man who was only half my father's age was Laurie Lee, who later became a well known English writer. He describes this meeting in his book As I Walked Out One Midsummer Morning (1969):

> That evening I was back on the job, playing to the open-air cafés [of Toledo's] Plaza de Zocodover—a sloping square of uneven cobbles which was also the town's main centre. No traffic, no radios—only the sun-down crowds quietly sitting and watching each other, the waiters mostly idle or flicking at flies with slow caressive movements.
>
> I'd not been there long when a special party arrived and made their way to a nearby table—a curiously striking group and immediately noticeable in the ponderous summer twilight. There were four of them: a woman in dazzling white, a tall man wearing a broad black hat, a jaunty young girl with a rose in her hair, followed by a pretty lacy child.
>
> They were clearly not Spanish, yet they had a Spanish air. I thought

---
[279] Anna remembers Laurie Lee playing a violin when the Campbells first encountered him.

they might possibly have been Portuguese. The man sat at the table with a distinguished stoop, while his companions arranged themselves gracefully beside him, spreading their shawls on the chairs and beaming round the darkening square as though in a box at the opera. I finished my last tune and began to take a collection, which brought me at last to their table. The woman asked me in French if I was German, and I replied in Spanish that I was English. "Ah," she smiled. "And so am I." And she invited me to join them.

The man shifted and coughed. He had a long scorched face and the eyes of a burnt-out eagle. He offered me a strong but shaky hand. "Roy Campbell," he said. "South African poet. Er—reasonably well known in your country."

His voice was musically hoarse, yet broken and interrupted as though being transmitted on faulty wires, and it seemed to quaver between bursts of sudden belligerence and the most humble of hesitations.

In a series of stuttering phrases he rapidly let it be known that he hated England, that all his friends were English, that English literature was an unburied corpse, that he was in Spain because England had no manhood any more; and was I broke and could he help me at all?

Apparently it was my father's saint's day, so they were celebrating. It must have been 31st July, St. Ignatius's day. Laurie Lee was invited to have supper with them:

When the girls had gone to bed, we woke up again and talked until early morning. Roy also read a few poems in his thick trembling voice, monotonous, yet curiously moving, and nothing could have suited me better at that hour, and at that place and time of my life. I was young, full of wine, and in love with poetry, and was hearing it now from the poet's mouth. It came out in agony, bruised yet alive, and each line seemed to shake his body. He read some of his shorter poems: "Horses on the Camargue", "The Sisters", "Choosing a Mast", and the words seemed to flare at the nostrils, whinny and thunder, and rise like steam in the air.

Half-dazed with sleep, I felt my eyelids falling, printed with succulent images: sisters called to their horses, naked in the dark, and met them with silken thighs; a rich Zulu nipple plugged the mouth of a child; mares went rolling beneath the hooves of stallions... What had I read till then?—cartloads of Augustan whimsy; this, I felt, was the stuff for me.

And here is a passage about my mother and sister:

In the Shadow of a Poet

Mary and little Anna lived in an intimate calm of their own, quietly busy with their spiritual chores, and could be seen in the morning going off to Mass, veiled and modest as shadows, and so native in appearance that when I met them in the street I often forgot and addressed them in Spanish. When they returned from their devotions they would come back transformed, light-footed and chirpy with gossip, their early silence now swept away and their eyes sparkling, as though they'd been to a party.

On the last day of his stay, my father took Laurie Lee to see El Greco's paintings and this is what he says:

We began by going to the Museo de San Vicente, to see the ANNUNCIATION. Campbell stood quietly before it, bare-headed, slightly bowed, his eyes blinking beneath their sun-bleached lashes; and I first saw the canvas as it were through him, by his physical stance and silence. Then muttering, without jargon, but with a kind of groping reverence, he explained what the painting meant to him. "A bloody miracle, that hand. And look at that light in the sky. Pure Toledo—only he was the first bugger to see it."

They parted on the last day:

Roy woke up in time to take me down to the bridge, by which I would cross the gorge of the Tagus. Here we said goodbye. "Write if you get short of money," he said, looking down at me like some puzzled and anxious parent. "Come back if you want to. Er—we might have gone to Mexico—but we'll always be glad to see you...." He coughed and shook hands. Crossing the bridge I looked back and saw him still standing in the road, legs astride, shoulders hunched, head drooping. He raised his wide-brimmed hat and held it high for a moment, then turned and stumbled back to town.

My father at the time was in one of his most drunken spells. He had just arrived in Toledo and got to know the Toledan wine, which must be one of the best in the world. Even I, who never drink wine, will drink that—it is a golden, rosy colour: wine made from sun-baked grapes from the plains. Its name is Valdepenas, and just the look of it carries one away. Of course my father did not live permanently in such an exulted and confused state as is portrayed in this description of him; this was just a spell while he was not writing.

Chapter 17
Airosas 13

My parents had been in Toledo a year now. After living in Calle Cardenal Cisneros, they found a more countrified house—Airosas 13. It was on high, with a terraced garden. Over the front door was a vast spreading vine, and in its terraced gardens were masses of rose bushes and honeysuckle on the walls. At the bottom of the garden, there were some large mulberry trees and a fountain. To come in from the street, one rang the tinkling bell at the heavy gate. Behind the house was a corral, with stables for the horses, and behind this, Toledo, rising crowned with convents and churches. It was a glorious situation, far from the busy streets and yet in the town and looking over the plains, towards the west.

I first got to know Toledo in early spring. It was a place, although I did not know it at the time, haunted by the influence of the Jews, the Romans, the Visigoths, the Moors, Ferdinand and Isabella, Charles V, St. John of the Cross and El Greco. It had been the capital of Spain until the 16th century. Across the way from our house was a square named after Recared the Visigoth, so dating back to the 6th century.[280] Our garden wall was part of the original Moorish battlements surrounding Toledo, and from our windows we looked onto the Old Puerta Visagra, one of the Moorish gates of the city.

As I said, my maternal grandmother, Tony and Kitty accompanied me to Toledo. We did the journey there by train, across France and Spain. We arrived at Airosas 13 at night under dim electric light. The excitement and magic of the place struck me when the bell at the gate tinkled (a long tinkle) as we entered the garden. From here in the dim light, one could see the house above on the

---

[280] The Visigothic king, Recared, who ruled from 586-601, had his capital at Toledo. Recared renounced Arianism for Roman Catholicism and maintained that orthodoxy. This great event of his reign marked the turning point for Visigothic Hispania. (TRADITION & DIVERSITY: CHRISTIANITY IN A WORLD CONTEXT TO 1500. Karen Louise Jolly. New York: M.E.Sharpe, 1997: 219. Also ART, LITURGY, AND LEGEND IN RENAISSANCE TOLEDO: THE MENDOZA AND THE IGLESIA PRIMADA. Lynette M. F. Bosch. University Park PA: Pennsylvania State University, 2000: 26).

In the Shadow of a Poet

last terrace. As events unfolded, my impressions became rather chaotic and mixed. There was my sister, whom I did not recognise because she had grown so tall, extremely thin and lanky, her cheeks hollow, her skin shrivelled and sallow like an old lady's. At the same time through this maze of sorrow at seeing my sister in this state, there was an otherworldliness emanating from the presence of the silent gypsy groom my father had employed. Not only was my sister gaunt and shrunken, but she exuded a strange smell of mould, which made me suppose the worst: that she had consumption. Later I found it was only the smell of an ointment against lice which she had contracted at school. Still, by then I no longer believed it was my sister and thought somebody else had been put in her place to save my desolation. Although this girl seemed in such a low state physically, I soon rediscovered my little sister by her burning spirit, which was as alive as ever and like no one else's. This was a great consolation after my solitary ruminations. Over the days and the weeks she recovered her normal self. Just before we had arrived, she had had a bout of tonsillitis with dangerously high temperatures.[281] She had been so ill that my mother at one moment had thought she had meningitis.

That same night, my first night in Toledo, the fascination of Toledo came upon me. There was some silent expression of something intangible, dreamlike. The Moorish influence around, the enormous scented roses like pink cabbages in the garden, the fountain with its gentle trickle, the dark burning eyes of the gypsy groom, all had the flavour of Arabia. There was such mystery and radiance in the gypsy's expression, it became the essence of the place.

After this rather emotional yet exciting introduction to Toledo at night, our life gradually established its rhythms and textures. Anna returned to school at the Ursuline Convent. We did a lot of riding. It took me three days to learn to ride our horses, and a few days after my arrival, Anna, the gypsy and I were galloping across the pampas outside Toledo.

Rodrigo, the gypsy groom, was my first love. Even though nothing came of it, it added glamour to life. I didn't want anything except to pay him back for the happiness his presence gave me and to let him know I loved him. This started a ritual. Every evening as the summer advanced, I used to go to the rose bushes in the garden and gather a few roses and scatter the scented petals over the hay, where Rodrigo would come to fetch the horses' last feed. He must have wondered where the petals came from and the horses must have been surprised at the special diet.

Since my parents had settled in our new home, for a year now, my father

---

[281] Anna says it was thought that she had contracted typhoid fever.

Tess and Anna, as *alguaciles* in Toledo bullring (Tess)

had been having strange adventures of all kinds and mixing with all sorts of people. He especially got mixed up with the pub life. He used to meet four or five beggar friends at the pub, who loved him. One of them could only crawl on all fours. They used to gossip for hours. Among these people there was a man called El Ranero, who used to fish frogs from the river and pull their legs off and prepare them for eating. He used to tell everyone with great relish that when the revolution came the capitalists were going to be treated like his frogs—which prophecy came more or less true.

One of my father's favourite pastimes was mixing with the gypsies. They are still in Toledo but no longer live nomadic lives and have settled in Toledo as citizens. There were two families, grandfathers and endless progeny. They were rival clans and unusual specimens of the human race. Some were well-to-do proprietors. My father spent much time with them. He had bad times and good. Once he came back from a fair with a good natured, orange coloured mule. It was young, healthy and fat. He was very pleased because he thought he had made a bargain. After a time the animal seemed stubborn and odd; it did not react as it should when told to advance or stop. To my father's disappointment the animal was deaf, so it was a dreadful nuisance as it was useless and very difficult to get rid of. The gypsies were skilled dealers and up to all sorts of tricks and my father was sometimes taken in. But his deals with them were more often happy than otherwise.

As in all places where my father lived, strange things happened to him. He had a knack for getting himself into unusual situations. When Anna and I were young, we didn't see the funny side of this and became indignant, especially my sister who believed in the good name of the family. In Toledo my

In the Shadow of a Poet

father had quite a few adventures, some dangerous. One of the less dangerous happened on a hot day when he came back from the pub. He had had one too many, and when he came home he sat on the edge of our fountain to rest. He lost his balance and fell into the deep basin. Just as he was recovering from his surprise, our landlord arrived and stared at my father in bewilderment. My father didn't turn a hair but pretended he was refreshing himself and splashed the water all over himself, crawled out and walked coolly into the house, looking like nothing on earth.

By now he was on very good terms with the gypsies. One day he came back home and said: "Kids, I have arranged for you to ride in a welfare bullfight as *alguaciles*." He explained that we were to ride before the bulls came in, which was a relief. The following weeks were spent rehearsing in the bullring. The gypsies helped us a lot. When the day came, my sister and I were dressed smartly in a long pleated, black skirt and bolero, over a sparkling white shirt with a tie and a *Cordobés* hat.

Our role was to ride into the bullring at the head of the bullfighters and receive the key from the mayor of Toledo to open the bulls' pen. We headed the parade to the accompaniment of a one-step, our horses dancing to the music. We approached the mayor who was in a box above the audience, and bowed, then we and the bullfighters went out. After this my sister and I came back alone and bowed again; the keys were thrown down to us. After galloping round twice we gave the keys up and exited.

My sister, who was only ten then, managed it better than I did. She had our best horse. Mine was a mare, hired from the gypsies, an Andalusian thoroughbred. She was almost as big as an English cart horse but not quite so heavy. She was white and so broad my legs could hardy reach round her. At one point I almost lost my grip with my knees and nearly fell off. It was a terrible moment but I managed to steady myself and was saved.[282] Then the bullfight began. We

---

282 Tess misspells this as *aguaciles*.

RC refers to this event with great pride in Light on a Dark Horse:

> [T]hey had the most amazing write ups in the Toledan and Madrid Press—"the enchanting little girls Teresa and Anna, riding magnificently on fiery coursers, for which they received resounding applause. They were of the age of ten and seven respectively"—El Debate. There were plenty of other such notices. It needs first-class riding on the part of the alguaciles to get any applause out of an expert bullfighting mob. One has to perfect certain mathematical evolutions, lead in the matadors with their trams or *"cuadrillas"*, catch the key of the bull's enclosure, thrown down from his box by the President, in one's hat, while rearing the horse, and return at full gallop simultaneously through the entrance. (339)

were taken into the audience amid great applause as we were rather unusual *alguaciles*. This was the second bullfight I had attended. Halfway through, my sorrow for the bulls got the better of me. I was in tears, and my father had to take me out. I never went to a bullfight again. I loved the horsemanship, the audience, the music, but couldn't understand the rest.

Chapter 18
Poppies and Hoopoes

During these three months after my return from England we were each having the time of our lives in our different ways. My mother, it being the first year of her conversion, spent much time in the Toledan churches, near the tabernacle which had a magnetic attraction for her, as it did throughout her life after becoming a Catholic. First things came first with her: "Thou shalt love the Lord thy God, with thy whole heart, with thy whole soul, with thy whole mind, and with thy whole strength." Once in church, she would gravitate towards the light near the tabernacle, the symbol of life, and settle nearby for hours.

On the rare occasions when I was with her, I wondered what on earth she was up to. Still, she knew. And later, I learnt that this silence was necessary. Soon, she joined the Third Order of the Carmelites[283] and took the habit, which consisted of a plain, brown woollen dress (which she wore in all seasons) and brown sandals. She said the long office every day and did a twenty minute climb up to the Carmelite church to attend the eight o'clock mass every morning. We soon got to know the Carmelite Fathers, some of whom were exceptional men, both physically and intellectually. They soon became close friends of the family.

My father having just completed his last work MITHRAIC EMBLEMS was relaxing and spent a lot of his time imbibing the golden, red, Castilian wine and making friends all over the place.

My sister and I, besides a few lessons, rode a lot, sometimes over the pampas and sometimes long distances to the hermitages in the hills round Toledo. In the evening after scorching days the whole family used to go on horseback to one of the sandy beaches by the river and bathe and have a picnic.

We also made whole day excursions to our maid's native village on the plains. On these occasions we would hire mules from the gypsies so that everyone would have a mount. At a certain point on the road, one saw the little village down on the swirling plain. It was called Casasbuenas, Goodhouses. It was a mass of low, whitewashed houses and a little church with a stork's nest with

---

[283] See note 43 above.

a stork in it on the belfry, and, in the distance behind, high mountains. On one of these excursions as we got down onto the plain, there were large, dense expanses of poppies, making the landscape bright and red. My father told us it was supposed to be a sign that battles had been fought there in the past. He was full of talk of battles at this time, both past and future ones.

There were also an uncommon number of hoopoes around, not only in the country but in our garden and about the ramparts of Toledo, and they sang a lot. They were very busy about something or other. According to my father their presence was a presage of war. I don't know where he got this superstitious knowledge from—perhaps the Zulus or the Romans or some other source. Hoopoes are mentioned quite a lot in his poetry at this time. One could tell by the way he talked that he was conscious of some stormy hell on the way, and he was right.

While we were engrossed in this varied and stirring life, as summer advanced the political situation in Spain became more and more tense. These months, from April to July 1936, had progressed from a simmering of unrest and confusion and had reached boiling point. After many disagreeable incidents, one fine July day, when we feared the rising sun in its silence and radiance—the civil war broke out. The inexplicable and uncalled for death of Calvo Sotelo,[284] the head of Catholic Action who was murdered in his bed on July the 12th, was the cause of the uprising. There was something ominous and momentous about his death, as all thinking people realised, and the alarm was sounded.

My father had been looking on in apprehension for months and had wanted to leave in the past few weeks but, as often happened in decisive moments in our family life, he took my mother's advice and stayed on, being convinced by her that it was only a passing disturbance. My father, as the head of the family, was responsible for us, so it was natural he should be more concerned. He was the more intuitive and instinctive of the two but my mother always won because she had stronger will power. It was often my mother's ruthless courage and tough decisions that brought added colour and adventure to our lives, but at a cost. On this occasion, instead of leaving in time and avoiding a lot of anxiety, we stayed on, although perhaps it was a more worthwhile adventure than otherwise—to have lived a few weeks near the siege of the Alcázar.

Despite my father's warnings to my mother that it was dangerous to go to mass now, she continued to wind her way up to the Carmelites every morning, until the eve of the outburst of war.

After the death of Calvo Sotelo it was clear some strong element had been let loose and meant business, and so the Nationalist rebellion started on the 18th

---

[284] See note 112.

In the Shadow of a Poet

of July. Then a man emerged who was fully equipped to deal with this overpowering menace—General Francisco Franco y Bahamonde. He only had half an army, the Moorish cavalry, no planes, hardly any ammunition, no navy and no money. What he had was an exceptional dose of faith, and with it he achieved the deathly blow to Bolshevism in Spain, the only one that was ever given. After this memorable date of 18th July 1936, a bloody, fierce civil war followed.

Chapter 19
Civil War

We were in Toledo during the initial weeks of the war. In the first days the confusion was great. We did not know what side Toledo remained on. After three days' fighting tooth for tooth and nail for nail, it was taken over by the Reds. We lived on lentils and lots of peaches and fruit that was smuggled to us; sometimes the maid managed to get as far as the grocer and baker and bring back some coffee and bread after standing in long queues. There wasn't any other food to be had. What she did bring back were diverse rumours: General Sanjurjo, one of the insurrectional generals, had been killed in a plane crash on his way to Spain; the Moorish guard had sided with Franco and was on its way to fight; the besieged Alcázar could not hold out long because they had no water.

As the days passed, my father looked more and more pale and worried. We couldn't go out because there were skirmishes in the streets and we didn't know how we would be received. We spent our time huddled in the centre of the house where the walls were thickest while the shells whistled over the house to land on the Alcázar with a thud. Our house was just under the line they took. In the streets there was shooting and looting. People who were hiding were discovered and brought out and shot. The churches and convents were sacked and left smouldering for days. We could see a large, steady stream of smoke going up from the Carmelite convent just above our house for days. There were bonfires everywhere of books, pictures and statues and other religious things. It was during these first weeks that some of our best friends were killed and the Carmelite friars were taken out into the street above our house and shot. All that remains now on the spot is a plaque giving their seven or eight names.

The atmosphere was desperate. On the third day of fighting we had a visit from the Red troops who had taken over. They were just ordinary civilians, bristling with arms. As they came into the house, their first remark surprised us: they said we were fascists because we had Dante on the bookshelf. Then they decided we were acceptable because we also had Dostoevsky and the Union Jack in the back yard. They were friendly after this, but terrifying nonetheless.

In the Shadow of a Poet

Some of the men sat down on the chests where we had hidden the Carmelite archives, but these were not discovered and, in the end, we managed to save them. As the rebels sat their pistols, revolvers and rifles bristled at us from all angles, and we were fearful that they might go off at any moment.

We have a BBC recording in which my father recounts how, while the militiamen were sitting on the chests containing the Carmelite archives, he prayed to St. John of the Cross and made a vow that if we were spared in this predicament he would translate St. John's poems into English. He managed to fulfil this promise fifteen years later and the poems were published in England in 1951. Little did we know at that moment how concerned he was about our fate.

After a lot of searching and questioning, the militiamen departed quite satisfied, and we settled down to a very unsettled state of affairs, not knowing what was going to become of us. The siege of the Alcázar had started and the post and communications were cut off. Our money was at an end—not even the British Embassy seemed to remember us. My father was extremely anxious, to put it mildly. We had been there now for two whole weeks without enough to eat, with no money, not knowing what was going to happen. We were at the end of our tether.

Then something did happen—something wonderful, something like a miracle. A boy appeared on our doorstep with a big packet of hundred peseta notes. It was like the fables: when good is done, the donor is paid back a hundredfold. We couldn't believe our eyes. He was a poor boy, and we couldn't imagine where he came from. He explained that he had been sent by a young Bolshevik friend of my father's. This young man used to come twice a week to our house to talk about poetry and learn something from my father. My father used to give him much time and advice. The way my father used to sit for hours talking to him never ceased to surprise me. They got on well enough although their politics were opposed; they kept off politics as much as possible. With this sudden outbreak of war, he must have guessed our predicament. He was our good angel and funnily enough his name was Angel, quite a common name in Spain. He was a shopkeeper's son who had a bent for poetry.

Later, we heard the tale about the money. It seems that after Toledo was taken over by the Reds, Angel was walking near the Puerta Visagra (which is the main entrance to Toledo from Madrid) when an old priest appeared in the deserted street, intending to escape from the smouldering city with the money from the cathedral; just then he was seen and shot by a militiaman, and when he fell the militiaman searched him and took the big packet of notes he had on him. Angel, who was nearby, happened to see the militiaman take the money off the priest, so the militiaman offered Angel half in order to keep him quiet. This was where this large amount of money came from. To us it seemed like a miracle, and we were infinitely thankful to our friend.

Chapter 20
Refugees

When this large packet of money fell from the sky, as it were, it was one of those strokes of luck which accompanied my father through life. He used to tell stories of things that had happened to him, and I used to distrust them for they seemed so incredible. However, as life went on, I witnessed many strange things that happened to him, so I no longer doubted them but knew they could be quite true. He told people stories which they thought far-fetched but which I had witnessed and knew to be genuine. Sometimes he exaggerated details, and once or twice put himself in other people's places, believing the adventures had happened to him, but that was rare.[285]

After receiving this money, the next move was for the militiamen to take us to Toledo station in a lorry. The drive was extremely risky as the last part was within the range of the Alcázar and the inmates fired onto the road. We made it though, and from here we were put on a goods train which at some time or other might have a connection from Algodor to Madrid. Lonely travellers, we

---

[285] Laurie Lee and others, including Campbell's biographers Alexander and Pearce, have said that Campbell's accounts are not always trustworthy or accurate. Anna (quoted in Pearce: 307) even goes so far as to say that the second part of LIGHT ON A DARK HORSE is "nonsense". Alexander says Campbell's two autobiographies "do not merely distort and conceal the truth; they substitute for it an elaborate and consistent un-truth" (ROY CAMPBELL: A CRITICAL BIOGRAPHY. Cape Town: David Philip, 1982: vii)

RC begins his first autobiography, BROKEN RECORD, with mention of the fictional deaths he, as a fictionalised character, has endured and then discusses his own efforts at self-representation:

> If it were true that men may rise upon the stepping stones of their dead selves to better things, I should be in the seventh heaven by now, instead of trying to haul my past out of the stable backwards by its tail, like a recalcitrant cow, and driving it to the market, where it has been more profitably sold so many times before, by others. (in COLLECTED WORKS I: 77)

Since for him "memory and imagination work as one", some "romantic adventures […] project into [his] imagination." He will not "bore" the reader "with a list of facts" but rather manipulate them "into some sort of design" (78).

arrived at Algodor railway junction in the middle of the night. We slept a few hours on some sacks in the station. Some time the next day we were picked up and taken to Madrid where we got to the British Embassy. The disorganisation and disorder were profound and small distances took ages to cover. When we arrived the door of the Embassy was locked but when we knocked they half opened it and were very pleased when they recognised us. Major Lance, who was later put in the Cheka,[286] took us in an open car across Madrid to a train which was going to Valencia. There, at Valencia, we joined a crowd of Britishers who had assembled from across Spain to embark on the H.M.S. MAINE, a hospital ship, for re-patriation.[287]

On the ship, the Royal Navy officers seemed like supermen or angels; they were so serene, tall and fair in their immaculate white summer uniforms. They seemed so blue-eyed, disciplined, beautiful and perfect after the extreme chaos, poverty and misery we had left behind. It was on occasions like this that one fully realised what the British Empire was. The British Empire at the moment I mention was a colossus of power and prestige, as the world had never known before and would probably never witness again; so it seemed to us when we encountered it at Valencia in all its splendour.

Just as we were about to embark, who should be waiting for us on the quay, but Angel, with his portmanteau and mackintosh on his arm, hoping to embark with us. But the authorities would not let him. We left him, a lonely figure, on land. We never saw him again. He later joined the Red Army and was killed at the front.

When we arrived in London we were news in the papers—there were articles by my father and photographs of my sister and me riding in the bullring. After staying in London with friends, we were generously offered a farm in Sussex by one of my mother's sisters.[288]

England was wonderful to us who had not only been starved of food but of any and every kind of luxury. It was heavenly to be there after our sad life of late. The farm was at its best, the orchards were heavy with soft Victoria

---

[286] During the Spanish Civil War, the detention and torture centers operated by the Communists were named *chekas* after the Soviet organisation. (E.H. Carr, (1958) THE ORIGIN AND STATUS OF THE CHEKA. Soviet Studies, vol. 10, no. 1: p. 1. Cited in http://www.nationmaster.com/encyclopedia/Cheka)

[287] Pearce (190) notes that Robert Graves and Laura Riding, whom Campbell had satirised in THE GEORGIAD, were fellow refugees. Although they accepted Campbell's apology for this, it would seem that there was no lasting reconciliation.

[288] This was Marsh Farm. It was owned by Lorna and Ernest Wishart. See notes 100 and 101 above.

In the Shadow of a Poet

plums and many kinds of apple. There was thick cream on the milk, fresh butter and eggs, and fresh vegetables in abundance in the kitchen garden. To me at this time food was especially appreciated as I was growing and perpetually ravenous. Indoors, the creature comforts were beyond belief, with expensive linen on the beds and hot baths. We had never enjoyed such sumptuousness and plenty, nor would we ever again.

When my aunt returned from her summer holiday, we moved into one of her relation's cottages on the property.

While here, every day we avidly read about five different newspapers of divers political leanings to get an idea of what was happening in Spain. We were fervent Nationalists.

My father had read a great deal of Communist literature. When in London, in the 1920s, he was given free access to the British Museum Library.[289] There he had read the works of Lenin. He, like Franco, had studied the machinations of Communism. Spain was apt ground for exploitation because of her social inequality. Often, in my socialistic ruminations, I suggested to my father that it might be better if the inequality and poverty in Spain were settled by Communism. He would answer that years ago Lenin had said that Spain must be the first convert to Communism because it was vital for the fall of Europe. He used to say: "If you notice in Spain, the discontented and revolutionaries are not the poor, they are among the factory workers and lower middle class, because they have been pumped with propaganda, which is all a plan to take over Spain and Europe." He would continue: "Was this equality which was suggested sufficient reason for religion to be stamped out of whole nations, a totalitarian regime imposed, and all the rest of what Communism entailed?" He felt compelled to oppose this inhumane tyranny, just as Solzhenitsyn did, when he made a superhuman effort forty years later.

My father called his epic poem FLOWERING RIFLE, "A Poem from the 'Battlefield of Spain'", but the essence of the inspiration sprang from the consciousness of the violation of the human spirit under the totalitarian Soviet regime. Although written and published years before Solzhenitsyn's deportation and confinement, it was the sort of experience which Solzhenitsyn was to later undergo that inspired FLOWERING RIFLE. For this awareness of the desolation and destruction of those many thousands of souls in Russian life, my father was known by most of the intellectuals of the world as a fascist bully.

FLOWERING RIFLE is a violent explosion in verse, the composition of

---

[289] The British Museum Library holdings are now held in the British Library, established in 1973.

which shook and devastated my father. He was compelled to take a stand even if no one else did, just as Solzhenitsyn, who was accepted, understood and acclaimed by the world, was compelled to. My father died just about the time Solzhenitsyn was released from his exile in the concentration camps. How my father would have exulted in the Russian's heroic testimony and how he would have gloried to see him rise, in his moral splendour, above the murky confusion of the world.

My father was so tormented and disturbed at that time by the attitude of the Saxonic nations about the conflict in Spain that he felt a barricade should be erected against Soviet propaganda.[290] Although he considered FLOWERING RIFLE his greatest work, it is not as finished or perfected as his other work because of his agitation and urgency. It was thrown into the arena like a wild bull. He felt that radical change in the world's attitude to Communism was imperative.

Ironically, my father's philosophy and way of life were much more like a Communist's than the views and practices of many who join the party. He lived his Communism in his Christianity and that was his ideal. He was a workman who depended on his earnings for maintenance and certainly lived a frugal life.

The Spanish Civil War was a cruel war, it has left an indelible scar on Spain which will be noticeable for years to come, but it was the first swift and effective defeat of Communism. Something people don't realise is how right Franco's rebellion was. If there had been no insurrection in Spain, Communism would for years have been stronger in Europe, especially after the occupations of the eastern European countries after the last great war.

The only practical conclusion one can come to is that Communism is a sharp and powerful reminder to humanity that we should try to find a better alternative. The socialist, humanitarian, well-meaning, expensive system does not seem

---

[290] Reflecting back on these times, Spender wrote in 1994 that "it is quite wrong to be nostalgic about the Thirties on the grounds that during that decade many young people felt there were political causes worth fighting and dying for." He adds, "In the work of this particular generation there is always a certain shamefacedness about the fact that we had been drawn into political activity"—in his case, anti-Fascist (1997: xiii). In the autobiography he makes another frank—and perhaps surprising—disclosure regarding his rejection of Nazism (which he refers to as Fascism):

> there were moments when I felt that there was a conspiratorial relationship between the evil passions of the Fascists—which I so profoundly understood—and my own anti-Fascist virulence. On a more superficial level, the existence of this vast immoral spiritual demonism [...] dwarfed my own moral problems. However bad I was, Fascism was worse; by being anti-Fascist, I created a rightness for myself beside which personal guilt seems unimportant. (1997: 186)

For Spender's discussion of the reservations he felt about Communism, see pp. 132-3.

In the Shadow of a Poet

to work either; it only seems to sow confusion, discontent and misery. The Christian ideal of the reform of the individual might help if that could come about.

To go back to our repatriation. During those six months' exile in England, every evening my mother, father, sister and a Spanish girl (a refugee whom my parents engaged as our governess) and I used to say the rosary for the victory of the Nationalists. It was my first experience of impassioned prayer. We felt after we had finished that the "Insurgents" had advanced ten miles along the whole front. ("Insurgents" was what Spain's patriotic troops, under a patriotic leader, who were trying to clear their country of a foreign invasion of erroneous ideas were called by the British press and most of the world.) After three years when they were victorious, we put it down to this quarter of an hour's prayer we said every day, as we had kept it up through the war.

Throughout that English summer while we were at this cottage, the Alcázar at Toledo was holding out against all odds, but the siege could not last much longer and it was doubtful whether Franco would be able to relieve it in time as conditions were becoming deplorable. During this time our rosary prayer in the evening became fierce with ardour. We put our minds to prayer as it was the only means we had of helping the besieged and promoting the cause.

Franco decided to abandon his important project of marching on Madrid and moved his forces towards Toledo instead. This delayed his final victory immensely but he thought the sacrifice imperative. In September 1936, the third month of the siege, the great day came, and by some miracle Franco's forces reached the Alcázar before it surrendered. When we got the news, what news! What thanksgiving!

As the story of the siege of Alcázar of Toledo has been scantily divulged and it was such a strange story, I will give a brief outline of what happened; it deserves to be better known.

In modern times, a surrealistic story like this could only happen in Castile. Here part of what I have tried to express about Castile and the Castilian people was realised. Having happened in Spain, not much was said about it abroad, partly because the Spanish people are so insular—their Spain is their world. The story did get abroad, but little importance was attached to this extraordinary event mainly because it was one of the Nationalist victories. One of the most extraordinary stories of this century, the event was a test of faith and endurance lived out by a group of people.

These officers of the Military Academy in Toledo had retired into the fortress of the Alcázar with their families and with what was there: sacks of grain, cisterns of water, a few mules and a few arms. They withstood the onslaught until the grim end. From the beginning, they were shelled all day. As this did not work, they were bombarded from the air. Having no result, the Reds then tried to exterminate them by mining them from underneath. The amazing thing was that throughout this they carried on a normal life—publishing a daily paper, hearing mass, doing surgical operations on the wounded, retaliating and defending themselves, slaughtering the few mules they had for meat, baking bread. Half-way through the siege they became short of grain. This did not disturb them; they made a successful sally into Toledo and provided more. Two babies were born.

The height of heroism was in the beginning, when the general in command, General Moscardó, whose son was held hostage by the Republican forces in Madrid, communicated with his son who told him he would be shot if the Alcázar did not surrender. The general told him to shout "Long Live Spain" and die, and so he did.

The fortunate thing about this siege was that the Alcázar was a fortress of great strength, with five stories of basements underneath, and in the case of the mining there were fine mathematicians among the officers who calculated an area of safety from the sound of the drill being used to tunnel from underneath. They also had fine doctors and surgeons with them to deal with the injured, otherwise matters might have deteriorated more rapidly.

In his autobiography, LIGHT ON A DARK HORSE, my father sums up this paradox of the riches and poverty of Toledo and the turbulent story of the siege of the Alcázar:

> Only Maurice Barrès, it seems, and myself *of all the foreign writers* who have visited Toledo knew that she was really stripped and cleared for action, and far more alive and awake than any of the modern towns. She is still the heart of Spain, the imperial capital of the Spains, and when she accepted us as Toledanos, as she had up till then accepted no other foreigners, it was because we could recognize the sleeping phoenix before she put on her flames of martyrdom.
>
> Toledo was the whole embodiment of the crusade for Christianity against Communism and I felt it the minute I set foot in the city. There is something victorious in the very look of the place, and inherent in its very poverty. But clouds were closing in.
>
> *By every sign the times were known*
> *Humanity by day benighted,*
> *The flesh defiled, dominion slighted,*
> *Blasphemed the high majestic throne...*

In the Shadow of a Poet

[Penguin edition, 1971: 329. Italics in original.]

The victory at Toledo was a spiritual and religious triumph, it was the living faith of these people that provided the power to endure and overcome. It was one of the examples of the supernatural working during the Spanish war.

Chapter 21
Life in Portugal

From what one could gather, this war in Spain was going to be a prolonged and problematic matter. Spain was gradually turning into an international battlefield. As can be imagined, my father felt remote and cut off in England so soon the whole family was on its way to be nearer the conflict. We had been in England six months.

In January 1937 we went to Portugal. We left Southampton in bitter cold, sleet and snow, and battled against a storm in the Bay of Biscay and nearly sank. For a day and a night the boat was silent except for loud heavings and sudden dives into the gigantic waves. We thought our end had come, and everyone on the boat was sick. My father, however, never felt better. The wilder the sea and the further away from land the better he felt. He was a solitary passenger walking the decks. At first I accompanied him. I had never believed waves could be so vast or so high. I had always thought the waves in the MOBY DICK illustrations exaggerated, but these were just as big, if not bigger. I had thought that if my father could, I would also be able to manage the deck, but when I got there I lay down on the spot. I felt dreadfully ill and nearly fainted, while every now and then the chilly spray covered me. My only wish was to go down to the warm cabin. For a day and a night we succumbed, tossing on our bunks, groaning, taking it in turns to be sick. Quite early on the first day we had nothing left in our stomachs. The boat braved the storm, but the boat that went before us broke in half and sank.

After rounding the Cape of Finisterre there was a sudden lull and a tropical anticyclone enveloped us. All the way down the Portuguese coast we languished prostrate in deck chairs, weak after the agonies of sea-sickness. The climate became soft and warm. At night we lay gazing at the stars—the whole sky was just stars. What peace and quiet after our tortured existence of the past hours. Gradually our poor bruised spirits and appetites came back, sharper than ever.

Our stay in Portugal was peaceful, full of varied experiences and happiness. First we settled at the typical fishing village of Sesimbra, at a pension, the Pensâo Chic. It was anything but *chic*, but clean, bare and airy, just a street away from

In the Shadow of a Poet

the ocean. It was winter, the climate alternated between hot sunshine (so warm we were bathing in February) to wild misty days. The tropical mists which rolled in from the Atlantic were so thick one couldn't see across the street, and the breakers came thundering in for days and nights on end. Everything became soaked with this mist.

The essence of Portugal comes from the sea—a cruel, savage, beautiful sea. Everything is tainted with

Tess, Estombar, Portugal 1937 (Francesca)

Painting of Estombar by Tess, using pseudonym Diana for the Garman family magazine (Tess)

iodine, which makes it different from any other European country. The hardy race that springs from its shores is not only fearless but strong and beautiful. We often watched the fishermen jumping into their little boats, with a wild sky and sea behind them, battling against the waves, going out in search of their daily living. Their business is the sea, and they seem to understand it better than the land. Sometimes sailors are never seen or heard of again, but this doesn't seem to deter the others.

Life at Sesimbra was quite new to us. We had never lived near the ocean, except for a short time in South Africa. Here fish was abundant and varied, and we got a taste for it, especially grilled and fried pilchards and sardines. This wonderful food became our staple diet as it is for the Portuguese nation.

We loved to go down to the fish market in the evening. The fishermen would display their catch of the day in rows on the sand. There were deep-water fish with outsize eyes to see in the dark, big fish, small, strange, ordinary fish, sharks, skates, sprats, eels of all descriptions and sometimes rare specimens. The diversity was amazing, all sparkling in the sunset light. After this exhibition the fish was packed and delivered all over Portugal.

My sister, Josephine and I soon found the Portuguese had a special gift for making the most of life and enjoying themselves—more than any other people we had mixed with. They took work very seriously, but they also knew how to make the most of parties and festivities. In the summer on the beach we made many friends; we would form groups, and the different groups would hire big motor boats and we would go round the coast on all-day excursions to fabulous beaches, bays and caves that could only be reached by the sea. On these excursions the families and fishermen that accompanied us would cook sumptuous *caldeiradas* (a kind of Portuguese *bouillabaisse*). Then, when we were well weighed down with food and wine, as only the Portuguese know how, someone would emerge with a concertina and everyone would take partners and dance. One of the caves we visited was so immense that it made a wonderful ballroom. To us young people, this dancing was inspiring as we all had our flirts.

Some of my best moments at Sesimbra were spent painting watercolours. It was wonderful to have some spare hours to paint a picture I had imagined the night before. It was at this time that I sent a little picture of fishing boats in the transparent blue-green water of a little bay we knew to an exhibition of the paintings of the children of geniuses in London. My picture was exhibited with Freud's grandchildren's. A review in REYNOLD's NEWS picked out my painting and said about it that it expressed more sensitive poetry than my father's. This was probably a dig at my father who was not popular at the time

In the Shadow of a Poet

because of the Spanish Civil War. Still, it was good praise and it pleased me.

During our stay at Sesimbra we rented two houses, staying about six months in each. We lived frugally, mostly on fish and fruit which was abundant and cheap. Josephine used to give my sister and me lessons of French, Spanish, Spanish history and mathematics. She helped us to perfect our Spanish and French.[291]

My mother, even in this short space of time, managed to establish herself so that she could work for the church. She used to play the organ and train the choir for the services in the parish church and also made friends with the nuns of the Misericordia Hospital at Sesimbra (the State hospital). She visited the sick and afforded them what relief she could. The nuns were like little white angels in their habits, ministering to the sick in bed. At that time in Portugal tuberculosis was rampant and there were many desperate cases in these hospitals.

All this time the Nationalists were advancing in Spain, yard by yard. My father went over the border several times and tried to enlist with the Nationalist forces but Franco turned him down and told him he would be more useful with his pen than with a bayonet. In the end he managed to get a permit to work as a reporter for THE TABLET, a Catholic magazine in England. He used to visit the various fronts. These visits relieved his spirits. He would bring back tokens such as Requetés'[292] red berets or even a twisted ankle from his narrow escapes at the front and be laid up for weeks. It was from these firsthand experiences that he got a lot of the material for FLOWERING RIFLE.

From Sesimbra we moved down to a roomy house in the picturesque village of Estombar, in the Algarve. If the coast round Sesimbra was fascinating, the Algarve coast was even more so, and the sea calmer and better for bathing. In those days there were no tourists there and very few foreign residents. It was mostly populated by farmers, peasants and fishermen, primitive in every way. The only meat to be had was mutton and even this was scarce.

Here also we made many friends among the more cultured families and

---

[291] As a result of their stays in France, Spain and Portugal, Tess and Anna were fluent in French, Spanish and Portuguese. Tess told me that as a child, her French was better than her English, but that their home language was always English.

[292] The Requetés (from the French requêté, "hunting call") were the Carlist militia (supporting the Nationalists) during the Spanish Civil War. Wearing red berets, they mostly came from Navarre and were highly religious and conservative with many regarding the war as a Crusade. They resisted capitalism, centralisation and modernity. See FRANCO AND THE SPANISH CIVIL WAR, Filipe Ribeiro De Meneses (London: Routledge, 2001: 34) and DEMOCRACY AND CIVIL WAR IN SPAIN 1931-1939, Martin Blinkhorn (London: Routledge, 2002: 15). RC claimed that he offered to join the Requetés; he did not offer to join Franco's regular army (Alexander, 173, 189). The distinction is important.

farmers' families. It was greatly owing to Josephine that Anna's and my social life was so animated. She made friends easily and was a great mixer.

We used to form parties of about fifteen young people for excursions. These jaunts were not by sea but by land. Each one mounted on a donkey, mule or horse, we would go along a donkeys' track for miles and end up at a lush farm on the outskirts of Silves. Called Matamoros, it still had marks of the Moorish settlement there. In this paradise we would spend part of the time up the loquat trees which were weighed down with deep orange, ripe fruit. Then we would have a big picnic lunch.

We also used to go further inland by taxi into a mountain paradise, Monchique, for picnics with our parents and foreign friends. We went at the time of the flowering of the mimosa which fell in cascades, all interwoven and clustered with camelias which flowered at the same time. These flowers were a sight, and amidst this magnificence we would have our picnic.

As we had no car, soon after arriving at Estombar we bought two rather wild horses to serve as transport. One was a black mare, with a smooth trot, and the other was a small Arab horse which was only half broken in and started rolling on its back whenever he got onto sand, whether he had a rider or not, so he was not very comfortable to ride. Someone in the village offered us a cart to harness to the black mare so that the family could travel together. My mother volunteered to drive it as she had driven a cart and horse during the war, delivering bread in the streets of London. So, on one occasion, all the family and Josephine got into the cart to take us to a nearby village. The journey was smooth until we had nearly reached our destination but then the mare started a tremendous struggle. We couldn't think what was up, when suddenly we realised the poor animal was being gently lifted off her feet, so we quickly scrambled out. We never tried a cart and horse again.

The whole length of the coast of the Algarve, with its beaches which are perfect for bathing, has now been turned into modern towns, with hotels, skyscrapers and luxury flats. Nothing of this existed in our day; there were just limpid beaches and bays baking in the hot sun. The Algarve is also famous for another reason—inland the landscape is covered with almond orchards. To me one of the Seven Wonders of the World is the Algarve in almond blossom time. The small hills and valleys are coloured with a fairy white and pink mist of blossoms.

Chapter 22
FLOWERING RIFLE

It was at Estombar in 1938 when suddenly one day my father shut himself up in his room and told us he wanted only thermoses of hot tea made for him every now and again. He started writing his epic poem FLOWERING RIFLE. This poem of 103 pages comprising five books was written in two weeks, my father lying on a mattress. He only rested to drink the tea which he came out to fetch. After two weeks he came out thinner and paler for the wear, but triumphant. It seemed a record of abstinence and absorption. Here his room was just as he liked it, completely bare; this one didn't even have a bed, just a mattress on the floor.

FLOWERING RIFLE stands apart from the rest of my father's works. It is more a vision of things past, present and future. Its tone is rather apocalyptic. It is not quite so difficult to decipher as Nostradamus' prophecies but every line is loaded with meaning. To the common reader, it may be almost unintelligible. It is subtitled "A Poem from the 'Battlefield of Spain'," and this is putting it mildly. It is really a summing up of European ideas since the Renaissance, as its main aim was to show the great power of endeavour or the spiritual power in man when entirely and rightly channelled into one cause.

To my father it was an important work because someone had to write it. He felt even in those days that Solzhenitsyn and company were rising somewhere, and he had to support them. It was spontaneous exasperation put into rhyme. To him it was significant also because in it he expressed his philosophy and it dealt with solemn truths and concerns. He also wrote this poem to correct the unfair interpretation of the happenings in Spain by the intellectuals of the world. From beginning to end, it takes for granted that Franco would win the war. It was written in the middle of 1938 and published in 1939, almost a year after the war ended. The poem seems heavy and repetitious, but it is powerful and will be better understood in the future.

In this chapter there is a chance for me to put an end to any idea that my father or Franco were Fascists or had Fascist leanings. To both of them the Spanish Civil War was a necessity, a Christian crusade against Communist atheism or Marxism. Franco did what any conscious Christian would have done when confronted by Communism. Both my father and Franco were labelled Fascists by Communists, but neither of them were. They were just two devout Christians defending what was most vital to them.

Spain is actually the only country in the world to have the honour of having routed Communism before Communism routed itself. German Fascism helped to defeat Communism in Spain, and Franco accepted its help. But when the time came for Franco to help German Fascism during the World War he refused to co-operate. He was astute. Hitler had asked Franco to allow him free passage through Spain, to North Africa, which would have been a tremendous asset to the Germans, but Franco refused to give his permission, though this would in fact have been an opportunity to advance the cause of Fascism. Isn't his refusal evidence enough that he wasn't a Fascist? Franco's rule in his old age did end up employing force, but nothing compared with the kind of force used by the Communists.

What was amazing—and the world seems never to have given it a thought—was the recovery of Spain after her war, with millions of her men dead, the most active of the race, with all her gold exported to Odessa, Mexico and Mont Marson in France, and then the World War which isolated her from the rest of the world. Although Spain managed to defeat Communism and keep her faith, the Church paid a heavy price for this freedom; no less than twenty thousand religious people and priests and six bishops were killed.

Funnily enough it was Opus Dei, a part of the Catholic Church hardly known and sparse in numbers, that after the war fostered the revival of Spain. It was due to the brilliant brains and discipline of some of the members of this organisation that Spain recovered and was able to stand on her feet and now, after having been one of the most backward countries in Europe, she has reached the level of the rest.

The principal idea of the Opus Dei movement is that all members must carry out their roles in life as perfectly as possible. That means that any role a person may have in life, no matter what it is, must be worked to perfection. Mothers, wives, husbands, fathers, must be just that. Mothers and wives have to take their place in the home, minding what is their real business, and not leave their children and husbands to outsiders. They cannot be absent from the home all day, as they are in modern societies all over the world. This is bound to strengthen a nation—it has made of Spain of all industrialised countries the one that counts least divorces and separations among married couples.

Chapter 23
Fatima

An important thing happened while we were at Estombar: my parents went on a pilgrimage to Fatima. Fatima, the shrine where Our Lady appeared to the three little shepherds, is situated on a high plateau, more or less in central Portugal. At the time it was far away from the bustle of modern life, but it is changing rapidly.

It is apt that this appearance of the Virgin should take place in Portugal as the Portuguese are an essentially spiritual people. The story of Fatima is long and complex. It is one of those stories only the Catholic Church seems to produce. Some people believe the story, some are sceptical. The average Portuguese peasant believes in it entirely, probably because their lives are lived more in accordance with the supernatural. The story has many facets: the message the Virgin wants transmitted to mankind, the warning of the future danger of Communism, the utter surrender of the children's will to the Almighty.

Apart from the supernatural side of the story, there are the nuances of the human side, such as when the mother of Lucia, the eldest of the children, tries to punish the nonsense out of them, whereas the old father of the two younger ones, who is a drunk, believes and defends them. Then there are the difficulties they have with the public, like the story of the mayor of Vila Nova de Ourem (the children's native town) who had them locked up. There was also the strange detail that the children had these visions in different degrees: sometimes all three had the whole vision, other times Jacinta and Francisco could only see fragments of it, and sometimes the boy, Francisco, saw little or nothing.

We moderns complain that in our days God does not manifest Himself as he used to do in olden times, but this manifestation was made in the old style, as in the Bible, through the human soul or psyche.

One of the details that is particularly striking is the children's mention of Communism and the importance they gave it. Why in the world were these three Portuguese children, tucked away in the back of beyond, so concerned about Communism when no one else was to that extent? How did they know, in the July of 1917, that the revolution in Russia would take place in October and Communism would be established? This revolution might have fizzled out like so many revolutions do, but this one was to prove as important as the children divined.

At the end of her short life Jacinta, the youngest, foresaw her premature death and predicted to the day the death of most of the people round her, which did not make her very popular.

Yes, Fatima is an extraordinary story and an extraordinary place, not only for the mystical things that happen there but because it attracts all sorts of people, strange or normal, from all the walks of life and from all over the world. It must be the most international spot in the world besides St. Peter's Square in Rome.

The Portuguese have been able to represent the Virgin of Fatima well. The image is spread across the country, in the chapels and churches. These depictions are enchanting and some are exquisitely inspired—the faces are very lovely and spiritual. However, since about 1950, these statues are mass produced and very poor and ordinary in comparison to those created in the past.

It was in 1938, just before my father wrote FLOWERING RIFLE, that my parents went to Fatima with some Portuguese friends. My father went partly because he was drinking heavily at the time and couldn't give it up. He felt the Virgin would help him (he had a great devotion to the Virgin). I seem to remember he went off half confused, repentant and in a depressed state of mind—in a kind of trance, not at all enthusiastic.

A few days later when they came back they had a strange story to tell. As they were reaching Fatima by car, my father stopped at a tavern as was his custom and ordered his pig skin bota, to be filled with half water, half wine, and paid for it. When he went to drink it later, it was only water. This gave him such a shock he did not touch a drop of wine for two years and made a vow to the Virgin he would not drink again until Franco had won the Spanish Civil War. He considered it to be a miracle the Virgin had worked. He kept his vow through every temptation.

My father's heavy drinking at the time was brought on, I think, by exasperation and longing to go back home, to Toledo, where we belonged, but the Spanish Civil War was far from ended, it just dragged on, and here we were, all of us, stranded with no definite home or plan.

But a lucky thing happened to us about this time. Our grandmother Campbell was on her second or third tour around the world. She was passing through Italy and a plan was made to go and meet her there at Christmas time. So instead of being stranded in Portugal, roaming around aimlessly, we travelled to Italy, and in the meantime the Spanish Civil War ended.

My sister's and my last few weeks in Portugal were spent at a little shack

In the Shadow of a Poet

on the cliffs near Carvoeiro, one of the beauty spots of the Algarve coast. Now, this part of the coast has become a tourist centre; in those days, only this little old house could be seen standing alone, above the little coves and beaches below. Our parents left us at Carvoeiro with a group of friends, while they visited Spain and prepared the way for our journey to Italy. Josephine had left us that summer, after being with us for two years. Her parents had been traced, so she returned to Spain.

After spending a few delightful weeks, bathing and sunbathing on those limpid beaches, gathering shells and diving from the rocks and enjoying Portuguese hospitality, which must be the most generous in the world, the father of the family took my sister and me to Estremoz on the frontier and put us on a bus, and we travelled alone to Seville, which was then the Nationalists' headquarters. We met our parents there.

Seville was buoyant in spite of the war. In the evening the centre of the town was flooded with soldiers and officers on leave, many bandaged up, others limping on crutches, recovering from wounds. The young girls and women were radiant, one never saw a plain female among them. Still Sevillanas are renowned for that. I have a theory of my own about this, and it is that this perfect physical beauty is due to the fact that future mothers spend so much time in church with the virgin in mind that it affects the child.

On September the 14th of 1938, we took a ferry from some port in Spain to Gibraltar and stayed there a night, then boarded the third biggest ship in the world, the REX, Fascist Italy's great pride at the time, which sailed into Gibraltar harbour at night, looking with all her lights on like a burning city. We travelled third class and had a blissful voyage across the Mediterranean.

Chapter 24
Italy

Naples, to me the most appealing of Italian cities, was burnished by the autumn glow when we landed in 1938, but we weren't going to stay here and soon left for Rome.

Now that we were going to settle for a time in Rome, the great centre of the arts in the world, there was a chance for my sister and me to study them. There seemed to be more possibilities here than in other places.

By the age of twelve, my sister had decided to pursue ballet as a profession. She was a born dancer and had the necessary physical attributes for this, being perfectly proportioned and very pretty. The only drawback was that she was starting rather late, as the right age for starting ballet is six or seven years old or even earlier, so there was some doubt about whether she would succeed in her career. She did get into difficulties later, but for other reasons as well, one being that when we went back to Spain there were no ballet schools functioning. She was willing to sacrifice anything for ballet. When the family left, Anna would happily have remained alone in Italy to continue the classes and dedicate her whole life to ballet but she was only twelve years old and we had no real friends or relations to leave her with.

The only training she ever had was three years in London during the war. There she dedicated the whole day to it, but she was already fifteen years old—too late to master the art successfully.[293] From there she went straight onto the stage and joined ENSA in some of the ballet companies that toured England and Europe to entertain the troops.[294] This was done under great stress, and a few years after the war she abandoned ballet as a profession. This was an immense shame as she had a rare gift for dancing. I remember all through her life she could dance anything instinctively, from ballet to Sambas and Rumbas.

Still, while we were in Italy she did manage to have her innings in this way. There was a good school of ballet in Rome and also of drawing, and so soon she

---

[293] Anna says that her mother would not allow her to continue with lessons as these were expensive.
[294] See note 179.

In the Shadow of a Poet

was studying ballet and I was studying drawing in an art school. This drawing was a serious business—just drawing, drawing, drawing all morning and all afternoon and sometimes in the evening instead of the day. There were models of every description, old peasant women, with their pronounced wrinkles, young men and women in the nude, old men with beards. The school was run by an old Polish teacher who had considerable expertise. After six months of this, I had really learnt something about drawing.

One of the things I remember most about Rome, besides the drawing, was eating cream buns. There didn't seem to be any cream in Portugal or Spain in those days; we never saw cream except on our rare visits to England, and I loved it. We were starved of cream so the buns in Rome were memorable.

After our day of classes, my sister and I would meet at a cosy café in the Via Babuino, one of the central streets of Rome. I recall our rendezvous on icy, winter nights, when the warmth and hot tea and fresh, sweet buns were a tremendous treat for us after studying hard all day. After this we would go to an English lending library just up the street to choose books. There was a great variety. My sister would choose healthy serious literature, mostly Dickens. I remember one fascinating book that I picked—Maria Bashkirtseff's Diary.[295]

While reading this book I got a sudden longing to be what I wasn't—delicate, spiritual, attractive. I didn't want to be a smashing beauty but I wanted to be different from what I was. I didn't like my face covered with freckles, or my English complexion, or my rather strong bandy legs. I wanted to be more delicate. I mention this book here because it made a strong impression on me. It was a time when something grave began to happen to me; it was to affect me and the whole family for years. The innocent book was not the cause of the trouble but it struck deep somewhere and had a great influence on my downfall. Adolescence is a vulnerable phase in the span of life when one can pick up all sorts of disorders.

Since my stay in England at school, I had depended on laxatives. Here in Rome, three years later, I was still taking them every night. I think this state of affairs was one of the causes for the long illness I was to suffer later. At this time I never felt normal. I was depressed and by then, at sixteen, my system was probably poisoned by so many liver pills, cascara sagrada, senna etc. Nowadays,

---

[295] Born Nov. 11 1860, Ukraine, Russia, died Oct. 19 1884, Paris, Mariya Konstantinovna Bashkirtseva, a Russian émigré artist is best known for her sensitive and girlishly candid autobiography in French, JOURNAL DE MARIE BASHKIRTSEFF, AVEC UN PORTRAIT, 2 vol. (1887) (MERRIAM-WEBSTER'S ENCYCLOPEDIA OF LITERATURE, Philippines: Merriam-Webster, 1995:110). The English title is, MARIE BASHKIRTSEFF (FROM CHILDHOOD TO GIRLHOOD). This is now in the public domain: www.bibliolife.com/opensource.

less harsh, more natural remedies have taken the place of laxatives. At that time I was not aware of the damage I was doing, and cream buns were the last thing I should have been eating. I did not know that in this state one should eat wholemeal flour, not refined flour, wholemeal bread, not white, fibrous vegetables, roughage, fruit. I was totally ignorant of the importance of nutrition in so many spheres of health, as everyone else was, and as so many people in the civilised world still are. So much ill health, so much suffering, so many complaints could be avoided with the help of a little information on this subject.

I seemed incapable of changing my condition. There was nothing I could do except be depressed. Nevertheless, life was thrilling in so many respects.

Strangely enough and quite unexpectedly in this city which was quite unfamiliar to us, my parents were suddenly drawn into its high society because of the right wing leanings of FLOWERING RIFLE which had just been published. My father was received as a great hero and invited to the grand salons of the famous Roman families—the Sforzas, Colonnas and Rospigliosis.[296] My mother, having only her Carmelite habit in the way of clothes, was forced to have some smart clothes made. My father went to all these parties and cocktail parties. Some of them were specially in his honour, and he never had a drop of drink.

We had come to Italy to meet my paternal grandmother. She arrived at about Christmas time, so we celebrated Christmas with her at her swanky hotel in Rome. Then she took us to visit Venice and Florence.[297] We saw Venice under snow, then went to Florence to visit the Uffizi galleries before she left to continue her travels.

In early 1939, the unexpected happened in Spain. The government forces were gradually crumbling before the slow but steady advance of the Nationalists, and one by one, the strategic points were falling into Franco's hands. By March of that year, the Spanish Civil War had ended, so we made our plans to return to Toledo.

---

[296] These families exercised considerable power in the Middle Ages.
[297] See the cover photo, it was taken on this trip.

Chapter 25
Special Interlude

The solid golden Toledo we had known had changed shockingly, even its contours against the sky had changed. It had no shape, it was a mass of rubble. Its atmosphere had changed, and there were no more cool patios or gardens. Everything was smutty and shabby, blighted. The people, those who had survived and stayed, seemed aimless. And there were all sorts of new people. Gardens, vineyards, olive groves, were a silent testimony of devastation and conflict. For three years, life had been interrupted in a grizzly struggle for survival.

My father's ever-discerning and hopeful spirit was groping among the shambles. He was conscious of what lay behind the ruins. Spain had routed one of the most formidable powers the world had ever known. Here his favourite theme, the one explored in THE FLAMING TERRAPIN, had realised itself in front of his eyes: Man's endeavour and faith against all odds, displayed clear cut against the horizon. One had to be conscious of the significance of victory. Whatever the world may say about the Civil War in Spain being a war of classes, the wealthy against the oppressed, there were other factors just as important at stake, such as freedom of expression and freedom of worship.

From the start it was a struggle for life or death on either side, and if the Reds did not win, it was because the different factions were always fighting amongst each other. By human standards the Reds should have won. They had one of the greatest military powers behind them, part of the army, the Navy, the International Brigade, and all the gold of Spain. The Nationalists' victory was solely due to discipline, determination, unity and faith.

Back at Toledo, our lives gradually fell into place, and soon after we arrived we heard all the fantastic local stories, some hair-raising, some of heroism, some of martyrdom. One was the story of Captain Alba. He was an officer from the Alcázar (the father of Anna's best friends at school) who, disguised as a peasant, set out from the siege, across the plains, to take a message to Franco. But on his way through one of the villages he was recognised and shot. There were lots of other heroic stories of many of our friends: the story of the Angel of Alcázar who lost one of his arms in the last desperate onslaught of the Reds and went on fighting without an arm. He died a few days later, after the siege was relieved. We also learned of our friends the Carmelite Fathers, eight of whom were taken out into the street next to their monastery and put against the wall and shot.

My mother, as usual full of her spiritual fervour, got down to relieve the misery around. She went down to the most miserable quarter in Toledo and, in her quiet way, initiated projects to assist. She started sewing sessions with the women. The women of the quarter were given material and sewed clothes for themselves and their families, while one of them read the gospels aloud. This was the main object of the sessions—evangelisation. (She had had good practice of this kind of work, for at sixteen she did it among the miners in the Midlands in England.) Later she got funds for the materials, and the whole venture grew into a big thing. In the end all the parishes of Toledo took it up. She even managed to have the chapel of the quarter functioning with mass on Sundays and Catechism for the children. Her quarter was the most difficult, the misery being rampant and the women all Reds. She could dedicate a lot of time to this, as Anna was at boarding school in Avila and I had private lessons all day.

Spain was depressing in its present state, but it still was Spain. Fundamentally it had not changed. For us there were incomparably happy interludes, such as the summer holidays when we relaxed from our various activities.

We spent part of our holiday the summer following our return to Toledo on a *dehesa*, a Castillian farm, one of the most remote and enduring things on earth. One felt it would take hundreds of years before they would change. We only managed to stay on a *dehesa* because we had intimate friends who had one, otherwise we would never have known one; they are so remote and the Castilians keep them to themselves. Sometimes the nearest village is two or three hours' ride on a donkey. For our holiday we were taken by car along dusty roads.

The building of a *dehesa* is rather like a fortress, large and spread out; the stables and courtyards are in one block, attached to the main house. The land is flat and arid, with big tufts of grass among which, in those days, literally thousands of big, fat partridges scurried as there had been no one to shoot them for years. We almost trod on them as we walked about. A ten minute walk from this farm took one to the Tagus, to a sandy beach, where we bathed in the cool, swirling water. The most wonderful thing about these farms is the atmosphere, so clear, so limpid, so light, because they are on this high Castilian plateau. One is nearer the sun, the moon and the stars. In summer from the early dawn, everything is hushed and luminous, waiting for the great sun god to rise and ignite every-

In the Shadow of a Poet

thing. Then it becomes even more still and hushed, except for the scintillating life of the birds of which we saw an infinite variety.

During our stay we camped out in the sheep's corral and slept on clean straw. From here at night one could see the harvest moon rise, so enormous, so orange, so near and clear, one felt one could reach out and touch it with one's hand.

My mother still insisted on going to mass every morning. The only way she could do this, because the heat was so great, was to leave in the cool of the morning at about six and get back before the sun got too high. She would have the donkey saddled and set out alone to do the five mile trek over the plains to the nearest village.

Everything we ate came from the premises. The farm was self-sufficient and even the bread was made from its grain and baked in its oven. Big *cocidos* were made everyday for everyone. A *cocido* is a big (usually) earthenware pot containing broth, made with whole chickens, chick peas, tomatoes, potatoes, sausage and bacon all boiled together. The sausage and bacon were also made from the pigs on the premises. And every day we had gazpacho, the cold salad soup of Spain, made with garlic, cucumber, vinegar, oil and tomatoes.

The hottest hours of the day we spent in the hay barn, reading. We had just received a big parcel of new books from England, for all our tastes, which we had ordered specially for the holidays. The heat was intense, so as soon as we could go out, we rushed down to the river and bathed. How delicious those bathes were in those days. Now one cannot bathe in the Tagus any more because the water is polluted. This holiday, on this *dehesa*, was the most captivating and pleasurable one we ever had.

The rest of the summer we spent in going to Segovia which, with its fairy-like castle and rocky streams, was rather a contrast to the *dehesa*. Here the speciality was roasted sucking pig. As there was a dearth of food in Spain at the time, this seemed a great luxury. My father ate this plentifully, but more than this, he exulted in the deep red wine of the region and soon recovered his natural colour and became his old rollicking self again. He had had anaemia after his long abstinence from drink and was very pale and thin.

We ended our holiday by going back to Altea to visit our old haunts and friends. Here things were very much the same as before the war as it had not been troubled by the fighting.

Chapter 26
Anorexia Nervosa

*S*ince we had been back in Spain, I read in magazines about treatments for straightening legs, fading freckles, and slimming. None of them worked, except the slimming, so I took to this in a big way, and the less I managed to eat the more triumphant I felt. It was fine in the beginning, I felt light and clear-headed, but after years of this I had a nervous breakdown. I thought by doing this I would become more elegant, more distinguished and energetic. The family looked on and didn't know what to do; my father would try with great kindness and compassion to make me eat more, but nothing was to any avail.

Anorexia Nervosa in those days was an uncommon complaint, and not much was known about it. Since then, the number of cases has grown and it has become quite common, and many, especially young girls, suffer from it. There are quite a few fatal cases, when the patient dies of weakness. I escaped this but never recovered entirely, always thereafter being under par.

After our holiday through Spain, our parents had arranged for Anna and me to be boarders at the most expensive school in Spain, the Assumption Convent in Madrid. This was done so that we would have adequate food, because as I said before, there was a great dearth of essential foodstuffs at that time. Here I continued banting[298] and passed on to Anna half of my meals for which she was thankful. At the convent the nuns were special women and some of them very witty. I had two special dispensations there. One was to go out into the streets of Madrid once a week; I went alone, as no other girl was allowed this privilege. The other was to have Holy Communion only once a week, as daily communion overwhelmed me.

One morning at the convent a strange thing happened to me. As usual

---

[298] Banting is a method of dieting named after William Banting (1797–1878), an obese Londoner, whose high protein and fat, low-carbohydrate diet was a splendid success. Eager to spread the good word, in 1863 Banting published a pamphlet in which he described the wonder diet. Soon the term "banting" entered the English and Swedish languages (Barry A. Groves, WILLIAM BANTING: THE FATHER OF THE LOW-CARBOHYDRATE DIET, http://www.second-opinions.co.uk/banting.html).

In the Shadow of a Poet

we girls got up at 7:30, washed, dressed and lined up to enter the chapel for mass. That morning just before waking, I had a clear dream. I saw the host at the time of the communion fall and go rolling along the polished floor of the chapel. To my surprise, that morning, as the priest gave the communion, a host fell and went rolling along the floor just as I had seen it in the dream. Was this coincidence or premonition?

For some reason or other I was always hankering after the insalubrious. LA DAME AU CAMELIAS, with Greta Garbo, had just been released. I had seen her in CHRISTINA OF SWEDEN and had a great admiration for her. The snag was the film was on the Index;[299] it was mortal sin to see it. Still, I was determined to sell my soul to the devil to see Greta Garbo fading away. That it was on the Index only gave it extra glamour. I went alone to see the film, accompanied only by my determination. For a long time after, the film served as another Maria Bashkirtseff beckoning me to annihilation. This film made me want to fade away more than ever.

If I had been a working class girl, without enough to eat, how different matters would have been. There wouldn't have been time to think about what I looked like, the struggle for existence would have kept me on the right road. But as things were, they led to misfortune.

When World War II engulfed an ever-enlarging portion of the world we all felt we should be doing something towards the war effort and so we left for England in the autumn of 1941, my father going on ahead. He went with a convoy across the then-dangerous seas to England. The rest of us remained in Lisbon. We stayed with some Portuguese friends we had made in Sesimbra in 1937. They offered us a flat where we stayed until a fairly safe journey could be booked to Ireland. In late 1941 we boarded a biplane which was waiting on the Tagus. We disembarked on the river Shannon in Ireland, and from there we crossed over to England.

We have a paper-cutting of this time of a report by a journalist who met my father on his arrival in England, and this is what he says:

---

[299] The Index of Prohibited Books refers to the list or catalogue of books, the reading of which was once forbidden to Catholics by the highest ecclesiastical authority. The last edition of the Index was published in 1948. In 1966 the Congregation for the Doctrine of the Faith (formerly, the Holy Office) announced that the Index and its related penalties of excommunication would no longer have the force of law in the church. (THE COLUMBIA ENCYCLOPEDIA, Sixth Edition. © 2006 Columbia University Press, Copyright © 2007 Yahoo!) See also CHRISTIANITY THROUGH THE CENTURIES: A HISTORY OF THE CHRISTIAN CHURCH, Earle Edwin Cairns (2nd edition) 1981: 348-9.

Back from Spain after an adventure or two is Roy Campbell, the poet. He came by the way of Gibraltar and lost no time in joining the A.R.P. One of the troubles in Spain at the moment, he told me when I met him this week, is the locust. The neglect of tillage has been responsible for this—the locusts' eggs have been allowed to breed, and they are not helping the crops. Mr. Campbell did not want to be left in Spain if trouble came between them and us, "When trouble does come —and if it comes", he said, "I want to be under the Union Jack".

This he said so as to define his politics clearly and show he had come back home to fight Fascism.

By the time we all arrived in London, my father was an air-warden, as reported, and we arrived in the thick of the Blitz. To start with, my mother and I were cook and parlour maid to an old lady who had a property near Petersfield, Hants. Anna continued her ballet lessons in London and came back for the weekends. My father then joined the Army Intelligence Corps. He was a commando and was sent to South Africa, but he was too old for the strain of such a service. During the last year of the war he was a sergeant and did coast watching in Tanganyika. We did not see him for years.

My ambition towards the war effort was to join the Land Army, but when I applied there were no vacancies, so I took what seemed to me the best thing, which was maintenance in the WRNS. I was stationed at Weymouth, a quiet port. There was little to do there apart from cleaning sparking plugs. Sometimes there were no sparking plugs, so rather than do nothing, I used to get the plugs from the garbage which would never be used again, and clean them. After a year in the WRNS I was invalided out with patches on my lungs because of my insistent banting. After a month of convalescing at Exeter Hospital, I was sent home and joined my mother.

My sister found it very hard to be alone in London, where she was studying ballet, with all the bombardments, so my mother decided to go and live in London to keep her company. We had to find a house. It would have to be large enough for us all and have a Catholic church near. That was always the paramount necessity with my mother. Here in London, even in war time and the worst war there ever had been on earth, there she was, thinking about the Church, and she managed to find it—of all churches a Carmelite church, with Carmelite fathers, the same order that she belonged to. This was so lucky, and the house was something special, two stories with a basement and a small terrace. It was in a line of old, typical London houses of the last century, facing the sun, so it was very sunny. It was a real find.

In the Shadow of a Poet

In the meantime the war was becoming more and more intense, and the sirens and blackouts more frequent. One night my mother and I were alone in the house (by then Anna was touring England in a ballet company), when a bomb made a straight hit on the Carmelite church. That was the nearest we ever got to a bomb in the bombardments of London. The blast was deadly and it almost annihilated the Carmelites. Suddenly, my mother and I heard the sound of rushing water. A pipe had burst in the roof and water was pouring down the main staircase, enough to destroy the house. What to do? I remembered a big tap outside, in the basement. So I went to it and turned it. To our surprise and relief not another drop flowed. After that there was silence. I don't know where the Carmelites were in all this. Still, some time after, the fathers and the services re-emerged, among the ruins.

Tess in WRNS (Tess)

After the invaliding out of the WRNS, I lived with my mother, but I was not what I should have been at that age: a strong and energetic woman. My banting for years now had got hold of my whole system. I was under par and felt ill and weak. Even eating normally didn't help, not that I did or could. Gradually I got completely demoralised and went downhill fast and ended up with a complete nervous breakdown. After that there was chaos in my whole being for years.

When the war ended and my father came back from Africa I was at my worst. From being his pride and comfort, I became his greatest worry and nightmare. He used to come and see me at the nerve-home where I was, already weighed down with trouble. My heart used to bleed to see him, and there was nothing

I could do to help my state, I only got worse.

After years of suffering all round (I think it was my father's greatest sorrow in life, it certainly was my mother's), after consulting many of the most famous psychiatrists and doctors in London, after being in many nursing homes and having all the modern treatments, electroshock therapy, insulin, to no avail, my mother very courageously decided to take me home. My father didn't want to, partly because he knew my state was desperate and also because he feared the affect this would have on my mother and Anna who were still sane.

But my mother had the power, the uncanny power, which made her do things other people couldn't do. After all, it was not for nothing she went to mass and communion every morning. It was her faith which gave her the necessary calm and courage.

This move brought on a crisis, but the crisis was the end of the trouble, as is often the case.

Through these years I had become a wreck, so weak I could hardly stand up. Every sound confused me. If I got up and tried to dress, I got so confused and felt so weak, I just went back to bed and lay there. The worst was I saw every member of the family weighed down with difficulties—my mother with a stomach ulcer, doing the cooking, shopping and housework; money troubles because my hospital bills had impoverished the family; my sister under strain because she was doing parts in ballet she had not had enough training for, travelling round England in ballet companies, living a life that stressed her nervous system, without adequate food; my father writing and doing odd jobs to keep us out of debt. On top of this they had to wait on me and bring me my food in bed. I was put in the basement near the kitchen to facilitate matters. But now I couldn't even eat because I couldn't digest food, nor could I sleep. It was a climax of hell which lasted for weeks.

A Carmelite father used to come and give me Holy Communion, the only communicating I did in the depths of depression.

Then, to cap the situation, the suicidal state occurred. One afternoon when the house was silent and my mother was absent, I took a few paces to the kitchen, got hold of the sharpest knife I could find, took it back to bed with me and started with the sharp blade to cut the veins on the inside part of my elbows—first one, then the other. Then I lay, the blood flowing slowly. In a kind of a maze, I heard my mother enter the house and come down to me. I was lying in a pool of blood. She phoned the ambulance, and I was taken urgently to Queen's Hospital, where I was operated on, saved and interned. After that I convalesced for two weeks and returned home. I did not die of

In the Shadow of a Poet

starvation or weakness, as many cases do, but I nearly died at my own hand.

Sometime after this serious event a marvellous thing happened. We had at Campden Grove a little old lady who lived next door, she was Irish and a Catholic, and she was concerned about me. One day she asked me if I would see her doctor. I said I would, but having seen many doctors in the last few years, I didn't have much faith. One evening he visited us. He was a Polish refugee, slight and dark. He got straight down to the matter. In his broken English he said: "What do you want most in the world?" I told him I wanted to go to a sunny, Latin country. He immediately said I could go, and he spoke to my parents, and although they had been pretty well broke for years with my expenses, they managed to scrape up enough money for us to go to Provence for a holiday. From that holiday onwards I slowly came out of the woods, and although we went back to London afterwards, I was able to lead a more or less normal life. So many times since I have remembered with immense admiration and gratitude the intuitive and direct way this Polish doctor diagnosed and tackled the problem and how successful he was, and I also remember our dear neighbour next door for having the bright idea of making us meet. And behind this I am sure it was my mother's prayers, fortitude and faith that worked the miracle.

The extraordinary thing about this happy ending to a sad story is that it was a spontaneous inspiration from a poor refugee who had the answer to the problem. Why should it be him to find the answer to my problem after I had consulted most of the eminent specialists and psychiatrists in England with no success? I suppose it was because the time had come—the war had ended, and he himself had just been through hell, escaping from Poland. This made him see clearly, soul to soul, in understanding.

Chapter 27
Recovery

At this point, early in 1950, our life began to change. The first days of our holiday were spent in Brittany with friends who had a house there. We used to go for short walks in the country and see the peasants living their calm lives. A glimmer of something seemed to revive in me; I don't know what it was—a vague joy, peace, happiness, hope, love. In any case, it was something. We were on our way down to spend the summer at Bormes les Mimosas in Provence. My father and I did this journey together, although I was just about fading out all the way, but I managed to pull through and we arrived at Toulon. On the journey my father introduced me to Birre and Vermouth which I drank with water, and this helped to lift my spirits. He was knowledgeable about all neurasthenic troubles, and his tips helped me greatly.

Bormes is some miles inland from the sea; a lovely hanging village with a view of the Mediterranean and the Alpes Maritimes behind. When we arrived, my mother

Roy, Bormes-les-Mimosas, Provence 1949 (Francesca)

and sister had rented a little villa on the slope, looking towards Le Lavandou and the sea. After a few days the change and the feeling of the hot sun on our skins started having a beneficial effect on us all. I began to feel a vague hope and had a slight idea of possible strength coming back to me. This state of spirit was owed a lot to my sister's company, she was so gay and kind. She used to set out bravely on foot towards the beach with me trying to keep up with her. Sometimes my head felt so vague I could hardly see, but when we got onto the hot sand and lay there, everything would fall into place again. With the help of the family, each in their different ways, I soon recovered a sort of balance.

My father had chosen Bormes to be near Richard Aldington, who lived at Le Lavandou at that time. They used to meet and have long talks and get rid of many of their grievances as they had a lot in common concerning modern trends in thought and politics.

We spent a whole splendid summer here, walking down to the beach, sunbathing, and gradually my depression dispersed. From then onwards my life seemed to take a turn for the better. We had rented the villa for a month but decided to stay on longer, so we moved into cheaper lodgings and rented an enormous loft in the village, which was kitchen, dining room, bedroom all together, and here we camped out. Our communal life was much more reassuring and satisfying than the conventional way of living.

This enormous, spacious attic was very homely, with our beds, a gas stove to cook on, a large wooden table for our meals. We started cooking a wonderful variety of Provençal and Spanish dishes. The fruit was delectable, and I remember the peaches there were something special. Outside there were the hot summer days and nights and drinks to lift our spirits. In this warm and loving atmosphere, we all started to breathe easier. My state of mind normalised and so we went back to London full of peace, new blood and Latin consolations.

Chapter 28
Life in London

My father by now was middle-aged. He had mellowed a lot and had lost a lot of the bitterness which was so evident in his earlier years. He no longer evaded civilisation with its fever, its noise. On the contrary, he encouraged social life. London seemed to suit him. What contributed a lot to this state of affairs was perhaps the feeling that he had fulfilled himself. He was an acknowledged and famous poet. He had changed physically, too. His lameness and sitting at office jobs and drinking beer had made him put on weight. He was very hefty. When people remarked on this, he would stick his thorax out and show with pride that this was more salient than his tummy. I also think that what contributed to his happy state of mind was that he had a good job as a Talks Producer at the BBC, which provided a much-needed a regular income, since he could not depend on his writing.

He soon made many friends in London and gradually formed a circle which used to meet every evening at the Catherine Wheel, a pub in Church Street, Kensington. Aimé Tschiffely,[300] the rider, and his Chilean wife, were some of my parents' best friends.

It was in early 1947 that we got to know Robert Lyle,[301] member of the Lyle sugar manufacturing family, whose discerning and keen spirit changed the course of our lives completely. It was through his friendship and generosity and help that my father was able to leave the BBC and dedicate himself to writing again. The outcome of this was the joint effort of Rob Lyle (who had just become a Catholic) and my father to edit a Catholic magazine, aptly called THE CATACOMB, at a time when any Christian belief was in severe decline. This undertaking made it possible for my father to take up writing again, and he was able to conclude two of his best works, his autobiography LIGHT ON A DARK HORSE and his translations of St. John of the Cross, both published in 1951.[302]

---

[300] See note 226.
[301] See note 2.
[302] As noted previously, RC described this autobiography as "autobuggeroffery" (COLLECTED WORKS III: 614 (note 1). Tess told me this attitude was probably due to his

These works were written in a little dark alcove at the back of our sitting-room. It was dark as it only had a long window which gave onto the basement steps below. Surrounded by high walls of flats, very little light could get in and my father had to write by electric light. For years he had craved to be really free to write; now he could, and his autobiography and the brilliant and outstanding translations were accomplished in this dark little hole. Anyone who knows Spanish can judge for themselves the perfection of this work which is a near miracle of a translation, rendered wholly in verse like the original. My father said of this work, that it wasn't he who translated it but St. John who spurred my father on: *"Arré burro!"* my father would hear him say in Spanish, meaning "Gee up, donkey!"

It was also to Robert Lyle that I owe a great part of my recovery from my illness. It was he, after our holiday in France, who offered me an easy job, because he knew I was keen to earn money but not strong enough to do a normal job. So he gave me some easy work in his office, helping with the subscribers of THE CATACOMB. He paid me two pounds a week, and this occupation contributed immensely to my recuperation.

As I said, from our holiday in France I slowly came out of the woods but progress was slow. Life on a holiday in Provence in summer is a decidedly different affair from a busy cold London in winter. I was still weak, nervous and apprehensive of everything except my easy job; every day I buckled down but once in the street, I kept my eyes glued on the pavement in case I might meet some surprise or person on the way. It was only when I finally got to my chair in the office that I felt safe. At that stage everything shook me, but day after day, being very brave, I was gradually able to face up to life and lead a more or less normal existence.

My father, having made so many friends, inevitably lived a prodigiously busy social life, partly due also to contacting people for THE CATACOMB. Besides our intimate friends, we came into touch with the Catholic ecclesiastical world, the Spanish Diplomatic Corps, and with the well-known writers of the London literary world, with Dylan Thomas, the Sitwells and others, as well as many, many artists and sculptors. In consequence we often had parties at home. Sometimes these parties were uproarious, when my father would exhibit one of his strongest characteristics—his humour. Then his store

---

sense that people shouldn't be concerned with his life, they should read his poetry, and also because it was written partly because he needed money, and it was in this sense "a bugger" of a job. Connolly says that RC referred to it thus because he was aware that it would scandalise some readers (218).

Tess also said she was unaware of why Anna claimed that the publishers of LIGHT ON A DARK HORSE had altered the manuscript in ways that made Roy unhappy.

of incongruous stories from the army world would come out and the house would almost come down with laughter. One night the uproar was so extravagant that our neighbours next door complained to the police who promptly came along to put an end to it. But it wasn't long before they also were drawn into the confabulation and forgot the reason they had been sent for and joined in the party, until the constable came. But by then it was time to finish up, and so it all ended happily.

With this lively social life, my mother had abandoned her tertiary's dress and went back to normal clothes. She usually wore dark colours with some scarlet or bright red which suited her. At fifty-two she was more delicate, more distinguished looking and more beautiful than she had ever been before. This was a great joy to my father who, although slap-dash about his own appearance, believed women should always make the best of themselves.

It was also here, during this hectic life, that my father used to sit for hours on end nearly every Sunday afternoon with the deaf and dumb South African poet, David Wright,[303] helping him, encouraging him, and keeping him company. The only way they could communicate was by writing. My father's dedication was deeply felt, just as it had been years earlier with Angel, the grocer's son who had a bent for poetry, in Toledo.

Something unexpected happened to me at this time. I got fat, very fat. My mother used to remark on it and say: "But Tess, you are getting too fat." I used to reassure her and say: "Don't worry, because it will disappear far too soon, you will see." I really enjoyed being fat now, it was a great consolation. It must have been the delayed action of the insulin and the plates piled high with fried potatoes that they used to give me as I lay in bed at the nerve home. It was a joy to be fat, and I hoped it would never leave me, but it did.

Another happening which speeded and helped my recovery at this time was a visit we paid to Spain. Two years after my recovery, in May 1951, my father had to go to lecture in Madrid. He asked me if I would like to go with him, and I agreed. It was the first time he or I had travelled by air. It seemed fabulous, it was so clean and fast, over and done in a few hours. In olden days it would have taken two or three days by train or boat. In Madrid we stayed in a pension where Charles D. Ley, the writer, was a resident. He was a professor in Madrid and a good friend of my father's.

After some time here, the people of the pension who were friendly and good-

---

[303] (1920-1994) South African author and poet, deafened as a result of scarlet fever, contracted at the age of seven. He wrote a short biography of Campbell (ROY CAMPBELL. London: Longmans, Green & Co., 1961).

In the Shadow of a Poet

natured, one day said to me with typical Spanish frankness: "Your hair does not look nice as it is. Why don't you go to the hairdresser? We know of one who will put you right:" So I agreed and they took me. The woman there, after taking a good look at my head, said: "You must have your hair cut short, like a boy." So that was what she did, and that is how I have worn my hair ever since, all through the years. She was right: I felt much smarter and more myself. It would take the Spanish to be so inspired.

Another thing I learnt on that stay was to be extremely wary in one's dealings with gypsies. One day I decided to go for a walk alone down to the Castellana, which is one of the main avenues of Madrid. There I was accosted by an old gypsy woman in black. She said she would tell my fortune. But at that time this was a rather sensitive question with me, so I said No. But I opened my bag and gave her a few pesetas. She never touched anything of mine except the money I gave her, and we parted. But by some magic she cleaned me of my money. When I got back to the pension I hadn't a penny left. It made me feel quite strange. A really uncanny power. I never got over it. After that I always kept clear of gypsies.

A change is as good as a rest, and this visit to Spain infused in me a new inspiration.

In London, all through my recovery from my illness, because it was gradual, my father was very understanding and tender. He used to give me little tips. When I felt low and depressed, he would tell me to lie down and hold my breath as long as I could and relax and make my mind a blank. He also said it was important to have warm feet and sometimes made me hot water bottles to put my feet on. He also told me milk was more digestible with a drop of water in it. When we went to pubs he would order me crème-de-menthe mixed with water which he said helped the digestion. Sometimes he would stroke my head with his exceptionally sensitive hands which used to revive me a lot. He was so knowledgeable about my afflictions, and these simple remedies helped immensely.

Tess and Roy, Madrid, 1951
(Francesca)

Chapter 29
Dreamer or Realist?

To most people my father is a conundrum, owing chiefly to his own reports about himself—the ones about him being a cattle-man, horse-dealer, bull-fighter, soldier at the front in the Spanish Civil War, and so on. He did have serious adventures in these spheres with friends and acquaintances, and some of these occupations were taken up with the idea of profit in some way or another, but without success. With fishing he did bring in a few fish, and this provided us with quite a few meals. With horse-dealing he did manage to provide us with one outstanding horse which he got for a bargain. With bullfighting he did get a prize of about twenty-five pounds for getting the *cocarde* off the bull's horns in the South of France, and so on. And the one about being a soldier at the front in the Spanish Civil War is true as far as going into the front lines, but never as a soldier.

Then there are the drastic judgements by his readers brought down upon himself by his virulent satire, concerning such subjects as Anglo-Saxons, Socialism, Communism, Jews and homosexuals. Accordingly, he was considered by contemporary left-wing writers and critics as a dreamer, a fascist bully, a Zulu, an outsider. All of this makes him mystifying.

It would be difficult or fairly impossible for a cattleman, horse-dealer, bullfighter or soldier to write lyrical verse as he did, or to do a translation of St. John of the Cross as he did, or even to write a few short books of critical prose as he did. No, he was essentially a poet, a scholar, a thinker and a prophet.

According to left-wing critics he was a romantic and a talking bronco,[304] but how could a man who was out of touch with reality prophesy so exactly the downfall and failure of Communism, both as an ideal and as a system, fifty years before it happened? There he was not only surprising but much more down to earth and realistic than his detractors. There was also the question of Apartheid in South Africa, a thing he condemned as far back as 1926;[305] this

---
[304] Spender's term for RC, which RC then used as the title for a volume of verse.
[305] Strictly speaking, apartheid did not become government policy until the Nationalist Party came into power in 1948. However, prior to this, the maintenance of white supremacy had been crucial to the formation of the Union of South in 1910, and numerous racist laws were passed and enforced. Separation of the races was known as the Colour Bar.

complex question has been resolved as he predicted it should.[306]

The only friend and intellectual who understood him entirely was Wyndham Lewis. In his book BLASTING AND BOMBARDIERING (1937) he says:

> Campbell has not any regulation political bias, I think. He may incline to Franco because he is a Catholic, and to the Old Spain rather than the New Spain because he likes bullfights and all the romantic things. But of politics he has none, unless they are such as go with a great antipathy for the English "gentleman" in all his clubmanesque varieties; a great attachment to the back-Veldt of his native South Africa; and a constant desire to identify himself with the roughest and simplest of his fellow-creatures in pub, farm, and bullring. Such politics as go with those predilections and antipathies he has, but it would be difficult to give them a name. He certainly is neither a communist nor a fascist.

As Wyndham Lewis says, it was my father's fidelity to Christianity in an age of atheism and social upheavals that made it difficult for people to follow him in all his unusual affinities and deviations from the beaten track.

As these memories are mainly about my father, I will try in this chapter to convey an impression of his nature and outlook on life.

From the moment he was born, there was animation. A calf with three heads was born at the same time in the vicinity. To the Zulus, it was a sign a genius had been born. So there was rejoicing and celebration. When he was a baby they went as far as to call him the "Messias", not because of the omen but because he was an extremely good and wise baby. That was how his career began.

My father was born and bred among the natives of South Africa. He got to love their wisdom and integrity. He respected them tremendously. To him they became as brothers, as with them he spent his happy childhood years and learnt a lot about life with them, and that gave him his clear insight into the South African problem. We were always surprised by his uncommon easy ability to mix with any company. He could sit down with peasants and fishermen and become one of them. This, my mother said, came from his early mixing with the blacks. The same happened with any company he was with.

For those who believe in astrology, he was born under the constellation of Libra. He was a typical Libran. Venus endowed him with beauty and a deeply balanced nature, although disturbed at times by nerves. He couldn't live without harmony in private life. This is also a Libran characteristic. This

---

[306] Apartheid refers to the policy of racial segregation devised by the Nationalist Party (in power from 1948–1994). Prior to 1948, a less extreme form of racism was known as the Colour Bar.

may sound contradictory for those who have read his satires. Perhaps it was his love of law and order that made him so brutal and disturbed in his satire. Although so belligerent in his work, in private life he could not endure discord, wherever it was. He did everything he could to make peace.

Any quarrel between my mother and him was always settled by him asking for forgiveness, even if my mother was in the wrong. She, on the other hand, was imperturbable; it didn't seem to matter whether they made peace or not. I can never remember her making up a quarrel. One of her favourite sayings was: "Angels never change their minds."[307] Their most frequent rows were about tipping waiters or porters. My mother would keep her purse tight shut. It was the only one there was. He wanted to tip all over the place but had no money. Still, he nearly always managed to squeeze it out of her in the end. Whenever porters or waiters came near, my sister and I would become apprehensive. It always meant a row, a serious one. Sometimes my mother would offer a shilling but he wanted five, and it would cause suffering all round. My mother was pretty immovable about this, too. She didn't seem to care much about tipping.

He had a tremendous sense of humour and this is what made him unusual and wonderful company. When he died, this is what my mother said she missed the most. There was no one to take his place.

He had a euphoric outlook on life, so much so that it was contagious to other people. Even Wyndham Lewis mentions this in one of his letters. He says that as he neared Martigues where he used to visit us in the nineteen-thirties, he had a feeling of elation.

My father was a great scholar. One of his greatest gifts was facility in rhyming. I was fascinated by this, as I lacked it completely. In this way he was a wizard.

When he was not writing, he would read; he could spend whole days and nights reading—propped up in bed, this was his usual position when reading. He read anything from detective stories to Homer, Dickens, Góngora. We still have a lot of his favourite books like THE LIVES OF PLUTARCH or Juvenal, without covers

---

[307] This would seem to reinforce the impression one gets from the 1929 photo (see p. 145) of Roy seated in a rather feminised position, gazing up at Mary, with unsmiling Mary standing over him, hand on her hip, in dominant attitude: although it is obviously a posed photograph, it nevertheless conveys the idea that Mary had the upper hand. I asked Tess about this: she said that although Roy could be strong when he wanted, Mary was "the very opposite of my father" and "had very strong will-power". Roy couldn't bear any ill-feeling; he was, Tess said, "very sweet that way; he loved peace" and wanted everybody to be friends.

Alexander, in reference to this same photo, says that at this time, Mary's dominance over RC and his dependence on her continued to grow: she controlled finances (giving him an allowance), made all major decisions and took care of practicalities (100).

In the Shadow of a Poet

from so much handling. If there was nothing left in the house to read he would fall back on THE DECLINE AND FALL OF THE ROMAN EMPIRE by Gibbon, and that he did not get through so easily. He must have been the best read man on earth.

From a diary kept up for a few weeks before he died, he gives a brief summing up of what he considers the greatest poetry:

> All these years I've been reading Calderón, Tirso and Shakespeare —and neglected the greatest of them all from my point of view, for if Shakespeare excels Lope as a playwright, Lope far excels him (as does Calderón) as a writer of poetry. For the sheer writing of lyrical or epic verse (as in Calderón's two plays about Daniel) I would put Dante, Calderón and Homer first; David and Solomon, Góngora, second; Lope third; Camões and Shakespeare fourth; Lucan, Lucretius, Virgil, Milton, Ovid, Claudius, Prudentius, fifth; Pindar, Marlowe, Jonson etc., sixth. At least that's what I feel like today. Where to put Ariosto? (But I would keep a special place for Gil Vicente, Chaucer and Dunbar.)

This is how he classified the finest poets of the world.

There was an essential paradox in his nature: on the one side an almost anarchic love of freedom, on the other a stern sense of discipline. Rabelaisian, extravagant, liberal in his way of life, he had an exalted approach to it and the world in general. He was an ardent lover, husband, father, poet.[308] He loved the world passionately and tried, while in it, to fill himself with all that it had to give. At the same time there was a deep stability and order in his nature. Perhaps one of the clearest expressions of this is in his handwriting—meticulous, every letter perfectly shaped, minute, clear and harmonious. This harmony was present also in his drawing.[309]

Although so free and unconventional in his behaviour, he was a great traditionalist. Writing in the age of free verse, one would imagine him an adherent to this form of writing poetry, but he adhered to the strictest rhyme and metre.

---

[308] I asked Tess about the strange chapter on marriage in LIGHT ON A DARK HORSE in which her father hardly mentions Mary. Most of the narrative is about how he outwitted and outcharmed his rivals. (I have written about this. See Coullie, 2001: "The Race to be Hero: Race and Gender in Roy Campbell's LIGHT ON A DARK HORSE". SCRUTINY2, 6 (2).) Tess said Roy refrained from discussing Mary because he didn't like to bring in private affairs. She pointed out that she and Anna are also hardly mentioned in the autobiography but that he adored his children. Her mother, she said, was quite unconcerned about domestic life. Roy, on the other hand, used to cook and "treat us very, very, very well."

[309] In correspondence with me, Tess suggested repeatedly that copies of RC's "perfect" handwriting and sketches be included in this book. See "Additional Illustrations" section of this book.

The other facet of his nature, the agitated and nervous state, was also present at times. There were moments of great conflict in his whole being, whether this came from his highly strung nature, from heredity, from drink, from a deficiency in his pituitary gland as one specialist claimed, or from an accident to his neck as he himself claimed. It may have been a combination of some of these things, but whatever it was, it affected him deeply. At these moments he was in a convulsed state and suffered greatly. I suspect it was a mixture of nerves, sometimes monetary worries and chiefly hangovers from drink. As a child I had seen him in these states, but no one was affected or took any notice. He seemed to take these trials for granted and so did we. These attacks, however, were rare and occurred less often as he got older.

He had some peculiarities. He loved music in the form of songs and dance music and sang a lot himself. He knew all sorts of songs by heart from beginning to end—nearly all the sea shanties in English, nearly all the Scottish songs, French songs, even ragtime Yankee songs, but classical music he avoided. I noticed this and asked him why he didn't like it. He said it had the effect of diluting or disseminating poetry and it wasn't good for poets to listen to it. When he said this he looked rather as I imagine sailors looked in olden days when they spoke of sirens. The nearest he got to listening to classical music was the BLUE DANUBE, and that he loved.

He was very particular about his writing material. He always wrote with a pen and nibs and ink. He didn't like fountain pens or biros. He was perpetually buying nibs, which he chose with great care, and different kinds of writing paper. This was very important to him.

My father's religion was very simple. My mother had read the theologians, old and new. He read some of them but never pretended to know much about theology. People in England and even in Latin countries wondered how he could belong to such an "old fashioned" and "outdated" institution as the Catholic Church. He did because instead of focusing on the human weaknesses of the Church, its faults, its abuses, its Inquisition, he focussed on the miraculous, the confounding, the sublime side of the Catholic Church, with all its crazy hosts of martyrs and saints, its St. Augustine, its St. Catherine of Sienna and St. John of the Cross and the endless multitudes of others who gloried in and manifested the essentials of Christ's teaching, and he found in the Church the answers to his ideals and doubts. The Christian religion was so profoundly a part of him; he came from a thorough Presbyterian upbringing and deeply religious forefathers, but when he joined the Catholic Church he felt it was the real way of channelling Christianity. I don't know whether he would

In the Shadow of a Poet

have discovered and joined the Catholic Church officially himself, without my mother's influence. His sense of values and morality were so strong, he would not have thought it necessary for religion to have any special name, but I think he believed the Catholic religion emphasised the primary essence of the Son of God's message, more than the other Christian churches, and for this reason he found it valid. He was not a great churchgoer, but he went to mass on Sundays. His religion expressed itself more in action than in sacrifice.

At a time when science was taking the place of religion, he believed the spiritual force in man all-important for his proper development. To put it in the words of Christ: "It is not on bread alone that man lives but on every word that comes out of the mouth of God."

Living at the time of new revolutions, new ideas, new philosophies, throughout his life he stuck to the Christian ideal. For him there was only one revolution, the Christian one, one revolutionary Christ. He expressed this in so many words: "If it weren't for Christ, the world would be a howling wilderness." For him Christ's two greatest interpreters were St. John the Evangelist and St. Paul.

For him there were no politics except the reform of the individual. He attested this very definitely in an article he wrote for the Jesuit magazine THE MONTH in May 1950, "A Decade in Retrospect".

My father had a rosary and he said it devoutly. He used to say he was too great a sinner to pray straight to God, he needed an intercessor. His sense of guilt came from his drinking. It must have been the only thing he could not live up to, in the Church, although he had a great sense of self-preservation in this and seldom went all out. He never drank spirits, that was a rule, unless forced to under circumstances, and even so he would rather abstain altogether than drink then.[310] His usual drink was wine mixed with water—this he drank plenty of, or, when in England, beer. He never drank when busy on some work and went completely on the water wagon, overnight.

Although my mother used to try and prevent my father abusing drink, all through their life together she always kept him company in this. She loved red wine, she was a natural drinker, never wanting more than the measure. This was also one of my mother's gifts which helped their married life, because some women don't appreciate alcohol. Drink affected my parents differently. While my mother could drink three full glasses of red wine neat and only just feel its effect, my father with half a glass of neat wine was already tipsy.

My father and I agreed about nearly everything in life but there was one

---

[310] In his youth, RC was known to drink gin because it was cheap.

thing I could not understand in him, and that was the virulence of his satire.[311] He used to read aloud extracts of his work to my mother, and where there was satire, she would tell him to take it out or tone it down. I also was shocked by it and said, "Poor people, leave them alone", and he would answer, "But they ask for it", or, "They deserve it." He would not change anything. When not in satire, the same topic could be treated differently. Nearly everything he was disturbed about in satire had another side to it when not in satire.[312] Saxons, England and the English—they were frequently the butt of his mockery, and yet a broadcast he gave in South Africa in 1942 made up for anything he ever said antagonistic about the English. There could not possibly be greater praise for England and the English. Here, in its entirety, is "Calling South Africa":

> On arriving from the Axis-ridden continent some months ago I discovered England. Though it wasn't my first visit I'd never seen the real England before. All I had seen on those previous occasions had reminded me of a glorified Home for Cats and Dogs where human beings took a back seat. Though like all Dominions folk I secretly revered the British as my ancestors, I had hitherto preferred to revere that sphinx-like nation at a respectful distance.
>
> What I had seen of England previously compares to the present reality just as a dull grey chrysalis compares to the winged and fiery form which it subsequently releases. I had not the intuition to see more than the external preservative and protective sheath which has proved so deceptive to our enemies, who mistake it for inertia, stupidity, or frivolity. But England grew her wings in the first moment of adversity, and it's now easy for me to see and admire the emerging strength and beauty.
>
> I'm learning here the difference between a warrior nation (like England) and the militarised nations of the continent. The Englishman is a born warrior and his apparent over-domestication vanishes at the first emergency. Let's take for example the magnificent work of the volunteer fire-fighters during the most terrible fire in history. These men and women had had no experience except that which slept in their veins, yet they brought to that emergency the skill, resourcefulness, and courage of veterans. They were immediately at home in the atmosphere of sudden danger: it exhilarated them.

---

[311] Alexander argues that satire allowed RC "to externalize those aspects of himself he found unacceptable, to step away from them and attack them" (72).

[312] Of RC's vindictive invective against his fellow South Africans and subsequent hatreds, Alexander avers that these seem "almost always to have been purely theoretical" (77).

In the Shadow of a Poet

That's where one sees the difference between a warrior nation and a militaristic one like Germany. Nazi Germany is naturally militaristic, whereas the British have to be roused before they want to fight. Their martial ardour is there all right, but, until the call to action comes, it's dormant—they're more concerned with the arts of peace. Aggressiveness and show are the chief characteristics of the militaristic nations. But the British have the memory of a thousand victories in their blood. With that memory goes the knowledge of what victory costs, in human suffering, both to victor and vanquished, and that makes them reluctant to start quarrelling. Their reluctance is mistaken by outsiders for half-heartedness or fear. In reality the bowler hat and umbrella of the Briton are just as much of a disguise as the plumes and brass buttons of the goose-stepping Italian conscript, who in his bones is no fighter. The Briton normally invests himself in a sort of pedestrian drabness, not only in dress but in speech and manner. But he carries—sheathed and concealed in that drabness—a beautifully tempered sword. And when the steel is drawn it flashes and cuts like no other in the world. Many of us Dominions people acquire a flamboyancy of speech and manner, perhaps from our native landscape, and we thereupon misjudge the Britishers' reserve and lack of spirit. But once that reserve is discarded, as it is now, we witness something like a miracle.

The various conflicting ideologies which have desolated Europe on the pretext of producing ready-made Utopias make little impression on the British consciousness. Yet a vast social revolution has taken place in England without any of the bloody upheavals that invariably follow such changes elsewhere. From the quarters whence one would expect them least, the nationalism of the poor and the socialism of the rich have fused, with a minimum of friction, to form one class, one race and one nation. It has happened without any self-conscious effort. When any nation clears its decks for action there must always be a great deal of restrictions; but the measure of freedom that still remains is astounding.

The finest music I have heard for years, after my sojourn among the tongue-tied continentals, was the sound of somebody grumbling. I just lay back in my chair and listened voluptuously as if to some long-forgotten and enchanting melody. The person was grumbling about his ration cards in front of officials themselves: and I could scarcely believe my eyes or ears, for the officials took it with a sort of amused sympathy. I revelled in the harmless growling of this gentleman. It had all the solemnity of thunder without its fatal lightning. For the Grumble is perhaps the finest of all emotional safety valves. It has kept more people out of lunatic asylums than any other form of mental relief, though, on the continent, it has probably sent as many people to prison and to the firing squad. Compared with that sort of life which I had just left, the amazing bounty, wealth, and freedom of English wartime life struck me very forcibly. For this man was grumbling about rations and food; and he was a very lucky man to have any rations to grumble about. Where I had come from we were reduced to stewed thistles and roasted acorns and we were fined, or imprisoned even for referring to the fact. Wherever the "Ginger-Locust" appears (as the German is called in Spain), whether he appears as an invader or a friendly protector, his voracity is the same—and he leaves you no bread to grumble about. It was a truly dazzling sight to see loaves of bread in all the bakeries here—stacks of it. I had volunteered to come over and share in the privations and misery of the British as represented by Axis propaganda in Spain. But I found I had really come to share the bread and laughter of the healthiest nation alive!

If you go up on the roofs of the loftiest buildings of London you can see vast patches of what seems a lunar landscape blasted by fire and earthquake. Then you get an idea of what the Londoners have been through and are ready to face again. At night during the black-out, especially by moonlight, the effect is uncanny; except for rare flashes of distant antiaircraft fire one has the impression of a vast necropolis. But the stillness there is vital, as when there is a dead calm and you feel the ocean hatching out its thunders. Yes, London is like that: like a great calm indestructible ocean nursing deep in its heart the thunderbolts of victory.

There is also in this broadcast a mention of a social revolution. In his satires, the mention of the word socialism always sends him off the deep end. Here he praises the way socialism has come about in Britain.

It is the same concerning the Jews. Here is a little passage from the last chapter of LIGHT ON A DARK HORSE, the only one I have at hand, about a Jew in Toledo: "Manuel had a typically Toledan Jewish face with very fine sensitive nostrils, a high forehead, and long eyelashes like a girl's, though he was a manly fellow, and had a very nice wife and a fine-looking little son, also Manuel." The man is special because he has Jewish blood. One can find many allusions to the Jews in his writings which contradict his satire. There were always two sides to his way of thinking. During the war, five of his best friends in the army were Jews.

In the Shadow of a Poet

Chapter 30
Beatific Portugal

After ten years of London, five during the war, and five after it, we all felt an urge to live abroad again. By then Robert Lyle was an inseparable friend of ours and we did everything together. It was a choice between Cyprus and Portugal, as all other countries entailed difficulties or dangers, and we were taking a lot of children.[313] It was a good thing we didn't settle in Cyprus because a few years later trouble started there. Portugal seemed the most peaceful and reliable country to live in. So one fine day in May 1952, my father, Mrs. Lyle and I set out for Portugal, to a large house near Sintra, which my parents and the Lyles had chosen a few weeks earlier when in Portugal.[314] We had never seen such a place for sheer voluptuous, natural beauty. It was a large rambling house, with about fifteen rooms, stables, cellars, and a coach house which we used as a garage. It had a terraced garden which when we arrived was a tangle of roses, syringa, wisteria, a jungle of fruit and flowers as we had never seen before. Below the terraced garden were orchards of plum and apple. Later I counted seven different types of pears. There were peach trees, orange trees, persimons, loquats, four kinds of plum, figs, damsons and the rarest of all fruit, nectarines, growing among the carnations and syringa. In the hilly woods round, the vegetation was fantastic: the heather grew into trees, primroses and violets grew among the tropical plants. In autumn once I counted twenty-four kinds of mushrooms, but there were many more.

The farm was called "Quinta dos Bochechos", which means cheekful of water or hiccups.[315] Still, whatever it was, it meant superfluous water, which was the riches of the place. It had three springs bubbling straight out of the ground. These joined a stream which ran down to a little river which ran through the property. The wells and streams in the district could dry up in a drought, but

---

[313] These must have been the Lyle children.
[314] Tess says that of all the countries they lived in, Spain was the one they really considered home, partly because of the religion. They didn't return, though, because they'd had enough of wars and revolution and Portugal seemed to RC the only country that had a bit of peace under Salazar.
[315] Alexander gives the meaning as "Gurgling Farm" (223).

these springs bubbled perpetually. What makes the vegetation so lush in this spot is that in summer the Sintra hills are covered with a thick mist which, with the effect of the hot sun, makes the place like a hot house and plants thrive.

As I said, when we first arrived it was May and the garden was heavy with the scent of white and mauve wisteria which hung from the pink walls of the house. The terraced garden was full of roses. There were at least five kinds of ramblers and behind, near where the springs were, there were loquat trees laden with fruit. The weather was unusually hot and fine. We three pioneers had the time of our lives during the ten days' wait for the rest of the party. We strayed about this paradise; the time was never enough. For the night Mrs. Lyle and I retired to lodgings in another Sintra Quinta or farm belonging to some friends of ours. Here we were waited on hand and foot. Enormous breakfasts were brought to us in bed. There were hot baths and every comfort. We had a sumptuous time, while my father slept on a mattress in one of the empty rooms of our new house.

After a year when we got the farm going it was unbelievable, the strawberries were the size of one's fist, the tomatoes weighed a pound each. My mother went in for farming in a big way and planted seeds from Suttons. The combination of the first class seed, strong sunshine and plenty of water produced the most astounding effect. The most wonderful of all were the outsized peas of every shade. We also had vegetables of every kind. In the end we became self-sufficient and even made our own bread with the wheat we had grown which had been ground at the nearby mill.

This busy farm life inspired one of my father's last poems, "November Nights",[316]

Bochechos 1953 (Francesca)

---

[316] This appears in COLLECTED WORKS 1: 482. The editors note that it was written in 1956 (CW I: 661, note 158). In the poem RC refers to the pain of old injuries: "It is the time the weather finds the wounds of bygone wars,/ And never to a charger did I take

In the Shadow of a Poet

which gives one an idea of the temperamental climate of Portugal. To end this poem, my father brings in his long life of devotion to my mother and in it he says what he repeated so many times in conversation—that every year my mother became more precious and beautiful to him.

We have never regretted our decision to settle in Portugal. It has proved to be the most stable and peaceful country in Europe in spite of their revolution which was radical and, for such a wholesome one, carried out without bloodshed, which is typical of this race.

The most striking thing about Portugal is the grace of its people. It would be difficult to ascertain where this comes from, whether from their discoveries in the 15th and 16th centuries; their mixing with all sorts of races and religions in Africa, India, China, Japan and Indonesia; their assimilation of some of the ancient, deep wisdom of eastern religions which is apparent in the usual Portuguese mixed with intense Christianity.

The strange happenings at Fatima may also have some influence in producing this quality. The national pilgrimages to the shrine twice a year certainly breed a keen supernatural atmosphere. At least there, the soul comes into its own for a few hours, away from the bustle of modern life. As it is, mostly peasants attend these gatherings and, as they are the moral backbone of the country, a great deal of the grace they possess may be attributed to this fact.

Here are a few everyday remarks one hears and examples of what I mean about the grace of the Portuguese people.

I remember one freezing, raw day in winter saying to a maid of ours, "Aren't you cold in that cotton dress without sleeves?" and she answered, looking at my woollen clothes, "We have a saying in Portugal which goes like this: 'God gives the cold according to the clothes you have.'" She was a girl from the north.

Another of our maids from the north said, as we had finished sowing our seeds in the kitchen garden: "My mother always says a blessing over what she has sown. It is like this: 'May all this yield, to feed a lot of virtue.'" Most of the peasants, especially in the north, are in a permanent state of grace or in the presence of God.

Another example of this deep rooted state of affairs or of the soul was one afternoon in our village grocer's. Two bedraggled figures suddenly came into the shop full of people waiting for their turn, one, a younger brother with a sack of potatoes on his back, followed by an elder spastic brother. They had

---

as I have done/ To cantering the rocking-chair, my Pegasus, indoors." It is the post-harvest time of his life; he continues: "For my olives have been gathered and my grapes are in the tun." Yet it is the love of his life who makes this time richer than any: "But for the firelight on your face I would not change the sun,/ Nor would I change a moment of our winter-season, no,/ For our springtime with its orioles and roses long ago."

bare, dirty feet and clotted hair, and they were extremely scruffy. They belonged to a family of saltimbancos[317] visiting the village. They wanted to weigh their potatoes. As they entered a silence fell on the shop. I waited for the reaction. It was miraculous and instantaneous, everyone rushed to help them, as if two princes had entered, and they were attended to before anyone else. Here one feels the real spirit of Christianity in action at times. I am glad to have been in time to witness this because I feel that as soon as Portugal is industrialised it will not be the same.

Roy and Mary in Portugal 1953 (Tess)

---

[317] Saltimbanco: literally, one who leaps or mounts upon a bench; a mountebank; a quack.

In the Shadow of a Poet

Chapter 31
Bochechos

At Bochechos my father settled down to a lot of translation and wrote a book on Portugal. Here he had a large room on the first floor, which was the model of every other room he had had. Wherever he was, his room was always very simple, with nothing in it except a bed, a chair and a table to write on and keep his papers on, which after a time started falling off and spreading over the floor, until it was a sea of papers and one could hardly open the door. This went on until he had a tidy-up, which took three days at least. It usually took place after he had completed some works. At Bochechos it was a much larger room, so the sea of papers was colossal. No one was allowed into the room except the family, and we knew how to behave when in there. No papers could be moved or tidied up in case he mislaid or lost something.

After the passing of years my father had not changed much although he was older. All through his life he had a natural simplicity in his possessions and habits. He only possessed the bare necessities of life. He had no wardrobe except a suit my mother kept in a cupboard for interviews, lectures or important occasions. It was a natural disposition, in this way he was freer and lighter to concentrate on the only thing that mattered to him, poetry. The only luxuries he went in for were leather belts which he bought at Spanish fairs and leather bound editions of Spanish writers which in Spain are quite cheap. He was also keen on head-gear. Wherever he was, he wore what the local people wore. He ended up by acquiring *Cordobés* hats which he wore with great style, whether in America lecturing or in London or at home.[318] Besides these things he possessed nothing.

With this vast room at Bochechos and life flowing fairly smoothly for us, as I said, my father settled down to translating and some prose writing which he called "pot-boilers". Most of his translations from French, Spanish and Portuguese writers were done here—Baudelaire,[319] Eça de Queirós, Camões,[320] Fer-

---

[318] RC started balding when still in his twenties.
[319] See notes 13 and 199.
[320] See note 172.

nando Pessoa,[321] Lorca,[322] Horace[323] and Lope de Vega.[324] He also went on lecture tours to universities in America, South Africa and Madrid and Salamanca in Spain.[325] It was a quick way of making money and we needed it badly. I also think he settled down to this kind of work partly because his own source of inspiration had dried up somewhat, or perhaps it was because there was need of more security and peace for this—he knew he had to speed up earnings. Translations and prose work came easier than original poetic inspiration, so he settled down to it.

Mary, Spring 1953 (Francesca)

The chief work among these was the translation of Baudelaire's LES FLEURS DU MAL. As he says in a note about this book: "Having had considerable success with my translation of a Saint, St. John of the Cross, I determined to translate a fellow-sinner who is hardly less a believer, even in his rebellious and blasphemous moments, than the Saint himself. I have been reading Baudelaire since I was fifteen, carried him in my haversack through two wars, and loved him longer and more deeply than any other poet." He says further on: "If I have not made as good a translation of Baudelaire as in the case of San Juan it will not be so much from lack of striving but for want of supernatural aid for in the latter case the Saint only needed to raise his stick and say *"Arré burro!"* ("Gee up, donkey!") to me —and the

---

[321] RC's translations appear in COLLECTED WORKS II. (For a discussion of RC's translations see THE PRESENCE OF PESSOA: ENGLISH, AMERICAN AND SOUTHERN AFRICAN LITERARY RESPONSES, George Monteiro, University Press of Kentucky, 1998.)

Fernando António Nogueira de Seabra Pessoa (1888-1935) published poetry in English and Portuguese (under his own name and under heteronyms). In the early 1900s, Pessoa was a pupil at the same high school in Durban as RC. See Jean McBean's "DHS: Cultural Desert/ Cultural Oasis?" in CAMPBELL IN CONTEXT (Coullie and Wade, 2004: 596).

[322] See notes 200 and 201.

[323] Son of a freed Roman slave, Horace influenced many great poets after him, including Lope de Vega, Shakespeare, Goethe and others.

[324] See note 153.

[325] In 1953, a lecture tour to North America involved lectures in twenty-seven cities in two months. The pressures and his heavy drinking caught up with him (Alexander, 229-30). I can find no verification for any lecture tours in South Africa.

In the Shadow of a Poet

Roy and Mary, Summer 1953, Quinta dos Bochechos (Francesca)

Donkey trotted."

Baudelaire was my father's favourite poet. My father felt he was *the poet par excellence* but with LES FLEURS DU MAL on the Index[326] it was forbidden to Catholics. Still, he seems to have reconciled his conscience to the problem.

The prose he wrote at this time was a rather original book on Portugal, dealing with many periods of Portuguese history and culture and the life of its people. The work was published after his death.

We all had a very busy time at Bochechos, Galamares. My mother with the help of a farm labourer really got the farm going. Besides growing farm produce which made us self-sufficient except for oil and sugar, we also had goats, chickens, rabbits, pigeons and— in the end—pigs which we fattened up and sold. My mother, when not weeding and helping in all the ways she could, was overseer. I also helped with the animals and housekeeping.

A great joy in my father's life was my sister's little daughter, Francesca. She was the prettiest little girl ever seen, with bright brown eyes and a mischievous face although she wasn't naughty at all. He was very proud of her because she was the great-great granddaughter of Castanos, the Spanish general who was the first to beat Napoleon.

With me, although outside myself and all around there was this teaming paradise, with all these splendid surroundings and no lack of food for body or soul (I say for soul because as Catholics there was no lack of church services or religious practices)—with me the more spiritual food of this kind I had, the more depressed I became. With all this luxury and beauty, my soul was drying up. My heart was growing smaller and colder every day. There seemed to be no way of thawing. There was a cold sadness and emptiness about everything.

All through the years ever since I was eighteen my father introduced me to many of his acquaintances and friends both young and old, hoping something

---

[326] See note 288.

Tess's wedding to Ignatius Custudio, 7 August 1954 (Tess)

would happen in the way of marriage. I never faced marriage seriously or practically at that time. My excuse was I was not in love with the men. He always said one only falls in love after marriage. It seemed sensible but quite contrary to my romantic ideas about marriage. In any case, with all my years of illness, I did not feel sure of myself, so nothing came of these efforts.

Now at Bochechos, in this empty state, I suddenly woke up to the fact that I was getting old and had better get married, otherwise it would be too late. I was thirty-one then. My ambition had been to have at least five children—it looked as if I would have none. How could I have five children without marriage? During the best years of my life I had been an invalid—from about twenty-two to twenty-eight.

Unexpectedly one day a completely new element turned up on our doorstep. He was a friend of a friend of ours.

Roy and Ignatius 1955 (Francesca)

In the Shadow of a Poet

Tess with Frankie, 1960 (Tess)

The first I saw of him was as he was coming down our staircase at Bochechos, speaking to someone above; I was struck by a kind of harmony that emanated from him. There was an extraordinary beauty and detachment about his whole person which made an immense impression on me.

This person was completely different from any we had encountered so far: no fears, no preconceptions, no inhibitions, generous, fresh, authentic. He was as free and open as the plains of the Alentejo where he came from. So in this drastic state and almost unconscious with misery, I decided to take the risk. We decided to marry[327] and before I knew it I was going to have a child.[328]

From then on my soul was filled with ineffable peace and plenty. When my father returned from a four months' tour in South Africa, he was astounded at the developments in my affairs. He was rather upset he had not been consulted but soon recovered and joined in the rejoicing. Four months later I was married.

---

[327] They were married on 7 August 1954. They were married in the Catholic Church, despite the groom's protestations (Pearce says he was "bitterly anticlerical", 320).
[328] Francisco (known as Frankie), the son of Tess and Ignatius Custudio, was born at home at Quinta dos Bochechos on 6 January 1955.

Pearce quotes RC who says Ignatius insisted on naming the baby after Frank Sinatra (Pearce, 320). RC's neice, Gillian Tatham, says she remembers hearing that he was named after Frankie Laine, the singer. In response to his father's neglect, Frankie assumed the Campbell surname. Tess and Frankie lived with RC and Mary and then, after Roy died, Mary supported Tess and her son for the rest of her life.

Here my life branches off into an endless story of satisfactions, joys, disappointments, miseries, happinesses and frustrations. Another long, long book it would make.[329]

---

[329] Like Anna, Tess did not want to focus attention on her own life, independent of her relations with her parents, but I did ask her to elaborate a little. She told me that Mary disapproved of the marriage because Custudio, a miner's son, could not find work and thus was unable to support his wife and child. Mary believed he did not want to work. The situation was hard on Mary, Tess said, as she had to support them and pay for her grandson's schooling. When Francisco was nine, his father "got a wonderful job" in the Volkswagen factory in Germany. His departure caused a rift between himself and his son, and Francisco took the Campbell surname. At the time, Mary threatened to disinherit Tess if she followed her husband. Being financially dependent on her mother, Tess obliged but told me that, "My mother should never have done that. No."

In the Shadow of a Poet

Chapter 32
End of Bochechos

There was one great snag about Bochechos, Galamares. It was exceptionally damp, being a spot where in winter the mist pours in from the Atlantic, and the hills form a kind of barrier, so that the mist from the sea is obstructed and settles there. Even in summer the sea steams with vapours which rise from the freezing water which comes from the North Pole—the contrast of the tropical sun on the icy water of the ocean produces a mist which rises and settles over Sintra, so that in summer there is really no dry weather either. Besides, the *quinta*[330] had a river passing through it and we also had the springs of water coming from the hills behind the house. Altogether this damp was too much for my father's rheumatism which was getting worse and worse. At Galamares he still walked a lot and on his good days walked to Sintra and back, but as his rheumatism increased, he was less and less able to do this.

My father suffered from sciatica caused by a bullet which had lodged itself in the upper part of the femur, and the bone socket was gradually wearing away. If he had been younger he could have had an operation which would have cured it, but a specialist said he would not be able to stand a serious operation because he was too old. There was also another problem. Although the farm was going well, the expenses mounted. The rent of the property was high, it being very large. There were the wages of the farm labourer and cook and maid to pay, besides all the expenses a farm demands. We were living beyond our means. For some time now my father and I had been telling my mother it was not wise to go on with the farm but she was determined to make it pay. To tease her, we used to tell her the place for us was a little ruin further up on the side of the road.

Then a disastrous thing happened. The head labourer fell from a ladder and broke his leg. Unfortunately he was not insured. He was in hospital for months for the operation to his leg, and following the operation, while still in hospital, he contracted pneumonia through neglect. This made his case desperate. Still, after all this being put into the hands of the law, the matter was settled by us

---

[330] Country house.

giving him an indemnity for life—a big sum of money with which to buy cows for his family and himself to make a living of. So the matter was settled, but it was very bad luck on both sides. This put a definite end to Bochechos.

Before this accident with the farm labourer, for some time now because of my father's rheumatism, we had been considering moving to the other side of the Sintra hills where there was much more sun and less mist. My mother found a bungalow there to let, in the village of Linhó.

As can be seen, this last year at Bochechos was very hard on my father. His sciatica was nearly crippling, but he had to write pot-boilers. His tours of the USA exhausted him: Yankee hospitality nearly finished him off—as it did finish off Dylan Thomas. The final blow was the labourer's accident, as we were already more or less ruined at the time. We kept going by my father getting advances from publishers on translations he did. In this state, he used to take masses of aspirin and Vegamin to ward off the pain of sciatica. He often took bromide[331] to calm his nerves and drank at the same time. So he was in a shocking state.

Then we moved to the other side of the hill which relieved us all in many ways, and it was amazing how much my father recovered.

Sometime before this happened at Bochechos, my mother had bought a cheap plot of land, overlooking the village of Linhó. She meant to build a house and settle there with my father for the rest of their lives. It was a beautiful spot and she had chosen it so that my father would have a peaceful place to finish all the works he had in mind. My mother at that time had a little money invested in England, and with this she managed to buy the land, and while we lived in the bungalow in Linhó, the house was built.

As if these many worries and problems hadn't been enough at Bochechos, there was another stone round my father's neck which I didn't mention: although both his daughters were married, neither of them had a husband. This also affected his state of mind. Both our husbands' financial backgrounds were in a worse state than ours and both were unemployed. There was no way of them supporting their wives and children, so I remained at home and my sister was self-supporting—a painful state of affairs. The only consolation my father could find for this misfortune with his sons-in-law was to repeat to

---

[331] There are many varieties of bromide and it is unclear which RC was taking. Because of dangerous side effects, since the 1950s in most Western countries, bromide is no longer sold as an over the counter sedative.

When in New York on a lecture tour in 1955, RC became extremely disorientated. The "mixture of drugs he was taking indiscriminately combined with alcohol to produce a near stupor" (Alexander, 237). He was taken to a doctor who diagnosed an overdose of bromides.

In the Shadow of a Poet

himself and to other people when they were listening, that the Cid Campeador had been in the same situation with his two daughters—both married but without husbands.

After four years at Bochechos and all of these happenings, around the autumn of 1956, we moved to the bungalow at Linhó.

Chapter 33
The House Made of Granite

Linhó is a spread-out village among some cornfields. It has a herd of sheep that graze along its lanes and on the hillocks around. It has an impressive convent, with the ever-changing Sintra hills behind. It was in this sunny spot that my father lived the last year of his life. We lived in the little bungalow in the village and soon started building the little house on the site, up in the woods, with a vast view over to Lisbon and the sea. There was one thing special to Linhó—it had a prodigious wind that blew from the north in the summer. No one liked it because it was too cold, ruthless and relentless. It could blow for days on end, but my father delighted in it because it cleared any cobwebs or clouds from the sky or anywhere else they might be and made the atmosphere limpid. He used to come out of the house on purpose to breathe it in and feel its strength.

There were three humble pubs in the village where he used to make friends among the people. One special friend he nicknamed Camões because he only had one eye, like the poet. My father made a pact with him that when he died he would leave him one of his eyes. It would have been a great success, as his eyes were blue like my father's, but unfortunately my father's death was so sudden, no one remembered the eye.

Nearly every day my father used to wind his way up the quiet, sunny path to the site where the house was being built. It was busy with stone cutters and masons. The house was made out of the granite rocks round. Gradually as it took shape, he would take great pleasure in going over it and planning the rooms with my mother, who had designed the whole thing with care. Sometimes on Sundays, we would take a picnic up there, with the maids and grandchildren. Here he would make a fire in the open and roast *boboches* in his old way.

It was the building of the house[332] that inspired my father to keep a diary, the one I quoted from in the last chapter—the only one he ever achieved. Unfortunately it was only kept up for four intermittent days. On March 3rd

---

[332] Mary had designed the house and felt that it would provide Roy with the peace and stability necessary for his work. He never lived in the house.

(this was a month before his death in April) he wrote about the site:

> The well is finished. The water comes in at about 36 feet down. It is lovely to see Mary so happy and proud about it, as if she were the naiad of the spring which but for her flair and determination would have remained undiscovered. The water is worthy of her—Amanzi[333]—as clear as crystal and as ice cold as she is fiery and beautiful. It comes clean out of the cleft in the granite of the mountain side and filters through the finest cream-white shingles. Mary has also found a rustless submergeable pump for less than two *contos* (we were going to pay six) which will send the water straight up to the house. It takes her!

He also started an original poem inspired by the gigantic, granite rocks he saw at the site. It has none of the usual flare. One feels that something had died in him. It is jotted down on a little writing pad. On many pages there is a line or two in miniscule handwriting. He would get as far as two verses and start over again in a new version. There is nothing strange in this, because this he always did this to form a poem. He might have been successful in the end if he had been able to work at it. It was left unfinished because of his death.

He had also started writing THE HISTORY OF THE SPANISH CIVIL WAR and a translation of THE SONG OF SONGS.

Of late, my father had been getting more and more nervous about driving with my mother. He was almost reluctant.

---

[333] is Zulu, meaning water.

Chapter 34
Death

In April of 1957 my parents decided to go to Seville for the Holy Week. They were going to tour round southern Spain first and then stop at Seville. It was with this idyllic plan in mind that they managed for once to unite the necessary factors—with enough money to pay for the expenses, they were going to tour Spain together and be with the Spanish people who interested them both so much, and they were also going to join in a religious gathering which was the main reason for their journey.

They set out for their last adventure together, after a turbulent life. In all this my father seemed to guess his approaching death. My mother said that during the whole voyage my father was unusually quiet, serious, sober and suffering, not at all his usual self. As I said before, although my father was very religious he was not an arduous churchgoer, but for this Easter he was a teetotaller and complied with all his Easter duties: confession, communion and mass.

My father was killed near Setúbal on his journey back home. The little Fiat 600 we had ran into a tree because one of the front tyres burst. The inner tube was worn and should have been replaced. They were going along an avenue of trees; my mother was going quite fast, and the car, being rather light, lurched to the side into a tree with the tremendous weight of my father. The impact was so strong my father died a few moments later. He didn't even have a scratch. His death must have been caused by internal haemorrhage.[334]

When I arrived at the hospital the following day, my mother had been in a coma for hours and my father lay in the chapel.[335] I was led to the chapel by one of the nuns and left with him alone. Then, only then, did I realise that he was dead and if I spoke to him he would not answer. I burst into paroxysms of sobbing and hugged him. He, who had been so restless and untiring in life, could not move any more. I couldn't believe the size of his shoes and the size of his body. He seemed so gigantic. He lay there a big mass, as if stuffed, with a slight smile on his face. I couldn't make out if it was an idiotic senseless smile of death

---

[334] Pearce says RC's neck was broken (329).
[335] Mary's foot was crushed and her arm, ribs and front teeth were broken (Pearce, 329).

or a triumphant smile to show he had overcome the last battle. There was profound peace in that spot and from that tremendous physical weight emanated a different kind of weight, that of the artist, man, erudite scholar, poet.

In a way my father's death was a blessing to him because his sciatica was steadily becoming worse and he could bear it only by taking painkillers.[336] It would have meant years of suffering. The last two years of his life were not fortunate or happy, but up till then it was what he made of it—a life of absorbing interests, rich experiences and daredevil risks. It was a Dionysian span of life, lived at full steam, rather in the style of his poetry—flowing, vital, vigorous and colourful.

In spite of the many infelicities, ill health and problems of the past few years, my father still had a firm hold and control of his senses at the end, and he concentrated on that which is most essential, eternal and absolute.

His last few days on earth were dedicated to the spiritual practices of the Church. Easter, the great spiritual celebration of believers was spent in entire dedication. This is a sign that after much sorting and taking and leaving, he did attain what he judged the absolute of life.

---

[336] Tess, who was about 36 when her father died, says that Roy was diabetic and an alcoholic; death was almost a relief for him.

Chapter 35
Boycotting and Justice

Just two days after my father's death there was an article in a British magazine called FRIEND stating that my father joined and fought for the British Union of Fascists. My mother promptly replied, denying my father had ever joined such a Union. In answer the FRIEND wrote this apology:

> The attention of the FRIEND has been drawn to an error of fact contained in an article published in the issue of April 25 on the late Roy Campbell. The article stated that Roy Campbell joined and fought for the British Union of Fascists. This is incorrect.
>
> The FRIEND regrets any inconvenience that might have been caused by the publication of this statement, which was taken, in good faith, from a source which it had every reason to regard as reliable.

It is a shame to bring Fascism and Communism so often into this book. There is nothing more boring than politics, but I mention this article from the FRIEND to eradicate the strong notion that my father was a Fascist and also to show how strongly propaganda can work. This myth came about from his many enemies. No one would ever have dared call him a Fascist while he was alive.

Long before Perestroika, years before, there were two people who had a clear notion of what Communism was and meant and how it would end up—General Franco and my father, and they put up a fierce fight against it. For this they were both severely sabotaged and boycotted. Franco was boycotted because he wanted to save his country from Bolshevik rule. England and all the world condemned him for this. England would have welcomed Russia taking over Spain but if the menace had been toward England they would have reacted differently and put up a fight—and what a fight, for even the English left wouldn't have allowed that. Is no justice ever be going to given to Franco over this?

The myth about my father and Franco being fascists was pure Communist propaganda. In the modern world it is the way to annihilate anyone because of Hitler's dictatorship and his persecution of the Jews. If my father and Franco were on the same side as Fascism it was because they felt it was the weaker of the two forces, and that by fighting Communism with the help of Fascism they could defeat Communism, which was their aim because Communism was atheist and they were two ardent Catholics. It was vital to both of them to free the world of this menace. It was the Christian element that made them fight, not the Fascist.

During my father's last years, besides the physical pains and mental worries he had, in the background, there had been for years from England this systematic boycott of his person and his works because of his siding with Franco in the Spanish Civil War. In those days it was not only England that was Red, it was the whole world—all the most advanced countries, almost all the intellectuals, all the great organisations. The left had the influence and the say. It was a strange state of affairs because at the same time there was this "cold war" going on between Russia and the West. In essence, these two forces were totally alienated, but this inexplicable flirtation with Communism was the fashion, a kind of illusion; not a thing to be taken seriously and put into practice or to be brought out into serious reality, but a permanent illusion and dream—as long as it was far away— but fearful to handle. While this state of affairs held, my father died.

Some years later, my father was succeeded by another famous writer trying to enlighten the world. In the 1970's Solzhenitsyn appeared on the scene, with his sensational works and his testimony. The world was surprised by what he reported. Even so, it was not taken seriously because it was the left that was accused of terrorising and torturing. However, with Perestroika and the disappearance of the Wall in Berlin, the truth about the Soviet Union came to light, even the information about Stalin's millions of deported, starved, tortured and dead.

The boycotting of my father in the past by left-wing writers, poets, public, critics and publishers was unjust, especially as he was so convinced of the futility of Marxism: it failed, as he said it would. And this was sixty years ago! This myth from many countries about my father being a fascist affected him and completely undermined his career and consequently his earnings. It was partly due to this that he was so ruined at the end of his life. Both my father and Franco were severely penalised for their convictions.

Franco managed to save Spain and it was with the help of Germany and Italy, two Fascist countries. During World War II he showed many times he wanted Spain to be reconciled with the allies and he succeeded to a certain extent, even after his adventures with Hitler and Mussolini. Franco would probably never have won the war without foreign help as the odds were too great. My father did the same: immediately Spain was saved from the Red menace he joined the British Intelligence Corps to defeat Fascism.

Now that Communist Marxism and Bolshevik Leninism have proved a failure, after sixty years of fierce boycotting from these forces, justice ought to be restored to both Franco and my father as two of the most enlightened and courageous men of the 20th century: Franco for his clear thinking and precise action when he took on his almost insurmountably difficult war against Communism, and my father for his solitary up-holding of Franco in his fight for freedom.

Anyone who has read my father's works will realise that this ardent boycotting of him came from many motives: it was a way of avenging many wounds and slights caused by his bitter satire. This, of course, is true, but it should also be recognised that his early and accurate condemnation of Communism was exact and correct and for this reason he should not be labelled a Fascist.

Now to end this long chapter is a letter written by my mother to the editor of the magazine ENCOUNTER:

Linhó, Sintra, Portugal,
Jan. 23
To the Editor of ENCOUNTER

> Sir,
> *By chance I happened to read Arthur Schlesinger Jr.'s article on "Authors take sides on Vietnam". In the ages of great literature it seems that prophecy (not in a political sense) and poetry go hand in hand.*
>
> *In 1935 there appeared a poem called "The Fight". It was by Roy Campbell and was a prophecy of the outcome of the Spanish War. The author was ostracised by literary England for writing and fighting for Franco, and suffered great damage to his literary career in consequence. He had studied the writings of Lenin and had a clear vision of what would happen to Europe if the Iberian peninsula became a satellite of Russia (as he also had in 1944 when the western armies were not allowed to go forward to the Russian border or later when General McArthur was recalled from the Far East before he could consolidate his victories).*
>
> *In 1936 the English poets dubbed Campbell a "fascist" and that stigma has remained although he was one of the few poets to join up and fight in 1940. Surely there must be someone honest and courageous enough to make "amende honorable" to his memory now it is proved that he was right!*
>
> *Mary Campbell*

In the Shadow of a Poet

Chapter 36
Fears and Hopes for the Future of Humanity

A lot of what I have said about the sabotage of my father's career and boycotting of my father's work is true. He brought much of it down upon himself because of his strong opinions which he put into mordant, bitter, virulent satire which, as I said, offended and outraged many sensitivities. In the end the damage he received from this, together with the political slander he received for being on the right, more or less put a finishing touch to his reputation for a certain part of his readers. There was, and still is, an élite who read him and who are great admirers of his pure, lyrical poetry and who are all with him and all for him in his convictions and opinions, but these are few.[337] In the political field he was an independent. Only in the religious sphere could one call him well-defined—he was a Christian.

He had many antagonisms, some of the strongest being against apartheid,[338] Marxism, Communism, Socialism, psychoanalysis and pedantry which were the main butts of his satire. His opposition to these practices, systems, solutions and cures for humanity's problems sprang from the fact of them (at the time he was living) being one-sided—there was always the lack of spiritual considerations, for they always dealt with the physical and even mental and material side of trouble.

Take apartheid, for example. My father with a few other young South African intellectuals of his time started his career as an anti-apartheid [strictly speaking, anti-racist] activist when he was very young. That was in 1926. He

---

[337] Given the fact that RC not only shifted position "in his convictions and opinions" but also made contradictory statements, it is more likely that his admirers nevertheless distance themselves from certain of RC's stated standpoints.

[338] RC's anti-racist politics are evidenced so cuttingly in THE WAYZGOOSE; nonetheless he made several racist observations in his autobiography, LIGHT ON A DARK HORSE and elsewhere (such as his implied support for the Nationalist Government's policies in his Honorary Doctorate acceptance speech). Tess says that while his position might have shifted somewhat in the intervening 30 or so years since the mid-1920s, due to the fact that the idealism of youth was tempered by the more mature realisation that things are not as simple as one had imagined, Roy was nevertheless consistently anti-racist.

was one of the first South Africans to point out the error of this policy. Towards the end of his life when living in the bungalow at Linhó in Portugal, apartheid was one of his last major worries; he seemed desperate that it be solved. He used to go about the house saying the Portuguese were the only nation that knew how to colonise and who would be able to deal with the black question in Africa. This was just before his death, about forty years before the massacres, terrorism and serious trouble started there. By his behaviour it seemed he already felt the unfathomable, inconceivable, unaccountable, indescribable difficulties ahead. This confidence in the Portuguese sprang from a kind of spiritual outlook they possess, an unaffected and natural attitude they have always shown to the different races and nations they have subjugated and dealt with all over the world, a kind of acceptance and appreciation on the spiritual plane, on the level of the soul, of which the Portuguese are very conscious and which other nations don't bring into consideration.

Here is an example concerning racism: according to my father, the Portuguese saw no difference in colour, they do not discriminate, there is no effort, everyone is the Almighty's creature.

In the twentieth century there was a tremendous reaction in the world of ideas to all that had gone before. Some of the great innovators in the world of ideas were Marx, an atheist, and Freud, an atheist who founded psychoanalysis. Science made great strides forward. The new ideas and sciences refuted the supernatural. They felt they would throw off all limitations, restrictions or fetters to sound alone the mysteries of the Universe. All desired a change from the old yoke of Christianity. They no longer included God or deities of any kind in their programmes but concentrated purely on the physical, mental, visible and material spheres.

My father was all for progress in all fields but he would not put all his trust and hope of progress in the purely scientific, physical and material way. These had to be accompanied by spiritual strivings or endeavour, as well. Poets in history have always been the torch-bearers of nations, trying to enlighten and lead the way. They succeed at times, but humanity is always striving and searching for something in the infinite. Humankind never rests, it always wants change and advance, it goes forwards or backwards to change, on to the Alpha and Omega it is searching for and cannot find. Science now, at the end of the twentieth century, is more prone to go along and try and fathom the mysteries of the Universe with a mixture of the natural and the supernatural. Progress purely and solely in the physical, material and scientific way has proven insufficient and annihilating.

In the Shadow of a Poet

In my father's poetry the *vaquero*, the open spaces, the mountains, the hills, the sky and horses are unexpectedly and strangely brought onto the scene every now and again; these are emblems of anti-pollution and anti-progress of a type. In his life he tried to keep to these natural consolations. This emphasis on the traditional and beaten track are natural impulses of his, as if he were a very insistent contemporary ecologist, trying to impose his laws on his fellow men (this was sixty and seventy years ago) before the ecologists came into fashion. All this vociferation of his came insistently from a wild desire to keep safe and not to go all out for scientific progress only.

Here, to illustrate what I have written, are a few paragraphs from an article my father wrote for the MONTH, a Jesuit magazine, in 1950. In this he sums up in his own words the only way he feels man will be able to make progress:

> In the last ten years I have noticed a considerable accentuation of the *contrasentida*—the working-out of all concerted political effort into the opposite result from what was intended. Ever since the French Revolution this has become an axiom. That foul volcano of blood and pus was intended to unite humanity, but only succeeded in dividing the once-great country of its origin into two irreconcilable halves, each so intent on persecuting the other that it welcomes any invader who will help it to do so. Marxism, intended to eliminate the top-dogs, Nietzscheism, intended to eliminate under-dogs, has filled the world with far more pitiable under-dogs than either were intended to eliminate.
>
> In the next fifty years this tendency of all concerted purpose to work out with the opposite results from those intended will increase, I think. Everything we have known for the last fifty years will be repeated: Leagues of Nations, UNO's, UNESCO's, and other lucrative, liberaloid, levantine-masonic money-rackets; which, if they do not destroy us by precipitating us into another world war, as they did in the previous two, will eventually, by a sort of "reductio ad absurdum", teach people that there is no such thing as concerted "progress" and finally force us to look within ourselves; for salvation is not a collective thing but happens (if at all) separately in each individual. Everybody will get sick of the repetition of the fact (obvious enough by now in all conscience!) again and again disastrously illustrated, that socialistic politics are ridiculous and unhealthy for humanity. The less politics of any sort, the better. People will have to begin minding their own business, and reforming themselves before they try to reform others. Minding one's own business is an all-time job too! So it may be that through non-interference, things will

be allowed to look up, and life to circulate normally. At no other time, nevertheless, was it ever more thrilling and enjoyable to be alive than it is to-day, when the life of the whole planet is triggered by a hair, and the roar of chaos is challenging from us all every atom of our faith, hope, charity and courage, in a measure which our Maker has never before done us the honour of expecting and demanding from His creatures.

In the Shadow of a Poet

Chapter 37
My Mother's Last Years

My mother outlived my father by twenty-two years. For a few months after the accident my father lost his life in, my mother was as if stunned; she was recovering from a broken ankle and had to employ a chauffeur as she could not drive.[339] After being a widow for a few years, at about sixty-five, she got the notion that old people were going to die and therefore the best way to shorten their life was to have less nourishment. So she started eating meagrely and got depressed, pale and weak, so much so that she could hardly walk from one room to another. She was rheumatic and her fingers crooked with arthritis and very painful.

At this time a remarkable book, LET'S GET WELL by Adèle Davis, the American nutritionist, was published, and Robert Lyle, now my brother-in-law, introduced us to it. My mother took to this book in a big way. Soon she was taking all the vitamins in massive doses and eating all the food recommended to become strong and healthy and rid herself of arthritis. Besides her usual food, the food recommended was wholemeal bread, yoghurt, brewer's yeast, B-pantêne, milk. She even baked little cakes for herself consisting of wholemeal flour, almonds, honey, eggs and vegetable oil, and nibbled at these between meals. In six months she was and looked a different person. She filled out, looked fresh and rosy and young, her fingers gradually straightened out and in time her extreme weakness and arthritis disappeared. So she had a new span of life. Four years after this she was busy, dynamic and happy, doing all the things she had most wanted to do in her life.

Since her return to Portugal she had done a lot of painting at Bochechos.

---

[339] Tess told me that Mary's financial situation deteriorated markedly after Roy's death. There were, for a time, also her two daughters and two grandchildren to support, as Anna and Tess and their respective children, Francesca and Francisco, lived with Mary. (Anna's marriage—the wedding was in 1951—was clearly already in trouble at the time of Tess's wedding in 1954, as the wedding photograph shows Anna alongside Rob Lyle. Anna's husband, Francesca's father, is not in the picture.)

Tess added that money obtained from the Killie Campbell Museum through the purchase of documents from Mary, was their salvation when they were really hard up.

After recovering from my father's death and the accident, she spent most of her time painting. Some of her best work was done then. She also become the foundress of the ecumenical movement in Portugal and organised regular gatherings in Lisbon every month of churches of all denominations and drove into Lisbon alone or with me to preside at them. She also did charitable work among the poor of Linhó. She managed to get funds from many of the prosperous families of the surroundings and quantities of powdered milk from the U.S.A. through the American Women's Club, in Cascais, near Sintra.

One day when out painting a landscape, she spotted a very elaborate, ancient, stone chapel, among a group of houses. It was evident it had been out of use for decades. It was a perfect spot for worship. My mother soon unfolded a plan of action around it. She would have it opened and functioning and feed the poor families in the houses round. The usual idea in a situation like this is to feed the hungry people in the houses and leave the chapel closed, if possible. My mother's ideas were reversed, they started with the chapel and ended with the people being fed. Here among the people she started sewing-sessions, as she had in the poor quarters of Toledo years before, after the Spanish Civil War. Mothers of the families were given materials to cut out to make clothes with and one of the women who could read would read the Gospels aloud to the others. In time she got the chaplain of the prison nearby to come and say mass every Sunday, and she got the nuns from the Linhó Convent to come once a week to give Catechism classes to the children. Twenty years after the chapel was opened, this religious life at Ribeira, the centre she opened, still goes on regularly.

As I have emphasised all through this book, my mother had an unusual streak in her nature. Different from us all in the family and different from most of the people we knew, she had a vivid interest in religion and the occult.

To the family, she was just like all wives and mothers going about her activities but at the same time dipping intensely into spiritual matters and going to church a lot. It was rather like having a drunken member of the family disappearing to the pub every now and again and coming back rather tipsy, but instead of going to the pub she would go to church. She was very refreshing in the way that although she went to church a lot and was deeply religious, she did not expect other people to be like her.

Nowadays when I come across her little office book of the Third Order of the Carmelites, it is a complete mystery to me how she could say this long prayer every day. To me as one of my generation, it is surprising to see the length and detail of the book and the prayers it entailed. I wonder how she trained herself to do such a task. She said it in stages, through the day, early

In the Shadow of a Poet

in the morning and sometimes at night, but it was always said. This long job only took place after her joining the Third Order of the Carmelites when she was thirty-eight, in Toledo. The Third Order of the Carmelites involves many other prayers, penances and disciplines. Sometime through our life together, I remarked on this rough and severe treatment of herself, and she answered: "The more serious the illness, the more severe the treatment."

Yes, she was definitely different from us all in the family. She had a mystical streak to a high degree. This came naturally to her. Even as a child she was always improvising religious games and making altars and taking the part of the priest. She would organise processions and make her brothers and sisters the congregation. For this reason she was nick-named Popy in her family—derived from the Pope.[340]

No soul on earth was ever less bored with existence than she. Any kind of boredom that may be present in so many millions of lives and souls on earth, was never present in her because she always had this infinite source of interest in this world of the spirit to explore, either in experience, occupations or books.

Her great discovery, for her entire satisfaction after her conversion to Catholicism, was the tabernacle in Catholic churches where the body of Christ remains permanently present. It was there, near the tabernacle, that my mother could spend hours absorbed, and it was there that she found satisfaction and consolation.

After my mother's conversion to Catholicism at Altea, in Spain, in 1934, she started going to mass every day.[341] At Altea, she walked to the village church about two kilometres away, there and back, before breakfast. From then on, all through her life, she went to daily mass and communion, unless prevented by illness or travelling or some other insurmountable difficulty. We were used to it and took it for granted, but when I come to think of this nowadays, this devotion to worship was almost unique.

In England sometimes it is difficult to find a Catholic church near. During World War II, when we rented a little cottage near Petersfield, Hants, in midwinter, with intense cold, she would cycle through the blizzards and snow to church, three miles away. In Castile, in mid-summer, as I said before, she would ride on a donkey before sunrise, about six in the morning to escape the heat, to celebrate mass six miles away, and she would be back before the sun got too high.

At our last home, in Linhó, when my mother was about seventy-six, one day there was a tree which had fallen across the beginning of the drive and

---

[340] Tess added that as a teenager in the bleak mining town where she lived, Mary used get the miners together and read the Gospels to them.
[341] Mary chose Mary Magdalene for her patron saint. Her saint's day is 22 July. The apostles Luke and Mark note that Jesus cleansed Mary Magdalene of seven demons.

no one could lift it out of the way and the car could not pass. My mother was ready for mass, but I thought it would be a good excuse for her to have a rest. She wanted the car put on the drive, but there was no way of doing this. There was a short cut through the trees which bypassed the fallen tree, but there was a bank to jump and uneven ground. I didn't dare to do this manoeuvre with the car as I was afraid of damaging it and possibly injuring myself. So she got in, drove over the moss and turf, through the trees, and then, with a jump like a rabbit, the car landed on the drive, and off she drove at top speed down the very steep hill that led to our house, as it was getting late for mass.

During the last few years my mother had three serious accidents going to mass but escaped from all three without a scratch. Her last accident was with a motor-bike which went shooting over the car and landed on the other side. The motor-bike was coming too fast round a long curve in the road, my mother was crossing the road and did not see it coming, so they crashed. After the formalities were over, the police had been, and the crowd was at its thickest, my mother appeared and said: "Please let me pass, the mass is nearly over." Someone in the crowd said: "But the man has got a broken leg." Off she hurried, walking towards the chapel, leaving the car by the side of the road with the people and the police. The fault of the accident was on both sides. Insurance saved the situation and paid for the operation to the man's leg and the hospital. The man was back at home after a month. The more my mother advanced in age, the more important the sacraments and mass became to her. All this may sound exaggerated and fanatic, but to the beholder it was not at all when one saw the amount of patience, sacrifice, courage and hardships she would go through to obtain these things.

My mother's last ten years of life were very happy. She settled down to an old age of enjoyment, still finding immense pleasure in worldly satisfactions as she had always done. She loved whiskey, which she drank twice a day, she continued going to mass and communion and spent many hours a day listening to Mozart records. When we had finished the stocks in Portugal, we started sending to His Master's Voice in London for the rest, and in the end we had the whole collection of his music, operas included.

My mother had always read a lot. At this time she got very interested in extra-sensorial experiences. She sent to Hatchards, the bookseller in Piccadilly, for any books she wanted to read. She found one on this subject which fascinated her. In this book was a passage where it was mentioned that flowers were sensitive to music, so she conducted some experiments. She would play Mozart on her gramophone during the end part of the morning, so she used to

In the Shadow of a Poet

open her window and let Mozart's music pour out loud onto the garden, and strangely enough a giant kind of daisy we had gradually turned their heads towards the window. We couldn't believe our eyes.

Earlier on she had discovered the writings of Teilhard de Chardin.[342] After a time she had all his works and used to discuss him with her friends. Even I was drawn into this attraction for Teilhard because of his belief in evolution. The story of the Garden of Eden had always worried me, even as a child, because I could not believe in it, and now there was an important thinker in the Roman Catholic Church who proclaimed how our life on earth had come about— gradually, through evolution. It is believed now the story of the Garden of Eden and many other stories in the Bible are more the story of the gradual opening up of the human spirit at certain stages in evolution, the serpent I suppose being our free will and the evil inside us and the six days' work the necessity of work and the seventh day for rest and worship of God, the creator of evolution and all, from the beginning.

At this time my mother could afford these luxuries—books, records, whiskey—because she had just received, from the Queen of England, a widow's pension for my father's service in the army during the war.

This idyllic life lasted until my mother fell and broke her arm. Then everything changed because she was such an ardent and active person that when she could no longer drive or do anything for herself she got deeply depressed. Still, she carried on bravely, and ten days before her eightieth-first birthday, she died of a heart-attack.

In her old age my mother used to say Roy and herself were the first Hippies, and this is true to a certain extent, but she did realise where the difference was. In Spain once I remember her picking on an article in a paper, the title being: *"Los Hippies—pero donde esta el forro?"* ("Hippies, but where is the lining?") At that my mother said: "Yes, and where?"—meaning they were non-productive, were, in a way, negative, not inspired. In this way they were quite different from my parents, who were just the opposite—very positive and inspired. Of course, the Flower Children couldn't care less whether they were productive or inspired. What they wanted was to be absent. My parents may have been the precursors of the Hippies but with another clear difference, that instead of taking to hard drugs, they went back to "the opium of the people", as Karl Marx called religion. For the intellectuals of their time this was a very neglected and unpopular practice.

---

[342] (1881-1955) French philosopher and Jesuit priest, trained geologist and paleontologist. His work was denounced by the Holy Office in 1962.

Tess's watercolour painting, in the style of Roy (Tess)

As regards my father, English literature of the twentieth century would have been much poorer without him. He brought a verve and colour to English poetry which would have been missed had he become a professor of physics or doctor of medicine or whatever it was he was supposed to have taken up as a career when he left Oxford.[343]

---

[343] Tess said sadly that her grandchildren and her niece Francesca's children (RC's great-grandchildren) are hardly able to read English and thus do not know RC's poetry.

Appendix I:
Roy Campbell Timeline

Appendix I
Roy Campbell Timeline

1850 March 29	Wiiliam Campbell, grandfather of Roy Campbell (henceforth RC), sets sail from Scotland for Durban
1861	Samuel George Campbell, father of RC, born in Durban
1886 February	Samuel George Campbell and Margaret Wylie Dunnachie marry in Edinburgh
1889	Sam and Margaret Campbell travel to South Africa
1898 March 18	Mary Margaret Garman born in Wednesbury
1901 October 1	Royston Dunnachie Campbell born in Durban. The Anglo-Boer War was drawing to a close
1916	RC tries unsuccessfully to enlist in South African Infantry, using a false name
	Mary, with her sister Kathleen, runs away to London
1917	RC matriculates (with a third class pass) from Durban High School
1918 December	RC leaves South Africa for England
1919	RC visits maternal grandparents in Scotland, then studies at Oxford University (preparation for Reponsions, i.e. the entrance exam)
September	RC fails entrance exam
December (or early January 1920)	RC leaves Oxford with T.W. Earp

Roy Campbell Timeline

1920	RC travels to London and Provence, works on fishing boats, damages his neck
1921 September	RC returns to London
October 10	RC meets Mary Garman
1922 February 11	RC and Mary are married
	They move to Ty-Corn, a cottage in the village of Aberdaron, Wales
November 26	Their first daughter, Teresa Mary, is born at Ty-Corn
1923	Campbell family move back to London
1924 May	THE FLAMING TERRAPIN is published
	RC sails to South Africa
December	Mary and Tess join RC in Durban
1925	Family moves to Peace Cottage, Umhlanga and then to Sezela, on the Natal south coast
	RC makes plans to create a literary journal, VOORSLAG
	RC meets William Plomer and later Laurens van der Post
1926 February 1	A second daughter, Anna Margaret, is born at Sezela
March 12	RC's father dies
June	First issue of VOORSLAG appears. RC announces resignation of editorship in third edition
August	Campbells move back to family home in Musgrave Road, Durban
November–December	RC writes THE WAYZGOOSE, a satire of colonial Natal
December 22	RC and his family set sail for England

1927	RC begins receiving £20 per month from his father's estate
May	Campbell family move to village of Sevenoaks Weald, Kent and meet Vita Sackville-West and Harold Nicolson
June	Holiday in Provence with Augustus John
September	Mary and Vita Sackville-West become lovers
October	Campbells move into cottage on Vita's estate
November	Mary tells RC about her affair with Vita
December	Vita goes to Europe to get away from repercussions of the love affair
1928 February	RC is hospitalised for appendicitus
April	RC leaves for Martigues, Provence
May 12	Mary joins RC in Martigues
June	Mary returns to England to see Vita and to collect children from Kent
November	Mary visits Vita and is rebuffed
1929	RC begins work on THE GEORGIAD, his satire of Bloomsbury
	RC becomes a member of Martigues water-jousting team
	Around this time, Mary receives inheritance of £100 per annum
	Campbells move to small farmhouse at Tour de Vallier
August	RC's ambitions to become a professional matador are crushed: twice at Istres he was caught by a bull
1930	ADAMASTOR and THE GUM TREES, anthologies of poems, published by Faber
	POEMS published in Paris by Nancy Cunard

Roy Campbell Timeline

1931	THE GEORGIAD, NINETEEN POEMS and CHOOSING A MAST published in London
	RC writes monograph on Percy Wyndham Lewis
autumn	Britain abandons gold standard; pound loses value against other major currencies
1932 Spring	Afrikaans poet, Uys Krige, becomes tutor to Tess and Anna
	Campbells move to Figuerolles. They are living on credit
	TAURINE PROVENCE and POMEGRANATES are published
1933	RC writes MARINE PROVENCE. Publisher ran into difficulties and it was not published. MS is lost
	FLOWERING REEDS is published
	RC completes first autobiography, BROKEN RECORD
summer	Mary pays one of her regular visits to England; children go to their grandmother. Plomer claimed that Mary made a pass at him
November	RC, Mary and Uys Krige leave France for Barcelona. Tess, Anna and Therese (their governess) join them a month later
1934 January	Bomb blast in Barcelona
	A few months later, the family leave Barcelona for Altea. They part ways with Uys
	RC and Mary convert to Catholicism
	THREE PLAYS by Helge Krog ("translated" by RC)
1935 May	RC's widowed mother visits, sends Tess to a school in England (in June) and persuades family to move to a city for Anna's education
June 24	RC, Mary and Anna are conditionally baptised, which is done in cases where it is not certain that the orginal baptism was valid. RC and Mary are re-married in Catholic Church

Roy Campbell Timeline

	The family move to Toledo
July 31	Meet Laurie Lee in Toledo
1936	Mary and RC are confirmed in the Catholic faith by Cardinal Goma
March	Riots break out in Toledo
April	Anna is very ill
May	Tess returns from England
July 17-18	General Franco launches military coup against the Spanish government
	Carmelite monks ask Campbells to safeguard papers of John of the Cross and Teresa of Avila
July 22	Spanish Civil War begins
	17 Carmelite monks befriended by Campbells are executed. RC discovers their bodies
August	Campbells escape from Toledo. Arrive in England 11 August and stay with Mary's sister's family in Sussex
September 27	Seige of Alcázar ended by Nationalist forces
October	MITHRAIC EMBLEMS published
1937 January 29	Campbells go to Portugal. Settle in Sesimbra for 8 months
June	As reporter for The Tablet, RC travels around Spain. Damages his hip in Talavera
September	Campbells move to village of Estombar
1938 May	RC and Mary go on pilgrimage to Fatima. RC gives up alcohol for a year. They also visit Toledo
September	RC writes FLOWERING RIFLE (published 1939) in support of Franco's Nationalists

Roy Campbell Timeline

	RC and Mary visit Mussolini's Italy. Travel Italy with RC's mother
	While in Italy, Tess studies art and Anna studies ballet. Tess develops eating disorder
1939 February	FLOWERING RIFLE is published
March 27	Franco's Nationalist forces enter Madrid
April 1	Franco announces that Civil War is over
	Campbells return to Toledo. After a time, Anna and Tess go to School of the Assumption in Madrid
September 3	Britain declares war on Germany. The very next day, RC tries unsuccessfully to enlist with British Army in Madrid. He works briefly for British Intelligence
1940	RC begins translating the poetry of St John of the Cross
	Tess gets pneumonia
1941 July	Campbells travel to Lisbon. Mary, Tess and Anna wait for a flight to England
	SONS OF THE MISTRAL published by Faber
August	RC leaves for London. Volunteers as an air-raid warden
December	Mary, Tess and Anna join RC in England
1942	Early in the year, Mary, Anna and Tess move to Petersfield
April 1	RC joins British Army as a private in the Royal Welsh Fusiliers
June	Mary visits RC in Wales
July	RC is transferred to Intelligence Corps Depot near Winchester. Trained on motorcycles
October	RC is transferred to Wentworth, Yorkshire, for training in map reading and orienteering

Roy Campbell Timeline

	Sometime in 1942, Tessa joins the WRNS. She is stationed at Weymouth
1943 February	RC is promoted to sergeant
March 24	RC leaves for East Africa
April	RC arrives in Durban. Has two weeks with family before traveling overland to Kenya. Attached to King's African Rifles, as military censor, then with 12th Observation Unit
July	RC injures hip again. Declared unfit for active service and becomes a coast-watcher. Suffers recurrent bouts of malaria
	While RC is in Africa, Tess is invalided out of WRNS and Mary moves to Kensington
1944	RC is sent home, too ill for active service
May	RC spends a month in Durban, before returning to London in late June
September 24	RC is discharged from the army
	Tessa is placed in psychiatric ward at Guy's Hospital, then an asylum at Epsom
	Tess and Mary live for a time in Oxford. In the autumn they return to Campden Grove, London
October	Anna tours Europe with ballet company
November	RC employed as clerk on the War Damage Commission
December	Tess returns home from asylum. Seems she was later readmitted to a home
1945 January	Anna's ballet company is called up by ENSA. Tours Italy for 3 months then dances at the Prince of Wales Theatre
	RC becomes Talks Producer at BBC and is later appointed to BBC's Literary Advisory Committee. He is with the BBC for 4 years

Roy Campbell Timeline

May 8	VE Day
Autumn	Anna is exhausted. She and Mary vacation in Switzerland
1946	Anna joins Anglo-Russian Ballet
May	TALKING BRONCO is published by Faber. RC and Louis MacNeice come to blows
	RC spends much time with Dylan Thomas; through RC's efforts, Thomas is a regular contributor to BBC programmes
November	Attends Inklings meetings with Tolkien and C.S.Lewis
1947 February	RC meets Rob Lyle
	Around this time, meets Australians Geoffrey Dutton and Alister Kershaw and South African Alan Paton. Begins correspondence with Richard Aldington
	Between 1945 and 1950, RC works on translations of work by St. John of the Cross, Lorca, Calderón de la Barca and Baudelaire
1948	RC's translation of Lorca's play, BLOOD WEDDING, has a run in London
	RC suffers recurring bouts of malaria
Summer and after	Anna has a serious breakdown. Mary takes her to Italy. When they return, Mary takes Tess home to nurse her. Tess attempts suicide. Mary has a stomach ulcer
October	RC delivers lectures in Barcelona
1949	Volume one of COLLECTED POEMS is published
April 14	RC storms the stage and punches Stephen Spender
June	Renews friendship with Edith Sitwell
	RC becomes editor of THE CATACOMB, a Catholic magazine founded (and funded) by Rob Lyle. Mary and Tess also assist
	RC begins work on second autobiography, LIGHT ON A DARK HORSE

Roy Campbell Timeline

August	RC is listed in the Gallery of Catholic Authors
September	RC resigns from BBC
1950	RC completes four volumes of translations of Lorca, translations of poems of St John of the Cross and manuscript of LIGHT ON A DARK HORSE. Also completes children's novel, THE MAMBA'S PRECIPICE
Summer	Mary and Anna visit Rome for Holy Year, then in July travel to South of France. Holiday with Tess and RC for 2 months. Tess's health improves
September and December	At the end of the month, all return to London
November	RC's hip injury forces bedrest
1951	Anna marries Viscount Jaime Cavero de Carondelet
May	RC lectures at Salamanca and Madrid. Tess acompanies him
December	THE CATACOMB closes
	LIGHT ON A DARK HORSE and THE POEMS OF ST JOHN OF THE CROSS (translated by RC) published
1952 January	RC wins Foyle Prize for poetry
March-May	RC meets South African writers Alan Paton, Laurens van der Post, Enslin du Plessis and Uys Krige. They sign an open letter denouncing the attacks on democracy by the apartheid government
	RC and family leave England for Portugal to set up house with the Lyle family near Sintra
	POEMS, A TRANSLATION OF BAUDELAIRE and LORCA are published
May	Anna gives birth to a daughter, Francesca
1953 October	RC sails to North America on a lecture tour

Roy Campbell Timeline

	THE MAMBA'S PRECIPICE and COUSIN BASILIO by Eça De Queirós (translated by RC) published
1954 March 20	RC receives Honourary Doctorate from the University of Natal
	RC's sister Ethel dies while he is in Durban
	While RC is in South Africa, Tess falls in love with Ignatius Custodio. She becomes pregnant
June-July	RC returns to Portugal. Over the next few months, RC translates works by Eça De Queirós, Lope de Vega, Calderón de la Barca, Lorca and Tirso de Molina
August	Tess and Ignatius Custodio marry in Sintra on the 7 August. They are separated not long after the wedding
October –January 1955	RC lectures in Spain and visits Toledo
October 1954	Mary and RC visit London
	NATIVITY published by Faber
1955 January 6	Tess gives birth to a son, Francisco, at home (Quinta dos Bochechos)
	In January, RC is diagnosed with diabetes
July-August	With Mary, RC travels around Portugal to research a book on that country
August	Edith Sitwell is received into the Catholic Church. RC and Mary are her godparents
October	Although ill, RC travels to North America for a second lecture tour. The tour is cut short because of his illness
December	RC returns to Portugal and is confined to bed for several weeks
	THE CITY AND THE MOUNTAINS by Eça De Queirós (translated by RC) is published

1956 January	RC's mother dies, aged 92. She leaves him a few thousand pounds. RC and Mary buy 2 hectares of land in Linhó, 7 miles from Cascais and begin building a house
Autumn	While building, Campbells rent a bungalow in Linhó. Towards the end of the year, RC's sciatica is so bad he can barely walk
1957	RC completes proof corrections for the second volume of his COLLECTED POEMS. It is published later in the year
	RC submits manuscript for PORTUGAL. Published in the same year
April 5	RC and Mary drive to Spain to attend Holy Week ceremonies in Seville. They visit Toledo
April 23	Near Setubal, Portugal, a tyre bursts and the car crashes. RC dies. Mary is injured
April 27	RC is buried in the cemery of San Pedro, near Sintra
1960 to mid-1960s	Third and final volume of RC's COLLECTED POEMS and NOSTALGIA, A COLLECTION OF POEMS by Paco d'Arcos (translated by RC) published
1961	ROY CAMPBELL by David Wright is published by Longmans
early (through to 1990)	Mary, in her mid-sixties, becomes depressed, thin and arthritic. With Rob Lyle's help, her health improves and she begins painting again
	Mary founds an ecumenical movement in Portugal and has a chapel restored. She works among the poor in Linhó
1970	Tess works on her memoirs. In about 1985, the final version is sent to a London publisher. It is lost. It was her only copy. She had to begin again from earlier versions
1972	LYRIC AND POLEMIC: THE LITERARY PERSONALITY OF ROY CAMPBELL by Rowland Smith published by McGill-Queen's University Press
1979 February 27	Mary Campbell dies of a stroke ten days before her 81st birthday

Roy Campbell Timeline

1980	The Campbells' house in Linhó is sold
1982	ROY CAMPBELL: A CRITICAL BIOGRAPHY by Peter Alexander published by David Philip
November 8	Anna and Rob Lyle marry. Many years previously, Rob's wife had left him. Anna and her first husband were divorced a year or so previously
1986	Anna's memoir is published by Typographeum (150 copies)
2001	BLOOMSBURY AND BEYOND: THE FRIENDS AND ENEMIES OF ROY CAMPBELL by Joseph Pearce published by Harper Collins
2002	International colloquium on RC held in Durban. Correspondence between Tess Campbell and editors of the CD CAMPBELL IN CONTEXT begins. Judith corresponds with Tess until her death
November 22	Anna Campbell Lyle dies
2003	ROY CAMPBELL, EIN SOLITAR: INTERPRETATIONEN SEINER VERSDICHTUNG by Michael Hanke published by Universitsverlag Winter
2004	CD-Rom, CAMPBELL IN CONTEXT, edited by Judith Lutge Coullie and Jean-Philippe Wade published by University of KwaZulu-Natal, Killie Campbell Africana Library Series
	THE RARE AND THE BEAUTIFUL: THE LIVES OF THE GARMANS by Cressida Connolly published by Fourth Estate
2005	Judith Coullie visits Tess in Estoril and Francesca in Sintra, Portugal
2006	CAMPBELL AND THE ROMANCE COUNTRIES by Michael Hanke published by Wissenschaftlicher Verlag
December 13	Tess Campbell dies in Estoril
2007	ORDERING EMPIRE: THE POETRY OF CAMÕES, PRINGLE AND CAMPBELL by Nicholas Meihuizen published by Peter Lang

Index

Index

NOTES

RC = Roy Campbell
Illustrations/drawings/portraits/ photographs = **boldface**
poems, individual = in ""
poetry, anthologies, publications, articles = *italics*
books = *italics*

Aberdaron, 13, 164n, 306

Addison, Paul, viii, 114n

Africa, xviii, 112, 131, 171, 254, 274, 293, 311

Africana library. *See* Killie Campbell Africana Library

Akerman, Antony, xivn, 175n

"Alan Paton, Knocking on the Door: Shorter Writings" (Gardner), xxin

Alba, Captain, 248

Alcázar, 57, 62, 62n, 69, 70, 71, 75, 76, 82, 83, 97, **146**, 211, 223, 225, 226, 228, 232, 233, 248, 249, 309

Alcohol abuse. *See* RC, drinking

Aldington, Richard, 2n, 117n, 127, 127n, 128, 258, 312

Alexander, Peter, xin, xiin, xiiin, xivn, xix, xx, xxn, xxin, xxiii, xxiiin, xxvi, 2n, 8n, 10n, 13, 13n, 14n, 15n, 16n, 17n, 20n, 26n, 34, 36n, 37n, 40n, 41n, 47, 48n, 54n, 67n, 74n, 97, 104n, 110n, 121n, 122n, 123n, 124n, 126n, 129n, 133n, 164n, 171n, 181n, 191n, 198n, 201n, 204n, 228n, 238n, 265n, 269n, 272n, 277n, 283n, 315

Alexandria, 130

Alfonso XIII, King of Spain, 92

Algarve, 90, 91, 101, 238, 239, 244

Algodor, 76, 77, 228, 229

Alicante, 47, 54, **147**, 202, 203, **206**, 206

Altea, 47, 48, 52, 55, 64, 64n, 79n, 97, 203-5, 211, 250, 298, 308

America, 3, 13, 58, 115n, 123, 132, **154**, 276, 277, 277n, 283, 297, 313, 314

Anamaria (maid), 48, 55

Anarchy/Anarchists, iii, xx, 45, 59, 65, 69, 90

Anders, General, 119, 122

Andersen, Hans Christian, 182

Angel (poet), 75, 76, 77, 78, 226-7, 229, 261

Angelita (friend), 62, 68

Anglo-Boer War, 305

Anna Karenina (Tolstoy), 58n

Annunciation (El Greco), 216

Anti-colonialism. *See* colonialism

Anti-marxism. *See* marxism

Anti-racism, xi. *See also* negrophilism, racism.

319

Index

Apartheid, xviii, xxii, 3n, 263, 263n, 264n, 292, 293, 313. *See also* racism and RC, racism

Apes of God, The (Lewis, W.), 34, 34n, 36n, 198n

Arabia, 218

Ariosto, Ludovico, 266

Aristotle, 7n

Arles, 22, 26, 39, 181, 185

"Art of Biography, The" (Woolf), ixn

Art, Liturgy and Legend in Renaissance Toledo: the Mendoza and the Iglesia Primada (Bosch), 217n

As I Walked Out One Midsummer Morning (Lee), 214-215

Atheism, 45, 51, 69, 79n, 81, 95, 241, 264, 290, 293

Athens, 130

Auden, W.H., iii, xiii, 115, 115n

Audley, Maxine (actress), 123

Australia, xxiii, 127, 131n, 312

"*Authors take sides on Vietnam*" (Schlesinger), 291

Autobiography, viii, x, xin, xxii, xxiii, xxiiin, 6, 7n, 10n, 14, 20n, 25n, 30, 35n, 41, 84n, 115n, 121n, 123, 124n, 125n, 126n, 128, 173n, 175n, 200n, 205, 228n, 231n, 233, 246n, 259, 259n, 260, 266n, 292n, 308, 312. *See also* biography, memoirs.

Avila, 88n, 93, 249

Badajoz, 95n

Ballet. *See* Dancing and Anna Campbell Lyle, ballet

Banting, William, 251n

Barcelona, 41, 42, 43, 44, 46, 83, 92, 93, 126, 201, 308, 312

Barrès, Maurice, 233

Bashkirtseva, Mariya Konstantinova, 246, 246n, 252

Bastida, Gustavo Adolfo Domínguez, 211, 211n

Baudelaire, Charles, 8, 8n, 123, 123n, 276, 277, 278, 312, 313

B.B.C. *See* British Broadcasting Corporation

Bécquer. *See* Bastida

Beddoes, Thomas Lovell, 118, 118n

Belfast, 115n

Belloc, Hilaire, 119, 119n

Benidorm, 47

Bentley, Eric, 94n

Bento, Filipe (Francesca's husband), xxv, **160**

Bento, Francesca Cavero de Carondelet (Anna's daughter), ixn, xxiii, xxiv, xxivn, xxv, 10n, 115n, 120n, 129n, **136**, **156**, **160**, 171n, 278, 296n, 301n, 313, 316

Berlin, 290

Bevin, Ernest, 119

Binstead, Squire of. *See* Wishart, Ernest

Biography, iii, viin, viii, ixn, x, xn, xiiin, xx, xxn, xxvi, 10n, 13,

13n, 19n, 20, 20n, 27, 47, 114n, 116, 124, 175n, 228n, 261n, 315; Biography, viin; "*Biography: Cult as Culture*" (Schlaeger), xn; *Biography: Writing Lives* (Parke), xn; *Bloomsbury and Beyond: the Friends and Enemies of Roy Campbell* (Pearce), iv, 20n, 26n, 316; *Lyric and Polemic: The Literary Personality of Roy Campbell* (Smith), 315; *Roy Campbell* (Ley), 261, 261n; *Roy Campbell: a Critical Biography* (Alexander), xiiin, xxn, 10n, 13n, 20n, 228n, 315;

Rare and the Beautiful: the Lives of the Garmans, The (Connolly), xxvi, 19n, 21n, 316, *Unafraid of Virginia Woolf: the Friends and Enemies of Roy Campbell* (Pearce), iv, 20n. *See also* autobiography, life writing, memoirs

Birmingham, 9

Blake, Nicholas. *See* Day-Lewis, Cecil

Blake, William, 166

Blasting and Bombardiering (Lewis W.), 10n, 13, 264

Blinkhorn, Martin, 238n

Blood Wedding (Lorca), 123, 312

Bloomsburies, ii, xii, xiii, xix, 7n, 15n, 16, 19n, 34n, 88, 88n, 116n, 163, 307

Bloomsbury and Beyond: the Friends and Enemies of Roy Campbell (Pearce). *See* biography

Bloomsburys. *See* Bloomsburies

Blunden, Edmund, 16, 16n, 84, 96-97

Bochechos, Quinta dos, **128, 129, 154,** 272, **273,** 276, **278,** 278, 279, 280, 280n, 282-4, 296, 314

Bone family, 48

Boniface, Mr, 75

Bormes les Mimosas, 127-8, **257,** 257, 258

Bosch, Josephine (friend), 83-84, 86-89, 92, 237, 238, 239, 244

Bosch, Lynette M.F., 217n

Botticelli, 92, 132

Brideson, Mrs (landlady), 103, 112

Bridges, Robert, 121, 121n

Bristol, 101, 104

Britain, 13, 33n, 40n, 54, 58, 72 (Union Jack), 81n, 84, 96, 99, 100, 113, 115, 115n, 225 and 253 (Union Jack), 271, 308, 310

British Army, xviin, xx, 39, 103, 113, 116, 253, 261, 271, 300, 310, 311,

British Broadcasting Corporation (B.B.C.), 2, 40, 109, 116, 117, 120, 122, 226, 259, 311, 312, 313

British Embassy, 77, 97, 226, 229

British Intelligentsia, 19, 45, 97, 291, 310

British Institute, 92, 99n

British Museum Library, 230, 230n

British Union of Fascists, 84n, 289

Brittany, 127, 257

Index

Buenos Aires, 132n

Bull fighting, xiii, xxi, 29, 30, 39, 41, 43, 78, 130, 132, **147**, 181, 181n, 182, 183, 185, **219**, 220, 220n, 221, 229, 263, 264, 307

Burns, Robert, 21, 53, 164, 182

Burns, Tom, 7

Busoni, Ferruccio, 11, 11n

Buss, Helen, viii, viiin

Butler, Guy, 126n

Byron, Lord George Gordon, 3, 24, 129

Caballero, Largo, 82, 82n

Cairns, Earle Edwin, 252n

Calder, Angus, 114n

Calderón de la Barca, Pedro, 55, 123, 123n, 266, 312, 314

Calvin and Calvinism, xxi, 38n

Camargue, 26, 185, 215

Camões, Luis de, 17n, 110, 110n, 111, 266, 276, 285, 316

Campbell and the Romance Countries (Hanke), xviin, xxvi, 168n, 316

Campbell, Anna. *See* Lyle, Anna Campbell

Campbell, Archie (RC's brother), 53n

Campbell Collections, xxv, **4**, 131n, 163n. *See also* Killie Campbell Africana Library

Campbell, Bruce Patrick (RC's brother), 53n, **141**, **143**

Campbell, Ethel (RC's sister), 52, 52n, 53n, 131, 131n, 314

Campbell, Francisco (Frankie, Teresa's son), xxivn, xxv, 135, **156**, 176n, 280, **280**, 280n, 281n, 296n, 314

Campbell, George Gordon (RC's brother), 15, 53n, 64n, 107n, 130-131, 130n, **143**, **155**, **170**

Campbell in Context (Wade and Coullie), xviiin, xixn, xxiii, xxiiin, xxv, 52n, 163n, 171n, 178n, 277n, 316

Campbell, Margaret Roach (Killie, RC's cousin), xxiii, 131, 131n

Campbell, Margaret Wylie (née Dunnachie, RC's mother), 13, 15, 52, 53, 53n, 54, 54n, 55, 72, 92, 131, 131n, 132, **141**, **143**, **147**, **170**, 205-8, **206**, 211, 243, 247, 305, 308, 309, 314

Campbell, Mary Margaret (née Garman, 1898-1979, RC's wife), accident, car, 1, 134, 287, 296, 297, 299, 315; affairs, xiv, xivn, 20, 26, 29, 101, 174, 175n, 198n, 307; appearance, vii, xvi, ix, xxi, xxvi, 3, 11, 19n, 21, 25, 41, 58, 92, 135, 165, 167, 261, 274, 316; biography, xxvi, 13n, 19n, 20, 20n, 316; *The Catacomb*, 2, 120, 127, 128, 259, 260, 312, 313; Catholicism, ix, xv, 20n, 21, 51, 51n, 55, 58, 61, 62, 74, 83, 90, 100, 104, 112, 126, 134, 135, 167, 175n, 180, 201, 205, 212-4, 216, 222-3, 250, 253, 255, 256, 267, 287, 297, 298, 299, 308, 309; charity work, 94-95, 238, 249, 297, 315;

colonialism, 171; death and burial, viii, viiin, 3, 85, 135, **159**, 300, 315; drinking, xv (natural),135, 268, 299, 300; governesses, 9, 164; guitar, 32, 189; health, 1, 3, 17, 88, 88n, 235, 255, 287, 296, 300, 312, 315; home-making, 18, 134, 176, 273, 278, 299-300; horses/horseriding, 63, 85, 91, 239; housekeeping, 40, 122, 123, 235, 253, 255, 266n, 278; house-warming, 2; inheritance, 18, 132, 307, 314; job as van driver, 9; "Little Lord Fondleroy", 36; love letters, 21n, 175n; marriage to RC, vii, xivn, 12, 20n, 201, 265, 305; Mary Magdalene, 298n; meets RC, 9, 10, 11, 165-6; money issues, 18, 26, 47, 75, 81, 103, 120-1, 134, 163, 175n, 188, 200, 201, 226-8, 245, 255, 265, 282, 296n, 299, 300, 308; music, 32, 135, 189, 299-300; obituaries, Portuguese,11; painting and drawing, 9, 13, 26, 142, 176, 177, 180, 296-7, 315; parenting, xvi, xvin, 25, 26-28, 62, 100, 115, 171, 108, 108n, 173, 175n, 178, 254-5, 281n; photographs, **11, 17, 23, 33, 39, 53, 128, 143, 145, 146, 147, 154, 170, 178 189, 206, 275, 278**; pilgrimage, 204, 242; portrait of, 10, **10, 143**; promiscuity, heterosexual, xiv, 175n; promiscuity, homosexual, xiv, 20n, 175n; ran away from home, 9, 305; relationship with in-laws, 15; relationship with Vita Sackville-West, xii, xivn, 18, 18n, 19, 19n, 20, 20n, 21n, 22n, 26, 26n, 28, 29, 173, 174, 175, 175n, 195n, 307, role as RC's muse, vii, 163-4;

Sappho, 20; schooling, 9, 41, 43, 308; separation, 47, 47n, 102; Slade School of Art, 9; South Africa, vii, 14, 15, 17, 47, 81, 164, 168, 170, 171, 173, 237, 306, St Teresa, 41; support of RC and daughters, 280n, 291, 296n; as teenager, 298n; temperament, 11, 18, 20-21, 28, 77, 165, 180, 202; vision, 166, 184; widowhood, 135, 296-7, 299, 300; World War One, viii, 9, 164, 165

Campbell, Royston Dunnachie (Roy Campbell, 1901-1957) (RC), accident, car, 1, **157**, 287, 296, 297, 315; affairs, xiv, 20, 81n-82n, 132, 175n; air-raid warden, 102, 253, 310; anti-élitism, xi, 7, 73, 118-9, 174, 192; anti-marxism, xii, 3, 35, 73, 131n, 241, 290, 291, 292, 294; anti-Semitism, xi, xxi, 12, 110, 263, 271; apartheid, 292-3, 313; army, xiii, xvii, xx, 39, 89, 90, 97, 99, 103, 109-114, 116, 125, 238n, 253-4, 261, 263, 291, 300, 305, 310, 311; appearance, xvii, 6, 11, 12, 54, 77, 127, 128, 132, 166-7, 190, 215, 259, 261, 264, 276, 280, 287; arrest, 67, atheism, 79n, 264, 290, 293; authority, xx; autobiography, xi, xin, xxiii, xxiiin, 7n, 14, 20n, 30, 121n, 123, 124n, 128, 175n, 200n, 228n, 233, 259, 259n, 260, 266n, 292n, 308, 312; "autobuggeroffery", xxiii, 124n, 259, 260n; baldness, 12; beating, 65; bigotry, xi; birth, 53, 53n, 264, 305; bisexuality, xx; boasts. See self-characterisation; boycott of work, i, xiiin, 67n, 198n, 289,

Index

290, 291-2; Britain, 13, 58, 72, 84, 96, 99, 113, 269, 271, 310; British Army, xviin, xx, 39, 103-4, 107, 116, 253, 310, 311; British Broadcasting Corporation, 2, 40, 109, 116, 117, 120, 122, 226, 259, 311, 313; bullfighting, xiii, xxi, 29, 30, 39, 41, **43**, 130, 181, 182-3, 263, 264, 307; "bully", xi, 99, 230, 263; calendars, keeping of, 5: Calvinist, xxi, 38n; Catholicism, ii, ix, xx, 2n, 20n, 51, 51n, 55, 66, 68, 89, 90, 104, 105, 109, 175n, 205, 209, 212-5, 243, 264, 267-8, 278, 287, 288, 290, 308, 309; cattle-man, xiii, 263; childhood, 7, 54n, 163, 264, **141**; Christ, iii, xiin, 51, 73, 79n, 80, 83, 212, 267-8; Christianity, iii, ix, xiii, 34, 45, 79-80, 89, 231, 233, 240, 264, 267-8, 292, 293; circus, 14; clothes, 54; colonialists and anti-colonialism, xi, xx, 16, 168n, 293, 306; Colour Bar, xi, 171, 263n, 264, 264n. *See also* apartheid, negrophilism, racism; Colour prejudice, xi. *See also* apartheid, negrophilism, racism; communism and anti-communism, x, xi, xiii, xix, xxi, 35, 45-6, 89,125, 230, 231, 233, 241, 263, 289, 290, 291, 292; complainers, 27; death and burial, viii, xiii, 1, 2, 3, 3n, 13, 17, 35, 44, 83, 97, 108, 110, 116, 118, 120, 125, 127n, 131n, 132, 133, 134, 135, 157, **159**, 193, 280, 286, 287, 288, 288n, 289, 290, 296, 297, 315; defamation, 125; democracy, 7, 57-8, 90, 118, 191, 313; drawings, xxiii, 24, 38, 64, 108, **109**, **150-2**, **157**, 180-1, 185n, 197, 266n; drinking, xiv, xivn, xv, xvn, 12, 20, 26, 47, 54, 59, 62, 63, 67, 73, 87, 92, 104, 108, 126n, 131, 174-5, 177, 190-1, 201-2, 216, 243, 247, 250, 259, 267, 268, 268n, 277n, 283, 283n, 287, 288n, 309; Durban High School, xviiin, **4**, 277n, 305; East Africa, 99, 108, 109, 119, 125, 311; élitism, xi, xxi, 191-2, 264; enemies, i, iii, xiii, xix, xx, 16, 34, 82, 86, 99, 108, 125, 133, 185, 312; England, ii, iii, vii, viii, 7, 17, 67, 75, 99, 100, 101, 103, 116, 121n, 124n, 126n, 164n, 171-4, 174n, 215, 226, 232, 235, 238, 252, 268, 269, 289, 290, 291, 305, 306, 309, 310, 313; eyes, xvii, 6, 24, 25, 46, 62, 92, 121n, 166, 190, 215, 216, 285, 289; fascism/fascist, xi, xii, xiiin, 35, 51, 85, 99, 102, 115, 125, 263, 264, 289, 290, 291; father-son relationship, 14, 14n; fishing, 128, 181, 188, **257**, 263, 306; Foyle Literary Prize, 123-4, 313; friends and friendships, i, iii, xi, xx, xxii, 2, 13, 15-16, 17, 17n, 26, 30, 32, 34, 36, 36n, 40, 46, 49, 55, 60, 65, 71, 76, 83, 85, 86, 91, 92, 92n, 100, 104, 108, 112, 113, 114, 114, 115n, 120, 126n, 127, 127n, 131n, 132, 133, 153, **153**, 155, **155**, 173n, 176, 177, 181, 182, 185-7, 214-6, 219, 222, 227, 259, 260, 261, 271, 312; grandchildren, 129n, 278, 285, health, xvi, 2, 3, 5, 11, 14, 14n, 18, 20, 23, 51, 54n, 86, 89, 108, 109, 110, 113, 177, 181, 235, 267, 282, 283, 283n, 290, 288, 306, 307, 309, 311-5; home, xiv, 14, 17, 18, 27, 30n, 38, 40, 47, 49, 59, 62, 63, 64, 65, 66, 76, 91, 100,

104, 107, 109, 114, 120, 122, 133, 164, 170, 171, 173, 174n, 176, 177, 178, 179, 180, 181, 182, 184, 201, 204, 218, 220, 243, 253, 255, 260, 272n, 276, 283, 287, 306, 311, 314; homophobia, xi, 263; homosexuality, ix, xii, xiv, xivn, xxi, 6, 7, 7n, 19, 21, 115, 175n, 263; honorary Doctorate from the University of Natal, xiii, 38n, 129, 130-131, 155, 292n, 314; horses, xiii, 71, 89, 91, 263; housewarming, 2; humour, 46, 46n, 88, 110, 260-1, 265; industrialization, 50; influence on South African poetry, viii; inheritance, 18, 132, 307; inspiration, 24, 119, 163, 191, 200, 202, 204, 212, 230, 277, 286, 300; jousting, 25, 29, 30, 183, 185, 307, King's African Rifles, 108, 109, 110, 113, **150**, 311; lectures, 3, 46, 129, 132, 261, 276, 277, 277n, 283, 283n, 312, 313, 314; letters, xi, xxiii, xxiiin, xxiv, xxv, 5, 6, 13, 15-6, 33, 36, 38, 42, 43-4, 64, 88-9, 96-7, 99-100, 101, 102, 103-5, 107-8, 108n, 125, 126-7, 127n, 130-1, 132, **150**, 151, 152, 197, 313, 314; Libra, 264; luck, 30, 74, 179, 202, 228, 283; Marxism, 240. *See also* antimarxism; masculinity, xii, xvii, 215; materialism/materialists, 6, 18, 83; meets Mary Garman, 10, 11, 165-6, 306; meets Mary's parents, 12; Misericordia Hospital, 2-3; money issues, vii, viii, 3, 17, 18, 30, 40n, 47, 75, 81, 103, 104, 108, 163, 174-5, 175n, 198, 198n, 200, 201, 226-8, 255, 259, 260n, 265, 267, 277, 282, 283, 290, 308; motherson relationship, 53-4; Muse, i, ii, vii, 1, 25, 163-4; music, 25, 44, 52, 90, 201, 215, 221, 267, Negroes, xi, 37n; negrophilism, vii. *See also* racism; Nietzscheism, 294; Oxford University, xiv, xivn, 5, 6, 6n, 7, 7n, 14, 16, 38n, 51, 116n, 163, 300, 305; painting, love of, 24; parenting, ix; xvi, xvii, xix, 5, 6, 17, 23-4, 32, 54, 67, 108, 128, 172-3, 175n, 178, 181-3, 188, 251, 254-5, 256, 261, 262, 266, 266n, 278-9, 283-4; parodies, 121-2; photographs, **IV, VI, 10, 17, 23, 25, 33, 39, 117, 128, 129, 141, 142, 143, 144, 144, 145, 146, 147, 153, 154, 155, 170, 206, 257, 262, 275, 278, 279**; pilgrimage, 52, 204, 242; as poet, i, xiii, xviii, xviiin, xix, 1, 7n, 24, 25, 46, 47, 79, 89-90, 95, 118-9, 127n, 129, 133, 163, 169, 174, 191, 199, 200, 212, 215, 237, 259, 263, 265, 266, 276, 286, 288, 293, 294, 301; portrait by Mary, **142**, 180; prejudice, xi, xxii, 200n; progress, xxii, 45, 50, 293-4; as prophet, xiii, 263; prose, viii, 43, 124, 263, 276, 277, 278, 283; psychoanalysis, 292, 293; Quakers, xxi; racism and antiracism, xi, xix, xx, xxi, 168n, 171, 263n, 264, 292, 292n, 293, 313. *See also* Colour Bar, Colour Prejudice, negrophilism; relationship with Mary Garman, vii, ix, xivn, xxn, 1, 12, 20, 47, 47n, 101, 175, 201, 265, 266, 266n, 268, 274, 274n, 285, 306; Reponsions, 305; reputation, xiii, xiv, 3, 13, 107, 133, 164, 259, 263, 291, 292; reviews, xiiin, 13, 121;

Index

rivals, ix, 266; romantic, 29, 263, 279; royalty, 92; sailing, 7, 25, 90, 92, 100, 164, 171, 183, 188, 193, 244, 306, 313; satirist, xix, 19n, 32, 33, 34, 119, 229n, 263, 265, 269, 271, 291, 292, 306, 307; as scholar, xiii, 109, 178, 263, 265, 288; Secret Service, 128; self-characterisations, xiii, ix, xx, xxi, 124, 187, 263; sexism, xi; sexual promiscuity, xiv, 36n; slander, 125, 292; socialism, xix, xxi, xxin, 192, 263, 270, 271, 292; South Africa, iv, vii, xi, xviii, xviiin, xxii, xxiii, 3n, 14, 16, 17, 27n, 33, 47, 81, 107, 107n, 113, 116n, 123n, 125, 129, 130, 144, 164, 168, 170, 171, 173, 188, 190 (incl. South African accent), 191, 200, 215, 237, 253, 263, 264, 269, 269n, 277, 277n, 280, 292, 293, 305, 306, 312, 313, 314; "talking bronco", 263, 263n; as teenager, 4; temperament, ; 29, 46, 55, 72, 99, 110, 116, 177, 179, 180, 181, 185, 192, 223, 259, 263, 264-5, 266-7, 276, 286; as thinker, xiii, 263; translation, xix, 8n, 17n, 47, 48n, 94n, 123n, 124n, 135n, 169n, 259, 260, 263, 276, 277, 277n, 283, 286, 312, 313; Wales, vii, 13, 103, 163, 306, 310; War Damage Commission, xviiin, 114, 116, 311; "Zulu", 175, 263

WORKS BY ROY CAMPBELL

COLLECTED WORKS

Collected Poems, 90n, 312, 313, 314, 315

Collected Works (ed. Alexander, Chapman and Leveson), xin, xxiiin, xxvi, 8n, 13n, 29n, 33n, 34n, 35n, 39n, 53n, 67n. 80n, 89n, 107n, 108n, 110n, 118n, 123n, 124n, 131n, 133n, 228n, 259n, 273n, 277n, 312, 313

PROSE WORKS

Broken Record, ix, 29, 29n, 33n, 39n, 43, 46, 124n, 131n, 228n, 308

The History of the Spanish Civil War, 286 (not completed)

Light on a Dark Horse: an Autobiography, ix, xi, xiin, xxi, xxii, xxiin, xxiiin, 7, 20n, 26n, 36n, 37n, 38n, 48n, 123, 123n, 124, 124n, 126, 175n, 200n, 220n, 228n, 233, 259-60, 259n, 260n, 266n, 271, 292n, 312, 313

Marine Provence, 37n, 181n, 308 (manuscript lost)

Portugal, 276, 278, 314, 315

Taurine Provence, 181, 181n, 308

Wyndham Lewis, 308

CHILDREN'S BOOK

The Mamba's Precipice, 14, 105n, 123, 313

BROADCASTS

"Calling South Africa", 27n, 269-271

POETRY

Adamastor, 16n, 120, 120n, 307; "Autumn", ii; "Choosing a Mast", 40, 181, 215, 308; Drafts of poems, 158; "The Drummer Boy's Catechism", 121-2; "Faith", 212;

"The Fight", 79-80, 79n, 80n, 83, 212, 291, *The Flaming Terrapin*, i, ii, vii, xviiin, 7, 12, 13, 14, 163-4, 166, 171, 248, 306; "The Flower", 137, 137n; *Flowering Reeds*, 137n, 198, 198n, 308; *Flowering Rifle*, "A Poem from the Battlefield of Spain", xiiin, 35, 51, 89n, 90, 91, 92, 95, 96, 118n, 230-1, 238, 240, 243, 247, 309, 310; *The Georgiad*, iii, 19, 19n, 20, 21, 34, 34n, 57, 173, 198n, 229n, 307, 308; *The Gum Trees*, 307; "Heartbreak Camp", 108n, 109; "Horses on the Camargue", 215; "A Jug of Water", 198-9; "Junction of the Rails", 33; "A Letter from the San Mateo Front", 89, 89n, 90; "Luis de Camões", 110-111; "Mass at Dawn", ii; *Mithraic Emblems*, ii-iii, ivn, 67, 67n, 83, 133n, 204, 212-3, 222, 309; *Nativity*, 314, *Nineteen Poems*, 308; "November Nights", 273-4, 273n, 274n, "One Transport Lost", 107; "The Palm", 25; Poem fragment, 2, 157, 158, 286; *Poems*, 307; *Pomegranates*, 308; "The Rhapsody of the Man in Hospital Blues", 123; "Rounding the Cape", xviiin; "Saint Peter of the Three Canals", ii; "Satire and Fiction" 16; "The Serf", ii; "The Sisters", ii, 215; "A Song for the People", 192; *Sons of the Mistral*, 310; *Talking Bronco*, 107n, 108n, 118, 312; "The Theology of Bongwi the Baboon", ii; "To Mary after the Red Terror", 133, 133n; "To the Sun", iii, ivn; *The Wayzgoose*, xi, xin, 131n, 171, 292n, 306; "Zulu Girl", ii; "Zulu Song", ii

TRANSLATIONS

Blood Wedding (Lorca), 123, 312, 313

The City and the Mountains (de Queirós), 314

Cousin Basilio (de Queirós), 313

Fuente Ovenjuna (de Vega), 94n

Les Fleurs du Mal (Baudelaire), 8n, 123, 123n, 277, 278, 312, 313

El Médico de su Honra (The Surgeon of his Honour) (de la Barca), 123, 123n

Nostalgia, A Collection of Poems (d'Arcos), 135n, 315

Romancero Gitano (Lorca), 123, 123n, 313

St John of the Cross, 47, 123-4, 259-60, 277, 310, 312, 313

Three Plays (Krog), 308

ADAPTATIONS

Two poems by Rubén Darío, 201, 201n

PERIODICALS

"Decade in Retrospect, A", 268

Catacomb, The, 2n, 120-1, 127-8, 259-60, 263, 312-3

Jambo, 109

Month, The, 268, 294

Mount Olympus Magazine, 209-10

Tablet, The, 238, 309

Voorslag, 15, 168n, 171, 306

CRITICAL STUDIES BY ROY CAMPBELL

Lorca: An Appreciation of his Poetry, 123, 123n

Index

CRITICAL STUDIES ON ROY CAMPBELL

Alexander, Peter *Roy Campbell: a Critical Biography*, xiiin, xxn, 10n, 13n, 20n, 228n, 315

Hanke, Michael *Campbell and the Romance Countries*, xviin, xxvi, 168n, 316

Hanke, Michael *Roy Campbell, Ein Solitar: Interpretationen Seiner Versdichtung*, 316

Meihuizen, Nicholas *Ordering Empire: The Poetry of Camões, Pringle and Campbell*, 316

Pearce, Joseph *Bloomsbury and Beyond: the Friends and Enemies of Roy Campbell*, iv, xivn, xxii, xxiii, xxvi, 14n, 20n, 21n, 23n, 26n, 29n, 37n, 59n, 79n, 94n, 135n, 168n, 171n, 175n, 176n, 198n, 228n, 229n, 280n, 287n, 316

Pearce, Joseph *Unafraid of Virginia Woolf: the Friends and Enemies of Roy Campbell* iv, 20n

Smith, Rowland, *Lyric and Polemic: The Literary Personality of Roy Campbell*, 315

Wright, David, *Roy Campbell*, 261n, 315

Campbell, Samuel George, Dr (RC's father) 5, 6, **6**, 12, 14, 15, 18, 52, 53, 53n, 64n, 131n, **141, 143, 170**, 305, 306

Campbell, Teresa Mary (1922–2006, daughter of RC and Mary Campbell), adolescence, 54, 87, 90, 94, 198, 205, 246; anorexia nervosa, xvii, 246, 251, 310; "banting" (dieting), 95, 98, 114, 251, 251n, 252-6; birth, vii, viii, 13, 108n, 163-4, 306; bullfighting and bullring, **147**, 183, **219**, 220-1; Catholicism, ix; childhood, 28, 54, 83, 168-71, 173, 175, 175n, 177-80, 182-8, 193-4, 195, 197, 198, 200-207, 232, 244, 278; Christianity, xi, 52, 231-2; correspondence and visits with Judith Coullie, ix, xxiv, 185n, 316; dancing, 196, 237; death, xxiv, 316; depression, 95, 98-9, 112, 246, 247, 255, 258, 262, 278; "Diana", **236**; drawing/s, 64, 64n, 246; engagement, 129; 40n; grandchildren, 301n; guitar, 95; Guy's Hospital, 112-3, 311; health, xvi, xvii, xviii, 40, 64n, 68, 86, 95, 98, 99, 112, 114, 121, 126, 168, 184, 196, 209, 210, 235, 246-7, 251-8, 260-2, 279, 310, 311, 312, 313; horse riding, 78, 147, 218-220, **219**, 222, 236; hunger, xvi, 76; husband (Ignatius Custudio), 280n, 281n; lunatic asylum, xviii, 114, 311; marriage, ix, 135, 135n, 279, **279**, 280, **280**, 280n, 281n, 283, 314; music, 95; painting, 95, 98, 176, 185, 209, 210n, 236, 237, 238, **301**, 310; parenting, 174; pets, 34, 37, 38, 40n, 64, 180, **186**, 197-8, 201, 203; photographs, **vi, 1, 25, 33, 35, 143, 144, 147, 148, 156, 160, 170, 178, 186, 189, 219, 236, 262, 279, 280,** ; schooling, xvi, 54, 64, 68, 97, 98, 101, 102, 178, 183, 191, 198, 207-10, 249, 251-2, 308, 310; separation from Anna, 54, 68, 207, 210; South Africa, vii, xxv, 144, 168, 170, 171, 171n, 237; suicide attempts, xvi, 255-6, 312; Victoria Women's Royal Naval Service (WRNS), 103, 103n, 107, 112, 253, 254, **254**, 310, 311; vision, 184; work on *The Catacomb*, 260; writing, 209-10

Campbell, William (RC's grandfather), 305

Campbell, William Neil (RC's brother), 53n, 64, 64n, **141**, **170**

Campeador, Cid, 284

Canada, xxiii, 3, 119

Canary, Cardinal, 126

Cape Town, 17

Carlists, 45, 83n, 238, 238n

Carmelite archives, 226

Carmelites, 2, 21, 21n, 58, 61, 66, 67, 71, 88, 89, 112, 164n, 167, 222, 223, 225, 226, 247, 249, 253, 254, 255, 297, 298, 309

Carr, E.H., 229n

Carroll, Lewis, 120

Carvoeiro, 244

Casa da Serra, 3, 132, **132**, 134, 135

Casasbuenas, 222

Cascais, 297, 314

Castanos, General, 278

Catechism, 52, 121, 205, 249, 297

Catherine Wheel, 120, 259

Castile, 66, 202, 211-2, 232, 249, 298

Catalonia, 45, 200, 201

Catholic Action, 94, 213, 223

Catholic Church, iii, xiiin, 21, 51, 55, 85, 103, 112, 175n, 205, 212, 214, 241, 242, 253, 267, 268, 280n, 298, 300, 308, 314

Catholicism, ii, ix, xv, xx, 2n, 6n, 20n, 51n, 85n, 175n, 205, 217n, 278, 298, 308

Cauper (friends of RC and Mary), 90, 100, 101

Causley, Charles, 117

Cavero de Carondelet, Jaime, Viscount (Anna's first husband), 129n, 135, 296n, 313

Cecil, Lord Edward Christian David Gascoyne, 124, 124n

Cervantes, Miguel de, 44

Chabrol, Henri, 44, 117

Chambers, Colin, 114n

Chapman, Michael, xin, xix, xixn, xxn, xxiiin, xxvi, 13n, 110n, 123n, 133n

Charles V (Emperor of Spain), 57, 217

Chaucer, Geoffrey, 24, 266

Cheka, 71, 229, 229n

Chesterton, G.K., ii, iv

Chiaroscuro (John), 10n

"Childe Harold" (Byron), 3, 129

China, 53, 86, 122, 274

Christian Science Monitor, xxin

Christianity, iii, xi, xiii, 45, 51, 51n, 52,

Index

74, 79-80, 89, 231, 233, 264, 267, 274, 275, 293

Christianity through the Centuries: a History of the Christian Church (Cairns), 252n

Christmas, 40, 43, 66, 92, 103, 107, 114, 132, 243, 247

Churchill, Jennie, 77

Churchill, Winston, 119, 120

Cintra. *See* Sintra

City and the Mountains, The (de Queirós), 314

Civil War, Spanish *See* Spanish Civil War

Claudius, 266

Club de la Joyeuse Lance Martégale, **25**, 30

Cocteau, Jean Maurice Eugène Clément, 42, 42n

Coimbra, 87, 88, 90

Colette, Sidonie-Gabrielle, 42, 42n

Collected Essays (Woolf), ixn

Colonialism (and anti-colonialism), xi, xx, 16, 168n, 171, 306

Colonna family, 247

Colour Bar, 171, 263n, 264n. *See also* Apartheid, Colour Prejudice, Racism, RC, Negrophilism, RC, Racism

Colour Prejudice, xi, *See also* Apartheid, Colour Bar, Racism, RC, Negrophilism, RC, Racism

Columbia Encyclopedia, The, 252n

Communism, x, xi, xiii, xix, xxi, 35, 45, 67n, 69, 71n, 81, 81n, 82, 82n, 84n, 89, 90, 91, 93, 125, 229n, 230, 231, 231n, 232, 233, 240, 241, 242, 248, 249, 263, 264, 289, 290, 291, 292

Communist. *See* Communism

Condor legion, 96, 96n

Congregation for the Doctrine of the Faith, 252n

"Conjunto de Infantes", 96

Connolly, Cressida, xxvi, 15n, 19n, 20n, 21n, 22n, 26n, 40n, 81n, 85n, 101n, 175n, 198n, 260n, 316

Contensaint (Dr.), 26, 44

Coronation Medal, 130n

Costillo, José, 67n

Coullie, Judith Lütge, iv, xviiin, xixn, xxiiin, xxiv, xxv, 1n, 52n, **160**, 163n, 171n, 178n, 266n, 277n, 316

Council for the Encouragement of Music and the Arts (CEMA), 114n

Cousin Basilio (de Queirós), 313

Crane, Hart, 36, 36n, 37, 185

Crau, The, 26

Crowder, Henry, 37n

Cunard, Nancy, 37, 37n, 45, 102, 307

Custudio, Francisco. *See* Campbell, Francisco

Custudio, Ignatius (Teresa's husband), **279**, 279-80, 280n, 281n, 314

Cyprus, 272

Czechoslovakia, 84

Dancing, 29, 43, 61, 87, 101n, 113-116, **114**, 115n, 122, 128, 170, 179, 183, 196, 220, 237, 245, 267, 311

Daily Worker, The, 82

Dante, 73, 225, 266

D'Arcos, Joaquim Paco, 134-5, 135n, 315

Darío, Rubén, 201, 201n

Dark Outsider (Akerman), xivn, 175n

Das Kapital (Marx), 74

Daudet, Léon, 35, 88

"Daughter of the Storm" (Krige), 46-47

David Copperfield (Dickens), 93n

Davis, Adèle, 296

Day-Lewis, Cecil (pseud. Blake, Nicholas), iii, xiii, 115, 115n

Death in the Morning: a Woman's Experiences of the Civil War in Spain (Nicholson, Helen), 91, 91n

Death of a Hero (Aldington), 127, 127n

Decadents, 8n

De Cardaval, Marquesa, 132

De Chardin, Teilhard, 300, 300n

De Chirico, Giorgio, 181

Decline and Fall of the Roman Empire, The (Gibbon), 266

Decoration (Hewitt), 15n

De Fremenville, Comte Frederique

(Freddy), 26, 41, 43-44, 186, **189**

Dehesa, 249-50

De La Barca, Calderón. *See* Calderón

De L'Isle-Adam, Auguste Villiers, 92

De Meneses, Filipe Ribeiro, 238n

Democracy and the Civil War in Spain (Blinkhorn), 238n

De Molina, Tirso, 314

De Poitiers, Diane, 25

Depression, The, viii

De Queirós, Eça, José Maria, 276, 276n, 313, 314

De Vega, Lope, 60, 94, 94n, 266, 277, 277n, 314

De Zgliniski, Baroness. *See* Nicholson, Helen

"DHS: Cultural Desert/Cultural Oasis" (McBean), xviii, 277n

Diabetes, 314

Dickens, Charles, iv, 92-3, 93n, 95, 209, 246, 265, 209, 265

Diet. *See* Nutrition

Digital Innovation South Africa (DISA), xxvi

Discalced Carmelites. *See* Carmelites

Divina Commedia (Dante), 73

Dold, Agnes (RC's sister-in-law), 107n

Dold, Alice, 107n

Dolores (maid), 62, 63

Dominicans, 135

Index

Don Bonifacio, 60
Don Gregorio (priest), 48, 52
Don Jacinto (priest), 48
Doolittle, Hilda, 127n
Doré, Paul Gustave 73
Dostoevsky, Fyodor, 34, 73, 112, 225
Driver, C.J., 107n
Drury, Dr., 81
Dublin, 101
Duff-Cooper, Alfred, 119
Dukes, Ashley, 35, 35n
Dunbar, William, 266
Duncan, Patrick, Sir, 107, 107n
Du Plessis, Enslin, xi, 16n, **153**, 313
Durban, xxii, 5, 14, 17, 39n, 52, 113, 131n, **142, 143**, 170, 180, 277n, 305, 306, 311, 314, 316
Durban High School, xviiin, **4**, 277n, 305
Durrell, Lawrence, 2n, 117n
Dutton, Geoff, 131, 131n, 312
Dutton, Nin, 131, 131n

Earp, T.W., xivn, 7, 7n, 8n, 305
East Africa, 99, 108, 109, 119, 125, 311
Ecumenism, 205
Eden, Anthony, 119, 120, 120n
Edinburgh, 57, **141**, 305
Edinburgh University, **141**
El Debate, 220n

El Greco, 59, 67, 216-7
Eliot, T.S., i, xviii, 116, 116n
El Mizzian, Mohamed, 95, 95n
Encounter, 291
Encyclopedia Britannica: A Dictionary of Arts, Science and General Literature Vol. V, 21n
Encyclopedia of Continental Women Writers, An (Wilson), 82n
Encyclopedia of Life Writing: Autobiographical and Biographical Forms, (Jolly), viiin
"Engine Fight Talks" (Lewis, W.), 33
England, ii, iii, vii, viii, xxiii, 7, 9n, 17, 29, 54, 55, 64n, 67n, 68, 72 (Union Jack), 75, 99, 100, 101, 103, 112, 114, 115, 115n, 116, 121n, 124n, 126n, 129n, 135, 164, 167, 171, 172-3, 174, 174n, 184, 195, 195n, 196, 198, 207, 208, 210, 211, 213, 215, 222, 226, 229, 232, 235, 238, 245, 246, 249, 250, 252, 254, 255, 256, 267-70, 283, 289, 290, 291, 298, 300, 305, 306, 307, 308, 309, 310, 313
ENSA. *See* Lyle, Anna Campbell
Epsom, 114, 311
Epstein, Jacob (Kathleen Garman's husband), 54n, 59n, 209n
Epstein, Kitty (Kathleen's and Jacob's daughter), 54n, 59n, 100n, 102, 209, 209n. 210, 217
Epstein, Lady Kathleen (née Garman, Mary's sister), xxvi, 9, 12, 54n, 59n, 166, 209n, 305, 316

Estombar, 91, **236**, 238, 239, 240, 242, 309

Estonia, 39, 39n

Estoril, xxiv, 87, **160**, 185n, 316

Estremoz, 244

Étang de Berre, vi, 22, 176

Eusebio, Fr (priest), 66, 67

Evaristo, Fr (priest), 66, 67, 88, 88n, 89

Excommunication 252n

Exeter, 8n, 253

Falangists, 45, 95, 96

Fascism/fascist, xi, xii, xiii, 35, 45, 51, 71, 72, 73, 84n, 85, 96n, 99, 102, 115, 125, 225, 230, 231n, 240, 241, 244, 253, 263, 264, 289, 290, 291

Fatima, 91, 242-3, 274, 309

Faulkner, William, xviii

Faust (Goethe), 168n

Ferdinand, King, 217

Field, Sid, 115

Fields, Gracie, 114n

Figuerolles, 38, 39, **39**, 40, 46, 197-200, 308

Finishing Touches (John), 10n

"First Meeting with Roy Campbell" (Krige), 191, 191n

First World War, *See* World War One

Fleurs du Mal, Les (Baudelaire), 8n, 123, 123n, 277, 278

Flora (maid), 61, 70, 72

Florence, 92, 247

Food. *See* Nutrition

Foreign legion, 96

Formby, George, 114n

Foss, 38

Four Quartets, (Eliot), i

France, vii, 40, 92, 127, 171, 175, 183, 195, 200, 205, 217, 238n, 241, 260, 263, 308, 313

Franco, General Francisco y, iii, x, xiii, xix, xxi, 35, 69, 88, 90, 92, 93, 95, 95n, 96, 131n, 173n, 224, 225, 230, 231, 232, 238, 238n, 240, 241, 243, 247, 248, 264, 289, 290, 291, 309, 310

Franco and the Spanish Civil War (de Meneses), 238n

Free verse, xviii, 118n, 266

French Revolution, 294

Freud, Lucien, 85n

Freud, Sigmund, 237, 293

Friend, 289

Fuente Ovenjuna, 94n

Fuster, Antonio, 49

Gable, Clark, 32

Gallery of Catholic Authors, 312

Gambara, General Gastone, 96, 96n

Garbo, Greta, 252

Garcia, Angel, 117

Index

Gardner, Colin, xxin
Gardner, W.H., xx
Garman, Douglas (Mary's brother), xxvi, 12, 81, 81n, 82n, 316
Garman, Grandmama, (Mary's mother), 12, 17, 29, 38, 54, 64, 78, 86, 102, 103, 105, 164, 195, 197, 208-10, 217, 308
Garman, Helen (Polge) (Mary's sister), 12, 26n, 59n, **189**
Garman, Kathleen, *See* Epstein, Kathleen
Garman, Lorna (Mary's sister). *See* Wishart, Lorna
Garman, Mary Margaret. *See* Campbell, Mary Margaret
Garman, Mavin (Mary's brother), 12, 316
Garman, Rosalind (Mary's sister), 12, 316
Garman, Ruth (Mary's sister), 12, 196, 316
Garman, Sylvia (Mary's sister), 12, 316
Garman, Walter, Dr. (Mary's father), 9, 12
Garnett, Constance, 34
Garrett, Martin, 176n
Garth, John, 7n, 8n
Geneva, 115, 116
German, xii, 39, 43, 84, 86, 98, 99, 169, 200n, 215, 241, 271,
German Air Force, 96n

Germany, xxiii, 43, 84, 270, 281n, 290, 310
Gibbon, Edward, 266
Gibraltar, 92, 100, 244, 253
Glebe House, 82, 83, 85
Godfree, Edward. *See* Aldington
Goethe, Johann Wolfgang von, 168, 168n, 169n, 277n
Gogol, Nicolai, 73
Golden ratio, 60, 60n
Goldsworthy, Colleen, xxv-xxvi
Goma, Archbishop, 214, 309
Góngora, Luis de, 44, 265, 266
Gongorismo, 44
Goya, Francisco, 63
Grandmama. *See* Garman, Grandmama
Grandpère. *See* Polge, Marius
Graves, Robert, 229n
Greece, 7n
Greek drama, 130,
Grey, Cecil, 38, 38n
Grey, Lord, of Falloden, 12
Grounds of Contest: A Survey of South African English Literature (van Wyk Smith), xviiin
Groves, Barry A., 251n
Guardias de Asalco (police), 65, 69
Guggenheim, Peggy, 81, 81n, 82n, 85n
Guibert, Armand, 2n, 91, 91n, 185

Guitar (Lyle), 129

Guitar, 32, 52, 90, 95, 189, 214

Gypsy/gypsies, 43, 59, 60, 61, 185, 214, 218, 219, 220, 222, 262

Haley, William Sir, 117, 117n

Hanke, Michael, xvii, xviin, xxvi, 168n, 316

Hardy, Thomas, 10n

Hart, John, 164n

Hastings, Lewis, 124n

Heath-Stubbs, John, 117

Herdsman of Apollo (Lyle), 116, 121

Hereford, 29

Heseltine, Philip (pseud. Peter Warlock), 6

Hewitt, Jeanne (Garman) (Douglas' wife), 81n, **146**, 175n

Hewitt, Kathleen, 15, 15n, 41, 187, 187n

Hewitt, Lisa (Jeanne's sister), 81n, 175n

High Diver (Wishart, M.), 36 n

Hillier, Tristram, 37, 37n, 183

Hilton, 130

Hindus, 170

Hitler, Adolf, 43, 48, 84, 99, 241, 289, 290

Holms, John (Guggenheim's partner), 82n

"Home Front" (Addison), 114n

Homer, 24, 32, 265, 266

Hommage à Roy Campbell: Choix de Poèmes (Guibert), 2n, 91n, 117n

Homosexuality, xi, xii, xiv, xivn, xxin, 6, 7, 7n, 8n, 19, 19n, 21, 115, 115n, 263

Hood (boat), 92

Hopkins, Gerard Manley, 121, 121n

Horace, 277, 277n

Housman, A.E., 118, 118n

Hunger. *See* Nutrition

Huxley, Aldous, 36, 36n, 185

Ibáñez, Vicente Blasco, 104

Ibárruri, Dolores ("La Pasionaria") (communist leader), 67n, 82

Iberian Peninsula, 92

Identity in memoir writing, ix

Idiot, The (Dostoevsky), 112

Iglesias, Jose Enrique Varela, 83n

Il Messagiero, 126

Il Rex (boat), 92

Index of Prohibited Books, 252, 252n, 278, 278n

India, 274

"Indian Upon God, An" (Yeats), ii

Individual, viii, xvi, xxin, 232, 268, 294,

Indonesia, 274

Inklings, 312,

Index

Inquisition, 58, 267

Intelligentsia. *See* British Intelligentsia

Ireland, 101, 252

Irún, 93

Isabella, Queen, 217

Istres, 22, 30, 307

Italian, 41, 73, 90, 92, 95, 95n, 98, 132, 193, 245, 270

Italy, xvin, 38n, 92, 96n, 114, 115, 127, 243, 244, 245, 247, 290, 309, 310, 311, 312

Japan, 16, 39, 122, 126n, 206, 274

Jesuits, 105n

Jews, xi, xxi, 43, 110, 217, 263, 271, 289

John, Augustus, 10, 10n, 11, 36, 36n, 165-6, 176, 185, 307

Jolly, Karen Louise, 217n

Jolly, Margaretta, viiin

Jonson, Ben, 266

Journal de Marie Bashkirtseff, Avec un Portrait (Bashkirtseva), 246n

Jousting, 29, 30, 183, 185, 307

Joyce, James, xviii

Julius Caesar, 199

Juvenal, 265

Keats, John, 164

Kenny, Robin, 112, 119

Kenya, 107, **109**, 110, 311

Kershaw, Alister, 117, 117n, 127n, 128, 312

Kiev, 57

Killie Campbell Africana Library, xviiin, xx, xxiii, xxiiin, xxv, 171n, 180, 296n, 316. *See also* Campbell Collections

King, Mr (RC's boss), 102

Kirk, Eve, 101, 101n

Knocking on the Door: Shorter Writings (Paton), xxin

Knox, MacGregor, 96n

Krige, Mattheus Uys, xi, xxvi, 38, 38n, 41, 41n, 43, 46, 46n, 117n, **153**, 185, 189-91, 191n, 192, 198, 198n, 308, 313

Krog, Helge, 48, 48n, 49, 308

Kulaks, 34, 35

La Borracha, Maria, 63

Laine, Frankie, 280n

Lambert, Leonard Constant, 10, 10n

Lance, Major, 77, 229

Langley, A.S., xx

La Revoltosa (school friend), 63

Lawrence, D.H., 35

League of Nations, 294

Lear, Edward, 182

Lee, Laurie (Laurence Edward Alan), xiv, xxii, xxiiin, 26n, 59,

59n, 85n, 117n, **146**, 214-5, 214n, 228n, 309

Lehmann, John, 35, 35n

Le Lavandou, 127-8, 258

Lenin, Vladimir Ilyich, xii, 35, 45, 78, 81, 119, 230, 291

Lesbianism, 21, 28, 175n

Let's Get Well (Davis), 296

Leveson, Marcia, xin, xxiiin, xxvi, 13n, 110n, 123n, 133n

Lewis, Clive Staples, iii, 312

Lewis, Wyndham, xix, 10, 11, 13, 16, 18, 29n, 32-33, 33n, 34, 34n, 35-36, 36n, 83, 84, 85, 117n, 119, 120, 181n, 185, 198n, 264, 265, 308 (influence on RC, 33-34, 36)

Ley, Charles David, 117, 117n, 261

Life writing, viii, viiin. *See also* autobiography, biography, life writing, memoir

Lindeque, Linda, 38n

Linhó, 283, 284, 285, 291, 293, 297, 298, 314, 315

Lisbon, 1, 2, 86, 87, 91, 100, 101, 103, 115, 132, 135, **148**, 252, 285, 297, 310

Little Nell, xvn, 62

Liverpool, 9n

Lives of Plutarch, 265

Local Habitation, A: An Autobiography, 1945-1990 (Butler), 126n

London, IV, iii, 2, 9, 10, 13, 15n, 21, 33n, 34n, 39, 39n, 81, 83, 84, 101, 102, 103, 112, 115n, **117**, 122, 123, 125-9, **153**, 163, 164, 165, 173, 174, 176, 208, 229, 230, 237, 239, 245, 253-6, 258-60, 262, 271-2, 276, 299, 305, 306, 308, 310, 311, 312, 313, 314, 315

Long Barn, 18, 19, 21, 23, 173-4. *See also* Nicholson, Harold

Lorca, Garcia, 123, 123n, 277, 277n, 312, 313, 314

"Love in a Hut" (Neale), 164n

Lucan, 266

Lucretius, 266

Lusiads, The (Camões), 17n

Luther, xxi

Lyle, Anna Margaret Campbell (1926-2002, daughter of RC and Mary Campbell), adoption, 22n; appearance, 22n, 126, 187, 245; birth, vii, 15, 171, 306; bullfighting and bullring, **147, 219**, 220-1; Catholicism, ix, 55, 83, 126, 205, 216, 308; childhood, vii, xv, xvi, xvin, 6, 14, 18, 22n, 24n, 25-8, 31, 37, 39-40, 41n, 43-4, 46, 49, 52-5, 69-78, 94, 173, 175, 177-80, 182, 187, 188; confession, 68; dancing, 29, 43, 101n, 103, 113, 114, **114**, 115, 115n, 116, 119, 122, 128, 245, 245n, 246, 253, 254, 255, 310, 311, 312; death, xxiii, 316; depression, 63, 100-101, 101n, 102; Entertainments National Service Association (ENSA), **113**, 114, 114n, 115, 245, 311; godmother, 15, 38-9, 122-3, 171n; grief at RC's death, 2; health, xvi, xvin, xvii, 56, 62, 63, 67, 88n, 100, 101, 101n, 115, 123, 127,

Index

175, 210, 218, 218n, 235, 255, 309, 312, 312; horse riding, 24, 61, 62, 63, 71, 78, 91, 175n, 218-220, 219, 220n, 222; hunger, xvi, 76, 94, 115n, marriage to de Carondolet, 129n, 283, 296n, 313; marriage to Rob Lyle, 2n, 172n, 296n, 316; motherhood, **136**; nutrition, xv, xvi, 94, 97, 98, 99, 103, 122, 122n, 123n, 128, 177; pets, 37, 38, 42, 43, 44, 61, 62, 72, 180, **186**, 197, 201, 204-5; photographs, **vi**, 33, **35**, **136**, **149**, **156**, **178**, **186**, **189**; Prince of Wales theatre, 115, 311; proposals of marriage, 127; protectiveness of RC, xv, 31, 72, 87, 128; role as biographer, viii-x, xii, xiii, xiiin; schooling and learning, xvi, 25, 54, 62, 63, 67, 97, 98, 178, 198n, 209, 218, 248, 249, 251-2, 308, 310; South Africa, vii, 170, 171-2, 171n, 237; suicidal feelings, xvi, 100; job with Universal Aunts, 128

Lyle, Mrs (Rob's first wife), 272, 273, 313, 316

Lyle, Rob, 2, 2n, 3, 6, 27, 116, 117, **117**, 120, 121n, 123n, 124, 126, 129, 132, 172n, 259, 260, 272, 296, 296n, 312, 313, 315, 316

Lyric and Polemic: The Literary Personality of Roy Campbell (Smith), 315

MacCarthy, Desmond, 116, 116n, 117, 118, 119

MacNeice, Louis, iii, xiii, 115, 115n, 312

Madrid, xvi, 46, 55, 57, 65, 69, 70, 71, 74-77, 89, 93, 95-97, 99, 99n, 100, 129, 207, 208, 220n, 226, 228, 229, 232, 233, 251, 261, 262, **262**, 277, 310, 313

Maillot, Pierre, 185

Majorca, 78

Malaria, 94n, 110, 113, 125, 311, 312

Malraux, André, 82, 82n

Mallarmé, Stéphane, 8n, 44

Manchester Guardian, The, 99

Marie Bashkirtseff (From Childhood to Girlhood) (Bashkirtseva), 246, 246n

Marie-Louise (governess), 38

Maritzburg College Old Boys, 130n

Marlowe, Christopher, 164, 266

Marseille, 26, 30, 183, 189

Marsh Farm, 81, 82, 229n

Martigues, ii, viii, xiv, 16, 22, 22n, **23**, 26, 27, 30, 32, 36, 36n, 41, 175, 176-9, 181, 183-191, 195, 197, 199, 265, 307

Martin Chuzzlewit (Dickens), 93n

Marx, Karl, 73, 74, 293, 300

Marxism, xii, 3, 35, 46, 73, 74, 78, 80, 131n, 241, 290, 291, 292, 294

Mason, S.C., Major, 108, 108n

Maxwell-Scotts, 92

McArthur, General, 291

McBean, Jean, xviiin, 277n

McKenzie, Archie, **141**

McLoughlin, Fr Terence, 135

Mein Kampf (Hitler), 85

Memoir, iii, iv, viin, viii, viiin, ix, ixn, xiiin, xiv, xvii, xix, xxi, xxii, xxiii, xxiv, xxivn, xxv, xxvi, xxvii, 1, 27n, 84, 89n, 124, 124n, 135n, 161, 165n, 315, 316. *See also* autobiography, biography, life writing

Memoirists, ix

"Memoirs" (Buss), viii, viiin

Memories of a Dissident Publisher (Regnery), 124n, 135n

Meninsky, Bernard, xxv, 9, 37n, 143

Merriam-Webster's Encyclopedia of Literature, 246n

Merry del Val, Pablo, 89, 89n

Metre, 119, 266

Mexico, 36n, 216, 241

Michael, Archangel, 168n

Millington-Drake, Nelly, 135

Milner, Major, 114

Milton, John, 266

Mireille (Mistral), 179, 184

Misericordia Hospital, 2, 3, 238

Mistral, 22, 24, 32, 178, 179, 191

Mistral, Frédéric, 179, 184

Mithraism, iii

Moby Dick, 235

Modernism, xix, xviii, 201n,

Monarchists, 45, 67n

Monserrat, 44

Monteiro, George, 135n, 277n

Montgomery, R.G., 134

Month, The, 268, 294

Montpellier, 42

Moscardó, Colonel José, 62, 69, 70, 95, 233

Mosley, Oswald, 84, 84n, 85

Mount Olympus Magazine, 209

Moving of the Third Floor Back, The (Veit), 208

Mozart, 135, 299-300

Mrs Beeton, 29

Mulvey, Charles, 126, 126n, 132

Mulvey, Sylvia, 126

Mussolini, Benito, 96n, 290, 309

Mussolini Unleashed, 1939-1941: Politics and Strategy in Fascist Italy's Last War (Knox), 96n

My Life (Mosley), 84, 84n, 85

Myushkin, Prince, 112

Naples, 92, 245

Napoleon, 50, 183, 278

Natal, 15, 17, 39n, 130, 168, 168n, 306

Nation, The, 16, 16n

National Research Foundation (South Africa), xxv, xxvi

Nationalism, 270

Nationalist Party (South Africa),

Index

263n, 264n

Nationalists, 90, 95, 123n, 230, 232, 238, 238n, 244, 247, 248, 309, 310

Nature, 46, 60n, 164, 177, 178, 198, 293

Navarre, 238n

Nazi, 86, 125, 231n, 270

Neale, Gwyn, 164n

Negrophilism, vii. *See also* anti-racism, colour bar, colour prejudice, racism

Nelken, Margarita, 82, 82n

Nelson, Horatio, 92

New Statesman, 16

New York, 132n, 283n

Nice, 127

Nichols, Philip Peter Ross, 125, 125n

Nicolson, Sir Harold, xivn, 8n, 18, 18n, 19, 20, 57, 173, 173n, 174, 175, 307. *See also* Long Barn

Nicholson, Helen (Baroness de Zgliniski), 91, 91n

Nietzsche, Friedrich Wilhelm, 52

Nietzscheism, 294

Nigerian Regiment, 108n

Nimes, 22, 26, 185

North Africa, 120, 241

Nostalgia, A Collection of Poems, (d'Arcos), 135n, 315

Nuremberg trials, 120

Nutrition, xv, xvi, 27, 27n, 29, 32, 48, 49, 55, 90, 97, 98, 99, 100, 103, 104, 115, 122, 128, 179, 182, 183, 187, 195-6, 204, 208-9, 226, 229, 237, 238, 246-247, 249, 250, 252, 258, 263, 271-3, 296

Oakeswell Hall, 9

Oceanographic Research Institute, 130n

Odessa, 241

Odyssey, The, 115

Official War Artist, 9-10

O'Flaherty, Liam, 37, 37n, 185

O'Flaherty, Pegueen, 37

Oliver Twist (Dickens), 93n

Olver, Thomas, 169n

Only Paradise, The (Hewitt), 187, 187n

Opus Dei, 241

Order of Bards, Ovates and Druids, 125n

Order of Carmelite Tertiaries. *See* Carmelites

Ordering Empire: The Poetry of Camões, Pringle and Campbell (Meihuizen), 316

Origami. *See* Paper folding

Origin and Status of the Cheka, The (Carr), 229, 229n

Orlando (Woolf), 173n, 175n

O'Shanter, Tam, 21, 182

Our Lady of Sorrows, 52, 204

Outspan, The, 107n

Ovid, 266

Owl, The, 17

Oxford, 113, **114**, 311

Oxford Chronicle, 163n

Oxford Dictionary of National Biography, 114n

Oxford Poetry (Earp), 7n

"Oxford Style", 7

Oxford University, xiv, xivn, 5, 6, 6n, 7, 7n, 14, 16, 36n, 38n, 51, 113, 115n, 116n, 121n, 124n, 163, 165, 301, 305

Paca (maid), 48, 55

Pacelli, Cardinal, 92

"Pack up your troubles", 25

Paper folding, 53n, 206

Paper Toy Making (Campbell, M.), 53n

Paris, xvin, 2, 28, 37n, 127, 129n, 246n, 307

Paris Vécu (Daudet), 88

Parke, Catherine, xn

Paton, Alan, xi, xviii, xix, xixn, xx, xxi, xxiin, xxii, 2n, 117n, 153, 312, 313

Patrick Duncan: South African and Pan-African (Driver and Sampson), 107, 107n

Paul, Pope, VI, 134

Paulette (maid), 39

Payn, Bill, 131, 131n, 155

Peace Cottage, 306

Pearce, Joseph, iv, xivn, xxii, xxiii, xxvi, 14n, 20n, 21n, 23n, 26n, 29n, 37n, 59n, 79n, 94n, 135n, 168n, 171n, 175n, 176n, 198n, 228n, 229n, 280n, 287n, 316

Pessoa, Fernando António Nogueiro de Seabra, 135n, 276-7, 277n

Petersfield, 102, 103, 107, 112, 209, 253, 298, 310

Pietermaritzburg, 107, 130-1

Pilgrimage/s, 24, 52, 204, 242, 274

Pindar, 266

Plato, 7n

Plomer, William Charles Franklyn, xxn, 15, 15n, 16, 16n, **17**, **144**, 171n, 306, 308

Plutarch, 265

Poetic Justice, xiii

Poland, 120, 256

Polge, Katherine, (Kitty) (Laurie Lee's wife) 26n, 59n

Polge, Marius Baptistin (Grandpère), **23**, 26, 26n, 27n, 30, 30n, 31, 37, 44, 59n, 182, 186-8, **189**

Police. *See* Guardias de Asalto

Politics of Revenge: Fascism and the Military in Twentieth-century Spain, The (Preston), 95n

Pontet, Jean, 135

Pope Paul VI, 134

Pope Pius XI, 92

Pope Pius XII, 92

Porchietti, Italia Augusta, 99n

Port-de-Bouc, 26, 30

Porter, Anne, 53

Portimao, 91

Portugal, **VI**, iii, vii, xxiii, xxv, 1, 2, 85, 86, 88n, 91, 92, 95, 104n, 110n, 129, 132, 135n, 163, 176, 210, 235, 236, **236**, 237, 238, 238n, 242, 243, 246, 272, 272n, 274, 275, **275**, 276, 278, 291, 293, 296, 297, 299, 309, 313, 314, 315, 316

Possessed, The (Dostoevsky), 34, 69

Post, Laurens van der. *See* van der Post, Laurens

Potter, Beatrix, 196

Pound, Ezra, xviii, 35

Prado, 63

Presence of Pessoa: English, American and South African Literary Responses, The (Monteiro), 277n

Presbyterian, 205, 267

Preston, Paul, 95n

Primavera (Botticelli), 92

Primo de Rivera, 45

Progress, xxii, 46, 50, 293-4

"Prolog im Himmel" (Goethe), 168-9, 168n

Protestant, 50, 112, 205

Provence, ii, xiv, 21, 23, 26, 29, **35**, 36n, 38, **39**, 40, 41, 42, 43, 67n, **146**, 175, 176, 176n, 177-9, **178**, 181, 184, **189**, 192-3, 195, 256, 257, **257**, 260, 306, 307

Provence: a Cultural History (Garrett), 176n

Prudentius, 266

Puerta Visagra, 75, 75n, 217, 226

Queen Jeanne, 24

Queen's Hospital, 255

Queipo de Llano, Gonzalo, 89, 89n, 95, 95n

Queirós. *See* de Queirós

Quevado, Francisco de, 44, 60

Rabelais, François 24, 41, 266

Race. *See* Racism

"The Race to be Hero: Race and Gender in Roy Campbell's *Light on a Dark Horse*", (Coullie), xiin, xxiiin, 266n

"Race Memory" (Chesterton), ii

Racism, xi, 263n, 264n. *See also* Apartheid, Colour Prejudice, Colour Bar, RC: racism, negrophilism

Rare and the Beautiful: the Lives of the Garmans, The (Connolly), xxvi, 19n, 21n, 316

Ranero, El, 58, 219

Rations. *See* Nutrition

Recared, King, 217, 217n

"Red Baron", 96n

Reds. *See* Communism

Regnery, Henry, 124n, 135n, **154**

Republic. *See* Spanish Republic

Requetés. *See* Carlists

Revenge for Love, The (Lewis,W.), 33, 33n

Reynolds, Lewis, 15, 168n

Reynold's News, 237

Richard Aldington and H.D.: Their Lives in Letters (Aldington, Doolittle and Zilboorg), 127n

Riding, Laura, 229n

Rilke, Rainer Maria, 57

Rimbaud, Jean Nicholas Arthur, xivn, 8, 8n, 19

Riquelme, General, 69

Risk, Terry, ixn, xxv

Robilant, Count, 132

Robilant, Olguina, 132

Rodrigo (groom), 61, 218

Roman Catholicism. *See* Catholicism

Romancero Gitano (Lorca), 123

Rome, 92-3, 95, 126-7, 243, 245-247, 313

Ronsard, Pierre de, 25

Rospigliosi, Prince, 92, 247, 247n

Rospigliosi, Princess, 92, 247, 247n

Roy Campbell (Ley), 261, 261n

Roy Campbell (Wright), 261n, 315

"Roy Campbell, Before the Terrapin" (Voss), 163n

Roy Campbell: a Critical Biography (Alexander), xiiin, xxn, 10n, 13n, 20n, 228n, 315

"Roy Campbell: the Man and his humour" (Krige), 46n, 46-47

"Roy Campbell: Poet and Man" (Coullie and Wade), xviiin, xixn, xxi, xxin

Roy Campbell: Selected Poems (Pearce), ivn

Roy Campbell, Ein Solitar: Interpretationen Seiner Versdichtung (Hanke), 316

Royalties, xxivn, 18, 108

Rude Assignment (Lewis, Wyndham), 10n

Russell, John, 117

Russia, 34, 45, 57, 69, 71n, 81, 84, 85, 119, 122, 230-1, 242, 246n, 289, 290, 291

Russian Revolution, 91, 242-3

Rhyme, xviii, 98, 169, 192, 204, 240, 266

Sackville, Baron of, 18n

Sackville-West, Victoria Mary (Vita), xii, xivn, 18, 18n, 19, 19n, 20, 20n, 21, 21n, 22n, 26, 26n, 28, 29, 173, 173n, 174, 175n, 195n, 307. *See also* Long Barn

Saint Austin Review (Pearce), iv

Index

Saison en Enfer, Une (Rimbaud), 8, 8n

Salamanca, 88, 89, **155**, 277, 313

Salazar, António de Oliveira, 134, 272n

Salute to Roy Campbell (Kershaw), 117n. *See also Hommage à Roy Campbell*

Sammat, Henri, 26, 44

Sampson, Anthony, 107n

Sangre y Arena (Ibáñez), 104

Sanjurjo, General, 225

San Lazzaro, 126

San Mateo, 89

Santander, 208

Sao Pedro, 3, 135, **159**, 315

Saul, Miss (ballet teacher), 103

Schaafsma, Anneke, xxvi, 46n

Schlaeger, JÐrgen, xn

Schlesinger, Arthur, 291

Schubert, Franz, 59

Science, 178n, 268, 293

Scotland, 52, 53, 305

Scottish Chieftains, The (Porter), 53

Scrutiny2 (Coullie), xiin, xxiiin, 266n

Second World War. *See* World War Two

Segovia, 100, 250

Ségur, Comtesse Sophie Feodorovna Rostopchine de, 41

Sérafine (maid), 23, 25, 30

Serra. *See* Casa da Serra

Sesimbra, 87, 90, 235, 237, 238, 252, 309

Sète, 26, 30

Setúbal, 1, 2, 287, 315

Sevenoaks Weald, 18, 173, 174, 175, 307

Seville, 1, 2, 89, 89n, 92, 133, 244, 287, 315

Sezela, vii, **17, 144**, 168n, 171, 306

Sforza family, 92n, 247

Shakespeare, William, 1, 104, 164, 266, 277n

Shanghai, 39

Shaw, Bernard, 10n, 34

Shelley, Percy Bysshe, 164, 166

Sibbett, Cecil J., 17, 17n, 38-39, 122-123n

Siege of Numantia, The (Cervantes), 94n

Silves, 239

Sinatra, Frank, 280n

Sintra, viii, xxiv, xxv, 3, 129, 132, **159, 160**, 272, 273, 282, 283, 285, 286, 291, 297, 313, 314, 315, 316

Sisters of Charity, 87

Sitwell, Dame Edith, iii, 2n, 6, 6n, 126, 126n, 131, 260, 312, 314

Sitwell, Sir Francis Osbert Sacheverell (Edith's brother), 6, 6n, 126, 131, 260

Sitwell, Sacheverell (Edith's brother), 6n, 126, 126n

"Skylark and the Daisy, The" (Andersen), 182

Slade School of Art, 9, 37n

Smith, Rowland, 315

Snooty Baronet, (Lewis, P.W.), 33, 33n

Socialism/socialist, iii, xix, xxi, xxin, 7, 81n, 82n, 192, 230, 231, 263, 270, 271, 292, 294

Solzhenitsyn, Alexander, 230-1, 240, 290

The Song of Songs, 286

"Songs between the Soul and the Bridegroom" (St John of the Cross), 212

Sotelo, Calvo, 67, 69, 223

South Africa, iv, vii, xviii, xxiii, xxv, 3, 3n, 12, 14, 15, 16, 17, 27n, 33, 47, 54, 81, 107, 107n, 113, 116n, 123n, 129, 130, **144**, 164, 168, **170**, 171, 171-2n, 173, 188, 191, 200, 237, 253, 263, 264, 269, 269n, 277, 277n, 280, 292n, 305, 306, 314

South African Ambassador, 134

South African Association of Marine Biological Research, 130n

Southampton, 17, 86, 171, 235

South Harting, 112, 209

Southern African Literatures (Chapman), xixn

Southport, 113

Soviet Russia. *See* Russia

Soviet Union, 3, 34, 35, 45, 290

Spain, ii, iii, vii, xv, xxiii, 33n, 37, 41, 44, 45, 47, 49, 50, 51n, 52, 55, 56, 57, 59, 60, 61, 65, 66, 69, 70, 71, 74, 81, 82, 82n, 85, 87, 88, 90, 92, 93, 94n, 95, 96, 96n, 97, 99, 100, 103, 104, 104n, 125, 126n, 129, 131, 133, 189, 192, 198, 200-202, **206**, 208, 212, 214, 215, 217, 222-6, 229-3, 235, 238, 238n, 240, 241, 244, 245, 246-51, 253, 261, 262, 264, 271, 272n, 276, 277, 287, 289, 290, 298, 300, 309, 314, 315

Spanish Army, iii, xiii, xv, 70, 74-77, 89

Spanish Civil War, iii, viii, xiii, 13, 33n, 38n, 45, 57, 58, 59, 67, 67n, 69-70, 71-2, 75, 82, 83, 83n, 88, 90-1, 92, 93, 94, 95n, 96n, 97, 102, 123n, 125n, 192, 200, 223-5, 228-29, 229n, 230-5, 238, 238n, 240, 241, 243, 244, 247, 248, 250, 263, 274, 286, 290, 291, 297, 309

Spanish Republic, iii, 38n, 45, 62n, 65, 66, 67, 67n, 69, 82n, 83, 233

Spender, Stephen, iii, xiii, 25, 25n, 84n, 115, 115n, 118n, 124, 125, 125n, 173n, 231n, 263n, 312

Stalin, Joseph, xii, 34, 35, 74, 81, 119, 120, 120n, 290

St Andrew's University, 12, 52

Starkie, Walter, 99, 99n

St Audaire, 88

St Augustine, 267

St Catherine of Siena, 267

Stellenbosch University Special Collections, xxvi, 38n

Index

Stendhal, Marie-Henri Beyle, 41
St Ignatius of Loyola, 105n, 215
St Jacut, 126
St John of the Cross, 21n, 47, 51, 58, 66, 73, 123, 124n, 212, 217, 226, 259, 260, 263, 267, 277, 310, 313
St John the Evangelist, 268
St Mitre, 199
St Paul, 268
Strachey, Giles Lytton, 19, 19n
Strauss, Peter, 169n
Strike a New Note, 115
Strong, Mrs, 92
St Sebastian, 45
St Teresa of Avila, 20, 21n, 41, 51, 58, 66, 105n, 164n, 205, 309
Sunday Times, The, 118, 118n
Surgeon of His Honour, The (de la Barca), 123, 123n
Switzerland, 115-6, 119, 312

Tablet, The, 238, 309
Talavera, 60, 309
Tanganyika, 253
Tatham, Gillian (RC's niece), 131n, 280n
Taylor, Bayard, 169n
Teetotaller, xiv, 131, 131n, 177, 268, 287
"Telling the life story, anxiously: The memoirs of Teresa and Anna Campbell", viin

Theoria, 191n
Thérèse (governess), 30, 42, 43, 44, 46, 308
Thomas, Dylan, iii, 10n, 117n, 126, 126n, 132, 260, 283, 312
Thomas, Elizabeth (Tony), 17, 29, 64, 78, 86, 102, 163, 196, 209, 210, 217
Time and Tide, 83
Times Literary Supplement, 16n
Tintoretto, 181
Tirso de Molina, 266, 314
Toledo, viii, xiv, xv, 34, **53**, 55, 56, 57, 58, 60, 62n, 63, 64, 66, 69, 70, 71, 75, 75n, 76, 77, 78, 82, 83, 88, 88n, 89, 90, 92, 94, 96, 97, 99, **146**, **147**, 207, 211, 211n, 212, 214, 216-9, **219**, 220, 222-3, 225, 226, 228, 232-4, 243, 247-9, 261, 271, 297, 298, 308, 309, 310, 314, 315
"Tolkien, Exeter College and the Great War" (Garth), 8n
Tolkien, J.R.R., iii, 7n, 8n, 312
Tolstoy, Leo, 58n, 73
Tom Burnses, 7
Tony. *See* Thomas, Elizabeth
Torn del Benaco, 127
Toulon, 126, 257
Tour de Vallier, 22, 25-26, 30, 32, **33**, 176, 176n, **178**, 181, 184, 188, 193, 197, 307
Tradition and Diversity: Christianity in a World Context to 1500 (Jolly), 217n

Traditional Catholic Religious Orders: Living in Community (Wynne), 21n

Traditions, 50

Trafalgar, 95

"Tragic Poet, A" (MacCarthy), 118, 118n

Tree, Iris, 10, 10n, 166

Trexler, Robert, xxvi

Truman, Harry S., 120

Truth, x, 30, 34, 35, 96, 113, 123, 133, 228n, 240

Tschiffely, Aimé, 132, 132n, 259

Tschiffely, Marquesita, 132

Turbot Wolfe (Plomer), 16

Turner, Noleen, 204n

Ty-Corn, **162**, 164, 164n, 306

Uffizi Galleries, 92, 247

Ukraine, 9n, 246n

Umhlanga, 305

Unafraid of Virginia Woolf: the Friends and Enemies of Roy Campbell (Pearce), iv, 20n

UNESCO, 294

Union Jack. *See* Britain

Union of South Africa, 107n, 263n

United States of America. *See* America

University of Catalonia, 126

University of KwaZulu-Natal, xxiiin, xxv, 131n, 316

University of Natal, xiii, 38n, 130, 130n, 314

University of Salamanca, 129

University of Stellenbosch, xxvi, 46n

UNO, 294

Ursuline Convent, 62, 218

Vacances, Les (Ségur), 41

Valencia, 46, 47, 52, 57, 77, 201, 229

Valéry, Paul, xxii

van der Post, Laurens, xi, 15, 15n, **144**, **153**, 171n, 306, 313

van Dieren, Bernard, 9, 9n, 11

van Wyk Smith, Malvern, xviii, xviiin

Varela, José Enrique Varela Iglesias, General, 70, 83, 83n, 95

Vegetius, 84, 84n

Veit, Conrad, 208

Venice, 92, 247

Verlaine, Paul, 8n

Vespucci, Simonetta, 132

Vicente, Gil, 266

Vinceness. *See* Winsnes

Virgil, 266

von Richthofen, General Wolfram Freiherr, 96, 96n

von Schubert, Anna, 15, 39, **39**, 39n, 40, 122, 123, 171n

von Schubert, Paul, 15

Index

Vorticist movement, xix, 10n

Voss, Tony, 163n

Wade, Jean-Philippe, xviiin, xxn, xxiii, xxiiin, xxv, 52n, 163n, 171n, 178n, 277n, 316

Wales, vii, 13, 103, 163, 306, 310

Waley, Arthur, 126, 126n

Wallace, William, 53

War, Spanish Civil. *See* Spanish Civil War

War, World War One. *See* World War One

War, World War Two. *See* World War Two

Warlock, Peter. *See* Heseltine, Philip

Waste Land, The, (Eliot), i

Way Out, The (Krige), 38n

Weald. *See* Sevenoaks Weald

Wednesbury, 9, 95, 305

Wentworth, 106, 310

Westminster School of Art, 37n

Weymouth, 253, 310

Whiplash. *See* Voorslag

Whitman, Walt, 118, 118n

"William Banting: the Father of the Low-carbohydrate Diet" (Groves), 251n

Wilson, Katharina M., 82n

Winchelsea, 114, 126

Winchester, 105, 310

Winsnes, Erling, 48, 48n

Wishart, Ernest (Squire of Binstead, Mary's brother-in-law), 27n, 81, 81n, 82, 85n, 229n

Wishart, John Michael Garman, 36, 36n

Wishart, Lady (Ernest's mother), 82, 85

Wishart, Lorna (née Garman, Mary's sister), xxvi, 12, 27, 27n, 59n, 81, 81n, 82, 85, 85n, 229n, 316

Woolf, Virginia, ix, ixn, xviii, 21, 21n, 102, 173n, 175n

World within World (Spender), 25n, 84n, 115n, 173n

World War One, viii, 9, 16n, 25, 127n, 164, 165

World War Two, iii, viii, xviii, 27n, 100-110, 112-115, 119, 120, 125, 125n, 241, 252-254, 270, 271, 272, 290, 298, 311

Wright, David, xxii, 261, 261n, 315

WRNS, 253, 254, **254**, 310, 311

Wynne, Edward A., 21n

Yagüe, Yuan, 95, 95n

Yasmin (daughter of Laurie Lee and Lorna Wishart), 59n

Yeats, William Butler, ii, 35, 46, 67n, 84

Yiddish, xii

"Yongi Bongi-Bo" (Lear), 182

"Younger, Jimmy" (pseudonym),

115n

Zilboorg, Caroline, 127n

Zulu, 24, 175, 182, 204, 204n, 215, 223, 263, 264, 286, 286n

Other Titles of Interest

C.S. Lewis

C. S. LEWIS: VIEWS FROM WAKE FOREST—ESSAYS ON C. S. LEWIS
Michael Travers, editor

Contains sixteen scholarly presentations from the international C. S. Lewis convention in Wake Forest, NC. Walter Hooper shares his important essay "Editing C. S. Lewis," a chronicle of publishing decisions after Lewis's death in 1963.

"Scholars from a variety of disciplines address a wide range of issues. The happy result is a fresh and expansive view of an author who well deserves this kind of thoughtful attention."
—Diana Pavlac Glyer, author of THE COMPANY THEY KEEP

THE HIDDEN STORY OF NARNIA: A BOOK-BY-BOOK GUIDE TO LEWIS' SPIRITUAL THEMES
Will Vaus

A book of insightful commentary—Will Vaus points out connections between the NARNIA books and spiritual and biblical themes in our world, as well as between ideas in the NARNIA books and C. S. Lewis's other books. Each chapter includes questions for individual use or small group discussion.

WHY I BELIEVE IN NARNIA: 33 REVIEWS AND ESSAYS ON THE LIFE AND WORK OF C.S. LEWIS
James Como

Chapters range from reviews of critical books, documentaries and movies to evaluations of Lewis' books to biographical analysis.

"A valuable, wide-ranging collection of essays by one of the best informed and most accute commentators on Lewis' work and ideas."
—Peter Schakel, author of IMAGINATION & THE ARTS IN C.S. LEWIS

C. S. LEWIS: HIS LITERARY ACHIEVEMENT
Colin Manlove

"This is a positively brilliant book, written with splendor, elegance, profundity and evidencing an enormous amount of learning. This is probably not a book to give a first-time reader of Lewis. But for those who are more broadly read in the Lewis corpus this book is an absolute gold mine of information. The author gives us a magnificent overview of Lewis's many writings, tracing for us thoughts and ideas which recur throughout, and at the same time telling us how each book differs from the others. I think it is not extravagant to call C. S. LEWIS: HIS LITERARY ACHIEVEMENT a *tour de force*."
— Robert Merchant, ST. AUSTIN REVIEW, Book Review Editor

C. S. Lewis & Philosophy as a Way of Life: A Comprehensive Historical Examination of His Philosophical Thoughts
Adam Barkman

C. S. Lewis is rarely thought of as a "philosopher" per se despite having both studied and taught philosophy for several years at Oxford. Lewis's long journey to Christianity was essentially philosophical—passing through seven different stages. This 624 page book is an invaluable reference for C. S. Lewis scholars and fans alike.

Speaking of Jack: A C.S. Lewis Discussion Guide (pub 2011)
Will Vaus

C. S. Lewis Societies have been forming around the world since the first one started in New York City in 1969. Will Vaus has started and led three groups himself. Speaking of Jack is the result of Vaus' experience in leading those Lewis Societies. Included here are introductions to most of Lewis' books as well as questions designed to stimulate discussion about Lewis' life and work. These materials have been "road-tested" with real groups made up of young and old, some very familiar with Lewis and some newcomers. Speaking of Jack may be used in an existing book discussion group, Sunday school class or small group, to start a C. S. Lewis Society, or as a guide to your own exploration of Lewis' books.

Mythopoeic Narnia: Memory, Metaphor, and Metamorphosis in C.S. Lewis's The Chronicles of Narnia
Salwa Khoddam

Dr. Khoddam, the founder of the C. S. Lewis and Inklings Society (2004), has been teaching university courses using Lewis' books for over 25 years. Her book offers a fresh approach to the Narnia books based on an inquiry into Lewis' readings and use of classical and Christian symbols. She explores the literary and intellectual contexts of these stories, the traditional myths and motifs, and places them in the company of the greatest Christian mythopoeic works of Western Literature. In Lewis' imagination, memory and metaphor interact to advance his purpose — a Christian metamorphosis. Mythopoeic Narnia helps to open the door for readers into the magical world of the Western imagination.

C.S. Lewis Goes to Heaven: A Reader's Guide to The Great Divorce (pub 2011)
David G. Clark

This is the first book devoted solely to this often neglected book and the first to reveal several important secrets Lewis concealed within the story. Lewis felt his imaginary trip to Hell and Heaven was far better than his book THE SCREWTAPE LETTERS, which has become a classic. Clark is an ordained minister who has taught courses on Lewis for more than 30 years and is a New Testament and Greek scholar with a Doctor of Philosophy degree in Biblical Studies from the University of Notre Dame. Readers will discover the many literary and biblical influences Lewis utilized in writing his brilliant novel.

George MacDonald

Diary of an Old Soul & The White Page Poems
George MacDonald and Betty Aberlin

The first edition of George MacDonald's book of daily poems included a blank page opposite each page of poems. Readers were invited to write their own reflections on the "white page." MacDonald wrote: "Let your white page be ground, my print be seed, growing to golden ears, that faith and hope may feed." Betty Aberlin responded to MacDonald's invitation with daily poems of her own.

"Betty Aberlin's close readings of George MacDonald's verses and her thoughtful responses to them speak clearly of her poetic gifts and spiritual intelligence."
— Luci Shaw, poet

George MacDonald: Literary Heritage and Heirs
Roderick McGillis, editor

This latest collection of 14 essays sets a new standard that will influence MacDonald studies for many more years. George MacDonald experts are increasingly evaluating his entire corpus within the nineteenth century context.

"This comprehensive collection represents the best of contemporary scholarship on George MacDonald."
— Rolland Hein, author of George MacDonald: Victorian Mythmaker.

In the Near Loss of Everything: George MacDonald's Son in America
Dale Wayne Slusser

In the summer of 1887, George MacDonald's son Ronald, newly engaged to artist Louise Blandy, sailed from England to America to teach school. The next summer he returned to England to marry Louise and bring her back to America. On August 27, 1890, Louise died leaving him with an infant daughter. Ronald once described losing a beloved spouse as "the near loss of everything." Dale Wayne Slusser unfolds this poignant story with unpublished letters and photos that give readers a glimpse into the close-knit MacDonald family. Also included is Ronald's essay about his father, "George MacDonald: A Personal Note", plus a selection from Ronald's 1922 fable, The Laughing Elf, about the necessity of both sorrow and joy in life.

A Novel Pulpet: Sermons from George MacDonald's Fiction
David L. Neuhouser

"In MacDonald's novels, the Christian teaching emerges out of the characters and story line, the narrator's comments, and inclusion of sermons given by the fictional preachers. The sermons in the novels are shorter than the ones in collections of MacDonald's sermons and so are perhaps more accessible for some. In any case, they are both stimulating and thought-provoking. This collection of sermons from ten novels serve to bring out the 'freshness and brilliance' of MacDonald's message."
—from the author's introduction

BEHIND THE BACK OF THE NORTH WIND: CRITICAL ESSAYS FROM GEORGE MACDONALD'S CLASSIC CHILDREN'S BOOK (pub 2011)
Editors, John Pennington and Robert McGillis
 This collection of 16 essays by various scholars is the first compendium on a particular MacDonald book – AT THE BACK OF THE NORTH WIND. This novel makes a good representative study because it bridges the world of the "realistic" and the fanciful, including a fairy tale and some nonsense poetry. Plus it deals with a central MacDonald theme — death. Essays run the gamut from exploring MacDonald's Christian worldview, to examining the tension between fantasy and reality, to grappling with North Wind as children's literature. In every case, the essays illuminate a complex book. This book is also an excellent companion to the critical and scholarly edition of AT THE BACK OF THE NORTH WIND by Pennington and McGillis published by Broadview Press.

Other Titles

TO LOVE ANOTHER PERSON: A SPIRITUAL JOURNEY THROUGH LES MISERABLES
John Morrison
 The powerful story of Jean Valjean's redemption is beloved by readers and theater goers everywhere. In this companion and guide to Victor Hugo's masterpiece, author John Morrison unfolds the spiritual depth and breadth of this classic novel and broadway musical.

THROUGH COMMON THINGS: PHILOSOPHICAL REFLECTIONS ON POPULAR CULTURE
Adam Barkman
 "Barkman presents us with an amazingly wide-ranging collection of philosophical reflections grounded in the everyday things of popular culture – past and present, eastern and western, factual and fictional. Throughout his encounters with often surprising subject-matter (the value of darkness?), he writes clearly and concisely, moving seamlessly between Aristotle and anime, Lord Buddha and Lord Voldemort... This is an informative and entertaining book to read!"
  — Doug Blomberg, Professor of Philosophy, Institute for Christian Studies

THE EYE OF THE BEHOLDER: HOW TO SEE THE WORLD LIKE A ROMANTIC POET
Louis Markos
 Born out of the French Revolution and its radical faith that a nation could be shaped and altered by the dreams and visions of its people, British Romantic Poetry was founded on a belief that the objects and realities of our world, whether natural or human, are not fixed in stone but can be molded and transformed by the visionary eye of the poet. Unlike many of the books written on Romanticism, which devote many pages to the poets and few pages to their poetry, the focus here is firmly on the poems themselves. The author thereby draws the reader intimately into the life of these poems. A separate bibliographical essay is provided for readers listing accessible biographies of each poet and critical studies of their work.

www.ingramcontent.com/pod-product-compliance
Lightning Source LLC
Chambersburg PA
CBHW030300080526
44584CB00012B/385